Foreign News

The Lewis Henry Morgan Lectures / 2000

Presented at

The University of Rochester
Rochester, New York

FOREIGN NEWS

Exploring the World of Foreign Correspondents

Ulf Hannerz
Foreword by Anthony T. Carter

The University of Chicago Press   Chicago and London

Ulf Hannerz is professor of social anthropology at Stockholm University. He is the author of eight previous books, most recently *Transnational Connections.*

The University of Chicago Press, Chicago 60637
The University of Chicago Press, Ltd., London
© 2004 by The University of Chicago
All rights reserved. Published 2004
Printed in the United States of America

13 12 11 10 09 08 07 06 05 04   1 2 3 4 5

ISBN: 0-226-31574-6 (cloth)
ISBN: 0-226-31575-4 (paper)

Library of Congress Cataloging-in-Publication Data

Hannerz, Ulf.
   Foreign news : exploring the world of foreign correspondents / Ulf Hannerz ; foreword by Anthony T. Carter.
      p. cm. — (The Lewis Henry Morgan lectures)
   ISBN 0-226-31574-6 (cloth : alk. paper) — ISBN 0-226-31575-4 (pbk. : alk. paper)
   1. Foreign news.   I. Title.   II. Series.
   PN4784.F6 H35 2004
   070.4′332—dc21

BK
$ 44. 50

2003011743

52341570

CONTENTS

FOREWORD

U lf Hannerz delivered the Lewis Henry Morgan Lectures on which this book is based at the University of Rochester in November 2000. They were the thirty-eighth in a series offered annually to the public and to students and faculty at the University of Rochester by the Department of Anthropology. The thirty-ninth lectures were delivered in October 2001 by Lila Abu-Lughod. The fortieth were presented last fall by Deborah Gewertz and Frederick Errington. Elinore Ochs will give the forty-first Morgan Lectures in 2003.

The lectures honor Lewis Henry Morgan. In addition to playing a signal role in the creation of modern anthropology, Morgan was a prominent Rochester attorney. He never found it necessary to accept a formal academic position, but he was a benefactor of the University of Rochester from its beginning. At the end of his life, he left the University money for a women's college as well as his manuscripts and library.

In recent years, the Department of Anthropology has sought out Morgan Lecturers whose work is of interest to a broad range of disciplines in the social sciences and the humanities. We remain firmly situated in anthropology and continue to provide a forum for rich ethnographic description, but we also want to explore the shape of conversations across disciplinary boundaries and the ways in which anthropology may contribute to such conversations.

Ulf Hannerz's Morgan Lectures renew and extend a conversation with foreign correspondents. The anthropological contributions to this conversation include Mark Pedelty's 1995 *War Stories,* an ethnography of war correspondents in the latter years of the civil war in El Salvador, and ethnographies of media consumption by James Lull, Lila Abu-Lughod, and Purnima Mankekar. Other interlocutors include Pierre Bourdieu, the sociologists

Herbert Gans and Todd Gitlin, media critics such as Noam Chomsky and Edward Said, and, of course, journalists themselves in both their news reports and their reflexive and autobiographical writings.

Hannerz began to attend systematically to the flow of culture in and around foreign news in the years following the collapse of the Soviet Union. He completed a draft of this manuscript not long after September 11, 2001. In the past year, controversy has split the faculty of the Columbia University Graduate School of Journalism following the university president's claim that the school's curriculum overemphasized reporting and writing at the expense of training in "political theory and economics" (*New York Times,* May 14, 2003). As *Foreign News* goes to press, two national correspondents at the *New York Times* have lost their jobs as a consequence of violations of journalistic ethics. A committee of *Times* editors and reporters is reexamining newsroom practices and the paper's executive editor and managing editor have resigned. The United States Federal Communications Commission has voted to relax regulations concerning media ownership. At the beginning of the twenty-first century, particularly, there has been considerable uncertainty and debate about the story lines around which the news should be organized. But if the flow of culture takes place in acts of conversation, this is an arena in which the languages used may routinely be incommensurable, the participants have widely varying access to power, and the arguments concerning meaning are commonly discordant.

Hannerz's contribution to these sometimes raucous conversations is remarkably civil. A Swedish anthropologist reading foreign news in Swedish and German papers as well as in the *New York Times* and the *Los Angeles Times* and doing an ethnographic study of foreign correspondents with diverse perspectives in Jerusalem, Johannesburg, and Tokyo cannot be unaware of or unconcerned with debates about getting the story "right" and institutional bias. That this sort of critique does not figure largely in *Foreign News* perhaps may be taken as a reflection of anthropology's commitment to cultural relativism. If foreign correspondents are Hannerz's "tribe," then their biases and perspectives are as deserving of an effort to understand them in their own terms as are notions of female embodiment in The Gambia (see Caroline Bledsoe's *Contingent Lives*) or ideas about love and sacrifice in contemporary English shopping (see Daniel Miller's *A Theory of Shopping*).

Foreign News is first and foremost an original contribution to studies of globalization, our experience of the world "as a single place." Where others have focused on "the global in the local" or on commodity chains, Hannerz here examines an occupation. Like academics, artists, athletes, businesspeople, diplomats, missionaries, and the staffs of global nongovernmental organizations, journalists, whether staff correspondents (long-termers, para-chutists, or spiralists), stringers, or fixers, belong to a community of practice which is spread over the globe in an organized if notably uneven fashion. And, like anthropologists, foreign correspondents are engaged in producing and organizing flows of culture—as Hannerz puts it elsewhere, "the meanings which people create, and which create people" and "forms of externaliza-tion . . . in which [these meanings are] made public"—across considerable so-cial as well as physical distances. In addition to thinking about how the work of foreign correspondents makes the world "a single place," this exercise in "studying sideways" gives him an opportunity to reflect on the practice of an-thropologists. Journalists are "good to think with" as well as about.

Echoing Benedict Anderson's claim that newspapers were among the media that enabled the inhabitants of diverse localities to imagine themselves as members of national communities at the beginning of the nineteenth cen-tury, Hannerz suggests that contemporary foreign news enables some of us to imagine ourselves as cosmopolitans, persons who feel themselves to be "to some degree at home in the world." Feature stories on Saturday night disco dancing in Beijing and, regardless of their veracity, news reports concerning killings and disappearances in El Salvador or the U.S. occupation of Iraq may allow us to conceive of the world as filled with our contemporaries. Even if we sometimes experience "compassion fatigue," all of us are members of a global society, "taking each other into account."

Journalists may fail in this role, as when, for example, they wrote of the Iranians who held American diplomats hostage in 1980 as living in the four-teenth century. Though they aspire to make the familiar strange and the strange familiar, anthropologists undermine a cosmopolitan sense of being at home in the world's diversity when they write of the Other in the ethno-graphic present.

Hannerz also explores the ways in which journalism and contemporary anthropology converge around an interest in events and temporality. As Nicholas Lemann, the *New Yorker* correspondent and newly appointed dean of the Columbia University Graduate School of Journalism puts it, "[t]he first layer of journalism is just learning how to do it, to see life in terms of events" (*New York Times,* May 14, 2003). Similarly, though the ethnographic present removed time from anthropological writing, Sally Falk Moore observes that "in the past 25 years there has been a shift in attention [in anthropology] from structure to event." In both crafts there is interest in ongoing processes or contemporary history.

For all the parallels between them, however, the two professions man-age meaning from different perspectives. Most anthropologists would wilt under the pressure of the temporal demands of journalists' daily routines. Foreign correspondents commonly do what Laura Nader called "studying up," reporting on the activities of major political and business leaders. Working at a scale well above that of nearly all anthropologists, journalists are less likely to take an interest in the sorts of everyday events that anthropologists take as diagnostic of the sociocultural systems with which they are commonly concerned. When journalists do take an interest in such events, they are likely to write about them in feature articles cast in something like the ethnographic present—any Saturday on Bar Ilan Street in Jerusalem—that appear in the paper when the news of "real" events is slow. Conversely, it is difficult to imagine either newsmakers or the just plain folks studied by most anthropologists trying to time their activities to maximize—or minimize—their impact in anthropological "news cycles." If anthropologists are moving toward a greater interest in events, the curricular reforms put forward for Columbia by Nicholas Lemann suggest a move in journalism toward more attention to structure and analytic writing.

Nancy Munn, another Morgan Lecturer, has observed that people, including anthropologists and journalists as well as newsmakers and those about and for whom they write, "are 'in' a sociocultural time of multiple dimensions (sequencing, timing, past-present-future relations, etc.) that they are forming in their 'projects.' " I take Hannerz to be reminding us—anthropologists as well as journalists—that the global ecumene has a temporal character that is, in part, a consequence of our projects—the stories we write and distribute—and for which we are responsible.

On a practical level, if anthropology might be a useful component of a revised curriculum for aspiring journalists at the Columbia University Graduate School of Journalism, so anthropologists have much to learn from journalists about writing first—or at least very early—drafts of history. And about getting the story out to a wide audience quickly, concisely, and clearly.

Anthony T. Carter
Editor, The Lewis Henry Morgan Lectures

ACKNOWLEDGMENTS

This book is a considerably revised and greatly expanded version of the Lewis Henry Morgan Lectures that I gave at the University of Rochester in November 2000. In 1963, the year when the first Morgan Lectures were given, I was a newly arrived exchange student at another American university, taking some of my early steps toward becoming a professional anthropologist. Since then, I may have spent more time perhaps a bit idiosyncratically exploring what have been borderlands and frontiers of anthropology, rather than the heartlands, which Lewis Henry Morgan had an important part in defining. I was happy to receive the invitation to give the Morgan Lectures as a hint that I may have been doing something right.

I want to express my gratitude for the enormously generous hospitality of the members of the Department of Anthropology at the University of Rochester during the days my wife, Helena Wulff, and I spent with them; in particular I wish to thank Anthony T. Carter, the director of the Morgan Lectures series. I also want to note, sadly, that my Morgan Lectures were the last that Alfred Harris, who did so much to organize this series over many years, attended before his death in early 2001.

My warm thanks also go collectively to all those foreign correspondents and foreign news editors who made my study possible, by giving generously of their time to discuss their work with me and also by offering various other kinds of help and advice. Most of them, although not quite all, can be identified, since their names appear in the chapters that follow. It was invariably a pleasure to meet with them. Since they sometimes made the point that they made a living by asking questions and thus should gladly accept answering some, I hope they will now accept as a token of reciprocity my attempt to cast some light, from another vantage point, on their activities and working conditions.

Some colleagues had important parts in various phases of my project. Sherry Ortner, unknowingly, made me take an important first step when she invited me to give a lecture at the 1994 meeting of the Society for Cultural Anthropology in Chicago, thus providing me with a reason to test whether foreign correspondence was a topic I wanted to pursue more seriously. James W. Fernandez and Vincent Crapanzano encouraged me to go on and offered important contacts. My visits to Israel, South Africa, and Japan were aided and in various ways made even more pleasurable by a number of colleagues and friends: Henry Abramovich, Harumi Befu, Shmuel Eisenstadt, Don Handelman, Dan Rabinowitz, Pamela Reynolds, Steven Robins, and Moshe Shokeid. Brian Moeran offered me the opportunity of a brief visit to Hong Kong. Outside of anthropology but with their own insights into it, Jane Kramer offered invaluable introductions to newspeople in New York when I was still considering the feasibility of the project, and Fumio Kitamura kindly and effectively connected me with the foreign correspondent community in Tokyo. I met Ethan Bronner first as a particularly helpful Jerusalem correspondent; later, he participated in a panel that was also a part of the Morgan Lecture series in Rochester, and in addition he commented on the manuscript at a later stage, after he moved on to New York. Among anthropologists again, Roger Sanjek, apart from commenting on the manuscript, used his wealth of knowledge of the history of anthropology to draw my attention to some intriguing aspects of Lewis Henry Morgan's life, and Marie Gillespie, Garry Marvin, and Adrian Peace also pointed me toward some important reading and viewing. At a critical moment my sister Birgitta Brandenstein found references that I needed urgently.

I am very fortunate to have had some periods in the phase of organizing materials and writing during which I could give relatively undivided attention to the project. In the fall of 1998, I spent two months as a Fellow of the International Center for Advanced Studies of New York University, with Thomas Bender, director, as host. In 1999, Steven Vertovec, director of the ESRC Transnational Communities Programme based at the Institute of Social and Cultural Anthropology of Oxford University, invited me to spend two months as a fellow in Oxford. In 2001, I was able to devote three months to my writing, on a part-time basis, as a visiting fellow at the Stockholm Center for Organizational Research (SCORE), thanks to the hospitality of Nils Brunsson, chair of the board, and Christina Garsten, director. All of them, I should add, also introduced me to new and tempting local intellectual milieus, allowing stimulating excursions away from the desk.

During the years that I have been working on the project, I have also had a chance to present materials to, and try out interpretations and formulations with, a number of audiences. I am grateful for comments made in the context of lectures and in conferences at Amsterdam, Bayreuth, Belfast, Berkeley, Berlin, Chapel Hill, Chicago, Edinburgh, Frankfurt, Hamburg, Heidelberg, Lund, Madison, New York, Norrköping, Oxford, Rüdesheim, Södertörn, Swansea, and Uppsala. Some of these led to publications relating in different ways to the project: "Other Transnationals: Perspectives Gained from Studying Sideways," *Paideuma* 44 (1998): 109–23; "Of Correspondents and Collages," *Anthropological Journal on European Cultures* 7 (1998): 91–109; "Reporting from Jerusalem," *Cultural Anthropology* 13 (1998): 548–74; "Studying Townspeople, Studying Foreign Correspondents: Experiences of Two Approaches to Africa," in *Afrika und die Globalisierung,* edited by Hans Peter Hahn and Gerd Spittler (Hamburg: LIT Verlag, 1999); "Dateline Tokyo: Telling the World about Japan," in *Asian Media Productions,* edited by Brian Moeran (London: Curzon, 2001); "Among the Foreign Correspondents: Reflections on Anthropological Styles and Audiences," *Ethnos* 67 (2002): 57–74; "Macro-Scenarios: Anthropology and the Debate over Contemporary and Future Worlds," forthcoming in *Social Anthropology;* and "Being There . . . and There . . . and There! Reflections on Multisite Ethnography," forthcoming in *Ethnography.* This book draws on some materials, ideas, and formulations that are also spread over these publications, although it puts them together in other ways and adds a great deal more.

In particular, however, I wish to thank past and present colleagues and graduate students in the Department of Social Anthropology, Stockholm University, who have heard much about this project over a period of years and responded helpfully. My closest colleague in the department, Gudrun Dahl, has continuously shown an encouraging interest. A number of graduate students with media research interests and journalist backgrounds of their own have been stimulating conversation partners. Örjan Bartholdson, Peter Frick, Ronald Stade, and Per Ståhlberg have brought additional materials to my attention.

And then my wife and colleague, Helena Wulff, has lived with this project almost as much as I have, from beginning to end, coming along to Jerusalem, Johannesburg, and Cape Town and putting up, for one thing, with changed media consumption habits sometimes seemingly around the clock. She has heard a great many presentations of the materials and no doubt knows some of my phrasings almost by heart, but she has still been ready to give the written version conscientious and very constructive attention, remaining marvelously cheerful throughout. Perhaps that has been made just a little easier as she has realized that it is a project I have thoroughly enjoyed and which has therefore made me better company.

INTRODUCTION

Conversations with Correspondents

So there I am again, early on a Stockholm morning, barely awake, gulping down my coffee, scanning the newspaper, listening to the Radio Sweden news program, and a familiar voice comes on, which I have heard a great many times over the last couple of years. Now it reports on street riots in Karachi, or perhaps the newest military triumph of the Taliban in Afghanistan (this must have been in the mid-1990s), and then signs off: ". . . So-and-so, Hong Kong." Hong Kong? But that report was about something thousands of miles from there!

There was a time when I responded to this sort of listening experience with a mixture of outrage and amusement. No doubt my reaction to the suggested continental reach of certain newspeople had something to do with the habitual assumptions of anthropologists about the rooting of expertise in local personal presence and experience, assumptions related to our preoccupation with fieldwork. But at some point, having come to terms with the fact that media organizations such as Radio Sweden would have a staff member described as the "Asia correspondent" (and an "Africa correspondent," and a "Middle East correspondent"), my professional curiosity began to grow instead. How do they actually do it? As a journalist, how does one handle the responsibility of covering a continent, or some large chunk of it?

As I made my way to a more organized study of the work of news media foreign correspondents, in an attempt to answer that and related questions, it was against the background of a wider range of research interests. In the late 1970s and early 1980s, I had been provoked into an engagement with globalization (before that term was in much use), as I realized that my new acquaintances in the Nigerian town where I was doing local fieldwork often had their own imaginative horizons far beyond town limits. That West African experience became a point of departure for a series of inquiries, during the years that followed, into the ways anthropologists, as sociocultural theorists and as ethnographers, might view various aspects of global interconnectedness.[1] I thought and wrote about the cultural role of world cities, about the uses of network analysis in conceptualizing globalization, about cosmopolitanism, and about the changing place of "the national" on the social and cultural map of the world.

For a time, these were mostly conceptual and theoretical efforts, involving desk work rather than fieldwork. But then I felt that the time was ripe for a more concrete ethnographic involvement again, relating to issues of global and transnational interconnectedness, and that was when I began exploring the world of foreign correspondents.

There were some particular anthropological reasons for this choice. One was a sense that a concern with globalization ought to involve some experimentation with units of study. In retrospect, I could see that my work in the Nigerian town had been an instance of what had become one major approach to globalization, in anthropology among other disciplines: studies of "the global and the local." Obviously such examination of what happens to long-distance influences as they are handled in a local setting draws on major strengths of the tradition of ethnographic study. It turns globalization into something more tangible, gets us down to earth from some of the airy and sometimes dubious assertions of what one critic of the evolving field labeled "globalbabble" (J. Abu-Lughod 1991). Sometimes, however, the global-local studies also seem to be little more than a reluctant, minimalist adjustment of an ongoing anthropological habitus to the fact of increasing interconnectedness in the world; there should be other vantage points for considering that fact than those from towns or villages.

Turning to a study of an occupation made sense partly because much of twentieth-century globalization was literally globalization at work. Businesspeople, academics, diplomats, consultants, journalists, artists, athletes—all of them now extend their occupational communities and cultures across borders.[2] And a more specific reason for my curiosity about the foreign correspondents was that they seemed to be key players in today's globalization of consciousness. Their reporting for newspapers and newsmagazines, news agencies, radio, and television makes up a major part of that flow of information from and about other parts of their world which, for many of us, is a part of the rhythm of our daily routine.

Studying Sideways: Tension and Reflexivity

At the beginning of my project, when I made one of my first contacts with a potential informant, he giggled a little at the idea of being interviewed by an anthropologist. "So we will be your tribe," he said. But it is, of course, from an anthropological point of view, a very special tribe, in some ways rather like that of the anthropologists themselves.[3]

"Studying up" became a well-known figure of speech in anthropology some decades ago, through an essay in which Laura Nader (1972) noted that anthropologists have mostly engaged in studying people less powerful and prosperous than themselves ("subalterns," we might have said more recently), that is, studying down. The time had come, she argued, to shift the professional gaze. One could perhaps see research on the work of foreign correspondents as a matter of studying up, insofar as the public reach, and possibly the impact, of their reporting is considerable, and certainly greater than that of just about any academic monograph. Yet I am more inclined to see it as a case of studying sideways: not so much as a matter of power or rank, but rather as a matter of engaging with a craft that is in some ways parallel to my own. Like anthropologists, news media foreign correspondents report from one part of the world to another. We share the condition of being in a transnational contact zone, engaged there in reporting, representing, translating, interpreting—generally, managing meaning across distances, although (in part, at least) with different interests, under different constraints.[4]

For as long as their discipline has existed, anthropologists have occasionally become aware of some variety of other practitioners in that contact zone—missionaries, spies, tourist guides, more recently the consultant-entrepreneurs in the growing intercultural communication industry—and often with some irritation. As we have noted the affinity between the pursuits of such occupations and our own, we have mostly not been inclined to approach them as allies in the pursuit of knowledge and the enlightenment of publics; rather, we have quietly kept our distance. We do not want to be mistaken for them, and we want to make sure that our product is distinguishable from theirs.[5] Or we may protest vehemently when boundaries are blurred, when identities are mistaken or even brazenly manipulated. At times, strong fences seem to make slightly better neighbors.

Consequently, when we approach any such neighboring tribe, it is hardly an entirely innocent encounter. George Marcus (1997, 400) has dwelt on the problem of studying sideways in a discussion of what, with a term of Foucauldian derivation, he describes as power/knowledge regimes—"formal institutions of modernity that exercise power through the creation and management of knowledge." There are affinities between such regimes, Marcus suggests, and approaching others among them ethnographically and comparatively is a way of reflecting both on one's own condition and on one's own reflexivity. An anthropological inquiry into the work of foreign correspondents can thus also be good to think with as anthropology looks into its own mirror.[6] Foreign correspondents are a sort of anthropologists, or anthropologists are a sort of foreign correspondents, to the extent that they engage in reporting from one part of the world to another.

Clearly, there is a measure of tension across this boundary as well. Anthropologists tend to find themselves in a complicated interaction with the media news flow: occasionally scrutinizing it and trying to explain it, if they take on the part of public commentators, more frequently commenting on it offhandedly or at greater length as teachers in their classrooms, and certainly arguing about it among themselves. Especially when they have some specialized area experience to draw on—but sometimes without it as well—they are often inclined to be critical of foreign news reporting, perhaps finding it shallow, or incomplete, or sensational, or simply false. (If these are power/ knowledge regimes, the way we may tend to see it is that we have more knowledge, but they have more power; and perhaps we are still envious.)

Yet if anthropologists over the years have wanted to distance their work explicitly from what is sometimes labeled "mere journalism," some voices have recently signaled a readiness to rethink the difference. Liisa Malkki (1997, 93) notes that "news and culture seem to repel each other like oil and water—not least because they generally operate in such different temporal registers"; nonetheless, coming from the study of an African refugee camp, she acknowledges her dependence on journalistic sources as she tries to stay informed about her field area. And in an essay on the anthropological understanding of "the economies of violence," Catherine Lutz and Donald Nonini (1999, 104) suggest that ethnographic work on such a topic will have to look like "fine investigative journalism" in its skilled combinatory use of a wide range of sources of knowledge.

Rather more constructively, one may thus keep in mind some questions about the balance of closeness and distance between these lines of work. How do the ways media correspondents practice their craft in foreign lands compare with the fieldwork of anthropologists? How do the structures within which they operate affect their efforts? And what do they report? How do they mediate to their audiences the element of unfamiliarity and difference in foreign news? The parallels and the contrasts can provide some food for thought.

Circumscribing the Field

For the purposes of this study, then, how have I delineated this tribe of mine? I take the core group of foreign correspondents to consist of those individuals who are stationed in other countries than that of their origin for the purpose of reporting on events and characteristics of the area of their stationing, through news media based elsewhere (usually in their countries of origin). But though this is the core, in the real world of international news reporting, the edges of the category get a bit blurred, through variations in recruitment, geographical mobility, and audience definitions. At times the causes and consequences of such blurring themselves deserve some attention.

Within these limits, moreover, as part of my anthropological angle, I am more interested in the work of correspondents reporting over greater cultural distances, as it were: from Asia, Africa, or the Middle East to Europe or North America, rather than from Washington, D.C., to Stockholm or from Brussels to London. This focus actually excludes a large part of the world's foreign correspondents, who report across borders within the West.

Again probably in a way characteristic of anthropology, I am concerned with variations rather than with standards and averages. Consequently I have been interested in correspondents reporting to different countries through different media. But by far the larger number of the correspondents I have met with are western Europeans or North Americans, reflecting that structure of international news flow to which there will be reason to return.[7]

I have also focused on what I would describe as the mainstream media—probably it is reasonably clear what I mean by this. I have in mind those that seek large audiences that are, perhaps, relatively diverse internally, media that offer a rather wide range of news in political, economic, and cultural domains, and that in principle, as far as international coverage is concerned, do not focus strictly on any one region of the world. Generally, in western European countries and in North America, this means a handful of national or metropolitan newspapers, some newsmagazines, and some radio and television networks or national channels. Of course, on the one hand, not all major media organizations have the ambition of offering much of an independent, continuous foreign coverage. In the U.S. newspaper market, for instance, the *New York Times,* the *Washington Post,* and the *Los Angeles Times* count for a great deal more than mass market tabloids; in Great Britain, you turn for such coverage to, let us say, the *Guardian* or the *Daily Telegraph* rather than (despite the name) the *News of the World;* in the German-speaking world, to the *Frankfurter Allgemeine* or the *Neue Zürcher Zeitung* but not to *Bild-Zeitung*. On the other hand, a wide range of media and media organizations offer international news from particular professional, trade, ideological, religious, or other perspectives to more particular audiences—sometimes as an alternative to what may be described as establishment media, sometimes as exclusive and privileged in contrast to what is held to be information for general consumption. A closer look at these media, I am sure, could help us understand better the social differentiation of international news production and access and the volatility of media organization in times of changing technology. Despite my interest in variation, however, I have left the latter group out here; I concentrate on the foreign news readily available to the more average "informed citizen."

There is, moreover, a majority of print correspondents among the people appearing in the following pages. There are several reasons for this. One is that there still are, as far as I can see, more of them than of others. Another is that since I wanted to follow the reporting of the correspondents I met, print journalism was simply more practical to deal with. But also important, I felt that it had the greater affinity with anthropology. "What does the ethnographer do? He writes," Clifford Geertz (1973, 19) once noted, and although there has been more interest in other modes of representation since then (as Geertz suggested there should be), writing remains a very large part of our work, a fact about which late-twentieth-century anthropology also became increasingly self-conscious.[8] To a certain extent, then, I have been interested in foreign correspondents as ethnographic writers. Yet in these times one could hardly disregard the variety of channels that foreign news flows through or the relationships between them. Thus, as even that first paragraph above suggests, I listen to the radio, and I watch television; and while engaging in this study, I have been talking to radio and television people as well. And to news agency people, whose line of work does not fit altogether easily into such categories.

Consequently, a large part of the material for this book comes out of more or less lengthy, sometimes repeated, open-ended conversations with some seventy correspondents and also with the foreign editors of some major European and American newspapers (and the international editor at the New York headquarters of the Associated Press)—these latter in order to get some overview of the management of foreign news coverage and to get the perspective from the office at home.[9] Most of the encounters with correspondents were in Jerusalem, Johannesburg, Cape Town, and Tokyo, but on a more ad hoc basis, I seized the opportunity to do some further interviewing in places where I found myself mostly for other reasons: in Stockholm (even in my living room at home), New York, Los Angeles, Washington, D.C., London, Frankfurt, and Hong Kong.

Perhaps anthropologists are still often drawn to the classic temporal (perhaps more precisely, atemporal) practice of "the ethnographic present" as they write, but in describing the life of news workers, this would hardly be possible. My first conversations with foreign correspondents for this study took place in 1995 and the last in 2000. I was in Jerusalem in 1997, in South Africa in 1998, and in Tokyo in 1999. The particular reporting I will refer to will obviously reflect the positioning of the study within the flow of history.[10] Apart from that, there is the overarching fact that these were times when the world had recently come out of the cold war and when reporting thus had to grapple with new circumstances. Moreover, most of the gathering of materials for this book was done before the symbolically powerful date of September 11, 2001. I will refer occasionally to the events associated with it, however, and to the question of its significance for foreign news reporting.

On-Site and Off-Site Conversations

I have been told in a New York café about the assault on the senses involved in arriving at a gruesome mass murder scene in India, and in the cafeteria atop the *Los Angeles Times* building of the conditions on a Nairobi beat that also included covering wars in Somalia and Rwanda. Such accounts can give a vivid idea of a correspondent's personal experiences and allow for reflections on the craft and the beliefs and values that may go with it. Yet, strictly speaking, one may say that these are off-site; they are conversations with ex–foreign correspondents—people who have returned from a beat or a series of beats abroad but who are, at the moment at least, not practicing as foreign correspondents, even if it may turn out that later on they will go off on such an assignment again. Insightful and eloquent as these informants have often been in my meetings with them, there is a certain added value in meeting with their colleagues who are on site and who talk about particular considerations entering into their own dealing with events that are fresh in their minds. The routines and the mundane contextual factors of daily reporting were more easily brought out on the spot, in a reporting landscape that I could at least catch some glimpses of myself. In that way, there is some difference between interviews on the scene and those conducted elsewhere, with a retrospective view of past experiences.

One afternoon in Jerusalem, for example, I was talking to a senior correspondent of a major American newspaper. That evening, Benjamin

Netanyahu, the Israeli prime minister, and Yassir Arafat were going to meet at the Israel-Gaza border. It was some time after the Hebron agreement in early 1997, a phase of no real crisis but certainly still one of many unsettled issues. So how would my interlocutor handle this event? Would he travel to the border point, a couple of hours away, to get the story?

No, he said; he had a stringer—more about this category in chapter 3— working for him in Tel Aviv, closer to Gaza, and he had asked him to go. The stringer would call him at the end of the meeting—which would probably be a bit delayed, since these things were seldom on time—and then the senior correspondent could call Netanyahu's press spokesman, who had a cell phone, in his car going back. This would allow him to check details and ask for comments. Then he would sit down, as his deadline rapidly approached, to do his piece for the next day's paper.

The day after that Arafat-Netanyahu meeting, I was speaking to a correspondent working out of Jerusalem for another American daily. He had had a look at his colleague's story on the Internet. He did not seem quite sure whether the writer had actually been present at the Gaza border point or not, but he concluded that "he must have been up to 2:00 a.m. working on that." This correspondent's own paper did not expect him to cover such an event, and if it printed anything about the meeting at all, it would use materials from one of the agencies, such as the Associated Press. Talking to both of these correspondents about a particular current event, I could develop my understanding of their different ways of dealing with the local scene and their own views of these differences.

In describing my project to foreign correspondents, I have tried to make the point that I do not intend it as an attack on their work and its products. Indeed journalists often have a reasonable suspicion that academics generally are inclined to be critical of news work and sometimes to forget the implications of such constraints as deadlines and space limits. Among the foreign correspondents, as elsewhere, I have felt that it is a part of an anthropologist's task to make sense of "the native's point of view." In this case it would seem to mean that we should not take satisfaction in critique and complaint, but we should seek to understand the comparative ecology of reporting, the practical, spatial, temporal, and organizational constraints of foreign news work—which is not to say, obviously, that we can never allow ourselves to be unhappy about the ways in which these constraints operate or with their consequences.

It is a legitimate question what an anthropologist might usefully contribute, within the interdisciplinary division of labor in media studies, to an understanding of foreign news reporting. To begin with, I would note that in quantitative terms, the academic literature about foreign correspondence seems surprisingly limited.[11] Again, especially since the 1970s or so, there has certainly been much documentation and analysis of the overwhelming North American and European dominance in the overall structure of news production in the world. I see my own study basically as contextualized by such studies and feel no need to go into their preoccupations. They hardly engage, however, with the ethnographic issues of everyday reporting practices and conditions that I am concerned with.

Obviously, this is a study more involved with the production side than with the consumption/reception side of news flow (even if it may often be difficult in media studies to entirely disregard whichever side one is not primarily dealing with—I try to spell out some assumptions about audience responses to foreign news in chapter 1). In contrast, some work on foreign news, for example on war reporting, is less based on familiarity with reporting circumstances; it engages rather more in some variety of content analysis (in a broad sense), in practice home-based. There are, too, in other disciplines concerned with media studies, examples of more close-up studies of news reporting as production; but somewhat expectably, they focus mostly on local or possibly national news, at home, where journalists are more readily accessible to academics.[12] (One book by an anthropologist, Mark Pedelty's *War Stories* [1995], a study of correspondents in El Salvador toward the end of the country's civil war, is obviously an exception.) To place news work in an everyday organizational context, as such studies usually attempt to do, is certainly important, and this has been one of my aims. I want to throw some light on the continued ordering of foreign correspondent activity and the room for maneuver, improvisation, and choice within that larger frame just noted—a bit less structure, perhaps, and some more agency. The correspondents are hardly mere puppets of the world information order, even though the latter cannot be ignored.

As an anthropologist, however, I also wanted to see the foreign correspondents in interaction with their wider reporting habitat, as correspondents in Africa or as correspondents in Japan, with an eye to how their depiction of specific foreign places emerges. The large anthropological storehouse of writing on these places can provide me, for one thing, with complementary or alternative views of the things foreign correspondents choose to write about and, for another thing, with an opportunity to think about what kinds of phenomena they somehow do not get around to writing about. (Yet I should say that it can work the other way around as well—what do journalists pick out that ethnographers have so far not told me about?)

"Exploring the World of Foreign Correspondents," the subtitle of the book, should sum up much of this. I think "exploring" suggests both the sense of curiosity built into the anthropological enterprise and a certain modesty as one tries to grasp the characteristics of another way of life. And "the World of Foreign Correspondents" is both the entire world, as foreign correspondents portray it, and their own particular social world of relationships and practices.

I have enjoyed my conversations with foreign correspondents. It is perhaps in the nature of their business for journalists to be more or less sociable, and now and then one of them has made the point that since they are forever dependent on people's willingness to talk to them, they should certainly be ready to reciprocate when someone seeks them out. Most of the correspondents have been about my age or younger; normally I have some recollection of the news events they reminisce about in discussing their reporting careers, and at one time or another I have passed through some of the places where they have previously been stationed. This has undoubtedly been helpful in establishing rapport, and so occasionally has been the fact that I have happened to know someone from their dispersed collegial networks, past or present, and may even be able to offer a bit of news about someone they have not seen for a long time.

I also suspect that our conversations sometimes served a therapeutic purpose for the journalists. Reminiscing in an essay about the brief period he had spent as a *New York Times* reporter, the historian Robert Darnton (1975) once noted that he and his peers in the newsroom really wrote for each other. There, in "the snake pit," they would show their appreciation for an assignment well handled or would be vociferous in their criticisms. The problem for foreign correspondents is that in their daily lives, such relationships tend to be attenuated. Most of their contacts with the busy editors at home may be brief, to the point, more focused on upcoming tasks. Feedback is often limited, and there might not be much opportunity to share experiences and assumptions or for the give and take of more broadly defined face-to-face collegiality. So the brief appearance on the local scene of a sort of quasi-colleague who would encourage some autobiographical and situational accounting might sometimes have been a welcome break.

Correspondents are also often concerned with facts and with formulations. In other field research, in order not to disturb the flow of conversations, I have been inclined not to take notes during the interviews themselves; I have hurried immediately afterward to some place around the corner where I could reconstruct on paper the key elements of what had been said and then move on to write the elaborated field notes as soon as possible. I started out like this in my first pilot interviews with foreign correspondents, but after one or two of them asked, perhaps with some puzzlement, how I handled my note taking, I began to raise the topic at the start of the conversations. Taking my pocket notebook out, I would point to the difference between them and those other anthropological informants who would be less accustomed to talking to someone continuously scribbling. And that observation might have helped suggest to them a relationship between ethnography and correspondent work. There were also those moments when correspondents came up with some formulation that (I suspect) as professional wordsmiths they felt particularly pleased with—and when they seemed to steal a glance to make sure I did not miss it. Once when I concluded a conversation, as I often did, by asking whether I had failed to ask about anything I ought to have asked about, the correspondent said that was a question she often used, too.

Multisite Fieldwork and Polymorphous Engagements

That might suggest that my project is indeed a sort of hybrid between journalism and anthropology (and perhaps media studies and cultural studies). It entered my mind that since, somewhat like a foreign correspondent, I would come to a place, stay for a while, and move on when my business was concluded, I might even be doing a sort of "parachute anthropology" (more later about the relevant comparable correspondent practice, especially in chapter 2). But then as James Clifford (1997, 186), intellectual historian and in-house critic of anthropology, has pointed out, anthropological fieldwork is one kind of spatial practice, "articulated along a changing border with literary and journalistic practices," with the border "unstable, constantly renegotiated." It is a practice that has recently been under more intense scrutiny within the discipline than it may have been at any time since Malinowski established its dominant form.

In any case, with extensive research in three countries and additional engagements in about a half dozen others, my interactions with foreign correspondents have obviously involved what has become known in anthropology as multisite or multilocal fieldwork.[13] This is certainly not the only way of doing an anthropology of foreign correspondents. Mark Pedelty's *War Stories* is an instance of "deep hanging out," staying more or less in one place and dealing with it in greater depth, the way ethnographies are typically done. But even though I have my ethnographic inclinations, I have aimed here rather at an overview, a bird's-eye perspective on the foreign correspondents' line of work, seeing it as an interconnected field, stretched out over continents. Probably in most multilocal studies in anthropology, there is an element of comparison or contrast between the sites involved, and that element is here as well—correspondent work in Africa is not altogether like correspondent work in Japan. Yet I believe mostly such studies are not just multilocal but also translocal, concerned with relationships between sites. Here, then, I also try to take note of linkages that connect places in the world of foreign correspondents.

This has to a degree steered my choices of people to look for in different sites. Rather than single-mindedly pursuing diversity, I sometimes sought out the dispersed correspondents of the same organization, and also their editors at home, to get a view of the same news enterprise from different places and perspectives. In such encounters, too, the fact that the correspondents and I already had some shared background knowledge and some shared contacts could become an additional asset in interaction.

If my conversations with correspondents turned this into a multilocal field project, I was also attracted to this study because it could involve a variety of other materials, allowing a flexibility in its operation. It was obviously a part of the project to intensify my daily news consumption (although I may be somewhat addicted anyway), to try to keep up with the ongoing flow of news in the press, on radio, and on TV. The field was thus with me in some way even when I was not able to venture far from my desk in Stockholm. Once I had begun to think of the work of foreign correspondents as a potential research topic, moreover, I realized that I had already been taking a more than passing interest in it. I remembered time spent in movie theaters, with Alfred Hitchcock's *Foreign Correspondent;* with *The Year of Living Dangerously,* portraying correspondent life in an increasingly chaotic 1960s Jakarta; with an American newspaperman and his local assistant in a Cambodia overrun by the Red Khmers, in *Killing Fields;* and with a rebellious stringer in a Central American civil war, in *Salvador.* Popular culture has had its part in shaping the image of the foreign correspondent. (Apart from the films, even before Hitchcock, there was Evelyn Waugh's novel *Scoop,* first published in 1938 and apparently in print ever since—a satire of African war reporting that many correspondents are still quite fond of.)

More important, I noticed how many books by foreign correspondents had in fact surreptitiously accumulated on my shelves over the years. There is a sizable autobiographical and biographical literature, as well as book-length treatments summing up a correspondent's knowledge and experience from particular postings.[14] Even if the authors of some of these writings are a bit inclined to dwell on the adventures and dangers that are certainly prominent in the public image of foreign correspondents (as in the movies just mentioned), saying less about routine practices, this literature has added to my comprehension of correspondents' work and lives. It may be true generally, under the current conditions of anthropology, that the dividing lines between natives and informants on the one side and colleagues, peers, and competitors on the other get rather fuzzy. Studying sideways, that tendency becomes especially strong. Still, I should say that I have mostly looked at the large body of more or less autobiographical accounts by foreign correspondents as texts belonging among my ethnographic materials rather than as analytical explorations of the kind I try to do myself.

Again, then, with this variety of materials to think about, the style of work may have come to resemble that of the correspondents themselves, and of other journalists. Hugh Gusterson (1997, 116), moving on personally from an ethnography of one California nuclear weapons laboratory to a study of the entire American "nuclear weapons community," and looking intermittently at the counterpart Russian community as well, argues that contemporary ethnography often becomes a matter of "polymorphous engagements" —interacting with informants across a number of dispersed sites, doing fieldwork by telephone and E-mail, collecting data eclectically in many different ways from a disparate array of sources, attending carefully to popular culture, conducting "formal interviews of the kind often done by journalists and political scientists," and "extensive reading of newspapers and official documents." A degree of such polymorphousness will indeed be evident in what follows. Part of it is that after I had my own encounters with the correspondents in one setting or another, I could continue to read their stories in the papers, hear their voices on the radio, see their faces on television—these informants do not vanish from your horizon the moment you leave the distant field site. And that means that in a way, "parasocially" perhaps, the conversations with them continue.[15]

1 Media and the World as a Single Place

In 1871 Lewis Henry Morgan, the pioneer anthropologist whose memory the Morgan Lectures honor, traveled to Europe. He took copious notes and hoped to publish some of his observations, but as one of his biographers put it, he observed Europe "with that dry literalness and grave earnestness that served him well when studying the habits of beavers or the material culture of the Iroquois" (Stern 1931, 47).[1] Disappointed, his editor friend at home suggested to him that instead, if "you . . . just use your Yankee eyes to see and describe things as they are in Europe, or as they seem to you, you might do something worth having." That argument, about bringing a perspective from one place and applying it to another place, then reporting back to where it came from, is central to this book.

Before that, having dabbled in local Republican politics in Rochester, New York, Morgan had hoped to be appointed to a foreign service position. Another biographer notes that he would really have liked to be sent to Russia, where he would have pursued his research on forms of human kinship, but since he "realized that he lacked sufficient political stature to win the position," he requested a position in Sweden instead. Having failed to get that, he tried in turn for Peru, China, and Italy but was awarded none of them (Resek 1960, 119).

In the long run, however, we may see that a Chinese connection of sorts was established for Morgan, or perhaps Morgan's ghost. Early Communists discovered this Republican and brought his ideas into their view of human history. And so in the early 1990s, when a young Chinese-American anthropologist, Mayfair Yang (1996), set out to do fieldwork in the People's Republic of China, she found that her official hosts had firm opinions about what she could and could not study—and these opinions were guided by the concepts of human evolution developed by Lewis Henry Morgan. Lineages and ancestor rituals were defined as "back-ward," feudal or even more ancient, and consequently not good topics for a study of contemporary China. And so Yang concluded that moving from nineteenth-century Rochester to twentieth-century Beijing, some of Morgan's work had become a prominent example of what Edward Said (1983) has termed "traveling theory"—with Friedrich Engels, one may want to add, as travel agent.[2]

Through his more renowned scholarship as well as his failed travel journalism, Morgan exemplifies the kind of matters I engage with in the following pages: the passage of perspectives, but also the representation of distant events, people, and places (a matter with which many anthropologists have been preoccupied in recent times, under Edward Said's influence among others) and the development of a sense of humanity and the world as a whole. To reiterate, this book is primarily about news production rather than news consumption. Even so, it seems hardly possible to develop a perspective on news work in the world without any underlying idea of what the work is for and who it is for. So in this chapter I want to spell out some assumptions about the place of foreign news in our lives and about contemporary stances vis-à-vis the world, as well as about the nature of news and the qualities of news media.

The term "globalization" may too often have been hijacked to refer only to the expanding reach of market actors, mechanisms, and processes, yet we may insist on using it to denote a more general, internally varied, growing interconnectedness and a corresponding form of consciousness. With globalization, argues the sociologist Roland Robertson (1992, 6), one of the pioneers in this field of study, the world is turning into "a single place." In some quarters at least, there is a growing sense that what is needed is more of a global citizenship that involves people as active, responsible, informed participants in a public life that in one way or another transcends national boundaries and is concerned with the welfare of humanity. (Perhaps if Lewis Henry Morgan, also a scholar-activist—on behalf of the Iroquois Indians—and a public intellectual in his time, were with us now, this would also be his vision; he closed chapter 13 of *Ancient Society,* his most famous work, by professing to be "profoundly impressed with the dignity and grandeur of those great conceptions which recognize the liberty, equality and fraternity of mankind.") For such a citizenship to be possible, there would have to be structures of civic life through which active and effective participation could be channeled and through which actors on the global arena could be held accountable. What I am ultimately concerned with at this level, however, is the complex shaping of civic impulses in a more interconnected world, that entity

I have taken to describing as the global ecumene.[3] What is the part of the long-distance news flow in orienting us toward—or away from—that world?

Before getting to such matters in more general terms, we will have a first brief encounter with three correspondents and three of the specific scenes from which they have reported.

Jerusalem, Accra, Beijing

The first of these three stories is from Marjorie Miller, who was *Los Angeles Times* correspondent in Jerusalem when I met her. For Jerusalem correspondents, the continuous main story over the years has certainly been the troubled relationships between Israelis and their Arab neighbors, including those closest at hand, the Palestinians. But in recent years, growing attention to another divide within Israeli Jewish society has contributed to a more complex picture. The split between largely secular Israelis and the ultra-Orthodox, the *haredim,* has serious political consequences, resulting in the hard news stories of election campaigns and parliamentary confrontations. But it is also played out in Israeli everyday life and is evident in the streets of Jerusalem, where the ultra-Orthodox are a quickly growing proportion of the city's population.

And so for one report on this social cleavage, under the headline "'Sabbath War' Flares in the Holy City," in one of those celebrated "Column One" pieces that characteristically begin in the upper left corner of the *Los Angeles Times* front page and then meander through several pages of the paper, Marjorie Miller (1996e), presents a Saturday afternoon scene in Jerusalem's Bar Ilan Street, where a caravan of cars move along slowly, slowly, bearing signs with the greeting "Shabat shalom" (Good Sabbath). The response of the people lining the street consists of hurled stones and epithets—"Dogs!" "Garbage!" "You are not Jewish!" Police on horseback move between the cars and the demonstrators.

Bar Ilan Street is a main Jerusalem thoroughfare. The secular city dwellers want to see it primarily as that; they feel strongly that it should be open for car traffic during the Sabbath as at any other time. But it runs through neighborhoods largely inhabited by the ultra-Orthodox, who insist that cars should stand still between sundown Friday and sundown Saturday. And thus, Miller reports, there is this "now-weekly ritual of animosity." She hears a yeshiva student dressed in the black hat and frock coat of the ultra-Orthodox turn angrily to a secular Israeli in the crowd of onlookers and demand, "If the community asks for its street to be closed one day on Shabbat, why not?" And the other young man, in Bermuda shorts, sandals, and sun-

glasses, virtually a secular uniform on a warm Jerusalem day, replies disdain-
fully, "Because those of us who are not religious should not have to live according to the will of the religious . . . You give these religious people a finger
today and they want the head tomorrow."

So of course, this is not just a matter of rights over those twenty-four
hours of traffic, once a week, on a particular street. A Jerusalem city council-
man, representing a party of the secular left, points out to Miller that the fight
is not only for Bar Ilan Street: "Jerusalem is our face to the world. The question is whether it will be the face of Los Angeles, Paris, London and other
Western cities, or whether it will be Tehran. The religious want to take steps
toward Tehran and further from the world I want to belong to."

In the second correspondent report there is also a kind of long-distance
imagination and identification. The title of the piece is "Ulster-by-the-
Equator," and the author is Chris McGreal (1999e), Africa correspondent of
the British newspaper the *Guardian*. At the time of the report, McGreal is
based in Johannesburg, but he has been spending much of his time traveling
widely in sub-Saharan Africa. This time, he reports from Accra, in Ghana.
There is a lodge of the Orange Order there, which has been in existence since
the end of World War I. The members march through the streets of Accra on
July 12, in memory of the Battle of the Boyne, and commemorate King
William's landing at Brixham on November 5. For their parades they wear
dark suits, orange sashes, medals, and bowler hats if they can afford them.
But the members of the lodge in Accra are not Northern Irish Protestants;
they are Ghanaians. The grand master, a retired building contractor, goes to
Belfast for the July marches when he has a chance, and when McGreal meets
him, he is planning his trip to the next conference of the Imperial Order,
in Liverpool. McGreal is shown a picture of the swearing-in of the Accra
grand master, at a table adorned with the Orange exhortation: "Truth, Unity
and Concord. No Surrender." Although the lodge in Accra stands with the
Orangemen in Northern Ireland in their religious beliefs, however, the grand
master says, "[W]e have no problem with Catholics."

Rather than actually engaging very actively with the affairs of Northern
Ireland, it appears, the Orangemen of Accra are part of an active local ritual
and associational life in which the membership of their lodge may overlap
with those of Rotarians, Freemasons, Odd Fellows, and others. All of them,
it turns out, entered a difficult period when the young flight lieutenant Jerry
Rawlings seized power in Ghana and started persecuting organizations of
this kind. Their temples were destroyed, parades were banned, and membership was proscribed for civil servants. Then a bit later the Orange Lodge had
to suffer the criticisms of the visiting grand chaplain of the Scottish lodge,

who was very suspicious of the mingling of the Accra Orangemen with people of all those other associations, who could be of any religious persuasion or none at all.

When the grand master of the Accra lodge went to the Liverpool conference, he would join those others who campaigned for a name change from "the Imperial Order" to "the International Order"—"imperial" has unfortunate connotations in Africa. Yet the imperial connection still has some advantages. The Scottish lodge had contributed funds for a new temple, and when McGreal came to visit, the grand master hoped that Queen Elizabeth, on her impending journey to Ghana, would take up his invitation to visit the lodge. It would be very good for its membership drive.

Saturday night in Beijing: my third correspondent story is by a veteran China watcher, Göran Leijonhufvud (1998), writing in the Stockholm morning newspaper *Dagens Nyheter*. (I had missed seeing him when I was in Hong Kong, where he is based, but then because it turned out that Leijonhufvud was on vacation close to where I have my summer house in southern Sweden, I had the chance to spend a quiet afternoon with him at the edge of the forest, talking about his experiences in reporting from China over a quarter century.)

Leijonhufvud begins this Saturday evening in a bowling hall with a few young bachelors who express a preference for this pastime over discos and karaoke bars. The patronage of the bowling alleys is mixed: some middle-aged people, entire families as well. The foreign correspondent runs into an American who sells bowling alleys as entire packages and who claims that there is a bowling index of national development—as countries reach a certain level of prosperity, their people begin to go bowling. Yet Beijing people do other things as well on a Saturday night now, things unheard of twenty years ago. On the extremely crowded dance floor of a megadisco, the dancers jump up and down, up and down; and the visual memory of the Swedish journalist takes him back to Tiananmen Square in the 1960s, where the Red Guardsmen jumped up and down with Chairman Mao's Little Red Book in their hands.

In the Beijing of the late 1990s, however, Saturday night is only a part of another new concept—*zhoumo* (the weekend). People go shopping or get out of town to breathe less polluted air wherever they may find it. Or they are busy with practical matters at home. Now that they are able to buy their apartments, laying new floors, painting walls, and looking for new furniture have also become major weekend preoccupations for Chinese city people.

Three correspondents, from three countries, reporting between continents. What understandings of the world do we draw from them? How do they place Jerusalem, Los Angeles, Accra, London, Beijing, and Stockholm

vis-à-vis one another in the global ecumene? We will come back to these stories and these questions after taking up certain overall issues.

Cosmopolitanism, Thick or Thin

Just after the end of World War II, one of the pioneers in the sociology of
knowledge distribution, Alfred Schutz, wrote an essay on "the informed citizen" that more than a half century later may still strike us as remarkably up
to date, even though technologies and their associated speeds have changed:

> We are, so to speak, potentially subject to everybody's remote control.
> No spot of this globe is more distant from the place where we live than
> sixty airplane hours; electric waves carry messages in a fraction of a sec-
> ond from one end of the earth to another; and very soon every place in
> this world will be the potential target of destructive weapons released
> at any other place. Our own social surrounding is within the reach of
> everyone, everywhere; an anonymous Other, whose goals are unknown
> to us because of his anonymity, may bring us together with our system
> of interests and relevances within his control. (Schutz 1964, 129)

Already there was a sense of what it meant to be an informed citizen of the
world as a single place.[4] Schutz contrasted this social type to the "man in the
street," to whom what was relevant was what he needed to know for his
everyday life in his immediate environment, and also to the "expert," whose
system of relevances was defined quite precisely by the established problems
within his field. The informed citizen was inclined to restrict the zone of the
presumably irrelevant, for he sensed that he could not know when the information someone else might place there would be made relevant to him by
that possibly anonymous Other.

"Informed citizens," we may think, along such lines, are those who
place a value on a sort of habitual, well-rounded but not very specialized
scanning of ongoing events, not only those most near at hand, and have some
conception of how matters fit together. This would seem to be a desirable
quality of a citizen of the world. Yet citizenship may involve not only information, but also sentiments and commitments.

I believe the notion of cosmopolitanism is one we can use here. At least
partially in reaction to the narrowly economic conception of globalization, it
has gained a renewed significance as a keyword in arguments over increased
transnational interconnectedness. In one central sense, there is a politics of
cosmopolitanism, which by now we may understand to involve a sense of re-

sponsibility beyond the nation-state. It may entail support for political activities transcending national boundaries, as well as the growth of transnational and supranational institutions and organizations of a political and legal nature. Even if it is not exactly preoccupied with the construction of a cosmopolis, a world society, as some sort of politically integrated entity, the present revival of a politics of cosmopolitanism involves a response to globalization that emphasizes that human beings are not only to be seen as a labor force or as consumers. The cosmopolitan impulse tends to favor more inclusive arrangements of compassion, human rights, solidarity, and peacefulness.

But quite important, there is another sense of cosmopolitanism: a more cultural and experiential conception, referring to an awareness and appreciation of diversity in modes of thought, ways of life, and human products and to the development of skills in handling such diversity. This cosmopolitanism, we should note, does not intrinsically refer to national units; it may relate to diversity in the world or in one's neighborhood.

We can ill afford to disregard the fact that "cosmopolitanism" is an old term that has accumulated many and disparate meanings and which over the years has aroused mixed feelings.[5] It seems we will be better off seeing it as a cluster of ideas at the center of a field of arguments that also includes anti-cosmopolitanisms, rather than as some single thing. But in the two central senses just identified, I am inclined to be generally in favor of cosmopolitanism. In addition, I am interested in the relationship between the two, between the politics and the culture of cosmopolitanism. Often they are discussed quite separately from one another, and it could indeed appear as if there were two different sets of ideas only accidentally sharing a label. Yet I believe the two senses may also come together.

In an American debate not so long ago over cosmopolitanism versus patriotism, the philosopher Martha Nussbaum (1996, 15), though a protagonist of the former (yet at the same time seeing no necessary conflict between the two), could still recognize a certain weakness in a philosophical or programmatic cosmopolitanism of the more political kind. "Becoming a citizen of the world is often a lonely business," she wrote. "It is . . . a kind of exile — from the comfort of local truths, from the warm, nestling feeling of patriotism, from the absorbing drama of pride in oneself and one's own." Cosmopolitanism "offers only reason and the love of humanity, which may seem at times less colorful than other sources of belonging."

Nussbaum's critics tended to agree with her at least on this point, or to feel that she had not even made it strongly enough.[6] Yet I do not see why we should accept this. Patriotism and cosmopolitanism do not need to be so different in their qualities as Nussbaum suggested, and neither may be entirely of one kind. Return for a moment to nationalism and national identity, which have drawn such intensive attention across several disciplines in the last couple of decades. We have learned to distinguish between two basic types of nationalism, one sometimes referred to as ethnic and the other as civic—the labels vary. The ethnic variety is indeed based on ethnicity, or at least something very much like it. Belonging to the nation thus tends to be based on an ascriptive criterion and an assumption of cultural homogeneity and considerable historical depth—the debatable term "primordial" is also used.[7] Consequently, this is a kind of nationalism based on great symbolic density, a major resource in contexts where solidarity has to be mobilized. The other side of the coin, obviously, is that it is often rigid and exclusionist when it comes to membership, and for such reasons it is not seldom conflict-generating.

Civic nationalism is a more clearly political thing. What is needed for membership is above all a commitment to an overarching political order: a constitution, a republic. In principle, regardless of culture and history, you too can join. But then, admirable as such openness and flexibility may be, some would argue that in civic nationalism there is a certain cultural deficit. It may be too symbolically narrow and thin to gain full commitments.

It seems, then, that civic nationalism has much in common with the sort of cosmopolitanism that Nussbaum identifies—but can we not also recognize the possibility that a politics of cosmopolitanism may take on a greater cultural density? Just possibly, the contrast between thin and thick nationalisms has itself routinely been drawn in a way that attributes too exclusive cultural efficacy to ethnic or primordialist constructs. Not all the cultural density sedimented in senses of national identity and nationhood need be of a narrowly ethnic, conflict-oriented character. The political psychologist Michael Billig (1995) has pointed out that in stable, affluent contemporary societies, there is often a strong "banal nationalism," based on the recurrent but evolving practices and experiences of everyday life that come to define much of what it means to belong to a given nation-state. I have argued elsewhere, too, that ethnonationalism does not have a monopoly on central, deeply affecting experiences; for a probably growing number of people, personal border-crossing involvements with different places, cultures, and nations may well have such qualities (Hannerz 1993, 2002).

We should be aware of the danger of simply conflating political and cultural cosmopolitanisms. The two may exist apart—people may be pleased with their personal levels of connoisseurship with regard to cultural diversity without necessarily committing themselves to political activity, or even sympathy, transcending national boundaries. Yet along the lines suggested with respect to nationalism, we may well consider it possible, even probable, that there is an affinity between them. Rather than merely constituting some kind of individual self-indulgence, the cultural, experiential, sometimes esthetic cosmopolitanism could perhaps become so intertwined with political cosmopolitanism as to provide it with both an important resource base of affect and a sense of competence. And unlike ethnonationalism, such cosmopolitanism can be inclusive rather than exclusive or confrontational, emphasizing the achievement rather than the ascription of understandings and social relationships.

To use a somewhat paradoxical but increasingly popular formulation, it is a matter of being, or becoming, at home in the world. One may ask here, too, whether this is not as much a question of breadth as of warmth—to be at home in the world, ideally, may entail having a similar range of experiences out there, of others and of oneself, as one has closer at hand, in a local community or in a nation. Corresponding to Billig's phrasing, perhaps this can turn into something like a comfortably banal cosmopolitanism.

The World through the Media

Wider horizons, a curiosity about the world, and some sense of a wider civic responsibility and human compassion may be desirable qualities, but they cannot be taken for granted. In neither its thinner nor its thicker varieties is cosmopolitanism now something that follows automatically from globalization. Even if we accept Robertson's notion that the world is turning into "a single place," most people do not have personal experiences of very much of it. Rather than having been everywhere and seen, heard, smelled, tasted, and touched everything, people—including those aspiring to be informed citizens of the world—depend on the representations provided by various agencies of information brokerage, and the news media have a central place here.

Do the media then turn people into cosmopolitans? That is really not self-evident. To begin with, inside and outside critics of the news industry have pointed to what seems like a paradox. In an era of intense globalization, foreign news coverage in many media channels has recently been shrinking. In a late 1990s cover story, the somewhat upscale British-based newsweekly the *Economist* ("Here Is the News" 1998, 4) compared the contents of the *Times* of London on typical days in 1898, 1948, and 1998. In the first of these years, an issue had nineteen columns of foreign news (in no small proportion on the Balkan war of the time), eight columns of domestic news, and three about salmon fishing. Fifty years later, lead articles commented on Italy,

Canada, China, and the crisis in Western civilization. The front page in 1998 had six articles. One of them was foreign news: about the actor Leonardo Di-Caprio's new girlfriend.

"Remember that this is a dying occupation," said one of the first foreign correspondents I talked to, as we parted on a busy street. Too dark a view, perhaps. If in overall quantitative terms, there really has been a decline in foreign coverage in recent years, however, various reasons for it have been offered. "The accountants are cracking their whips," said a Jerusalem news veteran to me. "Forget the rhetoric: the news business sells a product that is blended and packaged, and the competition is cutthroat," writes an experienced insider commentator on foreign correspondence, Mort Rosenblum (1993, 8); "when the product doesn't sell, its marketers tinker with the mix." It is certainly a widespread view that generally, media organizations are more business-minded than ever, and in times when economic considerations play a very large part in management minds, the down-to-earth question is raised whether the high cost of foreign news, especially in the form of an extensive network of staff correspondents, is really balanced by more readers or advertisement revenue directly brought in by such coverage. For some organizations the answer may be simply no, and thus they may seek alternative ways of reporting on the world—or just do very little of it.

But not every organization takes the same view. A little further into my research, in a sixth-floor office of the classic Forty-third Street building of the *New York Times* in midtown Manhattan, I met with Bill Keller, who was serving for a while as foreign editor. He reminisced about coming back to New York a few years earlier to take up his new position. At the time he had been worried about his new duties, because it seemed to him that the recent congressional elections (those in 1994) were a sign that Americans were turning away from the world toward more parochial preoccupations. On his way from Johannesburg, where he had been based as a Southern Africa correspondent, however, he made a stopover in Paris and met with Flora Lewis, an old-timer in foreign news and commentary, who strengthened his resolve: "That's not a demand problem, it's a supply problem." She argued that the public would respond to political leadership and to media that took the world out there seriously.

Then Keller found that the national edition of the *New York Times* grew when the local edition did not and that readership surveys for the former showed that readers liked the foreign coverage, which was weak in their local papers. Those informed citizens with cosmopolitan inclinations were apparently out there. It seemed that the declining interest in international coverage on the part of some media organizations could widen this news niche for others.

But business considerations are only one aspect of any recent decrease in interest in foreign news on the part of the media. In 1998 the *Economist* ("Here Is the News") could argue in its cover story, "[T]he lack of foreign news is a measure of world peace as well as of rich world insularity . . . [T]he world is a relatively quiet place these days." It went on to note that an expanding category of news is what Americans call "news you can use." Foreign news often did not seem to be exactly that.

A relatively quiet place? Not in a later period, after September 11, 2001. It remains to be seen whether the events of that date brought with them an enduring change in attention to foreign news.[8] Anyway, clearly it is significant that much of the space devoted to such news in that 1898 issue of the *Times* used for comparison involved coverage of a war—a European war, even though in the distant Balkans. The space or the time devoted to foreign news in the media increase in such times, as does the number of people classified, if only quite momentarily, as foreign correspondents. (One may even sense that this category seems to be easily conflated with that of war correspondents.) It is hardly true that the world, even in the 1990s, was one without such violence, but if there was a decline in foreign coverage by then, it must be partly understood against the background of what went before.

Early in my study, in another Manhattan office, I had a chance to talk to Tom Kent, international editor of the Associated Press. He noted that not least for Americans, the end of the cold war had left much foreign news coverage without a major interpretive framework. In the mid-1990s, one complex of events in a distant land was close at hand as an example. "In the past," he said, "if there had been a war between the Hutu and the Tutsi, our first question would have been, who is ours and who is theirs?" And, he suggested, there was indeed some likelihood that one side even in such a conflict would have been getting its arms and its political support from one of the main camps of the cold war, and the other side from the opposite camp.[9] But now, if the news media were to make audiences far from the conflict pay attention at all, they would have to find other ways of telling audiences that story. Through its connections with all kinds of regional conflicts—including many little, hot wars—the cold war may have made much of the foreign news seem more immediately relevant, in a fashion, like "news you can use."

We cannot take for granted, then, that as globalization in all its varieties intensifies, foreign news reporting will automatically grow with it. Instead, we will have to be continuously aware that the latter is vulnerable to contemporary pressures. It is also true that we are in a period when the media land-scape is being reconfigured. One can now find one's way to more information, and more varied information, by consulting a range of more specialized pub-lications of different kinds—including, on the Internet, an almost infinite number of Web sites from all over the world. Those in the news business who question the need to provide so much foreign news for general audiences are inclined to point this out.

Certainly, people who are pursuing particular interests (probably like Schutz's experts) may well seek out such sources.[10] But I believe we can still assume that if they have only so much time in a day to set aside for being sat-isfactorily informed in a general way, as a kind of everyday ritual—it was Hegel's observation that newspapers are modern man's substitute for morn-ing prayers—the majority of people will tend to expect that they can rely on the mainstream media to offer them what they need.[11] I have already noted that in this book I focus on these.

It is true that the mainstream is not everywhere constituted in precisely the same way. "This is basically a one-paper town," said Simon Li, foreign ed-itor of the *Los Angeles Times;* "you should try to write for the academic and the bus driver, because both read our paper."[12] Try, that seems to suggest, to reach out to "the man in the street" as well. In many other places media au-diences are more segmented. Probably the editors at both the *Frankfurter Allgemeine* and the *New York Times* imagine their readerships rather differ-ently than Li does in this statement; and then there are the places where your choice of media outlets is more affected by political sympathies. If you are British, it is mostly not a matter of chance whether you read the *Daily Tele-graph* or the *Guardian.*

Nonetheless, despite what may be differences in education or political leanings, for example, it is probably somewhere among the mainstream me-dia that those who aspire to being informed citizens seek much of their in-formation on a routine basis. Indeed, these media are held to be worthy of some trust. Some commentators would suggest that the media are part of civil society (like globalization, another favorite turn-of-the-millennium concept). One could argue, certainly, over where civil society ends and business be-gins.[13] The *Economist* ("Stop Press" 1998, 21), for its part, suggests in its cover story that "there is nothing wrong with treating news as a product for sale; but you must treat it carefully, because it contains ingredients like trust and decency that spoil easily." We can discern that although some other pub-lications, and not a few Web sites, devote themselves to unsubstantiated ru-mors, conspiracy theories, speculations, and extreme partisanship, it is part of the public agenda of the mainstream media to be credible—which means that they are also vulnerable to criticism whenever they are seen to betray their audiences in this regard.

Back to the question now of the relationship between media reporting and cosmopolitanism. Even when the media do offer their audiences a noticeable quantity of foreign news, that relationship is not simple. Could the news media sometimes even foster an anti-cosmopolitanism?

In an oft-cited formulation on "imagined worlds," Arjun Appadurai (1991, 198–200) has argued that in recent times, especially by way of the media, the balance between lived experience and imagination has come to shift in many human lives. Fantasy turns into a major form of social practice as an increasing variety of alternative ways of living are vividly presented. Although Appadurai appears to have in mind primarily alternatives that could seem in some way attractive, and probably mostly works of fiction, the media certainly also make available views of disaster, war, and suffering. What are the implications of such reporting for people's stances toward the world?

For at least a generation now, there has been a growing critical preoccupation with the influence of media on views of the world generally and on the conduct of international affairs especially. The Vietnam War was the first one to be extensively televised; it became a "living-room war." Whatever was learned from this, there were later military confrontations in the world from which the media were more or less shut out, or where their presence was strictly managed to the extent this was possible. The Gulf War stands out as the major example.[14] Yet some newspeople escaped the leash, and the fact that particularly CNN reported from Baghdad as the bombs were falling was widely taken to mark the emergence of that media organization as an actor in its own right in the handling of world affairs. By the time American soldiers waded ashore on the Somalian coast, the newspeople were already waiting for them on the beach. Not all foreign media coverage, however, is devoted to wars and violent conflict. In the mid-1980s, television reporting on the hunger catastrophe in Ethiopia drew a massive response in Europe (especially Britain) and America, and Bob Geldof's Band-Aid campaign and the song "We Are the World" became the celebrated manifestations of the meeting of a cosmopolitan humanitarianism with Western popular culture.

The media, and television in particular, may have a part here in the growth of the sort of compassionate cosmopolitanism I referred to before; elsewhere I have described it as "electronic empathy" (Hannerz 1996, 121). When you see dying children on the screen, or emaciated bodies behind barbed wire in some newly discovered concentration camp, or a crew of fanatics willfully crashing a passenger plane into a crowded skyscraper, you feel strongly about it, and you may want to do something about it yourself or insist that some responsible party take action. Martin Bell, one of BBC television's most notable reporters during the war in Bosnia, discusses this in his memoir, *In Harm's Way: Reflections of a War-Zone Thug* (1996, 137–45).[15] The British foreign secretary at the time, Douglas Hurd, had made a speech in which he pointed out that "there is nothing new in mass rape, in the shooting of civilians, in war crimes, in ethnic cleansing, in the burning of towns and villages. What is new is that a selection of these tragedies is now visible within hours to people around the world . . . People reject and resent what is going on because they know it more vividly than before." Martin Bell retorts that it sounds as if "the world would somehow be a better place if the killing continued and yet we knew nothing of it . . . The mandarins' objection is not just to the power but to the impertinence of the upstart medium, which challenges their monopoly of wisdom, and rushes in where the pinstripes fear to tread." Later, he notes that television, at least in its BBC variety, is most likely to give a misleadingly restrained, sanitized view of real-world violence. The guidelines say there should be no blood before 9:00 P.M., as long as children are likely to be watching (212–20).

But then we are still not sure that empathy and activism are what necessarily follow from the experience, by way of the media, of other human beings' suffering violence, hunger, or disaster somewhere in the world. Another view, suggested by Arthur and Joan Kleinman (1996), is that suffering, broadcast on a daily basis as "infotainment," is distorted and thinned out, turned into another commodity. The journalism scholar Susan Moeller has devoted a book to the phenomenon of "compassion fatigue" (1999), recognized and labeled, it seems, by a *New York Times* correspondent already early in the 1990s, not so many years after everyone hummed "We Are the World."[16]

There are, then, various possible reactions. Presumably they depend a great deal on the wider social and cultural contexts of particular media experiences. The point is now made often enough in media studies that consuming is itself a kind of producing—interpretation is an active engagement with media content. We could undoubtedly learn more about the way people respond to news through the kind of ethnographic studies of media reception that are by now a prominent transdisciplinary research genre. Such studies, however, appear more often to engage with works of fiction than with news of the real world.[17]

We can identify yet another possible response to foreign crisis news. Since news of the world out there is so often bad news, news of conflicts and catastrophes, that world may seem to be above all a place to be wary of—one that on the basis of common sense the "man in the street" would want to have as little to do with as possible. You would prefer to keep your distance, and if people from out there knock on your door, you will want to send them away. Pierre Bourdieu (1998, 8), in a critique of television and journalism, took this view: "Journalism shows us a world full of ethnic wars, racist hatred, violence and crime—a world full of incomprehensible and unsettling dangers from which we must withdraw for our own protection."

If cosmopolitans are likely to go with the flow that creates the global ecumene, then isolationism, and even xenophobia—taking that "single place" apart—can be other reactions to bad news from abroad. I talked about this with Inger Jägerhorn, at the time the foreign news editor of *Dagens Nyheter,* Sweden's largest morning newspaper. She said she and her colleagues were aware of this possibility. In her imagery, her paper must make sure to distance itself from an ancient "troubadour tradition," that of wandering about spreading news only of what in Swedish could be the three *K*'s—*krig, katastrofer,* and *kröningar,* that is, wars, disasters, and coronations. With such emphases (with elections now taking the place of the coronations), the world could indeed seem mostly dangerous and unattractive. There had to be more reporting that portrayed everyday life elsewhere and allowed journalists more personal angles and engagements.[18] Moreover, she noted, television might naturally be committed to reporting the news through dramatic pictures. This did not have to be her priority as a newspaper editor.

The Medium as Message

Obviously much of current argument about media impact is not only about crisis news but also particularly about television. Yet media also to a degree constitute each other's environments—or, putting it differently, there is an element of competition and a somewhat fluid division of labor between them. For such reasons, one should not look at any one of them entirely in isolation.

A generation ago, when Marshall McLuhan published his *Understanding Media* (1964), many of his assertions may have been dubious, but it remains true that with his catch phrases—"the global village," "the retribalization of the world," "the medium is the message"—he very effectively drew attention to the wider social and cultural implications of media and to differences between them. Through vividly contrasting the electronic media with what he described as "the Gutenberg Galaxy," McLuhan suggested a concern with the comparative study of media cultural form.

"I feel like a monk in the age of Gutenberg," said one former Asia correspondent, now an editor in New York, taking a step even further back in the history of media technology. But he just liked the writing craft. Obviously there is now a quite intense awareness among media people of the opportunities and constraints of their particular tool kits. They try to use their possibilities to the fullest but also to overcome what may seem to be built-in problems, and one of their goals is to carve out their special niches within the overall ecology of reporting. Bruce Dunning, Asia bureau chief for CBS News in Tokyo, who started his journalist career with a suburban New Jersey paper in the 1960s, has worked with print, radio, and television and says he found the change from radio to television the most difficult—in both print and radio, you work largely with words, but in television you have to think in terms of pictures as well, which may require some imagination when the story is basically a rather abstract one. When import duties on rice are an issue in Japan, Dunning will send a cameraman to the harbor to shoot pictures of rice bags being unloaded from ships. George Alagiah of BBC television does a story from India on GATT negotiations over textile tariffs by starting with a colorful sequence from a Bombay fashion show, then showing busy workers in a textile mill. We may listen, too, to Cecilia Uddén, Radio Sweden's correspondent first in Cairo and later in Washington, D.C., pondering over the ways of establishing a distinctive voice, perhaps literally as well as metaphorically, in the midst of the buzzing soundscape; or reminiscing about how she reported on ever-shifting, yet rather tedious phases of Israeli-Palestine contacts by having an acquaintance, a West Bank tailor, speculate on whether the time had arrived for Yassir Arafat to order a civilian suit to replace his uniform. Not only could she insert a brief moment of another voice, in Arabic, thus dramatizing a sense of place. The sound of the tailor's scissors cutting through cloth—snip, snip, snip—could also make for good, lively radio.

The media relate differently to our senses, of course. Print turns sound into sight but mostly remains in the single symbolic modality of language. With radio sound comes back into communication beyond the immediate, face-to-face environment, although again only one of the senses is fully engaged. Television still does not allow us to taste, smell, or touch, but at least the combination of more natural-seeming sight and sound entails more of a sensual immersion, more of a feeling of "being there." This broader appeal to, or assault on, the senses certainly gives television a key role in shaping people's stances toward the world. If they do not literally have the experience of "being there" as a basis for that thicker version of cosmopolitanism, is it television that can most effectively substitute for it—or will it instead turn people away, in fright or disgust?

Yet perhaps McLuhan, in his preoccupation with the divergent sensual properties of media, went a little too far in emphasizing form and disregarding content. I am reminded of another of my first conversations within this project, when a veteran print correspondent talked admiringly about the exquisite story that one of his colleagues had once done from India on the full experience of the coming of the first monsoon rains.[19] Can the foreign correspondents of the print media, too, as writers, draw their readers into a feeling of personal acquaintance with people and places far away? Do they not also sometimes approximate in their writing that involvement of the senses which television may get to more easily? "You have to write more seductively," said one correspondent, on the topic of finding and keeping readers in a post-cold-war world. Playing on a sensual imagination may be one way of doing so. From another perspective, can freedom from a continuous preoccupation with dramatic live pictures also allow the people of the printed word more diversified modes of portrayal and comment?

Foreign News: Space, Time, and Understanding

Media can do different things not only by way of their intrinsic means of expression. They also differ in their handling of time. The fact that radio and television can communicate instantly, and the print media cannot, has become even more conspicuous as some radio stations and television channels have concentrated entirely on news broadcasting. The print media have had to come to terms with the limitation that, to attentive audiences, they can seldom be first with major hard news. So in part, at least, they have to deal with the news, perhaps even define the news, in some other manner.

The very concept of foreign news is worth inspecting at this stage. As for the word "news," it is interestingly ambiguous. It can refer to something that just happened, or something can be news mostly because we simply have not come across it before and find it interesting and even surprising. Certainly the news media are primarily oriented to the first of these kinds, "hard news," and foreign correspondents tend to take pride in, and be excited by, being present when "history is made." But that other kind of news has some particular possibilities for foreign correspondents. A situation or practice may have a long-term, even everyday presence in a remote country without our learning of it, until someone tells us. For such news, we might note, the technology of instant reporting is really not that important.

"Hard news" refers to major, unique events, temporally highly specified, with consequences that insist on the attention of newspeople and their audiences. The news trade has various labels for what is not exactly that— "feature stories," "enterprise stories," or the old term "human interest stories." The relationship of such reporting to time is generally more vague, and the decision whether it should be done at all, or published or broadcast, is more or less discretionary. At times it is directly tied to the hard news of the moment—profiles of "people in the news," for instance, or analysis and commentary that extends the time perspective by sketching some historical background, at least to jog the memory of the audience, and perhaps by daring some forecasting of future implications. But often in foreign news, feature stories can be news of difference, of people thinking, acting, or living in some unfamiliar way. So here we face the fact that the word "foreign," like "news," is ambiguous.

The simplest reading of "foreign" in "foreign news" is certainly that it refers to news from abroad, reported across national boundaries. In that sense, one may view it as a spatial notion; but it is a matter of space already socially constructed and regulated. Again, we can also entertain the idea that it involves news that is somehow alien, strange—that such news has crossed boundaries of understanding and is not unproblematically accessible in cultural terms. When foreignness is of this kind, the advantages of television are perhaps not so great, or they may even disappear. Electronic empathy may work when the images of despairing faces or of limbs destroyed by exploding land mines have an immediacy that may at least appear to render most interpretation superfluous: raw humanity seems to be involved. But not everything in the news from elsewhere is so easily grasped. Words, words, and more words may be required for an understanding. For an anthropologist, such news may have some special appeal—and at the same time, it may involve all the controversial bias toward exoticism that we have also been made aware of within the discipline, as we are urged, for example, to write "against culture" (L. Abu-Lughod 1991). It is, hardly surprisingly, a reading of the "foreign" in "foreign news" that has attracted me as an anthropologist to this study and to directing it primarily to news from more exotic beats.

With regard to our interest here in the bases of cosmopolitanism, feature stories may have some special significance. The three instances of reporting sketched earlier—Marjorie Miller's Jerusalem story, Chris McGreal's Accra story, and Göran Leijonhufvud's Beijing story—are of this kind, so let us now return to them.

None of these stories involve hard news; and though none offer remarkably good news, it is not especially bad news either. The foreign correspondents offer themselves in these stories as flaneurs on behalf of their readers. Or perhaps I should say that they play at being flaneurs, for the moments when correspondents show up at the concrete scenes to be portrayed may not really be moments of spontaneous discovery. Certainly serious professionalism can go into the making of apparently random and even playful observations. To the reader, however, stories like these may seem as if they were drawn from the unexpected encounters, the chance acquaintances, and the overheard exchanges between strangers that go with having all of one's senses open, no matter where one is.

If stories like these can contribute to a cosmopolitan stance, a cosmopolitanism of the thicker, denser, richer kind, it is not so much a matter of compassion in relation to suffering as of the feeling of being to some degree at home in the world. "Infotainment" again, perhaps, but of a more benign kind. The writers work with words, but they appeal imaginatively to varied senses, including the visual. They allow, too, for a range of sentiments—surprise, empathy, amusement, irritation—much as life generally offers. Admittedly, some people are classified as rather more other than others: the ultra-Orthodox seldom get the last word in stories from Jerusalem. Nonetheless, these are stories that make distant places and people less one-dimensional, more complex, than they may be in much hard news reporting.

Especially considered together, the reports seem to entail a play with distances, in space and time, and a play with relationships between form and content. As seen from Belfast or London, the West African Orangemen may seem not to know what they are doing, but in the Accra context they certainly do; as we see them from afar, again, what they do is somehow subversive of Northern Irish primordialisms. The local politician commenting on the Bar Ilan Street scene sets Jerusalem next to Tehran, suggesting that one fundamentalism is as bad as the other; and then he lines it up with Los Angeles. Göran Leijonhufvud finds 1990s Chinese perhaps "much like us" as they spend their weekends in the disco or busy with home improvements (remember that his own readers are the people who gave the world IKEA)— and then in the next instant he makes them very distant from us, when they turn out to be locomotionally much like 1960s Red Guards.

In a general way, too, as far as time is concerned, stories like these may also make the people and places involved in some ways more durable. They do not freeze distant places in time, but they intimate that there is an ongoing life beyond the fifteen minutes of fame or whatever these places are afforded in breaking news. Those street clashes between the secular and the ultra-Orthodox in Jerusalem take place not on one particular Saturday, but on any one of an indeterminate series of Saturdays, just as Saturday night in Beijing could be any Saturday at the end of the twentieth century. The presence of a lodge of the Orange Order in Accra may come as a surprise to Chris McGreal's British readers, but its history of ups and downs go back to a European colonial order that has left more varied traces than most of us are generally aware of. Moreover, the somewhat indeterminate and yet fairly concrete representations of time—any recent Saturday, or an unfolding series of events taking the Accra lodge of the Orange Order from the past into the

future—also allow a sense of simultaneity. The foreign correspondents reporting here pull our sleeve to point out something that is there now. Simply
absorbing their claims on our attention as an integral part of a forever fleet-
ing news experience may add to this awareness. These are our contemporaries out there, in bowler hats in Accra, disco fashions in Beijing, or frock
coats in Jerusalem, not people living in some entirely separate and distant
temporal order. The correspondents seem to avoid, that is to say, what has
been identified as a problem in the classic construct of an "ethnographic
present," the distancing that goes with placing people elsewhere in some different time altogether.[20] That also seems like a contribution to cosmopolitanism and to the sense of the world as a single place.

Intentions and Audience Understandings

If news stories do something to cultivate a sense of belonging in the world,
this may or may not have much to do with the correspondents' own intentions
or ambitions. Some of the correspondents are in any case skeptical about
their own influence on what the public will think. One of the former Moscow
correspondents I have met said that he and his colleagues during the perestroika period tended to agree that Gorbachev was a man who spoke terrible
Russian, "of limited intelligence and great courage"; but readers in the West
were in an optimistic mood and just loved their Gorby.

Marjorie Miller, when I met her in Jerusalem, said she had become a
foreign correspondent "mostly for selfish reasons"—she loved to write and
wanted to see the world. But she also felt a certain obligation to make her audience better informed. She had been an American studies major as a college
student in California, and she remembered that when she traveled in Mexico
after her graduation, she read in a Mexican paper about American involvement in a 1950s coup in Guatemala that she had never heard of in her own
country. She thought there was an inclination toward isolationism in the
American public, and by now it needed to be told about the responsibilities
of the one remaining superpower. Her *Los Angeles Times* colleague John
Balzar, sometime Nairobi correspondent, felt that Americans tended to have
made up their minds about many things and needed to have their presuppo-
sitions shaken up and to learn something from other places. Loneliness, he
noted, is one of the great problems in American life, but he had never met
any lonely Africans.

Some foreign correspondents, it seems, are quite self-conscious about
their cosmopolitan convictions, going to work with the hope to educate. Others would say they are merely "doing their job." No doubt there are news-

people, too, who are drawn to whatever may shock their audiences. And then one comes across, at times, alarmist or rejectionist voices seemingly warning of too much involvement with the world, or at least with parts of it. Abroad is a terrible place. Two examples come to mind. Malcolm Browne (1993), of the generation of Vietnam War correspondents, thereafter science editor of the *New York Times,* has a remarkable chapter in his autobiography titled "Beware the Third World." "I have seen the future and it doesn't work," he begins; "It's the Third World, and it's coming our way" (288). The Third World in Browne's view is unenforced laws and edicts, proliferating as rapidly as worthless money; it is people refusing to stand in line and generally the disappearance of altruism toward strangers; priests, mullahs, and witch doctors dominating society and suppressing dissent; police carrying automatic weapons; and endemic warfare over the basic necessities of life. In a peculiar twist of culturalist imagery, Browne suggests that the Third World has something in common with bacterial cultures and cancerous tumors—"In a bacterial culture, organisms propagate exponentially and without limit, as long as they have food and room to dump their wastes" (291). Yet above all, his Third World is overpopulation, and perhaps we may read into his striking formulations not just fear and loathing but also, after all, a concern that goes beyond isolationism.

The other example for a while drew more attention and comment.[21] In his memoir *Out of America* (1997b), Keith Richburg, another former Nairobi correspondent (for the *Washington Post*) and a black American, detailed his reporting experiences in Africa during the violent early 1990s. Richburg was born and grew up in Detroit, the son of an auto worker and trade unionist. He attended an integrated Catholic school (his parents had converted after moving north), always had white friends, went to work for a newspaper that was nothing if not American mainstream—or "Establishment"—and had little sympathy for some of the varieties of black consciousness and Afrocentrist fellow traveling that he observed among prominent members of the African American elite. So leaving Nairobi, after "three years walking around among the corpses," he was tired of the hypocrisy, double standards, and ignorance concerning Africa that he felt he was getting from some such people who had often never been there: "Talk to me about Africa and my black roots and my kinship with my African brothers and I'll throw it back in your face," Richburg warned in his preface, "and then I'll rub your nose in the images of rotting flesh." He certainly would not defend slavery as part of the history of America and of his own family. But provocatively, he thanked God that his ancestors had thus been taken out of Africa and that in the end he was himself an American.

On that note Richburg moved on, to a posting in Hong Kong. (He had already been in Southeast Asia before Nairobi.) When we met there, he acknowledged that his experience in Nairobi had not actually been all bad. But in his book he had had a point to make, and he had felt strongly about it. He saw his book above all as a forceful affirmation of his American identity, a patriotic manifestation, polemically aimed especially at certain other black Americans. The line between patriotism and chauvinism, however, is not always easily drawn.

So there are different ways of reporting and of responding as a correspondent to particular beats. Internally diverse and contradictory as tendencies in foreign coverage may be, though, one can still discern here and there a kind of cosmopolitan turn, an actual desire to make the vicarious experience of the world through the media a richer, more varied one.

At the *New York Times,* in our conversation, Bill Keller made the point that foreign correspondents should be interested in societies, not only in states. And his paper had been giving some serious thought to its international news reporting. His predecessor as foreign editor, Bernard Gwertzman, who oversaw the post-cold-war transition period in his paper, had written an important internal memorandum that pointed to new directions for his correspondents.[22] In the coming period, he suggested, there would be a broadening of reporting from political news to deal more with environmental issues, histories of ethnic friction, and economic developments that might no longer be confined to the financial section of the paper. As a matter of policy, he declared, "[w]e are interested in what makes societies different, what is on the minds of people in various regions. Imagine you are being asked to write a letter home every week to describe a different aspect of life in the area you are assigned." The feature stories by Miller from Jerusalem, McGreal from Accra, and Leijonhufvud from Beijing seem to be examples of such reporting—and since none of these correspondents work for the *New York Times,* we may sense that the interest in such reporting has been a wider one. (The foreign news editor of *Dagens Nyheter* in Stockholm, Leijonhufvud's paper, we have already seen, took much the same stand.) Such a suggested move in foreign reporting, away from total preoccupation with the events and the personnel of national politics, can be understood in both a stronger and a weaker sense. Do the correspondents merely have a license to take on a wider range of topics—or is it an obligation?

If it is the former, we can perhaps expect no more than a rather spotty, in large part opportunistic, probably infotainment-oriented view of societies elsewhere, as a complement to hard news. But if we should measure news media foreign reporting against the higher standard of cultivating cosmopolitanism, making audiences feel more realistically at home in the world, it becomes a more noteworthy matter when we identify biases, gaps, and misrepresentations. We should then consider how such weaknesses may have come to be built into the structure of reporting.

The Embedding of Foreign News

Yet in the end we also need to recognize that no matter what the media do, they can hardly stand alone in shaping cosmopolitan attitudes. There is probably often an interaction between immediate personal experiences and general enduring orientations, on the one hand, and, on the other, the knowledge and sensibility built up by the news flow.

Some correspondents and commentators on correspondence whom I talked to when I was in Tokyo made this point as they argued that there were differences in the ways major American newspapers covered Japan: a number of the stories that might work on the East Coast you would not be likely to find in the *Los Angeles Times,* which "has to cover Japan as if it were part of the LA metropolitan area." Sonni Efron, Tokyo bureau chief at the latter paper, thought that particular formulation might be too strong. But she agreed that because so many of the paper's readers in California have either business or kinship connections in Japan and have been to Japan themselves, her bureau's coverage of Japanese affairs had to be a bit different from that of her East Coast colleagues. She would not get away with so much surprise, real or feigned, in stories of difference, and there were other kinds of stories that were perhaps of greater concrete interest to the California readers.

Foreign news, in other words, can be quite differently embedded in our overall, background understanding of the world. Such embedding can vary along two dimensions, individually and geographically. Some people, more than others, have a great, varied store of personal experiences to which news stories may be related. But then such experiences are also more likely to involve some places and regions than others. There are places we have been to, perhaps even lived in, ourselves. Or we may know people who live there or who are from there. We may have learned about these places more extensively in school or through other kinds of instruction. The *New York Times* bureau chief in Jerusalem when I was there, Serge Schmemann, said that in preparation for his assignment, he had read his predecessor's reporting but also the Bible. There was a rich symbolic geography here, with names of ancient places and past inhabitants that could resonate in his readers' minds with his own twentieth-century reporting.

Any feeling we may have of being at home in the world, away from our most immediate, routine habitat, is thus likely to be quite unevenly distributed. There are regions for which that wider embeddedness of news reporting in knowledge of some other derivation may be strong, and others for which it is weak. In the latter case, what we know, or believe we know, will in unusually large part be based on what we read, or hear, or see, as media consumers. And the burden on media reporting to shape the world images of audiences then becomes especially heavy. Whether it is a burden it can cope with will in turn depend in no small part on the way media organizations arrange their own commitments in time and space. The next couple of chapters should cast some light on these commitments.

Whenever you find hundreds of thousands of sane people trying to get out of a place and a little bunch of madmen struggling to get in, you know the latter are newspapermen." This observation by an early practitioner of the craft is one that many foreign correspondents are fond of. Terry Leonard, the silver-haired Associated Press bureau chief in Johannesburg, told me he had had it on his desk for years.[1] Leonard started out working for a local paper in Texas, without much thought of a foreign career—his father had been in the U.S. Army in World War II and took part in the liberation of Nazi concentration camps, and as a child he had heard of this and seen pictures from the camps, but he had never thought he would experience anything similar. Then after joining the Associated Press and working on the international desk in New York, he was posted to Rome, operating out of there as a "fireman," the kind of reporter who is sent on quick journeys, with little or no advance notice, wherever there is an event urgently requiring attention. He was in Romania at the fall of President Ceaucescu in December 1989, witnessed the transition in Eastern Europe, and was in Baghdad just after the invasion of Kuwait. When he returned later in the year, before the Gulf War broke out, he, like others of his kind, had been declared persona non grata.

Next he covered the war in Bosnia. He remembered being caught in a cross fire in Sarajevo and, while hiding in an alcove, hearing a recording of "Für Elise" full blast from an open window. He saw children shot in the head by a sniper who seemed to have taken careful aim. The first trip to Africa was to Somalia, when the peacekeeping troops arrived. Then he was posted to Nairobi in 1994, and he returned to Somalia to report on the departure of those troops. Immediately after that, the plane carrying the presidents of Rwanda and Burundi crashed (probably

shot down), and hell broke loose in Rwanda. Much of his period of assignment in East Africa, consequently, was spent in that country. All together he
was in fifty countries and reported from thirty-five.

Taking a bird's-eye view of correspondents' lives, we can see them as
movements within a global landscape of news. This chapter sketches some
features of that landscape. Some of the moves, in particular those quick fireman, or "parachutist," excursions in and out of suddenly emergent trouble
spots, are more or less unforeseeable, which is why again and again, you have
those madmen trying to get in where other people are getting out. The more
stable features of the landscape include the places around the world where
correspondents are likely to be stationed for a longer period, often in considerable numbers—Johannesburg, Jerusalem, Tokyo, to mention the ones
most recurrently discussed here; there are perhaps a couple of dozen others.
The assumption about these places is that a fair number of newsworthy
events occur continuously in the immediate vicinity and that they are at the
same time places from which other potential news sites can be reached fairly
quickly and conveniently. But before we concern ourselves with any of these
kinds of sites, we should take note of the kind of center points from which the
landscape is, to some degree, organized.

Who Is in Charge?

Particularly in the 1970s, in a political climate more radical than that of recent times, there was a growing recognition of the imbalances of news handling in the world. Especially on the international arena of UNESCO, debates over the desirability of a New World Information and Communication
Order had their ideological and intellectual ties to notions of "cultural imperialism" and to dependency theory, and within the cold war framework, they
tended to align the Third World strategically with the Socialist bloc in opposition to an established order anchored in the West. A major resulting document was "the MacBride Report," *Many Voices, One World,* produced by a
UNESCO commission chaired by Sean MacBride, an Irish politician, winner
of Nobel as well as Lenin Peace Prizes. The language was fairly low-key, but
the commission affirmed that

> [i]n order to be really free, information flows have to be two-way, not
> simply in one direction. The concentration of news agencies, telecom-
> munication facilities, mass media, data resources, manufacturers of
> communication equipment in a small number of highly developed coun-
> tries does, in fact, preclude any chance of free flow between equals, a

> democratic exchange among free partners. A dependency situation still
> exists in a large part of the world, and there is a growing determination
> to transform dependence into independence as harmoniously as pos-
> sible. The developing countries also resent the fact that, because of
> their limited resources and means to collect and disseminate informa-
> tion, they have to depend on the large international agencies for infor-
> mation about each other. (MacBride 1980, 142)

The debate over the politics of global news flow no longer seems so intense,
but this is not because of any major changes in the balance of power. Although the proliferation of Internet Web sites allows energetic, technologi-
cally well-equipped information seekers to find a much wider set of sources,
for the routine news consumer such opportunities may not matter much, and
the distribution of new technological facilities continues to be very uneven.
There have been attempts, too, to set up alternative or complementary news
organizations, but these have mostly been underfinanced and understaffed
and have struggled to survive in the shadow of the established Western organizations.

    Among news agencies, three are still way ahead of all others in their
world coverage: Reuters, based in London; Associated Press, operating out
of New York headquarters; and Agence France-Presse (AFP). If, for example, Germany and Japan are major economic powers, not even their news
agencies, or others with a strong national base, really offer significant international competition for these three. Frequently, however, the dominant
agencies link up with other regional or national agencies of more limited
scope. What has happened, since the debates of twenty or thirty years ago,
moreover, is that these organizations have extended their operations into new
activities. They have become increasingly active in supplying news film for
television, absorbing more specialized organizations in the process. Reuters
has focused more and more on the global marketplace, but specialized financial news organizations have also grown spectacularly.

    A development of recent times that is more immediately accessible and
conspicuous to general audiences is the around-the-clock global television
news channels, particularly CNN International and BBC World. These, too,
are undeniably Western, even though particularly CNN in some symbolic
ways tries to make this a little less obvious. Perhaps it is partly because of this
development that the older American television networks, especially, have
retreated from more internationalist ambitions. They now have their own reporting teams in fewer places abroad, and frequently they simply do not offer their viewers very much in the way of foreign news.

Anyhow, if we look at who these people are, out there, reporting mostly to their home countries from elsewhere in the world, whether through print media, radio, or television, we find that they are in very large part western Europeans or North Americans. Other parts of the world get much of their foreign news by way of them, especially through those major agencies. There are the expected exceptions. Japanese media organizations, for example, sometimes have impressive international correspondent networks. Yet on the whole the foreign correspondent corps of the world is in much larger proportion white-faced than black-faced, brown-faced, or yellow-faced (although some of those with other pigmentation also now represent North American or European organizations). And as I have already pointed out, a great many foreign correspondents (whom I almost entirely disregard in this book) are primarily engaged in intra-Occident reporting, within Europe or across the North Atlantic.[2]

So much for the commanding heights of the global news landscape. The enduring macrofeatures of its political economy, as well as the ongoing shifts within it brought about by mergers and acquisitions between corporate conglomerates, have been well documented and analyzed by specialists, and there is no need to go into greater detail here.[3] We should continuously keep in mind, however, as we attempt a more close-up portrayal of the practices of foreign correspondents, that the wider frame is one of Western and Northern dominance. There is a structure of center-periphery relationships, but as is frequently now the case in such structures, centers are not necessarily the sources where everything originates. They are more like switchboards, controlling incoming and outgoing news traffic. In Johannesburg, Terry Leonard's Associated Press bureau coordinates materials coming out of the other African bureaus of his organization—in Nairobi, Abidjan, and Harare —ordinarily somewhere between five and fifteen stories per day. From there they reach the rows of computer screens of the international desk at the New York head office, in Rockefeller Plaza in mid-Manhattan. And from there they spread over the world.

Parachutists' Tales

But let us get back to the parachutists and their quick passages across the news landscape, to these on-and-off foci of the world's attention that so frequently tend to be trouble spots, sites of violence or disaster. Again, these passages are what correspondents tend to dwell on in autobiographies or other collectively or individually self-reflexive statements. The accounts of getting there, witnessing events, finding a way to file, and getting out are also tales of correspondent camaraderie, and a cumulative series of hotels and watering holes thus become famous: the Caravelle in Saigon, the Commodore in Beirut (with a celebrated parrot), the Intercontinental in Bucharest, the Sahafi in Mogadishu. Ryszard Kapuscinski (1986, 142), long a sort of free-wheeling one-man Polish foreign correspondent corps during the Communist era before metamorphosing into a best-selling author in the West, made some of his reputation from having reported from twenty-seven revolutions (probably more now—the twenty-seventh was the one in Iran in 1979).

Not all travel to temporary news sites is so sudden, so improvised, or for that matter so uncomfortable and dangerous. There are scheduled stops for which elaborate plans can be made long beforehand and which draw hordes of newspeople from far away. Six thousand accredited journalists attended the United Nations Conference on Environment and Development in Rio de Janeiro in 1994.[4] The handover of Hong Kong from British to Chinese sovereignty in 1997, it has been claimed, brought some eight thousand newspeople to the city (Knight and Nakano 1999). Similarly, as royalty or statesmen travel, elaborate arrangements may be made for reporters to go along; however, these are often not the regular foreign correspondents but people whose regular business it is to cover the doings of these dignitaries at home, those whose beats are just temporarily relocated.[5] When President Clinton was traveling in Africa in March 1997, he was accompanied by a number of journalists from the United States, and what the regular Africa correspondents sent back to their foreign desks became complementary to what such sojourners reported. Mike Hanna, CNN bureau chief in Johannesburg, whom I met shortly before, was about to go to Accra, in Ghana, to team up with Wolf Blitzer, the White House correspondent, and proceed with the Clinton entourage from there.

Much parachutist travel is to sites of trouble, though. Among the correspondents I have met with, a few had been long enough in the business to have reported from the war scenes of Vietnam and Biafra, in the 1960s and early 1970s, and from Bangladesh when it seceded from Pakistan in 1971. At least one had first arrived in Israel to witness the Yom Kippur War of 1973. Others had been in Afghanistan in the 1980s, at Tiananmen Square in Beijing in 1989, and about as close as one could usually get to report on the Gulf War in 1991. Several had observed the wars in Bosnia and Chechnya at close hand. While my study continued, some of those whom I had already encountered went on to describe the fall of Suharto in Jakarta in 1998, the Kosovo war in 1999, and the terror in East Timor after it voted to secede from Indonesia, also in 1999. One or two had been Latin America correspondents during the years when stories from there were in large part about guerrillas and contras. By the time parachutists came together again—some three thousand of them, it was said at one point—to report from Pakistan and Afghanistan in October 2001, I noted among them several whom I had met in other places.

Yet I found myself talking to correspondents especially about their 1990s travels and travails in Africa—because it was a continent in which I took some special interest and because Johannesburg and Cape Town were among my field sites, but certainly also because it was a troubled period in the continent.[6] The major confrontation that so many had expected in South Africa miraculously never took place. The early 1990s transition there was not entirely serene, but it did not amount to either revolution or full-scale civil war. Elsewhere in Africa, though, Somalia, Sudan, Ethiopia, Eritrea, Sierra Leone, Liberia, Rwanda, Congo, and Angola followed one another, or coincided, in the news of armed conflict.

A number of the correspondents I talked to, especially in South Africa, had fresh in their minds their experiences in Kinshasa, in what was then still named Zaire, in April and May 1997, waiting for the fall of President Mobutu. This was a major event, ending his several decades of despotic and glaringly corrupt rule, but it was only part of a sequence that had been unfolding for a long time already and which certainly continued after they left Kinshasa. There was no single definite starting point, but that air crash in Rwanda (in which two Central African presidents died) that Terry Leonard mentioned, occurring at the beginning of his assignment in Nairobi, marked a dramatic escalation. Just as most of whatever attention the world media gave Africa was focused elsewhere, on the final stage of the political transition in South Africa and on Nelson Mandela's ascent to the presidency, genocide was taking place in Rwanda. It is too simple to describe what happened as a clear-cut ethnic conflict between Hutu and Tutsi, although this is the way the outside world has mostly seen it; anyhow, after one faction of Hutu extremists had engaged in a systematic mass killing of Tutsi, an exile military force of Tutsi invaded from Uganda and seized power, driving a great many Hutu away. Many of them ended up in refugee camps where, as it gradually became clear, they were largely under the domination of the groups engaging in genocide, the terrorist bands known as the Interahamwe.

When I met him, John Balzar had finished his assignment as Nairobi correspondent for the *Los Angeles Times* and had returned to California, but he was also among those who had again and again traveled to Rwanda to report on the country's mid-1990s tragedy and to neighboring Burundi, into which the continuing story spilled over (although in the same period he also took over the paper's Cairo bureau briefly when the correspondent there had to go to Jerusalem, after the assassination of Prime Minister Rabin). Balzar was among those responsible for the *Los Angeles Times* coverage of the Gulf War, but he had never really aimed for a foreign correspondent career and took the Nairobi posting mostly to see what it was like and to broaden his field of vision. He was an admirer of Ryszard Kapuscinski's writings, comparing them to Hemingway's, and said he liked to take one of Kapuscinski's books along whenever he traveled.

A former U.S. Marine who had fought in Vietnam, John Balzar felt that he was tough and not easily frightened.[7] The assignment in Africa, however, was physically as well as mentally demanding. It was no fun getting up in the morning knowing that one would be heading for Somalia and quite possibly risking one's life. And he found Burundi a "devilishly spooky place." In one area where he traveled, he reminisced, bandits had killed a TV producer and his crew. A team like that could be traveling with twenty thousand dollars in cash, to cover all expenses in the most straightforward way—but if a local warlord discovered this, he would be tempted, since such a sum might be enough to keep his side of a war going for a month or more.

Reporting, Balzar said, has four main parts: contemplation, logistics, writing, and filing. Of these, logistics took much more time in Africa than elsewhere. Perhaps it was 60 percent of his work. One had to be one's own travel agent, in nearly anarchical conditions. But if one cannot make sure that one can file a story, it is hardly any use writing it. You could be in Goma, in Zaire at the Rwandan border, and hear rumors about something going on in Bujumbura in Burundi, so you would rush there—there were times when Balzar had hotel rooms booked in four different places and still ended up sleeping on the ground in yet another place. But the office in Los Angeles was understanding as far as expenses were concerned. And when the TV crews arrived somewhere with their sizable crews, they took every space available, so it was wise to keep those room reservations as a precaution. It would be necessary to hire a trustworthy driver, too, and interpreters, and since there was very little trust between ethnic groups (tribes, one would certainly say), different interpreters would be needed for different interviews.

During one period he filed stories almost every day for three months, while subsisting largely on french fries and Zairean beer. (He never got sick during this period, but he caught malaria another time.) Actually he was quite proud of his Rwanda reporting. There was the time, for example, when, very tired and after a fair amount of beer, he had written a beautiful story— "a tear jerker"—on orphans and sent it out from his computer by way of a satellite phone. Staffers in his Los Angeles newsroom were sufficiently moved to hold a fund-raiser for UNICEF. Then soon after, of course, there was a scandal in the local UNICEF office, with someone squandering money. Although in reporting from Central Africa, he sometimes thought of himself as "a cog in the world's humanitarian machine," he sometimes had mixed feelings about this. People in the refugee camps, including vicious war criminals, at times seemed materially better off than a great many ordinary people in Africa. Yet he thought it was more important to report on a war than to criticize the international relief agencies—although, he mused humbly, perhaps a better journalist than he could have done both at the same time.

As I was talking to John Balzar in Los Angeles, his correspondent colleagues were again assembling in Central Africa. In November 1996, hundreds of thousands of Hutu who had been living in another of those camps dominated by the Interahamwe, on the Zairean side of the border, suddenly returned to Rwanda, trying to make their way to their old homes. The Interahamwe had been defeated in battle by another force, which declared its intention to overthrow President Mobutu, in Kinshasa, far away across the country. The makeup of that force was not very clear, but an old-timer Zairean politician-cum-warlord, Laurent Kabila, had proclaimed himself its leader.

So the news media made their way to Goma, a major Zairean border town. It seemed to be precisely one of these "little bunch of madmen" situations, as not only the masses of Hutu but also a convoy of aid workers and United Nations officials were heading the other way. The correspondents reported on the chaos in Goma and then left again. For the next half year, they filed accounts off and on, from here and there, of the arrival of the rebel forces in yet another of Zaire's major cities: Kisangani, Lubumbashi, and finally Kinshasa.[8] (It does not seem, however, that any of them were accompanying these forces themselves.)

When the story moved on from Rwanda to Zaire, those media organizations that had Nairobi-based correspondents tended to let them continue covering it. Some came from farther away. One of the correspondents reporting from Zaire to the *New York Times* during this period was Nicholas Kristof, who was taking time out from serving as the paper's bureau chief in Tokyo; we will encounter him again later. One of the stories Kristof filed (1997a) was from Kisangani, about the local zoo; it was open, but all the animals had died. There had been no food for them, and since townspeople were very hungry, some of the animals had probably themselves been eaten, even including a smelly old crocodile.

But media organizations with their Africa correspondents based in Johannesburg or Cape Town sent them to Zaire. Chris McGreal, of the *Guardian*—whom we met in chapter 1, reporting on the Accra lodge of the Orange Order—had been to the country for the first time in 1991 and had been returning regularly since then. McGreal liked certain aspects of reporting from Africa. Things were more "up front"; there was less manipulation of news, lying, evasion, and spin doctoring than in more sophisticated places. Even Rwandans involved in genocide actually offered information, although they might then try to explain it away. For the events of 1996 and 1997, McGreal was in Goma, then Lubumbashi, then Kinshasa. A café in Lubumbashi where all the correspondents hung out served as a rumor mill, with fresh rumors being served up continuously by the waiters. One set of Mobutu's forces arrested McGreal and two other journalists as well as an interpreter and beat them up (the interpreter quite badly), but they were rescued by Mobutu's local security chief.

Then they all descended on Kinshasa, a little early perhaps, to wait for Kabila's army. Vincent Dahlbäck from Radio Sweden flew in from Cape Town. Several Swedish media organizations had requested assistance from their Ministry of Foreign Affairs in getting into Zaire, but Swedish representation in the country was minimal. The ambassador was based in Stockholm and had never even had an opportunity to present his credentials to President Mobutu. Swedish affairs were therefore managed in Kinshasa by a person employed on a part-time basis, who worked for the Pentecostal mission the rest of the time. But this person had arranged for a "fixer" to get the Swedes through customs and passport control at Ndjili Airport, which could otherwise be an exasperating experience in itself. Then the Swedish journalists mingled with everybody else, at one or the other of the two major hotels. Television people were mostly at the Memling, because the European Broadcasting Union had set up special transmission facilities there. Most others were at the Intercontinental, owned by the Mobutu family at least for another few days—which meant that those who were at that hotel had a particularly close view of the going and coming of regimes.

Dahlbäck recruited another fixer, the kind of multipurpose local resource person who so often is essential to the work, and at times even survival, of a correspondent in a new setting. This one was a teacher who had received no pay for several months but who had a car, a 1973 Datsun, so that they could get around a little. Dahlbäck thought the man was good but a bit careless, and because the demand for fixers quickly allowed the rates to go sky high (the large organizations such as CNN tended to set the limits), this fixer soon appeared in an elegant new denim suit, which he thought was appropriate for mingling with his new customers. (After the crisis was over, Dahlbäck later heard, this fixer and a companion used their profits to start a pig farm.)

Dahlbäck thought there were about a hundred journalists staying at the

Intercontinental, as well as members of the Mobutu family. One was Mobutu's son, chief of the presidential guard. The hotel, with its switchboard connected to a communications satellite, would charge the journalists for incoming as well as outgoing calls. Dahlbäck thought he could avoid this by using his own satellite phone, but then officials came up with the idea of requiring a license for such instruments, with a $450 fee. Food at the Intercontinental was uniformly dull, and thus once in a while one would try to get over to the Memling for a change, even though things were hardly better there.

Some perhaps enjoyed the stay in Kinshasa more than others. Alec Russell of the London *Daily Telegraph,* who had shared reporting journeys in Rwanda with John Balzar, had a veteran colleague in Johannesburg, Christopher Munnion, who was inclined to complain that the fun had gone out of Africa reporting since the immediate postindependence era—Munnion had offered a warts-and-all account of that in his book *Banana Sunday* (1995).⁹ But Russell told him that at the Intercontinental in Kinshasa, it had all been there: the conviviality and the exchange of hilarious or hair-raising rumors after the correspondents came back from their explorations around town.

Just getting out of the hotels was difficult. The Mobutu government had proclaimed a curfew, which was enforced in the sense that the journalists might have to bribe the soldiers to exit from the hotels. Then if they did, they were sometimes threatened and manhandled by policemen and soldiers in the streets. Vincent Dahlbäck's Swedish colleague, Leif Norrman of *Dagens Nyheter,* the largest Stockholm morning daily, was seized and carried off together with a Danish reporter on the back of a truck, into a forest, and he wondered very seriously what would happen to him next. It turned out they were going to another army camp. They were held for several hours, then bawled out by a colonel, and were subsequently released, at a fifty-dollar fee each.¹⁰

The print journalists agreed, however, that they were better off than the TV people, because they could move about reasonably discreetly, armed with just pens and notebooks. As always, the TV journalists and photographers were very conspicuous wherever they showed up, in teams, with all their equipment, and so they drew special attention from soldiers and policemen. Several of them were roughed up, and one was apparently kidnapped and threatened that his testicles would be cut off before he was eventually released. George Alagiah of the BBC Johannesburg bureau said he had had a hand grenade held to his mouth by a soldier. Was this his worst experience as a correspondent? No, not really—there was the time in Somalia when his own hired gunman threatened him in a pay dispute (reporters in Somalia had taken to riding around in cars with mounted guns); and the time in Afghanistan when he had just left his house and it was demolished in an explosion; and the time when he was caught in a cross fire in Monrovia as he went to meet the head of one of the Liberian warring factions, in what was supposed to be a safe house. Probably there had been a tip-off.

In Kinshasa there was a period of waiting and an apparent power vacuum. Mobutu's people had fled, and Kabila's troops had not yet arrived. A clique of officers tried to seize power but were murdered one night by another clique. The correspondents felt that total anarchy could break out if the inhabitants of the shantytowns came into the center of town to loot, but this did not happen. Then Kabila and his army arrived, and his people took over the Intercontinental. Gradually the correspondents realized that there was a conspicuous Rwandan Tutsi contingent in the incoming army. Chris McGreal reflected afterward that compared to what could have occurred, this was really a sort of velvet revolution; it was striking that a small country like Rwanda, which Mobutu had treated with contempt, could play such a major part in pulling him down. But then it was true that Mobutu was dying; his life in exile turned out to be short.

The new government held press conferences at the Intercontinental that sounded like half-baked 1970s Marxist lectures.[11] Rumors spread about massacres along the Kabila army's march through what now again became Congo—"Zaire" would be a name linked to the Mobutu era—and Kabila himself, who half a year or so earlier, in Goma, had come running after the foreign reporters to press on them his own constructions of reality, now made himself mostly inaccessible. The airport, which had been closed, opened for a Kinshasa-Lubumbashi line, served by rather decrepit old planes. From Lubumbashi, the departing correspondents could continue to Johannesburg.

One fact that one glimpses in the correspondents' reminiscences from Kinshasa in 1997 is the great technological change that has left its mark on their parachutist work, indeed on foreign correspondence generally, in the last couple of decades. It is true that at the Hotel Intercontinental, the management was still trying to make the most of its privileged access to telephone lines, by way of the communications satellite. Yet if the correspondents could get away with it, their own satellite phones allowed them to bypass this communicative bottleneck, and at Hotel Memling the television people also made their own technical arrangements. Things had been different in the past. Much has been written over the years by the foreign correspondents themselves about the frantic search for access to the channels of communication that would allow them to reach the home office—the competition over a few telephone lines, the clumsiness of old-style telex machines, the smuggling of hard-copy manuscripts and films, the mishaps, the triumph of getting through. When Pakistan broke up and Bangladesh emerged as a new state, remembered Werner Adam (who was the *Frankfurter Allgemeine*'s Delhi correspondent then; he was the foreign editor of the paper by the time I talked to him in Frankfurt), a hundred foreign newspeople had been locked up by the Pakistani army at Dacca airport. They were strip-searched and all their notes were confiscated, and then they were shipped out on a plane to Karachi. On the six-hour flight, of course, they all tried to write up their stories again—and when they landed, these versions were confiscated, too. But by then, having written them twice, the correspondents almost knew them by heart. And as a Hungarian journalist, who was apparently not treated so roughly, was flying to Zürich, he took the third version of Werner Adam's story along. Reminiscing about his experiences as a Moscow correspondent for the *Washington Post* during the late 1980s perestroika, David Remnick (who went on to become editor of the *New Yorker*) was also emphatic about the changes in reporting technology that had occurred since then. On his trips to the more distant Soviet provinces, he told me, as we had breakfast in an off-Broadway coffee shop, he would get on the phone to his Moscow bureau and read out his story, which would then be relayed to the foreign desk at home. Laptop computers, modems, and satellite phones had made a world of difference since then.

Where the Bureaus Are

It was not long before Laurent Kabila's Congo was once more an arena of military conflict, but the news media parachutists did not gather there in large numbers any time soon again. When Kabila was assassinated in Kinshasa some years later, it seemed hardly anyone was at hand who could quickly offer the world an informed report on what had happened. The news flow from the places where the parachutists go is discontinuous, and also there is a fairly rapid turnover of such places in the landscape of news. The lights go on in one of them, as it were, and then flicker and disappear. In the awareness of the outside world, it returns to darkness.

Other places continue to be better lit, particularly those cities of the world, capitals or other metropolises, where correspondents, often in considerable numbers, make something like homes for longer periods. Preferably they should in themselves be places where things happen that are worth reporting about. But again, they should also be reasonably strategically located, so that correspondents can cover quite large territories from there.

Different media organizations spread themselves thinly or thickly over this landscape. The Associated Press has some eighty bureaus outside the

United States and stringers in between them. The local bureaus of such a major news agency can be quite large. Nicolas Tatro, chief of the Jerusalem bureau, had 47 people on his pay list in a recent month when I talked to him, but he felt that in large part this merely showed what an amorphous entity such a bureau could be. His more stable organization involved some 25 people: writers, photographers, TV crews, and others, to cover Israel and Palestine, "a nation coming into being." And then occasionally there would be some interns, recent graduates from schools of journalism at one American university or another, who would come to the bureau for a couple of months to work very irregular hours, mostly for free coffee and donuts, to get some experience and something for their résumés. Terry Leonard, Tatro's counterpart in Johannesburg, had a writing staff of 3, all Americans, in his office and a Croatian photographer who had worked for the Associated Press in the Balkans. He was injured there and was sent to South Africa to recuperate but was then hired by the bureau. Leonard had some staff members in Cape Town and Durban as well, apart from his network of stringers elsewhere in southern Africa.

Major North American and European newspapers likewise have extensive networks of resident foreign correspondents, although not comparable to those of the large news agencies. Among that handful of American dailies that take foreign news coverage seriously, the *New York Times* has around 40 foreign correspondents, distributed over some twenty-five bureaus, and the *Los Angeles Times* has 25 correspondents in twenty bureaus — give or take a few, as there is some flux in such numbers. The *Neue Zürcher Zeitung,* the Swiss paper, has close to 40 correspondents, and the *Frankfurter Allgemeine,* notably, a little over 50. The *Daily Telegraph,* one of the British papers paying systematic attention to foreign news, has around 12 correspondents of its own, and apart from that a considerable number of stringers are closely tied to the paper. *Dagens Nyheter,* in Stockholm, also has about a dozen correspondents abroad. And then an American paper such as the *Boston Globe,* with the ambition of having some international reporting of its own as a complement to agency materials, but hardly a comprehensive coverage, has some half dozen correspondents scattered over the global landscape of news.

Where, then, are those more stable postings, those where media organizations are likely to have their own correspondents, where even the use of the term "bureaus" may indicate a claim to more durable presence? (Now and then, however, a bureau turns out to be empty, which in practical terms means nonexistent.) To repeat, there is a western European and North American dominance here, reflected in locating practices. Most organizations rooted somewhere within this area around the North Atlantic seem to have at least half their foreign correspondent staff within it. In Europe a large proportion is obviously in London, Paris, Brussels, Rome, and Vienna; those based in Germany have moved, with the national capital, from Bonn to Berlin. Just a little outside that core is Moscow, certainly a prime news site. In North America, the foreign correspondents are overwhelmingly clustered in New York and Washington, D.C. Only a few report regularly even on the wonders of California. The concentration in this Western area is further strengthened by the fact that some bureaus here have more than a single correspondent. In its major bureaus, the *Frankfurter Allgemeine*, for example, may have three correspondents—one for politics, one for the economy, and one for culture. It is also true that cities such as London, Paris, and Rome, with their excellent air connections, are favorable bases for parachute journalism. From those cities one can reach much of Africa, Asia, or the Middle East quite quickly, while leaving one's family in comfortable surroundings.

As far as the rest of the world is concerned, we could perhaps construe a kind of optimal, relatively ambitious distribution as including one or two places in South America, probably Buenos Aires and/or Rio de Janeiro; in Central America, possibly Mexico City; in Africa, most likely Johannesburg or Cape Town, a bit less likely, Nairobi, and even less probably, Abidjan; in the Middle East, Jerusalem and quite possibly Cairo; in South Asia, Delhi; in Southeast Asia, most likely at present, Bangkok; in China at least either Beijing or Hong Kong; in Japan, Tokyo; and possibly, in Australia, Sydney.

In these places more or less considerable numbers of foreign correspondents are thus resident. In between them there are fairly large gaps or some rather inconspicuous dots on the news map. Rowan Callick, more recently Hong Kong correspondent for the *Australian Financial Review,* remembered how he had gone out, after beginning his career on a provincial northern English newspaper, to become a "Pacific correspondent," based in Port Moresby in Papua New Guinea. There were only about a half dozen people reporting in an organized fashion on the Pacific to the rest of the world: apart from himself, a New Zealander or two, a few Australians, and one American.

Yet even those main news metropolises make up a somewhat uncertain, shifting geography. A part of the reason is that foreign correspondents with all the benefits of an employee of the organization, all the perks of a foreign posting, and all the expenses involved in managing a demanding beat, are often quite costly. There is thus some motivation to find substitutes for fully employed staff correspondents. Using agency materials is certainly one way. Rather more tenuous, but highly variable, arrangements with "stringers" is another, which we will return to in the next chapter. Yet another is to have people based at the foreign desk at home, or in some other bureau, with a special responsibility for some region of the world to which they are sent out whenever necessary—as firemen—and apart from that, on an occasional basis.

In recent years, when the era of guerrilla wars and flamboyant dictatorships in Latin America has seemed largely to be over, some European media organizations have thus tried to save on the coverage of this region. If not someone from the organization at home, then perhaps someone from the bureau in Washington, D.C., can visit once in a while. American media may lean toward reporting on Latin America out of their Miami bureaus, which in any case are likely to be responsible for the Caribbean. In Asia, South Asia may not have the highest priority, and however important Japan may be on the world scene, many European organizations find the price tag of correspondents there so unattractive that they will try to get away with either stringers or occasional visits.

A somewhat complicated reasoning, in any case, is involved in placing the correspondents where they are. Let us consider the two instances of Jerusalem and Johannesburg or, to put it differently, the Middle East and Africa.

"This place is like a Rubik's cube," said Lyse Doucet, BBC correspondent in Jerusalem. "You keep turning it, and yet it seems there is always a wrong color showing somewhere." She was in a relatively small city, but probably one that has among the highest densities of foreign correspondents in the world. A recent edition of the local *Who Is Who in the Foreign Press Association* lists 177 active members. Some of these are photographers and cameramen, and not all of them reside in Jerusalem; some are in Tel Aviv, an hour away. But not all correspondents for foreign media in Jerusalem are actually members of the association.

Why are there so many foreign correspondents in Jerusalem? The answer is fairly obvious, although multifaceted. First of all, there is the continuous Arab-Israeli conflict, with a stream of generally newsworthy events. Second, news from Jerusalem has a special cultural resonance because the city is a center of three world religions. Third, after the Holocaust, the continuing history of the Jewish people has been a matter of special concern to a large number of people, especially in Europe and North America, and Israel is the focal point of this concern. The consequence of all this is, as Nicolas Tatro, the local Associated Press bureau chief, put it, that if one were to redraw the map of the world so that the size of regions and countries reflected the amount of news they generate, Israel and Palestine together would be very, very large.

Again, some of the correspondents prefer to be in Tel Aviv rather than Jerusalem, but that number is probably decreasing, despite the fact that many would hold the former to be a more attractive city. Jerusalem is the site of government, a fact that that government has tended to become more emphatic about—and after all, much foreign news continues to be about "states" rather than "societies." There was some tendency for television people to remain in Tel Aviv, but the technical facilities in Jerusalem have been improving, so that is no longer so true. And as more news involves the Palestinians, Jerusalem, with its proximity to major West Bank towns, is also more strategically located.

For correspondents, the Jerusalem beat tends to be remarkably compact. Even brief visits to Gaza or the Galilee hardly entail more than day trips, and as one correspondent said, "you can go to Hebron to cover an incident and be back in Jerusalem in time for lunch." (Hebron Arabs and Jewish settlers clash frequently; more about this in chapter 4.) Many of the correspondents are designated Middle East correspondents, especially if their organizations have nobody posted to Cairo or elsewhere in the Arab world; but a dominant proportion of the stories they are expected to cover are from Israel or Palestine, so trips to other countries in the region may actually be infrequent. For some, it is true, travel to Cairo or to Amman is now more or less routine. The logistic and political difficulties of travel to, say, Baghdad and Damascus have usually been greater. Some make the occasional journey to such places by way of Nicosia, in Cyprus—neutral ground where one might shift from one passport to another, arrange visas, and find transportation to the next destination.

Even though Israeli-Palestinian affairs are a large part of their brief, some Middle East correspondents live elsewhere. In itself Nicosia is not a particularly newsworthy location, but because of its conveniently in-between position, it has had a small colony of correspondents with Middle Eastern assignments. Some of them transferred there from Beirut when working and living in that city became too difficult. There are some Cairo-based correspondents, but not very many, whose regional beats also regularly bring them to Jerusalem. Cecilia Uddén, regional correspondent for Radio Sweden for an extended period, succeeded somebody who had been stationed in Nicosia (and whose predecessor had been in Beirut), but she did not like that city and suggested a move. Why not Jerusalem, she asked, but her employer felt that Israel was not a politically appropriate base for a correspondent covering the entire Middle East. So perhaps she could live in *East* Jerusalem, she had responded, and make that very clear when she signed off after each broadcast? But she ended up in Cairo and was pleased enough; she had spent some of her youth there, when her father had represented a major Swedish corporation. As it turned out, because the peace process got under way, she traveled to Jerusalem more often than she had anticipated, every four or six weeks approximately. Some trips could be planned beforehand; some were more in the nature of fireman trips, following terrorist attacks and the like. Since only a handful of people reported on Israel out of Cairo, they at least developed a sort of nodding acquaintance. There was one direct Cairo–Tel Aviv flight per day, and one by way of Sinai, with Air Sinai.

In Jerusalem itself, the flow of news, opinion, and commentary is intense. Barton Gellman, correspondent for the *Washington Post,* felt that one reason to go out of town occasionally, say, to Cairo or Damascus, was simply to get an outside perspective. Israel was an "echo chamber," he thought—the same news and views bouncing back and forth, with a lot of unstated shared assumptions that could best be identified by getting a view from elsewhere. At the time I was in Jerusalem, there was some speculation whether the ongoing peace process might ever reach the point where the city would no longer stand out as a major international news source. Few seemed to think so. Instead, it was expected that the significance of Jerusalem to millennia of human history would remain. (Nicolas Tatro, for such reasons, foresaw oddballs from everywhere flocking to the city in the year 2000.) In more mundane and practical terms, moreover, it was also held that if lasting peace really broke out in the region, Jerusalem would become an even more practical home base for correspondents with a general assignment of covering the Middle East. It offered more attractive living conditions than most competing locations (especially for families), and the difficulties of visits elsewhere would be gone. Yet most correspondents were perhaps not ready to take the prospects for overall, lasting peace altogether seriously. The Rubik's cube of Middle East conflicts, they suspected, would keep generating new local business for them.

As Jerusalem has Middle East correspondents, Johannesburg has Africa correspondents. But there has been a problematic politics of location here as well. First of all, it is clear that for a long time, South Africa offered the major continuous news theme in the African continent—the story of apartheid and the struggle of black people against it. It was largely because of this theme, this story line, that on any news map of the world of the kind Nicolas Tatro in Jerusalem fantasized, South Africa would for decades have been quite large and the rest of the continent comparatively small. It is also true, however, that South Africa has been the country in sub-Saharan Africa where members of western European or North American media audiences were most likely to have some personal or business connection.

Nevertheless, South Africa was for a long time just as controversial a base for covering black Africa's news as Israel was for reporting on the Arab Middle East. Traveling between black Africa and South Africa during the apartheid years tended to involve obstacles, tricks, and ruses similar to those involved in Middle Eastern detours to Nicosia. Scott Kraft, *Los Angeles Times* correspondent in Johannesburg during the late apartheid period, re-membered pretending to be on his way from somewhere to Gaberone, Bo-tswana, by way of Johannesburg—and on reaching the latter city, throwing away the ticket for his fictitious further journey.

Furthermore, since the apartheid regime thought of at least a part of the European and American media apparatus as its adversary, it was not al-ways easy to gain entry into South Africa or to remain there. For such rea-sons, some of the foreign correspondents and their organizations found some other base in Africa, either as a necessary substitute or as a political state-ment. Nairobi served this way for some, and after Salisbury in Rhodesia turned into Harare in Zimbabwe, that was also an alternative. Yet when South Africa began its transition away from apartheid, it was a new phase in that major news theme, with the additional new circumstance that the inter-national media were now entirely welcome both to be present in South Africa and to travel between it and other parts of the continent. So to South Africa they went.

A considerable number of the new sojourners in the country, as well as many of those already established there, were called Africa correspondents —which, as job designations go, seems a bit of a scandal—or as one of the people involved put it, "really an impossible job." "Sub-Saharan Africa cor-respondents," which in all likelihood is what they were actually supposed to be, is not a great deal better. Many of the organizations that sent them had only one person for that entire vast region, and South Africa appeared to be the most important and newsworthy country, as well as the most convenient and comfortable one to live in and to travel in and out of.

For some other news organizations, there were ways of dividing Africa for reporting purposes. On the whole, the tendency seems to have been to place a second Africa bureau, if any, in Nairobi; the correspondent there might handle East and Central Africa and even West Africa, as John Balzar did for a period for the *Los Angeles Times*. If people transferred from Nai-robi to Johannesburg when this became politically possible, it was partly be-cause of technical circumstances. The communications facilities in Nairobi were mediocre. But clearly other qualities would also count. Nairobi tends not to be regarded as a very pleasant place to live or to go about one's business—for one thing, the Kenyan government has occasionally made things difficult for foreign correspondents or has threatened to expel them. Some of the Nairobi correspondents, said Vincent Dahlbäck, the South Africa–based correspondent for Radio Sweden, were actually thinking about moving to Kampala, in Uganda, because things were looking better there.

With someone in Nairobi, the South Africa–based correspondents would usually be left with southern Africa in their assignment. South Africa itself would certainly be the most important part of it, but definitely not all. Suzanne Daley, bureau chief in Johannesburg for the *New York Times,* with her journalist husband Donald McNeil in the bureau as well, had ten additional countries in the territory they shared between them: Swaziland, Botswana, Lesotho, Angola, Mozambique, Madagascar, Zimbabwe, Zambia, Malawi, and Mauritius.

Yet more rarely, as we have noted, there would be a third posting in black Africa, which then as often as not might be in Abidjan, capital of the Ivory Coast, in West Africa. This may seem a bit puzzling, since the Ivory Coast was seldom in the news until a series of uprisings occurred in the early years of the twenty-first century. Again, however, it has been largely a matter of practicality, with reasonable facilities and the possibility of a good life for correspondents and whoever they bring with them. Considering that Nigeria is by far the most populous country in West Africa, and one with a lively press scene of its own to inspire foreign reporting, Lagos could seem like a better choice for a regional correspondent. But as one long-time West Africa correspondent expressed it to me, "Lagos—forget it, too many coups, too expensive, nothing worked." Even when newspeople are allowed into the country, the Nigerian metropolis may be just too much of a hassle.

I will come back to the coverage of Nigeria. Returning to Johannesburg, this city is not an altogether self-evident base for a correspondent with a South African assignment either. Just as in Israel some correspondents prefer Tel Aviv to Jerusalem, in South Africa there are those who stay in Cape Town rather than in Johannesburg. But here the contrast seems rather greater. Whereas in Israel the two cities are an hour's drive apart, in South Africa the cities involved are more or less at opposite ends of a much larger country, and they may be even further apart in the political imagination than the two Israeli cities are. Cape Town, at least as long as one stays in its central parts or along the suburban shoreline, is to a striking extent still a city for white people. Johannesburg has quickly become black, with the exception of those northern suburbs conventionally described as "leafy." Johannesburg, too, is generally held to be uniquely violent and crime-ridden. Yet it is by far the largest city in the country, the economically most powerful (sitting on top of South Africa's gold), and the one most in tune with the political aspirations of the country's majority. So where should the correspondents be?

Some of those who are in Cape Town note that their city is where the South African parliament is and that after the political transition, this may be less of a rubber-stamp institution than it was during the apartheid era. But the parliament excepted, most of the government apparatus is in Pretoria, next to Johannesburg, and it seems less than certain that the parliament will stay in Cape Town, desert lands away from the larger population concentrations of the country. It will also be admitted that Johannesburg has the larger and better-connected airport, so that if one really has to cover the continent as a news worker, one should perhaps be in the more northerly city. Yet communications being what they are in Africa (mostly poor), that extra hour or so of flying time between Cape Town and Johannesburg rarely matters.

All the same, the things that quite certainly matter most for those who choose Cape Town are the quality of life and safety aspects. Leif Norrman, of the Stockholm *Dagens Nyheter,* was in Johannesburg for a couple of years before he moved to Cape Town, but he remembered, for example, the time when he was at the border between Kenya and Somalia, at the height of the Somalia conflict, and got a telephone call from his wife in Johannesburg, reporting that their garden was full of policemen searching for some criminals. It was a time when he did not really need any long-distance worries to add to his local predicament. Against that kind of background, when Dean Murphy of the *Los Angeles Times* arrived to take up a South Africa assignment, his foreign editor at home, Simon Li, told him that if he wanted to make a case for relocating the bureau from Johannesburg to Cape Town, Li would give it serious consideration. The Murphy family stayed in a Johannesburg hotel to begin with, and when his wife and children went to a shopping center, there had just been a robbery at the Woolworth store, so the place was crowded with police. Yet Murphy felt that because Johannesburg was a black city, to report from South Africa this is where one should be. Moving to Cape Town would be "making a statement" of the wrong sort. And so Murphy, having just moved from the bureau in Warsaw, out of which he had spent a great deal of time in Bosnia, found himself in a Johannesburg office in the same building with Terry Leonard of the Associated Press, another Balkan veteran.

To a degree, news centers rise and decline; foreign editors and correspondents are sensitive to such shifts. Johannesburg, and South Africa generally, became more attractive with the transition away from apartheid, but by the time the momentous events of that transition to a "rainbow nation" had occurred, the question arose whether anything equally newsworthy could possibly follow. In Jerusalem, again, people in the news community speculated what would happen if peace was finally achieved between Israel and its Arab neighbors. As long as there was an Iron Curtain across Europe, Vienna, just next to it, was a rather marginal place as far as news of interest to the outside world was concerned, but when that curtain rose again, it was the place to be for covering central Europe and the unruly Balkans. At one time, before it was possible or convenient for correspondents to base themselves in the People's Republic of China itself, Hong Kong was the strategic choice of China watchers. Then China opened up, correspondents set themselves up in Beijing, and Hong Kong was eventually absorbed, after a fashion, into the People's Republic; so it seemed increasingly open to debate what, apart from Hong Kong itself (whatever that might amount to), could suitably be covered from there. To some observers and participants, the answer might be "Southeast Asia." Yet Hong Kong was not really in that region, and there were competing possibilities. For a while, during the dramatic years of Ferdinand Marcos and the heroic People's Revolution, Manila was the base for some correspondents traveling in Southeast Asia. But after that the Philippines seemed to be, as one of them put it, on a "decent autopilot" and no longer so interesting. Singapore, of course, was a well located, comfortable place to live—but the Singapore government seemed to welcome foreign correspondents only (or mostly) so long as they did not write about Singapore itself. To report on the increasingly important Southeast Asian region, then, where would one settle? A fair number of correspondents and their organizations decided on Bangkok. Keith Richburg, *Washington Post* correspondent in Hong Kong, covered Southeast Asia from the latter city until the end of his posting in the area. But he suspected his successor would be in Bangkok. During his first tour as Southeast Asia correspondent, in the 1980s, Richburg was in Manila.

I talked to some foreign editors of major newspapers about the ups and downs of news beats and what they were doing to adjust to changes in the news landscape—or for that matter, to bring about such changes. Bill Keller of the *New York Times* was generally inclined to try to make coverage less Eurocentric than it had traditionally been. His own most recent initiative had been opening an Istanbul bureau. "You don't have to believe this stuff about a clash of civilizations," he said, with a passing implicit reference to Samuel Huntington, but he thought Turkey was an increasingly interesting meeting point between East and West and was strategically important for reporting on "the -stans" in ex-Soviet Central Asia—"these people don't want to be covered from Moscow." And so Stephen Kinzer, the first Istanbul bureau chief, began producing a stream of stories. Not long before that, the *New York Times* had added a Shanghai bureau to complement Beijing and Hong Kong, in response to the growing importance of China reporting. (Later, in Hong Kong, some would begin to wonder whether the Chinese government would so strongly favor Shanghai as an international economic center that this could also play a part in a possible decline of the Hong Kong news beat.)

Keller's counterpart on the American West Coast, Simon Li of the *Los Angeles Times,* Hong Kong–born, British-trained, and a man with a sense of irony, told me that his paper had tried a Brussels bureau but closed it again. It turned out that there was no way of writing about the complexities of the European Union machinery in a way that would interest Californians. Here, too, the trend was rather away from the European focus in foreign coverage. The paper had recently tried to post a new Southeast Asia bureau in Hanoi, but the Vietnamese government had not given its permission. As far as the *Los Angeles Times* was concerned, however, reporting on Japan had some special weight (as I noted toward the end of chapter 1). There were at the time three correspondents in the Tokyo bureau, one of them specializing in economic news.

Werner Adam, of the *Frankfurter Allgemeine,* felt privileged in that he did not need to be as concerned as many other foreign editors with the costliness of his international coverage—his paper received its main support from a foundation, well endowed by German business and industry. He wanted to open a bureau in Southeast Asia (previously it had been a part of the territory of the New Delhi bureau), and because his paper had a strong interest in economic affairs, Singapore might be the best location. To serve the German readership, however, providing a clear view of the changes in central and eastern Europe was of special importance. He had bureaus in Moscow, Warsaw, Prague, and Budapest, and the Stockholm correspondent was in charge of reporting on the new Baltic states. Moreover, he planned to open a bureau in Kiev, in Ukraine. Like his colleague at the *New York Times,* he was aware that the people in ex-Soviet, non-Russian states did not like to be a part of the Moscow correspondents' territory. In London, Stephen Robinson of the *Daily Telegraph,* with a smaller network of foreign correspondents of his own, made two changes after coming in as foreign editor. As a former Washington correspondent, he thought the reporting from the United States had been too biased toward the East Coast, with two people in Washington and two in New York and nobody anywhere else. So he moved one of these four to Los Angeles. In addition, he placed a correspondent in Sydney. There were strong links between Australia and Britain, after all, and the increasing contestation of those links was itself newsworthy. He found that readers responded very favorably to this reporting.

News Neighborhoods, Roving Reporting, and Serendipitous Stories

For their longer-term assignments, foreign correspondents do not only cluster in particular cities in the world. A close-up view of the news landscape sometimes shows them also concentrating, almost to the point of rubbing elbows, in particular parts of those cities. They may or may not actually have their living quarters close to one another, although in Jerusalem a fair number were either in the German Colony, a neighborhood established by a German religious order in the nineteenth century, or in Musrara, an old neighborhood close to the Damascus Gate, long inhabited by poor Oriental Jews until it began to gentrify in more recent times.

But the offices of correspondents are more likely to concentrate in local space. A large proportion of the foreign news media organizations in Johannesburg have their office addresses in two buildings a few minutes apart from each other in Richmond, a small suburban enclave close to two main thoroughfares and to the large South African Broadcasting Corporation complex, a little to the west of central Johannesburg. Many of them had been assembled in a single office building in central Johannesburg until a few years earlier, but they left it partly because the security situation worsened.

As you turn off Stanley Road at the shop sign of the London Pie Company and go slightly downhill along Menton Road, you will find Richmond quiet although a bit nondescript. There are some commercial establishments —a couple of car dealers, a computer equipment business, a photocopy and fax service, a liquor store, a small restaurant, and a couple of small shops selling newspapers and sundry groceries. Turning right from Menton at Napier Road, you find the Richmond Square building, with AP, CNN, the *Los Angeles Times, Newsweek,* and others. Continuing on Menton down the hill, you come to the rather larger building at 1 Park Road, Menton House, with a large, conspicuous dish on the roof. Some twenty-five to thirty media or media-related offices are here. A very large proportion of news out of Africa passes through these two buildings. There is a guard at the entrance to each of them, but this has not prevented some burglaries to occur, resulting in the loss of high-tech equipment.

The classic address for the foreign press in Jerusalem is Beit Agron on Hillel Street, named after a culture hero of Israeli journalism, Gershon Agron, the first editor of the *Jerusalem Post* (which began as the *Palestine*

Post, before the Israeli state was founded). A number of American, British, French, Canadian, and Japanese media are represented here. But this four-story building, with a small Israeli flag and a large and complicated antenna on the roof, is not the home of the foreign media organizations alone. The Israeli Government Press Office is also here, as is the Israeli Defense Force spokesman and the office of the military censor. A bulletin board in the lobby, mostly containing notices about apartment rental opportunities, suggests that much of the population in the building is mobile. Beit Agron is no longer what it used to be, however, as far as the foreign press corps in Jerusalem is concerned. Earlier, all the correspondents accredited with the Government Press Office had their pigeonholes here and would come by more or less on a daily basis to pick up messages and handouts. Now they get most of the information on the Internet, and those who do not have their offices in the building do not visit it so frequently—which also means that they run into one another a little less often. (It is a little like a village that gets piped water, where villagers therefore no longer meet routinely around the village pump.) The people involved with television and radio are increasingly concentrating in the Jerusalem Capital Studios on Jaffa Road, opposite the city's central bus station, which can cater to all their technical needs.

There are similar places in other cities. In Tokyo, many foreign news organizations find it practical to draw on the technical facilities of Japanese media, and thus they rent space in the media buildings. A corridor on the eighth floor of the *Yomiuri Shimbun* building in central Tokyo, quipped one inhabitant, Nicholas Valéry of the *Economist,* was a "*gaijin* ghetto."[12] Correspondents who have been stationed in Nairobi remember Lester House, a dismal place where the Kenyan government found it handy to keep them assembled for surveillance and occasional harassment.[13] In Harare, Mass Media House was at one time a lively place. Somebody went by there later, however, and the guard posted at the front door shook his head and said that only the Chinese were left there now. More recently yet, President Mugabe's regime made it clear that it just did not want foreign correspondents around.

But even the correspondents who have offices in such buildings certainly do not spend all their time there. The small one- or two-room offices in Beit Agron are often empty (unless there is another staff person who takes calls, listens to the radio to follow the stream of local news, and attends to varied other matters—see chapter 5). Some correspondents do much of their work from home, and in any case, they may be out on reporting excursions.

Often these do not take them very far—to repeat, from Jerusalem, you can go to Hebron and be back for lunch. But those responsible for larger territories may be on the road farther away and more of the time. Ethan Bronner was the Middle East correspondent for the *Boston Globe* when I was in Jerusalem. He calculated that he spent about 25 percent of his time away from Israel and Palestine. Later that year he was going to return to the United States, and before that he hoped to do some more reporting from elsewhere in the region—he had applied for a visa to Libya and thought of going to Algeria, perhaps to travel with an antiterror unit (this was at the height of Algeria's most violent period). He had been there once before, during the 1991 election campaign when it was becoming clear that the Islamist opposition would win. He also reminisced about a reporting trip to Yemen, to write about the boat refugees coming in from Somalia and receiving a very reluctant welcome from the Yemeni authorities. The refugees were giving up gold to get drinking water; Bronner had talked to a jeweler who had gone from middle-class life in Mogadishu to ruin in no time. While he was in Yemen, too, he had done a story on the mildly narcotic leaf called *qat,* the chewing of which is central to local social life. The story on the boat refugees had been on the front page of the *Globe.* Apart from that, his experience had been that it was his Israeli reporting that got such treatment by his Boston editors.

Most recently Bronner had been to Amman, where he had gone with Barton Gellman of the *Washington Post.* The original purpose of this journey was to report on a meeting between King Hussein and Prime Minister Netanyahu, but nobody expected anything much to come out of the meeting, so this was probably going to be fairly routine coverage. Then Bronner and Gellman decided that while in Jordan they might work on another topic as well. As things turned out, this actually became the main purpose of the trip. In a major tragic accident, two Israeli army helicopters crashed into each other in the dark, close to the Lebanese border; more than seventy soldiers were killed, and Netanyahu canceled his journey to Amman. So the two correspondents, who had already made all their travel arrangements, went there anyway (meanwhile letting their papers use agency stories on the helicopter crash and its immediate aftermath) and spent their time in the Jordanian capital talking to Iraqi exiles. It was at a time when Saddam Hussein's son Uday had recently been seriously injured in an assassination attempt in Baghdad, and rumors—in large part contradictory—were flying in Amman about what had happened. Uday had been in a white Porsche, or was it red? He was driving alone—no, there was a woman with him. He was shot by someone in the family, or perhaps by somebody else. In any case, two months later, everyone seemed to agree, Uday was still in the hospital.

The correspondents in Johannesburg and Cape Town spent varying amounts of time in more distant parts of their territory. Mike Hanna of CNN described his outfit as a "travel bureau": since CNN operates on the principle of extreme flexibility, unless he was busy with something in Johannesburg, he might fly in wherever there was a staff shortage, whether it was Jerusalem, Cairo, Moscow, or somewhere else. Most of the others at least tended to stay within Africa. They, and their editors, sometimes took varying views of how to balance reporting from South Africa with travel elsewhere in the continent. Alec Russell, of the *Daily Telegraph,* did rather more in other countries after the transition period in South African politics was over and when what followed did not require so much continuous attention.[14] In contrast, Dean Murphy, of the *Los Angeles Times,* noted that his predecessor had been spending a great deal of time on the crises of Central Africa, and now the foreign desk in Los Angeles felt it was time to do more feature stories from South Africa. Marika Griehsel, correspondent for national Swedish TV in Johannesburg, working out of two small, crowded rooms in Menton House with her photographer-husband Simon Stanford, said they did about half their jobs outside South Africa and were probably away from the building more than most of its inhabitants. What many of the Africa correspondents could agree on was that when there was no crisis requiring immediate fireman trips, much of the continent was underreported (a theme we will return to in chapter 4).

I took some special interest in finding out what the Africa correspondents had to say about Nigeria. Again, it ought to have been fairly prominent on the news map: it is the most populous country in sub-Saharan Africa, with 100 million inhabitants or so; its oil economy has at least some potential of making it one of the wealthier countries of the continent; and it has a livelier intellectual scene than most African countries. But I was also curious simply because I had done fieldwork there and thus had a long-standing preoccupation with the country.

I was talking to the correspondents about this, however, at the time of the dictatorship of General Sani Abacha, plainly not a period of close and consistent Nigeria watching by the world media. Mostly the correspondents were simply not admitted. One or two knew of colleagues who had faked invitations from someone in the country and had therefore been issued tourist visas, but the correspondents I spoke with had been reluctant to use such means themselves because it was unethical as well as dangerous. And they were not allowed in as journalists, they surmised, because the Nigerian regime knew it was better to have no publicity at all than bad publicity—which was what it would most likely get.

Chris McGreal of the *Guardian* was among those who had managed to do some reporting from Nigeria. He liked his visits and was fascinated by the complexity of the country. Once you were through the airport, there was actually very little internal surveillance, compared, for example, to what Zaire had been like under Mobutu. In 1996 McGreal flew into the country shortly after the author-politician Ken Saro-Wiwa was executed for his alleged role in the ongoing violent unrest in Ogoniland, in southern Nigerian oil country. It was an event that for once did draw world attention to Nigeria (in no small part because there was an environmentalist angle and the Shell Corporation was involved). Somehow nobody at the Ministry of Information had bothered to check whether he was properly accredited, and he even made his way into an official dinner where the dictator Abacha made a speech. Then he journeyed to the province of which Ogoniland was a part and struck a deal with the Military Governor's Office: he would travel with the governor to Ogoniland one day (which was itself an interesting experience) and would be allowed to go out on his own the next day.[15] The governor had wondered why so few foreign journalists came to see him, apparently entirely unaware that for the most part they were not allowed into the country. It all seemed to be an intriguing mixture of despotism and inefficiency.

It was after these conversations about the coverage and noncoverage of Nigeria that General Abacha died, under somewhat mysterious circumstances. (According to one colorful rumor, people in Abacha's inner circle who had secretly turned against him had flown in some especially attractive Indian prostitutes to entertain him, then poisoned his Viagra pills.) Nigeria was again on a path toward democracy and an elected government. During this period, when I was back in Stockholm, I had an unexpected experience. There on my television screen was the little town in central Nigeria where I had done fieldwork many years earlier, now visited by Catherine Bond, the Nairobi-based correspondent of CNN—and at about the same time, a story datelined there appeared in the *New York Times,* by its Abidjan-based correspondent Norimitsu Onishi (1999).

It turned out that the local emir, whom I had met several times, had died at the age of ninety-five, and this had brought alive again a very old ethnic conflict. The emir was a Muslim and a man of the Hausa people, and his dynasty had established its rather shaky dominance in the area in the early nineteenth century, when the Hausa came into the area for the purpose of slave raiding and the exacting of tribute from local ethnic groups. During the colonial period, the latter turned to Christianity on a fairly large scale and kept voicing their demand that the Muslim emirate should be dissolved. Now that the old emir had died, they hoped they would finally be able to take over, and when it was suddenly announced that he would simply be succeeded by his son, the local groups rebelled. Muslims' houses in the town were set aflame, the emir's palace was stormed, and the new emir had to flee.

This might well be regarded as a newsworthy set of events, but I strongly suspect that the reporting was an instance of news by serendipity—seemingly a common phenomenon in foreign correspondence, particularly where correspondents have very large areas to report from. Although they set off from wherever they are based with one major story in mind, along the way they may find time to do another couple of items as well. Some may be planned beforehand; others are not. In this case, the newly elected president of Nigeria had just been inaugurated in Abuja, the national capital, built in recent years from scratch on a site not so far from "my" town. Thus the world media happened to be at hand when something of interest happened nearby. The town has not been in the news since then and possibly will never be heard from through such channels again.

Two Asians in Africa

To repeat, international news reporting is a heavily Western-dominated field, but it is not entirely an Occidental enterprise; and so finally we encounter two exceptions, correspondents in South Africa for two major Asian newspapers.

Yuji Yoshikata, of the Tokyo newspaper *Yomiuri Shimbun,* has his office in Menton House, in that media-dense neighborhood in Johannesburg. A table is cluttered with copies of the *New African* and the *Economist,* and there is a pile of *International Herald Tribune*s. As Yoshikata meets me, he wears an Africa-inspired yellow tie with elephants and zebras on it. He invites me for lunch at a Japanese restaurant in a northern Johannesburg suburb, where most of the customers are Japanese businessmen in dark suits. At one o'clock Yoshikata makes a prearranged call on his cell phone to a government office in Tokyo to get some Africa-related information that he finds more readily available there than anywhere locally.

With some 11 million copies printed per day, all editions combined, *Yomiuri Shimbun* is Japan's largest newspaper. It has a very large network of foreign correspondents, possibly the largest of any paper in the world: some sixty journalists in about thirty countries. Compared to European and American organizations, as one might expect, it is represented more strongly in Asian countries, with bureaus in such locations as Phnom Penh, Hanoi, and Manila. But it is present in Europe and in the Americas as well—Yoshikata assumes that the Havana bureau exists mostly to wait for the post-Castro transition. Before Japan's economy stagnated, the paper had correspondents in even more places, for example in eastern Europe.

For sub-Saharan Africa Yoshikata alone is responsible, however, although he has a locally recruited reporter working for him, a young Afrikaner woman who also does a variety of office tasks. Yoshikata feels that he writes a lot, but not everything actually gets into the paper. On a normal day it has only two pages of foreign news. With so many correspondents, there is definitely a competition for space, and Africa can hardly be heard from every day. When the Rwanda crisis began, he recalled, he and his colleagues at the foreign desk at *Yomiuri Shimbun* (he was still in Tokyo then) took out a map to see where this unfamiliar country was located.

Yuji Yoshikata grew up in a small town in southern Japan and only visited Tokyo a couple of times as a school child. He returned to study education at a university—not to become a teacher, but because he was interested in educational research. Although he had not done terribly well in his studies, he was hired by *Yomiuri Shimbun,* to be trained on the job. First he spent a period as an all-around local reporter in a small town close to an American base (where he learned to distinguish between different types of American military aircraft). Then he was assigned to the foreign desk in Tokyo, primarily to read correspondents' pieces and do fact-checking. It was rather boring. In an internal reshuffle, he found himself shifted to the sports desk for a while, but then he went back to the foreign desk, expecting to specialize in the Middle East. Instead he was sent off in a hurry to replace the Johannesburg bureau chief.

Much of Yoshikata's reporting involves reading agency materials and rewriting them in Japanese, with some analysis and background added, on a word processor with Japanese script; this is then sent on a phone line to Tokyo. He gathers additional information by phone, often by calling Japanese, American, or British embassies in various African capitals. When I meet him, he is working on a story on Japanese aid in Africa, but most of his stories, he says, have no specifically Japanese angle. Yet he remembers that when he planned to go to Kenya in the fall of 1997 to write about the national election, he ended up staying in Johannesburg because South Africa just then broke its diplomatic ties with Taiwan, and in Japan this was a more important Africa story.

But Yoshikata also travels. Unlike many correspondents, who often move in pairs, he usually goes alone; and since he does his own photography, at least for feature stories, he does not take a photographer along either. But he tries to cultivate contacts with local sources, including the often well-educated but underemployed individuals who have been his fixers in various places. In order to keep them well-disposed, he often pays them rather generously. Because of bad communications, however, they are often difficult to get in touch with when he needs them.

He had been in Rwanda and had followed the crumbling of the Mobutu regime in Goma and Lubumbashi and Kinshasa; he had his own recollections of these events. There was the time somewhere in southern Rwanda when the reporters stood in line to use the single existing telephone booth. He had to wait for three hours, thereby missing the deadline for his paper's first edition. And in Lubumbashi Yoshikata, too, was held for several hours by Mobutu's gendarmerie. Taking an interest in the idea of peacekeeping forces, he went to Liberia to look at the Nigerian troops sent there as a part of a regional West African collaborative effort. Although he was not impressed, he thought they were probably better than nothing. As he also wanted to get into Nigeria, he asked the Nigerian commanding officer of the force in Liberia to write a letter of support for his visa application, but this was of no avail. Had he been allowed into Nigeria, he would have liked to investigate the local roots of Nigerian involvement in international crime, which extended to the Johannesburg scene as well. In South Africa, he had recently traveled with party members on the African National Congress's own bus from Johannesburg to Mafikeng, to report on the party conference where this party, dominant in the post-apartheid era, staked out its continued course.

At some point, Yoshikata hopes, he will live in Tokyo again. It has many things not available elsewhere in Japan—unlike his home town, for example, it has foreigners. But Tokyo is also very crowded, and it would be almost inconceivable for someone like him to live in a house of his own there. (Members of a Japanese delegation visiting South Africa were amazed to discover that the slum dwellers in Soweto could have four-room houses to themselves.) Yoshikata also wants to be posted to New York or Washington, D.C., sometime. He is interested in American diversity—"the melting pot"—and would like to write about how it works.

Now and then Yoshikata watches televised press conferences from the United States, but he notes that even when they are of an international nature, there seldom seem to be any Japanese journalists among those who ask questions. Are his compatriot colleagues perhaps a rather timid lot? He comments, too, that when a Japanese correspondent sends his report to the foreign news desk of his organization in Tokyo, and the editors at home find that it is not in total agreement with whatever they have received about the same event from some major Western news agency, they may simply change the report to conform with the agency version. Yoshikata's impression is that they are reluctant to stick their necks out. Yet in terms of the resources at their disposal, the main Japanese media organizations appear by no means disadvantaged compared to their Western counterparts.

The southern Africa correspondent of the respected Madras (now Chennai) newspaper, the *Hindu,* seems to operate under more modest material and organizational circumstances. M. S. Prabhakara, now in his early six-ties, lives in a high-rise apartment building close to the seashore in southern Cape Town and works out of his home. Journalism is his second career. He taught English at various colleges and universities in India and had a year as a Fulbright Fellow at the University of Wisconsin, studying, among other things, Old Norse. But in the mid-1970s, at the time of the state of emergency in India, he wanted to engage more actively with public life. For eight years he worked for that major Indian journal of opinion, the *Economic and Polit-ical Weekly,* in Bombay. Then he became a special correspondent for the *Hindu* and its affiliated newsmagazine *Frontline* in Assam, during a decade that was particularly troubled there. And when Nelson Mandela was released from prison in South Africa, Prabhakara began his own personal campaign to persuade his editor to make him southern Africa correspondent of the *Hindu.*

He suspects that among those who meet him fleetingly, many assume that the *Hindu* must be a local paper catering to the religiously inclined among South Africans of Indian descent and that he has been flown in from the old country as some sort of religious specialist. But that is really quite far from the truth. His paper is one of India's established quality papers and has more foreign correspondents than any of its competitors several of them on assignments in neighboring South Asian countries, but others elsewhere in Asia and in Europe and the United States. He, for his part, is an old Indian leftist, as secular as anybody; he has portraits of Lenin and Mandela on the top shelf of his book case. (On the shelves below, Prabhakara's academic background is again discernible, as they are well stocked with biographies and political and historical monographs relating to South African affairs.)

Although there are numerous South Africans of South Asian back-ground, they play no major part in his reporting to Madras. Perhaps he had done about ten such articles in four years. One was a humorous piece on a Member of Parliament who insisted on speaking Hindi in sessions, to make the point that it was one of the national languages. As I meet him, Prab-hakara is devoting most of his attention to the hearings of South Africa's post-apartheid Truth and Reconciliation Commission. Actually, it is far from every day that he has something in the paper. The competition for foreign news space in the *Hindu* is not so different from that in Yoshikata's *Yomiuri Shimbun.* Some of the South Asian stories may be run on national or regional news pages, but for the rest of the world there are regularly two pages, and a considerable part of those is taken up by advertisements. Prabhakara doubts that even the rather sophisticated readers of his paper care much for foreign news, except perhaps for news from the United States. Once, he reminisces, he was on the high-speed train between Madras and Bangalore, on which many of the passengers are affluent and well educated. Because he had a story in the paper that day, he tried to see if a fellow passenger, sitting next to him and reading the *Hindu,* was taking any notice of it. But no, the man cast a diagonal glance across the foreign news pages and then turned quickly to the sports page. In fact, that was where one of his stories had turned up once, and it had been a bit of a shock to him: he had written something about South African rugby and its relationship to apartheid from a very political angle.

Besides writing for the *Hindu,* Prabhakara does pieces once in a while for the *Economic and Political Weekly* and for *Frontline.* He reads *Time* and *Newsweek* regularly and the *Economist* occasionally. The national South African News Agency wire service is too expensive for his operation, but the Web site of the African National Congress gives him much of the political news, and he uses the Internet extensively to dig out varied information. Once his editors in Madras asked him to do something about the upcoming elections in Sudan, about which neither they nor he knew anything. But he found a home page belonging to a Sudanese politician in exile, E-mailed him, and received useful materials in return. That allowed him to file a story to go with the pictures from Sudan that his editors had liked so much and which were apparently the main reason for their sudden interest in the country.

On the whole, however, the editors made few such demands. Prabhakara writes on whatever interests him. His assignment in South Africa was simply a personal reward for services rendered earlier in his work for the *Hindu.* The paper had no correspondent in Cape Town before, and most likely he will not have a successor either. Thus, for the readers of this Indian newspaper, one light in the landscape of news, after shining for a few years, will probably go out.

W hen Dean Murphy was a graduate student in Washington, D.C., he already knew that he wanted to become a foreign correspondent. He went to talks by veteran newspeople, and when he asked two of them how to get his chosen career going, they gave him quite opposite advice. One told him he should go to a place where news was made or was about to be made, write as a freelancer, and make himself indispensable—then someone would hire him. The other told him to get hired by the best paper he could, begin by doing local news, and move on to foreign news whenever an opportunity arose.

Murphy took the latter route and joined the *Los Angeles Times.* He spent many years in Los Angeles, sometimes worrying whether he would ever get any further. Because he had grown up in Pennsylvania, however, getting to know California was a bit like being a foreign correspondent (and reporting on the Los Angeles riots was somewhat like being a war correspondent). Eventually he was posted to Warsaw and then to Johannesburg.

Anton La Guardia, of the *Daily Telegraph,* who was in Jerusalem when I met him, mostly went the other route—at least to begin with. He had a largely expatriate upbringing, started studying engineering in England but was bored, became involved with Amnesty International, and turned to journalism. He worked for a local paper in South London for a while but then decided to try to make use of his Philippines connection (his mother was a Filipina). So he went to Manila. He began as a freelancer and also served as a fixer for an American television network, marketing himself as someone who could build bridges between cultures.

Then came President Marcos's "snap election" in 1986, which Marcos evidently intended to steal through fraud. Vote counting seemed to go on forever. Most of the parachutist correspondents became bored and left—and then the People's Revolution broke out. La Guardia remembers that he could sell front-page stories to both the *Sunday Times* and the *Evening Standard.*

No doubt these were good for his résumé. Yet he then returned to London, to do some work for the *Guardian* and for BBC. When an offer came from the *Daily Telegraph,* he accepted it, partly because he realized that he preferred print journalism over other media. He reported out of Belfast for a year, then joined the foreign desk in London, covering the Foreign Office and taking an occasional reporting trip. Gradually he developed a Middle East specialization, because he saw that it was a news-rich region. While the regular Middle East correspondent was off covering the Gulf War, La Guardia was assigned to Jerusalem, and after that he was stationed there on a regular basis. When I met him, he had been there for six years—longer than he had expected.[1] The year after, when I was talking to Alec Russell, *Daily Telegraph* correspondent in Johannesburg, it turned out that Anton La Guardia was soon going to replace him there.

This chapter is about foreign correspondents' careers.[2] A career, as I use the notion here, is a path through life; but I do not assume that it can be entirely planned or predicted or that it always moves in some sense upward. It involves intentions as well as contingencies. We may be inclined to associate the idea of career mostly with working life, but the concept can be extended to other domains of life as well, such as domesticity: being single, teaming up with a partner or a succession of them, rearing children, perhaps being single again. And careers in different domains have a way of becoming entangled with one another. One fact, however, is basic to a concept of career: it entails passages, shifts, changes, discontinuities, phases.

One major shift is already exemplified by Dean Murphy's and Anton La Guardia's stories—that of entering into foreign correspondence. Even before that step, there may be a series of accumulating conditions and experiences that eventually lead up to it. And once that move has been made, there is a range of possibilities of continuity or discontinuity that reflect the internal diversity of the news media world. Do you move between modes of employment? Do you stay with one organization or shift between them? Do you remain faithful to one medium—say, print or television—or will you have readers in one phase and viewers or listeners in the next? And perhaps most significantly in relation to the global landscape of news, will you mostly stay in one place, or will your career take you through a number of postings on several continents? Finally, how does one stop being a foreign correspondent?

To start at the very beginning, we may be curious about what kind of people are likely to become foreign correspondents. It is difficult to establish any real pattern. One of my informants argued that they (perhaps journalists generally) were likely to be people who were curious about things, liked easy contacts with others, would be quick to establish rapport, and did not seek for depth in relationships. But others confessed that they had been very shy when they were young—one woman's father had laughed in surprise at his daughter's career choice, and one man said he had thought going into journalism might be a cure for this affliction. As a foreign editor, Bill Keller of the *New York Times* said, he would want to fill a foreign correspondent opening with someone who was adaptable, open-minded, willing to endure inconveniences, and able to talk himself through a military checkpoint—someone with "a taste for street reporting." A veteran American correspondent who had spent several decades in news work felt that the newsrooms in major media organizations had become too much like academic seminars, with an elite recruitment. I have come across both American and European correspondents with master's degrees or doctorates, in fields varyingly relevant to their work and their particular postings. But another foreign editor remembered having recruited a China specialist who had come with strong academic area expertise. "It didn't work," he said. "Too much knowledge. Too full of nuances." And then there are Chris McGreal of the *Guardian* and Leif Norrman of *Dagens Nyheter*, both ex-seamen who moved through adult education and local reporting at home before going overseas in their new capacity. Nicholas Valéry went to the *Economist* with a degree in engineering—even at this magazine, he commented, few correspondents seemed to have had academic training in economics. There were doctors and lawyers, but nobody was likely to be hired with just a fresh degree. The editors at the *Los Angeles Times* noted that several of their correspondents were former Peace Corps volunteers. Few of the correspondents I have met have gone through professional schools of journalism, and some explicitly offered the opinion that doing so would not have been of much use.

There are correspondents, like Anton La Guardia, whose expatriate childhoods may have served as a sort of anticipatory socialization, and here and there one even finds someone who turns out to be the child of another foreign correspondent. In contrast, we may remember that Terry Leonard, the Johannesburg bureau chief for the Associated Press, did not think of going into foreign news until he had already been long in news work; and that does not seem rare.

The Logics of Switching

People may come out of different backgrounds to join the foreign news trade, then, and they may have different reasons for doing so. Once they are there, under one set of circumstances or another, there is little certainty about the direction of their future career within it, either. Yet some passages, some switches, are more likely than others. In some way it makes more sense to move in one direction than in its opposite, and we may imagine some kinds of career moves that actually seem to occur very rarely, if ever.

Let us quickly take note of some of this internally diverse organizational logic of foreign correspondent careers. To begin with, there is the tendency to move from what we may see as an uncertain livelihood at the margins of the news business to the relative security and comfort of steady employment at its center; from what might often seem like the petty trade of freelancers, perhaps by way of more durable stringerships, to positions as regular staff correspondents for fairly sizable organizations. Freelancers and stringers make up what one might see as the informal sector of foreign correspondence. The terms are often used interchangeably, or at least with much overlap. But the term "stringer" tends to suggest at least a bit longer-term relationships with media organizations, although in a wide range of arrangements, from the quite tenuous to the rather stable working conditions of "super stringers," which approach those of regular staff.[3]

Again, there is no inevitable progression here. One may begin as a freelancer and remain one forever. It may entail continuously inventing and reinventing oneself as a supplier of what may also have to be invented and reinvented as news, and it may involve finding at least some of one's customers far from the large mainstream media. Some do it full-time, others flexibly in combination with some other means of livelihood and when opportunity arises.

Påhl Ruin, a stringer for *Dagens Nyheter,* the largest Swedish morning newspaper, had fairly recently arrived in Tokyo when we met. He also already knew that he would not be there for very many years, but for somewhat special reasons.

While Ruin was going to the university in southern Sweden, he began working in the summers for a major regional newspaper, and then he took an editorial position with the journal of Sweden's municipal authorities. Moreover, he married a young woman headed for a career in the Swedish foreign service. Soon after the birth of their first child, she was sent on her first foreign assignment, in Tokyo; and thus, while she went back to work, Ruin spent his first few months in Japan on Swedish parental leave. He had also arranged, however, to write for *Dagens Nyheter* during his stay in Japan, which would of course end when his wife was reassigned by her ministry. The paper was pleased with the arrangement. Although by the standards of Scandinavian news media, it has a respectable foreign correspondent network, it had not seen it as feasible to station one of its regular staff members in Tokyo, and it had been looking around among Swedish expatriates in Tokyo for a suitable stringer. But the income might be a bit unstable, so it was easier for Ruin than for someone else to take this on—there was someone else in the household with a steady income, after all, and the embassy provided him with a roof over his head. So he could do something interesting with his time as a diplomatic spouse and not be too worried about variations in income between one month and the next.

It is in the nature of things that there is a fairly rapid turnover in freelancing. Many may be drawn to it, but if there is not much success, and if one runs out of money, one may turn to something else or return home. Or, as for Ruin, eventually, there may be other reasons for bowing out. When there is a choice, however, many will prefer to move into news work positions where the pay is steadier and where some perquisites may go with the job—which is also where some fortunate people start out.

Nonetheless, occasionally someone may see fit to move in the opposite direction: less security, more autonomy. In Jerusalem I met Eric Silver, a freelancer in his early sixties who had arrived in Israel the first time in 1967, after the Six Days' War, as a temporary replacement for the regular correspondent of the *Guardian.* Silver himself was that paper's Jerusalem correspondent for more than a decade, starting in the early 1970s. Then the *Guardian* thought it was time for him to move on to another posting, so he went to Delhi for a few years in the mid-1980s. From there he was expected to return to London. But being Jewish, Silver and his wife had felt at home in Jerusalem, had bought a house there, and had had their children in regular Israeli schools rather than in the international schools where many of the expatriates sent their offspring. So after Delhi, they went back to Israel, and Silver became a freelancer—"I used to have a career, now I have a business." He suspected that he was more or less unique in Jerusalem in having made such a move.

A little surprisingly perhaps, his most regular customer was now probably the *Statesman,* in Calcutta; this was because its Indian foreign editor was a friend of Silver's from the time when they had met as young journalists at a small newspaper in the north of England. He also sold articles to several provincial British newspapers, to *Macleans,* the Canadian weekly magazine, and to various Jewish weeklies in the United States. (When it was possible in terms of audience interests, and when his different customers were obviously not in the same market and in competition with one another, he would sell basically the same story to more than one of the publications, a practice that was entirely accepted in the freelance business; at times this might mean that the Calcuttans and the Jewish-Americans, continents apart, would unknowingly share reading matter.) And he fairly regularly got to do some work for *Time* magazine, usually when there was more to do than the staff of its own Jerusalem bureau could cope with. This was useful not only because the pay was good. The byline in the magazine gave his name some high international visibility, which was beneficial for his overall business.

Just as newspeople may tend to move from self-employment to more secure salaried work—with someone like Eric Silver as an exception—they may also naturally be inclined to switch, when an offer comes along, from smaller to larger and more affluent organizations. Major American newspapers, it is sometimes said, can spot the talent among reporters for smaller papers and buy them with better pay and less materially constrained working conditions. There have been times, too, when particular organizations have expanded rapidly and gone headhunting on a rather large scale to fill new positions. The *Los Angeles Times,* old-timers remember, had a busy period of hiring in the 1970s, when its new publisher wanted to seriously compete with the *New York Times* in regard to foreign coverage. That expansion did not go on forever and was followed by some retrenchment in the early 1990s, but even later the paper's foreign desk sometimes recruited correspondents from other papers. There could indeed be people like Dean Murphy inside the organization who wanted to go abroad, but the editors also had a suspicion that many journalists just enjoyed the southern California lifestyle too much to be bothered with foreign assignments. Conversely, sometimes what appear to be ambitious new enterprises and highly attractive employers later take downward turns, so that their correspondents find it wise or even necessary to move on.

Another recurrent career pattern takes journalists from the major news agencies to other kinds of reporting. The agencies, with their huge correspondent networks, seem to have an insatiable appetite for new recruits, and some of these certainly stay on for their entire careers, perhaps to become, with time, as we saw in the preceding chapter, bureau chiefs like Terry Leonard in Johannesburg or Nicolas Tatro in Jerusalem. But many young reporters prefer to proceed to some employer who allows a little more freedom and considerably less anonymity.[4] For Ethan Bronner, writing from the Middle East for the *Boston Globe* when I met him in Jerusalem, there was also a matter of style. He had worked for Reuters, first in Madrid and then in Israel for a couple of years in the early 1980s, and was initially quite favorably disposed to the crisp, "just the facts" news agency format—he was irritated with the self-indulgence of some contemporary journalism. But with time he became increasingly dissatisfied, finding that the style concealed too much of the past of current events and carried interpretation surreptitiously between the lines. That was when he left for the *Globe.*

And then there is the possibility of moving between media, between print, radio, and television. Obviously, when an entire medium is new, rapidly growing, and diversifying its content, as television was not so many decades ago, it almost inevitably looks to older media for at least some of its first generation of professionals. Later, when media operate alongside each other in relative maturity, such crossovers may become less common. But here again, the rise of new organizations also allows for career switches. As CNN emerged as a major television news outfit, it hired some veterans away from the agencies. Peter Arnett, who drew the attention of much of the world with his reporting out of Baghdad during the Gulf War, had had much of his career with the Associated Press, including service in Saigon during the Vietnam era. Mike Hanna, the first Johannesburg bureau chief for CNN, started out in radio with the South African Broadcasting Corporation during apartheid but disliked its politics, as a "propaganda arm for the government," and went to work for a new small station in one of the black homelands. From there he switched to television, with a British commercial media organization, before CNN came along.[5]

A correspondent may have a definite preference for one medium over another. Chris McGreal, in Johannesburg for the *Guardian,* had gone over to that paper from the *Independent*—another London paper, the foreign coverage of which had taken a downturn—but before that had worked in local radio in Cornwall and then as a stringer for the BBC in Latin America and the Caribbean in the late 1980s. He had been happy to make the transition from radio to print. The former, he felt, was on the whole more superficial in its journalism, and he did not like having to deal with the technology of radio. Moreover, it was easier to work with only a single daily deadline.

Other newspeople may find a stronger sense of drama in radio or television and may prefer that. Even so, some spread their reporting over several media. Sometimes within a single organization, you may be expected to do work for both radio and television, as some BBC correspondents do. Others, especially freelancers and stringers, may work in different media for different organizations—something in print here, a piece for the radio there. Some of the stars of one medium, too, may diversify their reporting and commentary as an evolving part of their stardom. A British example is John Simpson, who in later years has complemented his long BBC television career with a column for the *Sunday Telegraph.* Some careers may entail changing one's media involvements, whereas in others one just adds to them.

Eric Silver, the veteran Jerusalem freelancer, is fundamentally a print person. He is somewhat unusual, however, in writing for publications in a number of different countries, as we saw before: Great Britain, the United States, Canada, India. Yet his niche in the news market is apparently all Anglophone, and this also suggests one pattern in correspondents' careers: despite the fact that the news business is in some ways obviously global, most foreign correspondents do their reporting in a single language. Often that means that they deal primarily with national news markets and make their career changes within these markets. Larger language areas obviously allow a bit more freedom of movement, as in Silver's case—if you write in English, French, Spanish, or German, your reporting may be immediately publishable in several countries, perhaps even on different continents; if you are a stringer supplying mostly, say, one Swedish paper, you may at least have some of your market in other Scandinavian languages as well. Since there are English-language dailies or weeklies, catering in large part to expatriates, in places where the national language is a different one, some correspondents may get a local foothold by writing for such a paper while at the same time cultivating more distant customers. Peter Arnett, a New Zealander by origin, describes in his autobiography, *Live from the Battlefield* (1994), how he moved from small English-language papers in Southeast Asia by way of the Associated Press to CNN.[6] And of course, writers for major international news agencies can expect to find their writing published, in translation, in a great many languages (although seldom credited to them personally). What seems to happen only very rarely, however, is that correspondents switch their primary allegiance from one language segment of the news business to another.[7]

Domesticating Foreign News Work

In the early 1980s, freelancers as well as regulars in foreign correspondence were drawn to Central America and its violent conflicts. The cold war was still on, and President Reagan warned that world Communism was only a day's drive or so south of the border. Newspeople, whether from the United States or elsewhere, often took other views of the situation, but the reporting of one correspondent, Raymond Bonner, became especially controversial, in a couple of different ways.[8]

At the time, Bonner was a newcomer in foreign correspondence. His professional training was in law, and he had worked in consumer advocacy for

Ralph Nader as well as in the district attorney's office in San Francisco, but he wanted to do something different, so he set off for South America to try journalism. As a stringer for *Newsweek* and the *Washington Post,* he reported on a brutal coup in Bolivia, but when he was informed that the junta that had taken power was displeased with his writing, he found it wise to move on. In El Salvador, where a civil war was going on, his services were in demand again. The chief of the *New York Times* bureau in Mexico City, who would in principle have been in charge of Central America as a whole, knew that he was personally not welcome in El Salvador, so Bonner was taken on for a brief trial period and very soon found himself hired as a regular staff correspondent for the paper.

His reporting soon drew attention, including attention from officials of the American Embassy in El Salvador, who found it reflecting very adversely on American collaboration with the Salvadoran government and army. The controversy reached a climax with Bonner's part in the disclosure of what became known as the El Mozote Massacre. A few days into 1982, Bonner, who had made contact with representatives of the main guerrilla movement, was taken with a photographer into their territory. Just a little later, another journalist, Alma Guillermoprieto, then a stringer for the *Washington Post,* also entered the area. Both of them learned of a recent Salvadoran army massacre of villagers, seven hundred of them or more, in El Mozote and other nearby hamlets. And both of them reported on what they had heard and seen.

Salvadoran and American officialdom both claimed that there was no reliable evidence that the massacre had ever occurred; they said the reporters for those two American newspapers had become instruments for a guerrilla propaganda maneuver. It was only long after the civil war was over that a team of Argentinian forensic anthropologists, investigating sites in the El Mozote area, could show conclusively that there was no room for doubt.

The massacre itself was obviously a focus of controversy; but so was Raymond Bonner's continued relationship with the *New York Times,* and that is what we are more concerned with here. After the disclosure of the El Mozote affair, Bonner's contacts with Salvadoran authorities as well as with American Embassy officials became increasingly strained. The executive editor of the *New York Times* during this period, A. M. Rosenthal, visited El Salvador and met with the American ambassador. Later in 1982, Bonner was recalled to New York, where he was assigned to the business desk. After some time, he left the paper.[9]

The forensic anthropology team conducted its investigation ten years later, and the matter became newsworthy again. The *Wall Street Journal,* which had attacked Bonner's reporting in the early 1980s, now found itself being criticized for this and responded that, after all, it was the *New York Times* that had removed Bonner from the scene. At this point, Rosenthal submitted a "letter to the editor," published in the *Wall Street Journal* (April 22, 1993), asserting that Bonner's reassignment from El Salvador to the New York office had not been politically motivated or the result of government demands—it had to do rather with "training and staff development, prosaic things, not plots and pressures." When he was hired by the *New York Times,* Rosenthal continued, Bonner had not been an experienced journalist, and although he had performed bravely, the editors had started feeling that they were in a way exploiting him by demanding so much from him, since he had not been given the journalistic training most of the paper's reporters would have acquired before being sent out on a foreign assignment. Bonner was asked to come back to New York in order to be equipped for future assignments. "The idea is to make the reporter familiar with the ways of the paper and its staff, part of the Times journalistic family, not an outsider on the payroll."

So it turns out to have been a career matter, one of organizational socialization. Actually, Rosenthal's argument may not have been entirely convincing, as Michael Massing (1993), the writer who was the main commentator/whistle blower on "the Bonner affair," has pointed out. Bonner had already spent an extended period in 1981 at the *New York Times* headquarters, on the metro desk, after being hired in El Salvador and before returning there as a regular correspondent. Moreover, Rosenthal was quite widely seen as a political hard-liner whose views on Central American conflicts were more in line with those of the Reagan administration than with Bonner's. Yet for our purposes, his depiction of Bonner's reassignment as standard operating procedure is interesting precisely because he thus identifies an organizational normality as a presumably uncontroversial basis for the step his paper had taken a decade earlier.

Indeed, news organizations are inclined to want to have foreign correspondents securely domesticated before they are sent out on possibly very demanding postings where their daily contacts with headquarters may be more tenuous. Occasionally, this may entail bringing a new employee back from a distant reporting arena. More often, as in Dean Murphy's instance, described before, the foreign assignment comes as a reward for successful work at home. In his monograph on the *New York Times,* Edwin Diamond (1995, 268–69) quotes another former foreign correspondent on the paper, Pamela Hollie, who refers to doing "the stations of the cross." To take a few more examples from among the correspondents I have talked to about their beginnings in the craft, Barton Gellman, in Jerusalem for the *Washington*

Post, was a courthouse reporter in the District of Columbia and then covered the Pentagon before going to the Middle East; Jörg Bremer, in Jerusalem for the *Frankfurter Allgemeine,* had a doctorate in German history before starting out as a subeditor to learn about his paper; Werner Vogt, representing the *Neue Zürcher Zeitung* in Johannesburg, worked on a small Swiss paper before doing five years in the head office in Zürich.

We may discern a few different aspects of such in-house socialization. One is quite concretely that a person learns the craft: practices fact-finding, writing, and editing. This may not have to take place in the organization one eventually works for. The first training ground may be on the staff of some smaller organization, as in Vogt's case. Perhaps somewhat more diffusely, another aspect involves absorbing an organizational culture—a history, background understandings, basic values. When Rosenthal, in arguing about Bonner's reassignment to New York, refers to the reporter's becoming a part of the paper's "journalistic family," one may sense that it is partly an appeal to such a wider sense of cultural sharing. A third aspect is the practical value of face-to-face acquaintance. It is a good thing if correspondents and home-based editors know each other personally and can draw on this even when their contacts are by way of E-mail or telephone.

Jeff Sommer, ex–Asia correspondent turned international editor of what was the New York *Newsday* when I met him, was emphatic about the value of basic, movable craftsmanship. He had developed an interest in Asia in college during the period of the Vietnam War, and when President Nixon went to China and that country began to draw more American attention, Sommer started studying Mandarin. He went on to get a master's degree in Asian studies at Harvard. But then he worked for local papers in New Jersey and upstate New York before joining *Newsday,* where he did another period of local reporting before being posted to Asia.

Especially for the foreign correspondent practicing parachutist reporting, Sommer argued, having ingrained routines to resort to could be invaluable when one might not have much in the way of a specific sense of place. "Every story is a local story"; one can therefore fall back on the regular structures of such stories, whether they are police stories or reports on industrial accidents.[10] One knows what details must be included, and asking the right questions even where one is actually a bewildered newcomer can be a way of establishing local credibility as well. Sommer remembered rushing into Bhopal, India, after the 1984 disaster at the Union Carbide plant and also arriving at the scene of a mass murder, likewise in India, seeing the corpses, and then going on to interview the people who were obviously the killers.

Serge Schmemann, bureau chief for the *New York Times* in Jerusalem, had not actually spent much time in the paper's office at Forty-third Street, Manhattan, by the time we met—perhaps four months altogether. He was a Russian specialist, with family connections going back to pre-Soviet Russia, and had been hired in Moscow in an emergency. After that he had been elsewhere in Europe and in South Africa. Yet the people in charge at headquarters, he pointed out, were now in large part former foreign correspondents of his own generation or slightly older, people like Joe Lelyveld and Bill Keller, whom he knew well. Especially the correspondents who had been stationed in Europe at the same time were often quite close. If they were ever in New York at the same time, they would try to get together. Schmemann believed in his paper as an institution, and in institutional values. One must always remember that the paper was more important than any individual correspondent.

Spiralists and Long-Timers

Of all the kinds of shifts that may occur within the career of a foreign correspondent, the ones that will receive most of our attention here are those that involve relocating within the landscape of news sketched in chapter 2. Primarily, we are concerned with changes of posting between the relatively stable focal points of foreign news work, between, say, Paris and Johannesburg, Bangkok and Tokyo; not with the quick excursions of parachutists. Some correspondents move about a great deal over their working lives, and others do not. This points to a major divide in the craft.

One may think of different labels to summarize central qualities of these variations in mobility in foreign correspondent work. For the people who move about a great deal, the term "expatriate" comes naturally to mind, since these correspondents are not strongly rooted in the territory where they reside for a period and may engage in a lifestyle and a pattern of social contacts that somehow do not quite belong there. If they are rooted anywhere, it is someplace else. "Sojourners" would also be an appropriate general label, and I will use it occasionally. They could perhaps be described as "cosmopolitans," in the particular sense of Robert Merton's classic distinction (1957, 387–402) between cosmopolitans and locals—they are people who tend to take their most important contacts and knowledge along as they move. (This notion of cosmopolitanism overlaps only in a limited way with that sketched in chapter 1.) I lean, however, toward the term "spiralists," coined by William Watson (1964, 147–51), from the classic Manchester school in social anthropology, to refer to the way social mobility within the hierarchy of an organization can be coordinated with geographical mobility.

The contrasting type of foreign correspondence, which involves remaining for a longer period—or even throughout the correspondent's life—in a single territory, one might call "local" (as in the cosmopolitan-local dichotomy). But that may be too vague, or in some ways misleading, or perhaps oxymoronic. "Settler" may be almost right but perhaps has unfortunate overtones, particularly in some settings. So I will call these correspondents "long-timers," referring to their more durable presence in a place.

In large part, the division between spiralists and long-timers reflects the economics of the news business and an organizational as well as spatial hierarchy. In the past it was clearly more common even in large, prosperous news organizations to keep correspondents as long as decades in major postings, especially in important European capitals. Such postings sometimes became rather like personal fiefs. There may still be some room left for such arrangements, but at present, long-timers are often in somewhat more modest positions—organizationally, locationally, or both. They may be freelancers (although certainly not all of these are long-timers) or stringers, rather than staff correspondents. And this may be because they work, even out of major news centers, for less affluent organizations or because they are in rather less important locations, where organizations find that some reporting presence is desirable, although not at any price.

The more affluent media organizations, which tend to rely largely on staff correspondents in many of the world's news centers—American media are prominent here, but certainly there are many such European ones as well, and also such Japanese papers as *Yomiuri Shimbun*—often believe in rotating these correspondents relatively quickly between assignments. After, say, three to five years on one foreign beat, the correspondent either moves on to another one or returns home. Spiralists, consequently, belong mostly in these organizations. They may be complemented with stringers in places of less importance—perhaps with the nearest major center's staff correspondent as an intermediary in the chain of news delivery.

Talking to spiralists where they are posted, as well as to their foreign editors at home, one realizes that arranging the shifts can be an intricate business. The correspondents, wherever they are, may be keeping an eye on the trajectories of their colleagues in the organization, because these may affect their own next moves. But since foreign assignments are usually attractive, there may also be worthy and impatient new candidates waiting at home, making their wishes known to the editors. Those who are already abroad may not be too happy with the idea of returning home, so for the editor at home, handling the reassignment especially of someone who has not been very successful as a foreign correspondent can be a touchy matter. At the *New York*

Times, Bill Keller said, the foreign editor would usually initiate a dialogue some time before an assignment was due to end, about what opportunities were coming up and about the correspondent's interests and prospects, but it also happened that the correspondent would open up the conversation.

Within the world news landscape, some postings are clearly considered more attractive than others, and although one probably will not get to a prime spot immediately, one may have such places in mind for later moves. Yet preferences depend on various criteria. Again at the *New York Times,* Serge Schmemann, after serving in Moscow and in South Africa and in Germany (covering the fall of the Berlin Wall—he earned a Pulitzer Prize for that), could perhaps have claimed a posting in London or Paris on the basis of his seniority, before he returned to New York. Generally, European and North American assignments are desirable because they are comfortable. But Schmemann thought these places were by now "kind of sleepy" as far as news was concerned, so he chose the Jerusalem bureau instead.

The status of postings thus also depends on their potential for the right kind of reporting. If you want to "write the first draft of history," or simply write for the front page, or make a reputation for yourself, you will prefer to be in a place where there is likely to be a stream of hard news. Jerusalem seems like a good bet here. Moscow or Beijing may also be good for events that make history. New Delhi, I have been told, does not count so highly. As one hard-nosed correspondent pointed out, you do not want your stories to be hidden away in the paper somewhere behind the brassiere advertisements. But with fewer pressures and with opportunities for feature stories, it could be a good place to try out a neophyte. Nairobi, too, has had a rather modest standing—not very comfortable socially or physically and less important than Johannesburg, and probably not worthy of a correspondent at all, if your organization is only going to have one in Africa. Perhaps it is another posting suitable for beginners—although as we have seen, in the later years of the twentieth century, Nairobi turned out to be the base for much of the coverage of Somalia, Rwanda, and Congo.

Fresh Perspective versus Local Knowledge

As the classic Alfred Hitchcock movie *Foreign Correspondent* begins, the powerful editor of a New York newspaper, the *Globe,* is dissatisfied with the reporting he gets from Europe, where World War II is about to break out. It is dry, colorless, cryptic stuff. Impatiently, he sends for crime reporter Johnny Jones, changes Jones's name to Huntley Haverstock (more appropriate for his new assignment), and rushes him off to Europe—about which Johnny Jones knows next to nothing but where Haverstock quickly finds himself in the thick of things, among diplomats, thugs, and beautiful women.

This happens to be a parody of one real-life mode of reasoning about how to manage correspondents. The assumption behind the preference for a quicker rotation of them is that "going stale" is a significant occupational hazard. The correspondents, like the bibulous veteran whom Johnny Jones encounters as he arrives in London, start taking things in their surroundings for granted, instead of seeing stories in them. They get bored when they have to do basically the same story the second, third, or umpteenth time. To some degree, there is virtue in innocence. The ideal correspondent, according to this view, has a fresh eye for the peculiarities of a beat—"a sense of wonder."

Moreover, that fresh eye should not be just any fresh eye. It helps not to lose touch with the audience at home, to retain a sense of its interests, experiences, and assumptions. A bit parenthetically, I would insert here that this may be difficult enough even when one has a clear sense of what "at home" is. Again, if you write for the *Los Angeles Times,* you should try to write at the same time for the academic and the bus driver. Things get even more problematic when that audience can be anywhere, as in the case of media with a self-consciously international reach. There is a widely circulating story about Ted Turner, founder of CNN, that he threatened to fire any staffer who used the word "foreign," as in "foreign correspondent"—nobody among the viewers of CNN should ever be made to feel that he or she lived in a foreign country. So CNN correspondents outside the United States were "international correspondents." Adjusting to this situation, Mike Hanna, CNN bureau chief in Johannesburg when I met him (and reporting from the country where he had spent most of his life), said that he really tried to avoid implicit assumptions about viewers, simply expressing himself as clearly as possible, not aiming at Americans or anybody else especially.

If there is a value in not "going stale" on an assignment, the other side of the coin is that the correspondent who moves rapidly between postings may not develop very deep local knowledge anywhere. Those correspondents who stay in a place, in contrast, may become very knowledgeable. They may have a longer-term perspective on stories, remembering what led up to them. Whereas the spiralists sometimes risk becoming encapsulated in their social lives in circles of expatriates and perhaps local ex-expatriates, the long-timers will frequently have wide and varied local networks that can be important resources in their reporting. Quite possibly they are also considerably more skilled in using a local language.

The respective advantages and disadvantages of spiralists and long-timers in reporting are obviously a topic of debate—possibly unending debate—in foreign correspondence. The two categories of correspondents may tend to have different organizational bases and may be somewhat differently distributed in the news geography, yet there are certainly a great many times when they work next to one another in the same place and in principle do the same work. Here the comparisons are closest at hand, and arguments are likely to be most intense.

It also matters that in some such locations, long-timers are long-timers not just because of their place in the organization of the news business. That organization may also exist in a symbiotic relationship with the individual identifications and commitments of particular correspondents. Rowan Callick, Hong Kong–based China correspondent of the *Australian Financial Review* after a start in the business as one of only a few "Pacific correspondents," thought that on the whole, his own journalistic curiosity was of a fairly generalized kind. He would be able to move on without any major regrets. In his opinion, there were really three main kinds of China correspondents. Some were like himself, basically the spiralist kind. Then there were those who arrived on an assignment, perhaps somewhat unsuspectingly, only to "fall in love with China." And third, there were those who were above all Sinophiles, who wanted to live their lives encompassed by Chinese culture and society and simply felt that working as correspondents was a way of accomplishing this. They were long-timers largely for intellectual and aesthetic reasons. Callick noted, too, that their commitments at times could make them somewhat blind to what did not fit in with their aesthetic impulses. (He felt, for instance, that they frequently refused to take any note of the growth of crime as an ugly fact of Chinese and Hong Kong life.)

Such strong preferences for place, with its varied social and cultural accoutrements, over organizational centrality and advancement appear to have a recurrent part in long-timer adaptations to foreign correspondent work. In Tokyo, there were numerous committed long-timers who had no desire to live anywhere but in Japan. Some had formed family connections there, and certain of them might even see their involvement in foreign correspondence mostly as a way of supporting themselves while remaining in the country where they wanted to live. They would rather change employers or jobs than move anywhere else. Among the Jerusalem correspondents, too, I found both spiralists and long-timers. In this case, the long-timers are often Jews who have made *aliya* (the ascent); they have gone to live in Israel because they want to be in their national homeland, but they have found an occupational niche in reporting for media in the country they left. In a way, they have reversed their diasporic attachments. (Eric Silver, who arrived in Jerusalem the first time as a spiralist and then returned to become a long-timer, is of course a special case here.) [11]

The long-timers I met in Jerusalem tended to emphasize the intensity and breadth of their knowledge, and particularly their personal involvement in Israeli society. They are more likely to live in ordinary Israeli neighborhoods, and their children go to Israeli schools. More than a few have done Israeli military service, which is a way of meeting people of many backgrounds in a very diverse society. Having been around for a long time, they can place new events in the context of old ones, and they know where to turn for informed comments. In addition, there is the language factor. In most instances (not quite all), the immigrants speak Hebrew fluently, whereas many of the spiralists do not. And so they are immersed in the daily flow of Israeli comment and debate.[12]

One example of an immigrant correspondent's personal path to a Jerusalem reporting life is that of Ramy Wurgaft, who writes for *El Mundo* in Madrid. Wurgaft is not originally from Spain but from a Chilean Jewish family. His father, a lawyer, decided to make *aliya* with his family in the 1960s, but it did not work out particularly well—his father, says Wurgaft, concluded that he was Chilean after all, and so they all returned to Santiago. The 1973 military coup in Chile was a traumatic experience, however, and Ramy Wurgaft decided to go back to the Israeli kibbutz where he had spent some years of his youth. He later attended Hebrew University in Jerusalem for a while, studying international relations and sociology, married an Israeli girl, was called up to do his military service in the Israeli Defense Forces, and had no job lined up when he was demobilized. So he became a restaurant waiter to support his young family. While in this business, by chance he became acquainted with a Scandinavian foreign correspondent, who after some time suggested that Wurgaft should try his hand at writing and gave him some support in his early attempts.

Once when Wurgaft was on his way to Chile to see his relatives and had a stopover in Madrid, he checked the papers in the newsstands and called the offices of a few of them. It turned out that at *El Mundo,* a rather new paper making a reputation through political muckraking, there was some interest in improving foreign coverage. The first piece he was asked to do was a nervous experience, as it dealt with arms smuggling from Israel by way of the Caribbean to a Colombian narcotics cartel—not a topic for which he felt he had much expertise to draw on. But soon luck came his way, in a peculiar sense. The Gulf War broke out, Iraqi Scud missiles fell on Israel, and there was Wurgaft, when he had his gas mask off, reporting to Madrid on reactions to the emergency in his modest Jerusalem neighborhood. The response at *El Mundo* was very favorable, and soon enough Wurgaft was assigned tasks such as traveling to Cairo to interview Boutros Boutros-Ghali, the United Nations secretary-general. But he still felt that his closeness to the local Jerusalem scene was his greatest asset.[13]

Among the Tokyo correspondents whom I met, there was certainly some understanding of the respective advantages and disadvantages of the two basic types of correspondent careers, but also some mutual irritation. One correspondent for a major American newspaper, who had been in Japan for a few years but who was approaching the end of his posting there, commented that certain long-timers were really walking advertisements for the value of not staying too long—they were world-weary and jaded in their views, and if they absolutely must stay in Japan, they really ought to turn to some other line of work. Those who had been around longer, and who were likely to stay on, for their part, were sometimes critical of the newcomers' evaluation of news and choice of stories. They suspected that they were more likely to conform in their reporting to the beliefs about Japan held by their editors at home and to become too dependent, in their search for information, on the "*gaijin* handlers," the experts on handling contacts with Americans and Europeans, who could now be identified in many Japanese organizations.

The Tokyo bureau chief of the *Economist,* Nicholas Valéry, in a sense did not belong in either category. His magazine usually rotated its correspondents every three years or so, but he was now back in Japan by choice for a third time. The first time had been in the 1970s, and between his Tokyo assignments he had had periods in the United States, on both the East Coast and the West Coast. (Before that he had been in Frankfurt and Moscow.) He valued his accumulated networks in government and business offices highly, but he also saw a problem with becoming too settled. When basically the same stories come up with intervals in between, you learn a great deal the first time; the second time you can do them confidently on the basis of accumulated knowledge; the third time you may find you know more than the people you interview. And when the stories that surface in a place cease to give you a thrill, Valéry thought, it might be time to move on.

Questions of Access

Certainly one's handling of a foreign news beat will depend partly on one's interactive and communicative abilities and partly on the social characteristics of the place itself. What role, for one thing, do language skills play in the work of foreign correspondents—spiralists or long-timers, or for that matter parachutists? *"Anyone Here Been Raped and Speaks English?"* is the title of one of the classics in the literature of foreign correspondence, the autobiography of Edward Behr (1982), of *Newsweek* and other organizations; Behr got the title from a question shouted by a British television reporter in the early 1960s, at a crowd of refugee European women and children escaping from civil war in the Congo. It seems to say something about what you can do with a language and at least as much about what you cannot do without the right one.

Jeff Sommer of *Newsday,* reminiscing about his experiences as Asia correspondent with both China and India included in his beat, noted that he still felt much more at home in China, where he kept returning. Knowing the language, he could listen in on conversations in the street, and he was sensitive to perspectives and reverberations.

Obviously correspondents' knowledge of the language of their posting —or languages, where there is more than one—is highly variable.[14] No doubt it is often greater among long-timers than among spiralists, but this is certainly not true in every individual case. There are correspondents who have been in Jerusalem and Tokyo for decades but whose ability to get by in Hebrew and Japanese, respectively, remains restricted. And there are others who arrive on a new assignment knowing that they will not be staying forever but who are already equipped with a working knowledge of the relevant language. What languages people already know can play some part in deciding what assignments they will be given. An Arabic-speaker, said Bill Keller at the *New York Times,* will quite likely be posted to the Middle East, but there are not many of them around. Certainly there are more Spanish-speakers, so it is easier to rotate people to Latin American postings. And although major American print media would now hardly assign anybody to Moscow who is not a Russian-speaker, this was not necessarily so in the past and, noted Keller, might still not be the case with television people.

Then, too, in a small number of instances, the news organization may allow a correspondent some language training before taking up a particular new assignment; but much time off for study, when the person in question accomplishes little else in terms of news work, is not a very appealing notion to the employer, or sometimes to peers, so it is not an ordinary practice. Major American newspapers now also find it desirable for their correspondents in Beijing to speak Chinese and for those in Tokyo to speak Japanese, but in postings like Delhi, Hong Kong, or Jerusalem, the expectation is that one gets by well enough with English. Barton Gellman, in Jerusalem for the *Washington Post,* knew a year ahead of time where he would be going for his first foreign assignment, so he had some time to read up on the Middle East and

Israel and to take Hebrew lessons, but he did not get any time off, and since his wife was expecting triplets, he might have been somewhat distracted. Sometimes, however, correspondents are told where they will be going next only a month or two ahead of time. And hardly any Africa correspondent, whether in Johannesburg, Nairobi, or Abidjan, is expected to know any African language.

The question may also well be asked whether the level of proficiency one reaches in a new language in a year or so of preparatory study takes one anywhere in serious news work. Sonni Efron, Tokyo bureau chief for the *Los Angeles Times,* had her doubts. She had actually majored in Japanese as an undergraduate, was reasonably fluent in speaking the language, and had some success as she struggled to read Japanese newspapers. But she wondered whether it did not make more sense to allow a prospective Moscow correspondent to study Russian for a while than to have someone about to be posted to Tokyo study Japanese for the same period—Japanese, for an American or a European, is much more difficult. Efron felt the money that might be spent on allowing an American time to acquire quite rudimentary Japanese would probably be more wisely used by hiring more local staff in the office—people who could translate and also help in news work.

To repeat, a normal period of assignment for a spiralist correspondent on a foreign beat is now something like three to five years. What kind of experience, insight, or understanding can one accumulate during such a period? I thought of this when I read the British journalist Jonathan Freedland's book *Bring Home the Revolution* (1999), which contends that Britain would be better off if at last it became more like the United States, its erstwhile colonial possession. Freedland had been the *Guardian*'s Washington correspondent, and this is how he portrays his encounter with American life:

> I spent four years travelling across the country, covering two presidential campaigns and the landmark congressional elections of 1994, when a Republican landslide swept away four decades of one-party control. I met suburban mothers in California's Woodland Hills and teenage heroin addicts in Seattle's Pike Street market, Christian fundamentalists in Dallas and peep-show strippers in Las Vegas—asking them about their home, their town, their country. I sat in a diner in Troy, North Carolina, and listened to the lunchtime chatter. I watched a baseball game in Baltimore and went on night patrol—in Haiti—with the soldiers of the 10th Mountain Division. I stood with the black Americans of the Million Man March on Washington and among the jackbooted neo-Nazis of the Aryan Nations in Idaho. I watched Ricki Lake

on TV and listened to Rush Limbaugh on the radio. I interviewed presidential candidates and kindergarten pupils, trudging through the
snows of New Hampshire and roasting in the desert heat of Arizona.
(Freedland 1999, 15)

Sometimes, it would seem, one can fit a great many things into three or
four or five years—perhaps even gaining a wider range of experiences than
many natives will have over a lifetime. Yet Freedland's American beat, huge
and diverse as it was, was undoubtedly on the whole quite accessible. It involved a society that by most standards is rather open, and although the argument of his book largely entails highlighting the differences between Britain and the United States, there certainly are similarities as well, not the least
of them a (more or less) shared language. Apart from that, given the place of
the United States in the contemporary world, one could question whether it
is really particularly foreign to any arriving foreign correspondent. A great
deal is likely to be known beforehand, even without much special preparation (and even though one may sometimes be wrong about what one expects
to find).[15]

Spiralist correspondents do not always find the expatriate condition
much like this. True, those stationed in Jerusalem, even when they do not
speak Hebrew, do not complain much about access to Israeli society. But then
there is the issue of how to deal with the Palestinian part of the assignment.
We will come back to that. Moreover, if their job is really to cover the Middle
East, the question of access to the beat in its entirety takes a different shape.

In South Africa, engaging informally with local society also has its
problems. Alec Russell of the *Daily Telegraph* had come to Johannesburg after several years in the Balkans, where most of his friendships were with
other foreign correspondents, but he had expected that the new posting, in
a country that was substantially English-speaking, would be different. Yet in
five years based in Johannesburg, he really felt he had made only two close
local friends, one black and the other Afrikaner. It was a society, many of his
colleagues also agreed, that was still highly segmented, not only by race but
by ethnicity and class as well—"Afrikaners, English-speakers, Indians, Zulu
. . ." One had to establish one's personal credentials again and again and engage in rather uncomfortable role-playing. Besides, the level of urban violence was such that one's movements became a bit restricted.

In Tokyo, correspondents would not face this hazard. Yet there, too,
gaining entry into local networks is seen as very problematic. But, to suggest
a rudimentary comparative understanding of problems of correspondent
access, if the difficulties in South Africa seem to be rooted rather more in

social-structural circumstances, those in Japan are perhaps more cultural. The sojourner correspondent finds that it takes a long time to get invited into a Japanese home and may come to suspect that Japanese contacts see little virtue in baring their souls to a foreigner. There is a basic cultural contrast, notes Brian Moeran (1989, 10, 18–19), an anthropologist specializing in Japanese studies, between *tatemae,* language used in public as a matter of "principle," and *honne,* language that "comes from the heart." Moeran himself found that the answers he got from his informants in formal interview sessions could be directly contradicted, for example, when he met them in drinking sessions; they had shifted from one code to the other. One may suspect that the frustrations the Tokyo correspondents often experience in finding quotable utterances tend to involve too much *tatemae* and too little *honne.*

Women Correspondents

Marjorie Miller was in her third year as Jerusalem bureau chief for the *Los Angeles Times* when I met her. She started out as a local employee of the Associated Press in Mexico City and was covering U.S.-Mexico border affairs for the *San Diego Union* when she was hired by the larger paper. Later she reported from Central America for five or six years and for a few years from Europe out of the bureau in Bonn. Now the end of her stay in Jerusalem was approaching. She did not intend to be an expatriate forever—perhaps one more posting abroad? She had two children and thought Europe would be good for them. (As it turned out, her next stop was as London bureau chief.) Before coming to Jerusalem, she had had six weeks in Bonn to prepare for the new assignment, and she had used some of the time to take some Hebrew lessons. Then she had a little time off in Jerusalem to get her family set up before taking charge of the office, which was on the two upper floors of an old stone house in Musrara, close to the Damascus Gate. She had taken some Arabic lessons as well. Although she knew she would never really learn to speak either Hebrew or Arabic, she at least wanted to be able to show some interest and politeness in both. By the time we met, she thought that perhaps some more commitment to Hebrew would have been a good thing, but then in Jerusalem most people were ready to speak English, and she had never intended to become a Middle East specialist. Yet it had been very different from the situation in Mexico, where she had been fluent in Spanish and could eavesdrop on what people said outside of interview situations. She also thought there was a typical progression in the kind of three-year posting she was in. The first year you are busy learning, the second year you are more secure and can give more texture to your reporting, and the third year you may be getting a little tired. She invited me to look at her collected stories out of Jerusalem to see for myself what she meant.

As a woman and a mother of young children, Marjorie Miller hardly conforms to the lingering stereotype of a foreign correspondent—still perhaps that of a lonely, hardened man, graying and leading a not-very-wholesome life, with a string of divorces behind him, moving in and out of brief liaisons along his way, and largely out of touch with any offspring. Some such men may still be around, but on the whole the people in the foreign news trade are now a more mixed group, and Miller is not so atypical.[16]

In fact there is a long history of women foreign correspondents.[17] Some of them are legendary: Martha Gellhorn, Marguerite Higgins, and a handful of others. Gellhorn established herself as an eyewitness of decades of war and peace in Republican Spain in the 1930s, where she wrote for *Collier's* and had the company of Ernest Hemingway, whom she later married. In the 1940s she reported on World War II; she reported for the *Guardian* in the 1960s from Vietnam and in the 1980s from Central America. She wrote for a range of different publications and found time for novels as well. Higgins made a name for herself in World War II; her reputation grew with her coverage of the Korean War and was perhaps rather diminished by her brief involvement in Vietnam reporting. She was more or less continuously connected with the *New York Herald Tribune* (and died not long before the demise of that paper).

Yet women like Gellhorn and Higgins were anomalies within an overwhelmingly male craft community. Georgie Anne Geyer, another American, entered foreign correspondence a generation or so later, writing first for the *Chicago Daily News* (defunct in the 1970s but with a respectable foreign coverage until then) and thereafter as a syndicated columnist. She reflects in her autobiography, *Buying the Night Flight* (1996, 66), that she was still "an interim woman journalist—a creature between the harder, tougher, and basically antifeminine generation of a few women journalists just before me, and the more fully liberated and very female reporters of today." Geyer returns repeatedly in her book to the theme of having had to choose between marriage and family, on the one hand, and the freedom of the roving correspondent, on the other. (Her favorite three words, one of her disappointed suitors had suggested, were not "I love you," but rather "room service, please.")

Perhaps the public fascination with some prominent women foreign correspondents, some of them war correspondents, even in recent times— Christiane Amanpour of CNN and Kate Adie of BBC, for example—has been that they have seemed to be women doing a man's job and excelling at it.[18] The lingering popular culture motif is that of Annie Oakley ("Anything you can do I can do better") in the musical, or Modesty Blaise of the comic strip. Women correspondents, too, often comment on the *machismo* of some of their male colleagues and competitors. On the whole, however, in the United States and, perhaps to a slightly lesser extent, in Europe, the influx of women into foreign correspondence in later years has been so considerable that they now form a sizable proportion of the entire correspondent corps.

In what ways might it matter whether foreign reporting is done by men or by women? Most of the women correspondents I have talked to seem to think that much of the time, their gender makes little difference. The nature of events and shared professionalism will determine what needs to be done. In the opinion of Sonni Efron, when she and Marjorie Miller, her *Los Angeles Times* colleague, had shown that they could report on the wars in Chechnya and Bosnia as well as anybody else, that marked their final full acceptance by their editors. But perhaps it is worth noting that one of their contemporaries, Sylvia Poggioli (1997), who reported from the Bosnian war for National Public Radio in the United States, has suggested that there was more attention to the prevalence of rape in that war compared to earlier wars because a large proportion of the press corps was now female.[19] And one might suspect that a male correspondent would be less likely to do the feature story Marjorie Miller (1997b) did, from Jerusalem, on Jewish women's frenetic housecleaning before the Passover holiday. Also in Jerusalem, Simonetta Della-Seta—working for Italian television as well as for the newsweekly *Panorama*—remembers the enormous immediate audience feedback she got after a report on Israeli techniques of no-pain childbirth.

Even when male and female correspondents themselves see each other as basically of one professional kind, it is a fact that gender conceptions in the societies where they work sometimes influence what they can do, where they can be, and how they interact with people. In Tokyo, Efron found that being a mother with small children could sometimes be an asset, since people in the street are more willing to talk to someone pushing a stroller. And when she took her children to the park on Saturday mornings, she could get a sense of what the Japanese mothers assembling there were concerned with, as they chatted while the children played. But on the whole, in Japan, it was not an advantage to be a woman correspondent. She could not go out and drink with bureaucrats or politicians on Friday evenings, when their tongues might loosen, and there are still very few women in prominent positions in Japan to whom she could have comparable access. This, she summarized, was still a society of "gender apartheid."

Suzanne Daley, bureau chief for the *New York Times* in Johannesburg, found both white and black South Africans quite sexist, in ways that could be both ludicrous and upsetting. She and her husband, also a journalist, would have dinner with a male South African colleague and his wife, and the South African journalist would keep addressing only Daley's husband. So what should Daley do—talk to the wife about her latest pair of sunglasses? When her managing editor, Joseph Lelyveld (himself a former Johannesburg correspondent) came to visit, she took him to see President Mandela; at the end of the meeting, the old president, apparently not aware of her status, patted Lelyveld on his knee and said, "In my country you would be laughed at if your wife is that skinny; she needs some extra pounds." Daley was only half amused. She suspected, too, that when the *New York Times* assigned a woman to be Johannesburg bureau chief, some South Africans took it as an indication that the paper did not take their country seriously any longer.

But then again, there are situations when being a woman reporter might be an advantage. Cecilia Uddén, comparing experiences in reporting for Swedish radio from Washington, D.C., and Cairo, said she thought being a woman made little difference in her assignment in the United States, but in the Middle East it was sometimes convenient to be able to move across the gender divide; she could be simply a journalist among the men, and then slip away and sit down among the women in a way her male colleagues could not. (It was a recurrent nuisance, however, not to be able to go to the hotel bar or restaurant the first evening in an unfamiliar place—too often, she had to rely on room service.) She also felt that women journalists were sometimes considered less threatening, not "out to get you." Lyse Doucet, reporting for BBC from Jerusalem on Israelis and Palestinians, and before that from Afghanistan, suggested that although tough military commanders could suddenly break down and cry in front of a female interviewer of the motherly type, they were not likely to do so with a male journalist. Georgie Anne Geyer, in her autobiography (1996), makes similar observations. In Latin America, in the troubled decades of the late twentieth century, guerrillas and political rebels could hate American men, because they were seen as representatives of American power; American women were not seen the same way. But then rapport could be a matter of a more female interviewing style as well. Geyer favored a sort of "empathic immersion," for which she found a parallel in psychoanalysis. With male correspondents, she noted, citing another observer, interviews could instead turn into pissing matches.

Domestic Lives

As far as career patterns in foreign correspondence are concerned, however, it may not be merely the entry of a larger number of women that makes things

different. It is true also that many of them, such as Marjorie Miller, Sonni Efron, and Suzanne Daley, also have families, often with young children—and
that, moreover, many of their male colleagues are in domestic situations much
like theirs, with similar familial commitments. Chris McGreal, in Johannesburg for the *Guardian,* had spent years traveling widely in Africa, but when I
met him, he concluded that because he now had a young family, he wanted to
be a father who could be relied upon to come home in the evening. Perhaps
he would take one more foreign assignment, but it would have to be one with
less constant travel. And he did not want to turn into the kind of correspondent, he said, who sat drunken in the hotel bar at age fifty-five, reminiscing
about Zaire in the 1960s, while all his younger colleagues yawned.

Indeed, a few years later McGreal was in Jerusalem, with its mostly
quite compact beat, requiring not much more than day travel. In the same
city, Barton Gellman of the *Washington Post* found the combination of foreign correspondence with family life very workable. He had his office at
home and could see a lot of his children. Often he could have dinner with
them and put them to bed before going back to his writing. Jörg Bremer of
the *Frankfurter Allgemeine,* also in Jerusalem, was a bachelor while reporting
from Warsaw during most of the 1980s, but then he postponed going abroad
again until he could return to foreign correspondence as a married man.
There were times, he confessed, when he chose to stay home for a chess game
with his ten-year-old son rather than setting out for another predictably dull
press conference. There were good schools in Jerusalem; and both Gellman's
and Bremer's spouses were lawyers who had found something worthwhile to
do in Jerusalem. Bremer's wife specialized in restitution law and could work
with Israeli lawyers on the claims of elderly Israelis of German origin, including cases involving the return of properties in eastern Germany. Gellman's wife, a civil rights lawyer, had a fellowship to study Israeli civil rights
legislation. She also had more time than her husband to learn Hebrew, because she could attend the quite efficient government-organized language
classes for immigrants.

Managing the working lives and career desires of spouses can certainly
be a major concern and is often one handled with some inventiveness. In
Cape Town, Leif Norrman's wife, who had met her husband when both of
them worked for *Dagens Nyheter* in Stockholm, started a small travel agency,
arranging tours for Swedish groups. In Johannesburg, where Alec Russell
worked for the *Daily Telegraph,* his wife did development work for a nongovernmental organization dealing with care for the elderly. In the same city,
Dean Murphy's wife stayed home with their children—she had agreed to ten
years of foreign correspondence, which would also be her years of full-time

domesticity. Murphy hoped to fit three postings, of which Johannesburg was the second, into that decade.[20] For Simonetta Della-Seta's husband, living in Jerusalem is not too inconvenient. He is a musicologist, and the work he does for a European producer of classical music he can in large part do almost anywhere. We have already seen how Påhl Ruin's term of stringing for *Dagens Nyheter* in Tokyo is coordinated with his wife's career in the foreign service.

Of course, it is not rare that newspeople marry other newspeople. For Marika Griehsel, a Johannesburg television journalist married to her photographer, Simon Stanford, the professional division of labor within the family worked out fine, although it did require some special domestic arrangements when the two of them were away on reporting trips together: sometimes her parents came down from Stockholm to combine babysitting with a vacation. Otherwise, in foreign correspondent marriages, the career of one spouse sometimes has to take precedence over that of the other; but perhaps they can take turns.[21] Rebecca Trounson, working with Marjorie Miller in the *Los Angeles Times* bureau in Jerusalem, had met her husband while working for one of the paper's suburban editions. Then he was assigned to the Beirut bureau, and she went along as a freelancer, reporting for CBS Radio News and the *Boston Globe*. After that both of them were back in the United States working for the *Houston Chronicle*. When she got the Jerusalem position with the paper both of them had started out with, it was her husband's turn to come along—to do some radio work for National Public Radio and write fiction. Göran Leijonhufvud, *Dagens Nyheter*'s China correspondent, returned to Sweden for a few years, got a doctorate in Chinese studies (with a thesis on the history of Chinese wall posters), and married a colleague from the head office. As the two of them moved first to Beijing and then on to Hong Kong together, his wife, Agneta Engqvist, became a stringer for *Dagens Industri,* a Stockholm business daily with a growing interest in Asia.

Most news organizations, of course, have only one correspondent in a posting, and besides, many of them have had nepotism rules that have made it impossible for spouses to work as correspondents for the same organization. Such circumstances have often made it necessary for couples who want to be in the same place and yet continue their careers to find work with different organizations.[22] This in turn could lead to further complications, if the organizations are in competition. In more recent times, especially those large and affluent organizations, mostly American, that have more than one correspondent in their bureaus have given up the nepotism rule, occasionally assigning couples to the same posting.[23] At the *New York Times,* this has become quite common. Nicholas Kristof and Sheryl WuDunn pioneered the arrangement, reporting first from China and then from Japan. In their steps have followed, among others, Suzanne Daley and Donald McNeil, reporting on southern Africa out of Johannesburg. In such instances, the combination of work with family life could be similar to Griehsel and Stanford's (although when there are two writers in the family, the cooperation over work becomes different, with possible domestic implications).

When correspondents have their families along in their postings, they may find the expatriate life more convenient in some phases than in others. Depending on where they are, life with small children is sometimes uncomplicated. If one needs help with child care, it may turn out to be neither difficult to find nor expensive. Arrangements for the early school years can often be handled rather readily as well, either in ordinary local schools, perhaps for the slightly more adventurous, or in schools catering to an international clientele. There are postings, certainly, where safety becomes an issue. Like many others, Suzanne Daley was concerned with the crime situation in Johannesburg. One morning when she and her husband came out of the house, they found that their car had been broken into, and since the steering wheel lay in the front seat, someone had apparently been at work for a good while trying to steal the car—next to the large bedroom window of one of their young daughters. So they put up a higher fence and installed more security gadgets.

It is often when children are moving into youth that correspondent parents begin to worry about getting them back into an ordinary way of life again and making sure that they can adapt to life at home. Yet it certainly also happens that the decision to give up the correspondent's life for domestic reasons comes earlier: a spouse may find too little opportunity for meaningful activities or may just turn, in a state of some culture shock, to complaining generally about life abroad.

Exits

When I met David Remnick in New York, he was a writer for the *New Yorker* (he later became its editor). In the late 1980s, during the years of glasnost and perestroika, he had been in the Moscow bureau of the *Washington Post*. It was an extremely demanding assignment, with long and intense work days, but he was newly married, without children yet, and found it a stimulating challenge. Soviet coverage was being reinvented, with the passing of old-style Kremlinology and its political conjectures based on who in the leadership was standing next to whom while watching Red Square parades. (Moreover, he enjoyed the competition with Bill Keller, who was in Moscow for the *New*

York Times at the same time and whose work he had a great deal of respect for.) But then later on, as a young father, he felt it would be nice to have some time for a family life, and besides, there was this creeping sense that the news beat was becoming a bit repetitious after all. So the time had come to move on. When he went to press conferences in the Kremlin, it struck him that Moscow seemed to be covered by a bunch of twenty-eight-year-olds (at least as far as the American media were concerned—the European correspondents were often a bit older). They would probably not think of this themselves, but Remnick, who had been around a little longer, noticed. And thus he and his family returned to the United States.

Perhaps the image of the foreign correspondent as a veteran, hardened by decades in the business, draws to some extent on the selective attention and memory of the audience. We may notice the veterans who are there apparently forever and forget that there have always been people passing through such work more rapidly. Yet especially among American foreign correspondents, there now seems to be a quicker turnover than in the past, and domestic considerations clearly have a part in this. There are also other reasons why people leave foreign correspondence. Some just turn out not to be so good at it and are therefore brought home again; there may be others within the organization coveting their place. If "going stale," losing one's cu riosity and one's sense of what is newsworthy in a place, is one possible occupational affliction, burnout is another. The continuous psychological stress of going on and on gathering news and getting one's writing done at a fast pace, in a setting where things keep happening, can wear a person down—especially when news work turns into a matter of personally witnessing violence and disaster.[24] "One strange and compelling aspect of a correspondent's life is the way everything in life becomes speeded up," Georgie Anne Geyer (1996, 57) writes. "Because you are covering, day after day after day, things that other people might see only once in a lifetime or never, you live in a distinctly different 'time.' Sometimes I have felt as though I had lived five years in five weeks; by the time I was thirty-five, I felt as though I were 150." On some beats, moreover, one may too often simply find good reason to be physically afraid. That may be another reason for going home.

What do ex-correspondents do? I asked one foreign editor, and he mused, "Someone ought to do a study of that." Certainly their continued career paths vary a great deal. One hears of some returning rather unhappily to headquarters, showing in small or more conspicuous ways their displeasure with new, unexciting tasks, even as a reasonably benevolent management may try to smooth ruffled feathers. Others come home to something more satisfying. If, as spiralists, they have pursued careers combining geographical with social mobility, the last upward step may be back to the center again. Some go into editorial work, often on the foreign desk, at least to begin with. We have already encountered Bill Keller of the *New York Times,* Werner Adam of the *Frankfurter Allgemeine,* and Stephen Robinson of the *Daily Telegraph,* all foreign editors and ex-correspondents. In some major media organizations, moreover, former foreign correspondents have with a certain regularity continued up the executive ladder. Examples are Joseph Lelyveld and A. M. Rosenthal at the *New York Times* (and Bill Keller after I met him) and Michael Parks, who began with the *Baltimore Sun* in Saigon in 1970 and spent some twenty-five years in about a half dozen foreign postings, mostly for the *Los Angeles Times,* but who was that paper's managing editor when we met. American newspapers with a national bureau in Washington, D.C., often find it useful to have an ex–foreign correspondent there, since the coverage of the bureau partly involves international affairs and diplomacy, which someone with extensive foreign experience can be well equipped to deal with. In the electronic media, some become news anchors. After meeting Lyse Doucet in Jerusalem and George Alagiah in Johannesburg, I have seen both of them in charge of BBC TV newscasts from London. Alagiah perhaps was not entirely excited by this prospect when he mentioned it to me, knowing that his assignment in Africa was approaching its end, but then he had also heard that he could combine being an anchorman with occasional fireman trips. And the opportunity for such side trips was not only his. There on BBC World radio news, as I turn it on one early morning at home, is Lyse Doucet's distinctive voice reporting from Damascus on President Assad's funeral; later on, there she is on television, interviewing the king of Afghanistan, about to return from a long exile.

There are also those who cross the boundaries of the media world to do something else, related or quite different. I met Salil Tripathi at a conference in Hong Kong, where he argued forcefully that the weakness of autonomous, critical media in the countries involved had played a part in the buildup, and then the recent crisis, of Southeast Asian crony capitalism. Tripathi, who had started out as a journalist in India, was by this time the Southeast Asian regional economics correspondent for the *Far Eastern Economic Review,* the authoritative news magazine published out of Hong Kong. We had breakfast together in the business hotel where he was staying. Actually he was supposed to be stationed in Singapore, where his wife and children were already in residence, but he did not yet have a work permit there—as usual, the Singapore government had turned out to be very restrictive with regard to having foreign newspeople around. So while he was hoping to work this out, he would go and see his family a couple of times a month. He said correspondents with families were otherwise rather pleased with life in Singapore; for example, there was little risk in that rather authoritarian environment that teenage children would be tempted to try drugs.

We talked about the news business in Hong Kong and in Asia. He sometimes found it useful to be an Indian—"as an Asian, you must understand . . . ," his interviewees would say—but it was not all-important. And though he worked only in English, he had both European and American colleagues at the *Review* whose Chinese was fluent. At that time there were no Australians on the staff, although they had long had a conspicuous part in journalism in the region. But clearly, said Tripathi, Hong Kong was still a frontier of opportunity for young foreigners hoping for a future in journalism. Arriving even in their early twenties, they would rent an apartment together, three or four of them, on the outlying island of Lamma or wherever rents would be low, and try their luck as freelancers. The *Asian Wall Street Journal,* published locally, was one outlet, especially in the weekly Hong Kong section devoted to such matters as local lifestyles, but sometimes they would get a little encouragement by whatever they regarded as their home papers as well.

A year or so later, I learned that Tripathi had moved to London and was working for Amnesty International. As one person leaves foreign correspondence, however, no doubt there will be another of those hopeful young people sharing an apartment on Lamma, ready to get started on a correspondent career.

Toward the end of 1987, the Palestinian uprising that became known as the intifada (and after 2000 as the first intifada) began in the occupied territories of Gaza and the West Bank. It seems that the Israeli military forces were taken by surprise. More important, for our purposes, so was apparently the foreign press corps in Jerusalem and Tel Aviv. Some years later, one longtime observer of the regional news scene published an interpretation of the reporting on the intifada by the American news media, suggesting that they had been paying insufficient attention to the preceding buildup of tensions within Palestinian society. Jim Lederman, who arrived in Israel from his native Canada in the late 1960s, just after the Six-Day War, and has been there most of the time since then, writing and broadcasting for a number of news organizations, argued in his book *Battle Lines* (1993) that the intifada was above all a youth rebellion. At the same time as it opposed the foreign occupation, it also rejected a crumbling Palestinian social order. The reason why this development was mostly ignored was that it was not clearly enough related to what was the story line of the region, at least since the Six-Day War: Israeli-Arab violent conflict over possession of land. Lederman also commented on the general significance of story lines in news work:

> The story line is a frame into which a journalist can place seemingly random events and give them coherence. It simplifies the narrative thread, reducing it to manageable dimensions by using a single overarching theme so that each dramatic incident can be highlighted as it occurs and each "chapter" of the ongoing story can be slotted in easily and given a context. It gives all who use it, be we hacks, ideologues, area specialists, diplomats, or scholars, a common

> reference point, a set of agreed bearings from which to set out into
> the unknown and through which to communicate with our audiences.
> (Lederman 1993, 12)

It is the way stories are selected, contextualized, and presented to portray regions in foreign news that we are concerned with in this chapter. Lederman's comments on the story line phenomenon may serve as a point of departure; it suggests one of the parallels between foreign correspondence and anthropology. We may be reminded of what Arjun Appadurai (1986, 357) has labeled "gatekeeping concepts," concepts that "limit anthropological theorizing about the place in question, and that define the quintessential and dominant questions of interest in the region"—for the anthropology of India, caste; among the Mediterraneanists for some time, "honor and shame." Like story lines in news work, the gatekeeping concepts of anthropology have led to a concentration on particular kinds of authorized topics and selective inattention to many others. But the identification of story lines and gatekeeping concepts can in itself be a first step toward scrutinizing them, noticing their limits, seeking their origins, discerning their blind spots; perhaps suggesting alternatives, but also discovering their varying uses. What can we say, in such terms, about reporting out of the news beats that this book is chiefly about— Israel and Palestine, Japan, Africa?

Jerusalem: A Story Line Continues

Ramy Wurgaft, the *El Mundo* correspondent in Jerusalem, was pleased with a story he had done on a camel-riding contest on the West Bank. He described it as a lively, colorful event. But then his account took another turn, as he revealed that the competitors belonged to a Bedouin tribe threatened with expulsion from its Jerusalem site, claimed for other purposes by Israeli authorities.

A story line may seem to be everywhere because it can enter reporting in different ways: both as focus and as context. Lederman (1993, 13) notes this, too—if you wrote about Israeli universities, soon enough you could get to the fact that students are off on reserve army duty now and then. Or if you described Christmas in Bethlehem, you would turn from an account of religious activity to local security concerns.

For Jerusalem correspondents, in other words, the dominant story line has remained the one identified by Lederman, that of Israeli-Arab conflict. It has had other components than possession of land, although, as the case of the Bedouin tribe in Wurgaft's story shows, land possession continues as a main ingredient. It has not been altogether continuously characterized by violence, either. In the 1990s, it included an uncertain, uneven peace process, with negotiations sometimes taking place locally, as at the Erez crossing at the Israel-Gaza border and sometimes elsewhere in the world. Yet there were also acts of terror, minor skirmishes, an occasional major battle, and then the second intifada, breaking out in the first year of the new millennium. Meanwhile, with regard to the possession of land, particularly in and around Jerusalem, Israeli government agencies, settler groups, and Jewish entrepreneurs from abroad cumulatively established new facts on the ground.

What we heard Lyse Doucet of BBC describe in chapter 2 as a Rubik's cube of Jerusalem coverage—you turn it and turn it, and always a wrong color shows somewhere—seems to be an infinitely varying story line. The correspondents there are inclined to feel that their assignment is very considerably "event-driven," and this predominance of hard news many of them evidently find a bit irritating, at times even boring—well, so if this is history being made, why does it have to move in such tiny steps, or back and forth?

Again, we are dealing here primarily with the reporting of the late 1990s. Watching Hebron is one of the durable ingredients of an assignment to Jerusalem in the period and up to the present. Apart from Jerusalem itself, no other place has a comparable symbolic load, and of the two, Hebron is even more conflictual. That city, south of Jerusalem on the West Bank, has the grave of Abraham, holy to Arabs as well as to Jews. Arabs massacred some fifty members of its old Jewish settlement in 1929, when conflicts between the two peoples were escalating in the British mandate of Palestine between the world wars, and then for many decades there was no Jewish presence in Hebron. After the Israelis occupied the West Bank in the Six-Day War, however, a new Jewish settlement named Kiryat Arba arose just next to the city, and in a rather sudden maneuver, Jews also occupied a number of buildings in its center. These settlers, both outside and inside Hebron, were militant and well armed and made no secret of their goal of taking over the entire city. The Arab inhabitants of Hebron were understood to be among the most vehemently anti-Israeli of all Palestinians; Hebron was a stronghold of the Hamas movement rather than of Arafat's PLO. In 1994, when a settler from Kiryat Arba opened fire in the main Muslim shrine in the city and killed twenty-nine Arabs before he was killed himself, Hebron renewed its claim on world attention. The other settlers in Kiryat Arba turned the assassin's grave into yet another local shrine, this one certainly not shared with the other faith.

As the peace process gets going, and growing portions of the West Bank and Gaza are turned over to the Palestinian Authority, Hebron is the last major urban center that the Israelis hold on to. In late 1996 and during the first weeks of 1997, negotiations over the fate of the city move painfully slowly. Meanwhile, street battles, minor skirmishes, and provocations between Jewish settlers and Arab townspeople continue in Hebron itself. Foreign correspondents find frequent reasons for visits and acquaint themselves with the more noticeable, vocal representatives of both sides. Nathan Shachar (1997), correspondent for the Stockholm *Dagens Nyheter,* tells his readers that news photographers are now so densely packed in strategic urban spaces that they can hardly document the everyday lives of Palestinians and Jews without getting each other into their pictures.

Shachar finds an old Jewish man to talk to who has arrived from London only a few months earlier. Jack Kurshior is in his late eighties and seems refreshingly nonideological—he is in Hebron mostly to be with his children and grandchildren. But before he has a chance to take Shachar around to show him the synagogue, his granddaughter appears and tells him sharply that he is not allowed to talk to a journalist. The settlers' leaders, having realized that the battle for Hebron is now a battle of quotes and sound bites, want to make sure that no unsuitable utterances find their way into news media notebooks or recordings. Yet in this instance, Shachar tells me, they must have changed their minds, since Jack Kurshior begins to appear in the news again and again. It seems he has become a propaganda asset.

A nineteen-year-old Israeli soldier takes it upon himself to try to halt the peace process and the negotiations over Hebron by opening fire in the city's main Arab marketplace. This leads to more international headlines but not to the intended results, and a couple of weeks later, in mid-January 1997, an agreement of sorts is reached. Most of Hebron is turned over to Palestinian control, while the Jews in the middle of the city will still be closely guarded by Israeli soldiers in an enclave that also includes a much larger number of Arabs. Most of the Israeli troops pull out rather discreetly, and for the moment, in this volatile city, that is about it. The English-language Palestinian weekly *Jerusalem Times* notes that to some it may have been a disappointment: "Foreign journalists and photographers flooded the streets of the city looking for scoops. Most were glad that a funeral of an old man who died earlier in the day, gave them something to do. A number of those photographers ran through the funeral procession route, taking pictures despite local people's attempts to explain to them that the burial had no value in their stories" (Zananiri 1997).

In the following period, the Hebron watch is no longer so continuous, although the tense copresence of Jews and Arabs still generates stories with some frequency. About half a year after the Israelis left most of the city, there are riots after a young female Jewish militant has gone around plastering

Arab storefronts with a poster depicting the prophet Mohammed as a pig stomping on a Koran.

Not much later, at the end of July 1997, the foreign newspeople in Jerusalem have another hard news story to share. Two young Palestinians, evidently dressed in dark suits and white shirts to look like Orthodox Jews, explode two bombs in the midday crowds of the Mahane Yehuda market in western Jerusalem, causing fifteen deaths, including their own. Print correspondents assemble largely similar stories. Whether their eyewitness accounts are from their own visits to the market, or from the news agencies, or from live television coverage, is not necessarily clear. The ingredients of their stories tend to be the same: dead and injured people, shattered stalls of fruits and vegetables, cheap clothing blown out of other stalls by the force of the explosion, ambulance sirens. The reporting includes comments from Israeli government spokesmen and from the Palestinian Authority, and from more distant observers in the world as well. There is a list, too, of other terrorist deeds in recent years. And then in the next few days, the correspondents follow up with more comment on the implications of the event and with reports on the investigation and resulting arrests. In the *Daily Telegraph,* Anton La Guardia (1997) adds a brief account of how radical Palestinian groups recruit and prepare suicide bombers for martyrdom.

There is more room for variation and personal initiative elsewhere along the story line. A week or so after the Mahane Yehuda bombing, Cordelia Edvardson (1997b), writing for the Stockholm daily *Svenska Dagbladet,* visits an Arab family in the West Bank village Beit Jalla, whose life is greatly complicated—indeed endangered—by the restrictions on personal movement, which become even more stringent after an event such as this bombing. The husband and father of the family, a mathematician who because of severe lung problems has been unable to work for several years, ran out of supplemental oxygen when access to Jerusalem was cut off by Israeli authorities after the bombings. He most certainly would have died if his wife had not been a nurse. She knew that it was essential to keep him awake until the next morning. By then she was able to pull strings so that she could pick up a new supply of oxygen in Jerusalem. Edvardson concludes by pointing out how Israeli collective sanctions affect innocent people, and she notes the bitterness this breeds.

About a half year earlier, in another of those long *Los Angeles Times* "Column One" stories, Marjorie Miller (1996c) moves about in East Jerusalem to describe the struggle of Palestinians to hold on to their houses, neighborhoods, and residence rights. From what remains of the hilltop summer residence once commissioned by King Hussein of Jordan, she has Khalil Tufakji, "the Palestinians' chief map maker," point out new Jewish neighborhoods, while bulldozers busily carve out new roads and housing blocks. "Every time I come here it makes me crazy," Tufakji tells her. "You can see the future of Jerusalem. What is there to talk about?" She meets a grandmother who, with her husband, bought their house in 1966, only to find herself the following year living in Israel and cut off from just about all her Arab neighbors by a major highway. Shopkeepers in Salah-al-Din Street, East Jerusalem's old commercial center, complain to Miller that their businesses are being strangled—for customers from the West Bank, it is difficult to get into Jerusalem, and those Israelis who used to shop there before the intifada have stopped coming across that invisible border so well-marked in the depths of everybody's mind. Arab banks are not allowed in Jerusalem, and movie theaters were closed down during the intifada. Building permits are difficult to get and prohibitively expensive. If Palestinians go ahead and build anyway, they may find their new houses razed. Hayyan Jubeh, a widower returning to Jerusalem from abroad after his British wife's death, finds his rights to live there and hold a vitally important Jerusalem identity card challenged by the government—it argues that his "center of life" is now elsewhere. Meanwhile, Ehud Olmert, Jerusalem's Israeli mayor, says in an interview that Jerusalem will remain a united capital: "When you make peace, you don't split cities, you don't build walls in the middle of cities. You break walls, you unite cities."

Two Israels

Meanwhile, Israel itself seems increasingly divided. The rift between the more secular and the more religious Israelis is by now evident in much of the reporting from Jerusalem. At times it turns into a tale of two cities, as Jerusalem itself is depicted as a center of strong religious sentiment, a desert mountain capital, in contrast with secular, cosmopolitan, hedonistic, Mediterranean Tel Aviv. Yet the divide is also conspicuously present within Jerusalem. We saw an example in chapter 1: Marjorie Miller's report on Saturday traffic on Bar-Ilan Street.

This rift, something of a culture war, has in effect become another story line, not entirely divorced from that of the shifting Arab-Jewish relationship (since the hard-liners opposing the peace process are often on the religious side of the divide), but far from a mere reflection of it. Strong feelings are involved, and stark visual impressions. Men in dark suits, frock coats, and black hats, with long forelocks—the *haredim,* the "Godfearing," the ultra-Orthodox—promise good pictures for photographers and pose a challenge for those who work with words.

Although not devoid of events, this theme involves a balance between hard news and feature stories that is different from that of the Arab-Israeli conflict; there is less of the former and more of the latter. But there can be a great many variations in each kind of story. Eric Silver (1997), the veteran staff correspondent turned freelancer, reports in *Time* magazine on the provocative call by two Israeli intellectuals, a novelist and a newspaper columnist, for the partition of Israel into two states: Israel for the secularists and a state of Judah for the religious. Writing for the *Washington Post,* Barton Gellman (1996) describes the uproar that occurs after the young rock idol Aviv Geffen—"who calls Bob Dylan his idol but wears enough eyeliner and lipstick for Madonna"—advises his fans to pack their bags and leave Israel. This, and Geffen's remark that a Pink Floyd record means more to him than the Western Wall, is too much even for many secular Israelis, and Geffen later retracts his first statement (which has done little to hurt the sales of his chart-topping album among his teenage fans).

Marjorie Miller (1996b) likewise finds the culture war being fought through secular popular culture, as she reports on the stand-up comedian Gil Kopatch's appearances on a Friday night TV variety show, presenting satirical versions of biblical events. In the Bible, Noah gets drunk on wine and falls asleep naked in his tent; on Channel 1 of Israeli state television, "Noah danced in his tent with his boulboul exposed." In the Bible, Sarah banishes her maidservant Hagar and Hagar's son Ishmael; on television, Kopatch notes that Prime Minister Netanyahu's wife, also named Sarah, likewise gives her servants a hard time. A deputy cabinet minister from a religious party protests that Kopatch "speaks with mockery and derision, abomination and cheek of Israel's most sacred matters." The comedian's secular following protests against proposals of censorship and wonders how the Orthodox could know what is on television on Friday nights anyway—they are not supposed to be watching then. The Knesset's education committee calls Kopatch in for a hearing, which turns into another comedy hour. The deputy minister invites him for dinner, and it turns out that a profane term for Noah's private parts has entered the minutes of the Israeli parliament for the first time.

There are also more personal dramas springing out of the religious and cultural divide. Miller (1996f) devotes one article to the experiences of Israelis who have left their Orthodox faith behind and have therefore been rejected by their families and communities. The price they pay can be high. Religious parents have been known to go through mourning rites for apostate children as if they were deceased. One man is thrown out of his father's funeral by his brother, a rabbi. A woman who began to question her religion when her husband, supposedly a pious man, had an affair with another woman

of the same faith, now lives a double life. To get her divorce accepted by a rabbinical court she has granted her husband custody of their children, and to
get to see them a couple of days per week she pretends on those days, by way
of dress and conduct, to be devoutly religious. The rest of the week she is secular. Yet those who leave Orthodoxy are not entirely without support. There
is an organization, founded with the support of American Jews, that offers
counsel and some practical assistance to "exitees"—finding them a place to
stay in a kibbutz, for instance. To the faithful, says Miller, the organization
represents the devil.

Nathan Shachar (1996), of *Dagens Nyheter,* too, offers a view of a
boundary transgression, a Romeo and Juliet story of an ultra-Orthodox girl
and a secular boy. Peri, the teenage girl, lives her life almost entirely encapsulated among the Gur Hasidim, one of the strictest groups in ultra-
Orthodoxy. But there is one passage through the outside world. Peri has to
take an ordinary Jerusalem city bus to the teachers' college she is attending.
And like a couple of other ultra-Orthodox young women recently, she falls in
love with a bus driver! His name is Oren. She travels on his bus again and
again. In the end, she accepts his suggestion that they meet, if only for a dis-
creet walk. Peri and Oren keep meeting secretly, but then Peri's mother listens in on one of their telephone conversations. Hearing about the relation
ship for the first time, her father, a judge in a rabbinical court, cries like a
child. Oren begins to get visits from dark-frocked strangers who come to his
door to talk him out of the relationship. At one time he is offered a check for
hundreds of thousands of dollars to forget about Peri. But the two remain
committed to one another. The police has to escort them to their wedding
feast, so that there will be no violent outbreak. Thus Peri begins her new life,
as a young married woman, in a suburban flat. Shachar notes that the Orthodox are expanding into ever larger areas of Jerusalem; he asks a demographer
at Hebrew University whether it is true that in the 2030s the Orthodox, having never committed themselves to the state of Israel, will form a majority
that can vote to abolish it. The demographer replies that the Orthodox have
many more children but that immigrants have been more often secular. But
then, he says, in this country something will always happen that nobody has
foreseen.

An Earthquake and the Soul of a People

On to Japan. It was on January 17, 1995, early in the morning, that the earthquake struck Kobe, which is one of Japan's commercial and industrial centers and has one of the busiest ports in the world. More than five thousand

people died, there was major physical destruction, and city life was severely disrupted. It was the kind of event foreign correspondents flock to. For the *New York Times,* most of the reporting was done by Nicholas Kristof, who had just arrived in Japan to become Tokyo bureau chief. It was not entirely clear from the beginning that Kristof would go to Kobe. When I met Sheryl WuDunn, his wife and colleague in the bureau, in Tokyo some years later, she reminisced that she had been very tempted by the opportunity as well. But in the end, she stayed in the office to coordinate the coverage from there.

Most foreign journalists, in typical parachutist fashion, probably went to Kobe as quickly as they could after the earthquake and left quite soon afterward. Kristof, however, keeps on reporting from there for several weeks. To begin with, the physical facts of death and destruction dominate, interwoven with an appeal to the reader's sensual imagination. The eeriest time is at night, when the back alleys are dark and one hears only endless distant sirens. Along the alleys are the shadows of abandoned, damaged houses and open spaces where piles of debris remain—some still contain bodies, or even perhaps a person still alive, still struggling (Kristof 1995j).

As time passes, the reporting gradually changes character. In an article in the paper's Sunday "Week in Review" section, Kristof suggests a background assumption for the continued coverage: "It is of course risky to generalize too much about differences in foreign cultures . . . Yet differences can be real, and sometimes the way people or nations react to disasters can open a window on their souls. The catastrophe in western Japan, and its orderly aftermath, with hardly a looter to be found, may offer some insights into life and society in Japan" (Kristof 1995g). As I quoted in chapter 2, "whenever you find hundreds of thousands of sane people trying to get out of a place and a little bunch of madmen struggling to get in . . . " Does Kristof's suggestion imply a parachutist privilege in looking into this kind of window?

Having just arrived in the country anyway, the correspondent sets out to explore Japan as seen through the disaster. Japan, he remarks, sometimes seems torn between two perceptions of itself; on the one hand it is an "irrepressible, unstoppable powerhouse, whose secret weapon is its own special characteristics," and on the other hand it is "the poor island archipelago with few natural resources . . . always living on the edge of one disaster or another." As Japan looks at itself after the earthquake, it is the second image that appears again. "One of the phrases the Japanese have used in describing themselves is 'gaman,' a term that has no equivalent in English but that roughly means a kind of stoical perseverance" (Kristof 1995g). Kristof notes the old contrast between guilt-based and shame-based societies and comments that the theory can be taken too far, yet points to the possibility that the sense of personal honor and the fear of being shamed may make the Japanese the ideal disaster victims.

Back in the streets again with Kristof, we find order and generalized reciprocity. Rumors of looting turn out to be almost always only rumors, and in the one case of a store clerk actually claiming to have seen looters, he asserts that they were foreigners (Kristof 1995j). Generosity, however, can be troublesome as well. One woman, sitting on a futon in a refugee shelter, worries about all the apples and rice balls and other gifts that friends have brought her: it could be a terrible embarrassment if one of them returned and found a gift moldering in a corner (Kristof 1995i).

About a week or so after the catastrophe, the army sets up tents containing public baths. These, Kristof (1995b) notes, "in a nation where cleanliness is almost a fetish and drug stores sell disposable underwear," are greeted with much satisfaction. "I've been cleaning myself with wet tissues, but now I can have a real bath," says one older woman; "I'm going to dash home and get my friends and get some clean underwear, and then I'll be back."

Thus we get a view of the Kobe disaster as refracted through the experiences of the homeless, the shop attendants, the mail carriers who cannot deliver the mail, the undertakers, the visitors to the temporary bath houses, and the woman who heard a neighbor die. Kristof and his colleagues draw our attention, as well, to the diversity and inequalities of contemporary Japanese society. In a wealthy neighborhood in the hills above Kobe, a surgeon's wife sees little damage to her home, although some porcelain was broken and an aquarium tipped over. Mostly it is the older wooden houses down below, with heavy tile roofs, that have been destroyed. Their inhabitants are among the relatively poor (Kristof 1995c). Assisting temporarily in *New York Times* coverage from Kobe, James Sterngold (1995b) reports that a gritty industrial ward, populated in large part by Koreans and the discriminated minority of burakumin, suffered some of the worst damage and also that a gangster syndicate, the Yamaguchi-gumi, is offering free food, water, and diapers to earthquake victims on its turf (1995a). But unlike the situation in 1923, when thousands of Koreans were killed in riots after the great Tokyo earthquake, there has been no real tension between Koreans and Japanese in Kobe in 1995. And in Kobe's Chinatown, its modern brick buildings not much damaged, business is thriving (Kristof 1995h).

Meanwhile, some forty miles away in ancient Kyoto, there is some worry about what Kobe's troubles will do to particular local enterprises. Miss Takada, seventeen, an apprentice geisha, notes that banquets have had to be canceled. Anxiety shows through the layers of white makeup on her face, and she pauses to adjust her red and purple silk kimono (Kristof 1995a).

Geishas, Samurais, Hara-Kiri

In its concern with difference and with a window on Japanese souls, Nicholas Kristof's vivid reporting on the Kobe earthquake also opens a window on themes in Japan reporting by western newspeople.

The highest priority for the Tokyo correspondents is clearly hard news, as it is for correspondents elsewhere. Some of the hard news is characteristically the bad news of conflict, violence, disasters. In 1995 two such stories came out of Japan: the Kobe earthquake and the poison gas attack in the Tokyo subway by the cult Aum Shinrikyo. Economic news is certainly also sometimes hard news. If anything has replaced the cold war as a global superstory, it is "the market," and Tokyo is a major site for economic and business reporting. Those American newspapers that have made a serious commitment to a foreign news coverage of their own usually have one staffer in their Tokyo bureau specializing in economic affairs, while their other Tokyo correspondents also do economic stories with some frequency. Werner Enz, the correspondent of the serious, journalistically conservative *Neue Zürcher Zeitung,* does almost entirely economic and political reporting—and when the paper adds a second correspondent in Tokyo, he says, the newcomer will do politics and Enz will concentrate on business and economy.

Yet a conspicuous part of reporting from Japan is not devoted to hard news and unique events but to a continuous thematization of difference itself. In Kristof's reporting from Kobe, the event seems to be placed in the service of a series of feature stories on Japaneseness, with a balance between unity and diversity: on the one hand the concern with honor, dignity, and appearance, the orderliness of social life; on the other hand the problematic presence of groups that continue to be at the margin of society (burakumin, Koreans, and Chinese). But for the American journalist, the orderliness and the lack of looting in Kobe contrast intriguingly with the scenes surrounding recent disasters and unrest in cities in the United States. And then the detour to Kyoto, to get a geisha's point of view, seems to be a sure way to dramatize the Japanese-ness of an event.

Stories that relate, or can somehow be made to relate, to classic and stereotypical Western notions of what is Japanese continue to attract foreign correspondents—and probably no less their editors at home. Geishas, samurais, hara-kiri, and kamikaze seem inevitable, although contexts may be updated and sometimes intriguingly anomalous. In the *New York Times,* Sheryl WuDunn (1999a, 1999c) has written both "A Japanese Version of 'Geisha'? Well, It May Sound Easy"—on the translation of the American author Arthur Golden's bestseller *Memoirs of a Geisha* into Japanese—and "Manager Commits Hara-Kiri to Fight Corporate Restructuring." When it comes to business reporting, Japanese economic and industrial organization can also suggest the theme of dramatized difference, whether it is a matter of success or of decline and failure. The keiretsu, "huge corporate alliances welded together by shared values, business ties, and webs of cross-shareholdings," as *Business Week* describes them in a cover story on the fall of Mitsubishi, are a case in point (Bremner, Thornton, and Kunii 1999).

This preoccupation with difference is noticeable not only in American reporting. In a critique of Japan coverage in British media, Hammond and Stirner (1997) describe it acerbically as a theme of "weirdness," with a multitude of expressions. It is not even a monopoly of Western journalists. The Japanese themselves have not been averse to dwelling on forms of national uniqueness—the entire intellectual field of Nihonjinron has been evidence of this.[1] Japan has been described, too, as "God's gift to comparative sociology," because of its capacity to offer early and continuous evidence that modernity can appear in other than Occidental forms. No doubt it is precisely the superficially familiar background of generally modern features that often allows the stories of difference to be told to Western audiences with particular effect. Kristof (1995g) could begin his "Week in Review" essay with a quick portrait of what kind of place Kobe had been "with its neon lights and heated toilet seats and cellular faxes, the great trading city of Kobe a week ago seemed a citadel of modernity and affluence and internationalism, an antipodean New York with more sushi."

Sometimes intertwined with the theme of difference, there is in Western reporting from Japan the theme of Japanese participation in World War II and whatever have been its continued implications. When the dateline is Hiroshima rather than Tokyo, stories involve one aspect of this war heritage. Another, coming up again and again in recent times, is that of Japanese war guilt: Will the representatives of Japan apologize, or won't they? Precisely how strong a vocabulary will they use? This is a theme that no doubt resonates particularly with collective memory in the countries that were Japan's war adversaries. Hammond and Stirner (1997) discuss it under the rubric "Fear and Loathing in the British Press." In the period of most conspicuous Japanese economic success in the late twentieth century, vestiges of older sentiments could mix with new fears in the "Japan-bashing" of both news commentary and popular culture. And when in the 1990s the issue was increasingly frequently raised of a renewed greater Japanese military responsibility in regional and even global affairs, and when at the same time the flag, Hinomaru, and the anthem, "Kimigayo," returned to greater prominence as national symbols, the historical background of reporting was unmistakable.

In early 1999, for example, the *Economist* ran a cover with three warships in dramatic black and white against a background of the red and white rising sun, over the words "Let Japan sail forth" ("Japan's Constitution" 1999). Påhl Ruin (1999e), the *Dagens Nyheter* stringer, reported to his Swedish readers about a suicide by a school principal who could not stand the cross-pressure when the school authorities (in Hiroshima) and the parents wanted the national symbols to be used in end-of-term ceremonies and the left-leaning teachers did not.

When Japanese politicians make statements relating to this theme, sometimes perhaps rather carelessly, often in ways judged as disappointing, it tends to become international news. Otherwise, Japanese politics is often deemed not particularly newsworthy. Werner Enz of the *Neue Zürcher Zeitung,* doing the occasional feature interview with leading politicians, concludes that on the one hand, they hardly ever say much of any interest, and on the other hand, they are likely to say different things for international than for domestic consumption.[2] One exception to the rule that Japanese politics makes dull stories, at the same time confirming it, is Kristof's story "Mr. 'Cold Pizza' Earns Respect in Japan with Deft Tinkering" (1999a). It turns out that when Prime Minister Keizo Obuchi (who died in office in 2000) took up his post, he was described by an American publicist as having "all the pizzazz of cold pizza." But since then, according to Kristof, although "nobody would describe Mr. Obuchi as charismatic," he had come to be more effective and more popular than expected.[3]

At times, the seemingly opaque, fluid, decentered nature of Japanese politics and government turns into another variation on the theme of difference. One long-time Tokyo correspondent, the Dutchman Karel Van Wolferen, who reported on East Asia for the Amsterdam *NRC Handelsblad* over a couple of decades, focused on this in his book *The Enigma of Japanese Power* (1989), which drew considerable attention in and outside of Japan. At the time of the Kobe earthquake, the matter showed up in reporting on the allegedly slow response of the Japanese government to the catastrophe.[4] In an article by Sheryl WuDunn (1995a), a political science professor at Tokyo University is quoted as explaining that this tardiness shows a weakness in the Japanese political system. The consensus style of management became unworkable as communication lines between bureaucracies and ministries broke down, and officials seemed reluctant to act decisively on their own. And Nicholas Kristof (1995d), in his Kobe reporting, notes that whereas normally "it is Western businessmen who gripe about bureaucratic stonewalling as they try to penetrate the Japanese market," after the earthquake Japanese officials seem to have been just as unwilling to accept foreign disaster assistance—arguing, for example, that the medical supplies offered might not be appropriate for Japanese bodies.

Featuring Families

Political peculiarities often become a nonstory, but the place where difference, and a play on similarity and difference, quite explicitly and continuously enters in is in reporting on family and gender—a conspicuous genre in feature stories by Japan correspondents in recent years. When Påhl Ruin arrived in Tokyo, he was a little impatient with the difference theme in Japan reporting and really hoped to do some stories with similarity as the main theme. Yet he could hardly ignore difference. So he reports on being on the streets of Tokyo on weekdays, on Swedish state-financed parental leave and in the company of his firstborn, looking for another father tending a baby (Ruin 1999a). He never saw one. And he describes a Japanese government campaign to get men to spend more time with their children and the mixed reactions to it. In another article, the focus is on Fuchino, an eighty-four-year-old woman living in her son's household; the main point is that every third household in Japan is still made up of three generations—but more and more younger women, especially as they hold on to jobs of their own, simply refuse to manage domestic lives of this kind (Ruin 1999b).

Mary Jordan and Kevin Sullivan (1999a), reporting from Tokyo for the *Washington Post,* have a similar story on the limited domestic involvements of Japanese fathers, and Jordan (1999) also writes on the aversion of Japanese couples to child adoption. WuDunn (1995b) observes that Japanese women increasingly find their male compatriots boring and sexist. There is something called the "Narita divorce": when young women arrive with their new husbands at Narita International Airport after a dull honeymoon abroad, they want to be rid of these disappointing spouses immediately. And both WuDunn (1996, 1999b) and Ruin (1999d) note that Japan appears to have been in no hurry to legalize the Pill—but quicker to approve of Viagra. WuDunn (1998), however, also points out that the government has issued guidelines against sexual harassment.

Why are all these stories about family and gender coming out of Japan now? Certainly, against the background of shared modernity, this is an area where Japanese society is noticeably different from western Europe and North America, and it is a kind of difference that just about every reader can relate personally to. Gender inequality (occasionally with some rather kinky expressions) and gender segregation form the basic story, together with intergenerational cohesion in families, and changes away from that baseline allow further variations on the theme.

But perhaps these interests are also of special concern to some foreign correspondents. I return to my comments in chapter 3 about the age and gender of foreign correspondents in the present period. If the correspondents had more often conformed to the stereotype of graying, lonely men, would they have been doing these stories? Less likely, it seems. The influx of women into the foreign correspondent corps—and often younger women, engaged in their own family lives, such as (in Tokyo) Mary Jordan, Sheryl WuDunn, and Sonni Efron—may have made a difference here. To them, one may surmise, family and gender differences between Japan and the West may be a striking personal experience.

The increasing number of women correspondents, however, is hardly the entire explanation for these stories. A number of youngish male correspondents, who grew up in Europe and North America in a period of changing patterns of personal relationships and with a great deal of public discourse over such issues in their home countries, may also be drawn to such reporting during their stays in Japan. Nicholas Kristof does not seem to have been noticeably less involved in gender and family issues in his writing than Sheryl WuDunn, his co-worker and spouse. He links one difference story, on Japanese civility, for example, to his five-year-old son's birthday party. Gregory and his Japanese friends from kindergarten were going to play a game of musical chairs—but the trouble was that Chitose-chan, Gregory's little girlfriend, was too polite to rush and claim a chair. When Kristof told her she had just lost the game, she looked at him, "her eyes full of shocked disbelief, looking like Bambi might after a discussion of venison burgers" (Kristof 1998). And this shows the difference: "American kids are taught to be winners, to seize their opportunities and maybe the next kid's as well. Japanese children are taught to be good citizens, to be team players, to obey rules, to be content to be a mosaic tile in some larger design. One can have an intelligent debate about which approach is better." [5]

The *New York Times* couple's contemporaries in Tokyo at the *Washington Post* bureau, Mary Jordan and Kevin Sullivan, are also a correspondent couple. And there is Påhl Ruin, whose wife is not in the news business, pushing a pram in Tokyo streets while on parental leave in Tokyo, before beginning his correspondent work. All of them, too, seem to be drawn to stories on Japanese schooling (see, e.g., Kristof 1997c; Jordan and Sullivan 1999b). Sullivan, when I talked to him, smilingly acknowledged that being of about the same age and in the same phase of the domestic cycle as the *New*

York Times couple could perhaps sometimes influence his and his wife's work—and when they identified a topic, they might try to do the story sooner rather than later, because it was quite likely that Nick and Sheryl would be attracted to the same idea. The couples met socially now and then and had their children in the same school. So when one parent from the *Post* team and one from the *Times* team took their children there in the morning and greeted each other, there might be some subtle attempt at tracking the competitors' stories—". . . and where is Kevin today?"

Nicholas Valéry of the *Economist,* back in Tokyo for a third period, is not of the same generation, but he now has a young Japanese wife and sometimes watches children's programs with their daughter, not yet two years old, on the bedroom TV set. There is a morning show with three rice dumplings on a stick, and the signature tune is always heard in the program; after listening to the tune at home, Valéry begins to hear it everywhere. It seems as if all Japan is humming it. And he reflects that the show conveys simple, optimistic, sensible values, a sort of Forrest Gump mood appropriate for harder times, just right for Japan at the moment. If the three dumplings had another life, they would only want to share a stick again, but perhaps with some nice gravy on top.

Tribes and Troubles I: South Africa after Apartheid

On the whole, Japan tends to be considered a largely homogeneous society; sometimes this is even emphasized as a characteristic. It is true, though, that such a portrayal has disregarded certain old internal differences and social cleavages, and with increasing immigration, legal as well as illegal, differences and conflicts over them have become another theme in Japan reporting. In their stories on the Kobe earthquake, Nicholas Kristof and his *New York Times* colleagues indeed gave some attention to the Koreans, the Chinese, and the burakumin minority, and Kristof (1995f) returned to the sensitive topic of discrimination against the burakumin soon again. When a Brazilian woman writer successfully sued a jeweler in a town west of Tokyo who had posted a "No Foreigners" sign in his shop, the correspondents in Tokyo took it as one example of the discrimination and xenophobia that especially South and Southeast Asians and Latin Americans encounter in Japan (e.g., Whymant 1999; Ruin 2000).

Nonetheless, group conflicts and collective violence are a minor theme in news out of Tokyo, whereas they have clearly been very prominent in reporting from Johannesburg or wherever Africa correspondents are at work. South African apartheid, starkly racial, was long a major story line, in its workings, in the resistance to it, in its international repercussions, and in its eventual dismantling—comparable in both drama and longevity to the conflict between Arabs and Israelis. The "winds of change" and the passing of colonialism elsewhere in sub-Saharan Africa had been a significant international news theme in the 1950s and 1960s, but by the time the transition to majority rule occurred in South Africa, a generation or more had been born and reached maturity in independent states in most of the rest of the continent. But then ethnic, or ethnicized, internal conflicts became a recurrent topic in African coverage, from the Biafra War of the late 1960s to the Rwanda conflict of the 1990s.

By the time of my encounters with Africa correspondents and my related closer monitoring of news from Africa, the reporting from South Africa was in a post-apartheid phase. In no small part, however, stories still deal with the handling of the past and with the markers of the extended transition.

The Truth and Reconciliation Commission chaired by Bishop Desmond Tutu is a prominent context for such reporting. South Africans are confronting the atrocities of the past. The correspondents report on some truths and some likely untruths and offer evidence of the uncertainties of reconciliation. In the *New York Times,* Suzanne Daley (1999b) describes the amnesty application, more than four thousand pages long, of Eugene de Kock, formerly in command of a counterterrorism unit and now serving two life terms, with another 212 years on top of that, for a variety of offenses. One dispute concerns precisely when de Kock smashed a shovel through a suspect's skull—was it before he shot him or after? Chris McGreal (1999a), in the *Guardian,* portrays "The Deeds of Dr. Death," the heart surgeon Wouter Basson, who was involved in a secret chemical and biological warfare program, in the murders of at least 229 people, and in some inventive assassination plans such as lacing one prominent church leader's underpants with poison. People like de Kock and Basson were obviously directly involved with the crimes of the apartheid apparatus. When it comes to the individuals at its apex, more remote from everyday repressive exercises, the questions are the usual ones asked when the most mighty come under suspicion—what did he know? When did he know it?

Elsewhere, Daley (1998a, 1999a) describes the qualms of an eleventh-generation Afrikaner father over what to teach his children about the heritage of the "white tribe of Africa"—"a culture in which covered wagons, German Mauser rifles, Wagnerian operas, Malaysian spices and African cattle all played important parts"—and the debate among the staff and directors of an Afrikaans-language daily whether they should apologize for having abetted the apartheid system. In another story, she tells of a small whites-only town where the inhabitants still dream of an Afrikaner *volkstaat*. Writing also in the *New York Times,* Donald McNeil (1997b), Daley's husband, reflects on the fact that in the prosperous and mostly white northern Johannesburg suburb where they live, the classmates of their twelve-year-old daughter Avery have no idea who Steve Biko, 1970s martyr of the anti-apartheid movement, was. McNeil uses this finding to "rail about white South Africans who refuse to leave their comfortable cocoons and face changing times." Then just a few weeks later, he discovers that Avery has never heard of Malcolm X.

The correspondents show that the post-apartheid era has its own large measure of violence. Lynne Duke (1998a) of the *Washington Post,* contemporary with Daley and McNeil in Johannesburg, describes a drunken white farmer's impulsive shooting of a black infant and reports how it subsequently dominates newspaper headlines and radio talk shows across South Africa. In the *Daily Telegraph,* Alec Russell (1998) tells his British readers about black high school students rioting in a small Afrikaner-dominated town after they are beaten by whites with raw-hide whips. Reporting on white fear in *Dagens Nyheter,* Leif Norrman (1998c) notes that more than five hundred white farmers have been murdered on their farms in the four years since the political transition and that many others now suspect that an organized force is behind the killings.

The violence touches not only small towns and rural homesteads. In another of his feature stories, Norrman (1999a) visits a Johannesburg white family, the Halsteads, portraying their comfortable living arrangements but also their preoccupation with danger. An accompanying picture shows the family, mother, father, and two children, in their car; the father has a handgun in his lap. The Halsteads are preparing to leave for Australia. A number of stories describe the changing face of downtown Johannesburg as white businesses, even the stock exchange, escape to the suburbs in reaction to street crime in what has supposedly become "the most dangerous city in the world."[6] And a report in the *Economist* ("Murder and Siege Architecture" 1995) notes that in those affluent suburbs, "defensive walls round the houses are climbing upwards, usually topped off with what South Africans call siege architecture: crenellations, electric fencing or just plain razor wire."

For a time, a big question is what will happen "when Mandela goes." Mike Hanna, CNN bureau chief in Johannesburg, who was born in colonial Tanganyika but has spent most of his life in South Africa, says he finds the question irritating. He hears it most often from visiting American correspondents, and he retorts that the same thing will happen as when an American president leaves office: someone else takes over. He thinks the reporters have built up a Mandela cult, and he argues that the new government machinery is quite well in place.

When the 1999 election (the first after the transition) approaches, however, the question becomes more acute. Some note the reemergence in the election campaign of Winnie Madikizela-Mandela, the old president's ex-wife, controversial especially because of her links to township violence during the late apartheid period, but with considerable personal grassroots support among the township poor. Ola Säll (1999b), writing for the Stockholm newspaper *Svenska Dagbladet*, attends a rally in Gugulethu, one of the grim townships behind Cape Town, and finds a couple of thousand enthusiastic women inside the meeting hall and just as many outside, listening to Winnie over the loudspeakers. Lynne Duke (1998b) reports from another of Madikizela-Mandela's appearances, at a business breakfast, that this guest speaker sees a "second revolution" sweeping South Africa—not a reassuring image to her mostly white audience.

Thabo Mbeki, about to become the country's second black president, appears in the election coverage as a rather enigmatic figure: he has spent most of his adult life with the African National Congress in exile, as an academic, technocrat, and diplomat, rather than in the township streets or in the dusty villages. Suzanne Daley (1998d), who follows him on the campaign trail, says that under normal working circumstances, he would rarely be seen "in anything less formal than a double-breasted suit and a silk tie." For the purpose of winning his first election as party leader and prospective head of state, however, Mbeki is apparently ready to do some relearning. Ola Säll (1999a), also reporting from Mbeki meetings, finds audiences delightedly surprised when the candidate dances on stage, but adds that he still wears socks. His campaign advisers have supposedly told him he would appear closer to the masses if he had his bare feet in his shoes.

In a way Mbeki personifies another social cleavage in post-apartheid South African society, that between black haves and have-nots. Among the former, not a few are people who have, like Mbeki, returned from exile. In the same article in which Leif Norrman (1999a) visits the white Halstead family, he also sketches the life and opinions of a black businessman who is now at home under similarly affluent suburban circumstances, after years abroad; his parental home is in Soweto, the sprawling collection of black townships south of Johannesburg. The businessman goes back there frequently, but he worries that his nice car will be stolen and is also upset by Johannesburg violence—perhaps it is time to reintroduce the death penalty? For a third portrait in the same article, Norrman goes to meet with a former student activist, still living under very modest circumstances in Soweto and bitter about corruption and nepotism within the new regime, for which he feels the returnees from exile are partly to blame. Whether they comment on the role of returnees or not, other correspondents also report on the same social gap. McNeil (1998) cites a local definition of "the Irish coffee problem": "blacks on the bottom, whites on top, with a sprinkling of black faces like cinnamon on the foam to lend respectability."

Before he left Johannesburg to become *New York Times* foreign editor, Bill Keller (1993) did a magazine story drawing on his earlier experience as a Moscow correspondent as well. He compared the role of the last apartheid president, de Klerk, with that of Gorbachev as a transitional figure. He also had time to note that the post-apartheid social fabric was changing in a variety of ways. "Apartheid's Gone, and Anything Goes," he headlined an article (Keller 1994); and the next cohort of correspondents have had much to deal with here. Since the new constitution guarantees equal rights irrespective of sexual orientation, Chris McGreal (1999a) contrasts the greater sexual liberalism of the new South Africa with the homophobia expressed by leaders elsewhere in the continent, including President Mugabe in Zimbabwe. But in another article he notes that when the Miss Gay South Africa pageant is staged in a small town, not all its residents are pleased (McGreal 1999c). Women's groups, McGreal (1999d) also reports, are finally insisting on drawing public attention to the alarming frequency of rape in South Africa. In a controversial television advertisement, a well-known actress who has moved on to Hollywood says that one woman out of three in South Africa will be raped in their lifetime and that men seem not to think it is a problem. There is a barrage of protests by men demanding an apology, and the advertisement is banned.

Smoking dagga, the local form of cannabis, has long been a part of township low life. Now harder drugs have entered the scene on a much larger scale than before, and in Johannesburg tough foreign middlemen, Nigerians prominent among them, are taking advantage of the loosening of social control to establish themselves in the trade with heroin and cocaine (MacLeod 1994). Like many others, as he follows an ANC campaign worker around the townships of Cape Town, Leif Norrman (1999b) points out that local gang wars have a great deal to do with control over the drug trade, even if there is also a component of Islamist protest.

When I talk to Suzanne Daley, the *New York Times* bureau chief in Johannesburg, she has just extended her posting there for another year. She finds the "size and rawness" of South Africa addictive, she says; and in comparison with it, when she and her husband went to France and Italy not long before for a vacation with friends, they actually became a bit bored. Every minute, every hour that South Africa stays together without blowing up is a good sign, she thinks—it normalizes peace.

Perhaps it is on such grounds that she and her husband make some effort to cover the less troublesome, more attractive, and even touching aspects of life after apartheid. Donald McNeil (1997a) reports on the rediscovery of an old protest painting in the London basement of a ninety-year-old white South African who went into exile as a radical in the early 1960s. It was an unconventional rendition of the Crucifixion, with a black leader (Chief Albert Luthuli, later a Nobel Peace Prize winner) as Christ, and two apartheid presidents, Hendrik Verwoerd and John Vorster, as Roman soldiers. In 1962 the picture had briefly hung in a little church near Cape Town, but a board of censors promptly banned it. Now it would finally come back to its country of origin. Daley (1998b), for her part, shows that not only the new black elite can make personal fantasies come true. Enos Mafokate, she writes, has loved horses and riding ever since as a young boy he was given the task of cleaning out stables. He dreamed of being a show jumper, but although he became an accomplished equestrian, he was never in those past days allowed to enter major competitions. In 1992, however, as the international boycott of South African sports was lifted, he was invited to accompany the national team to the Barcelona Olympic Games. Riding in the official parade there, Mafokate reminisces, he smiled so much he locked his jaw. Now, with a few horses of diverse characteristics that he has assembled from here and there, he has started a rather improbable enterprise: a riding academy in Soweto.

Tribes and Troubles II: The Rapid Construction of Primordialism

During the uncertain transitional years of the early 1990s, news reports out of South Africa often described violence between Zulu supporters of the Inkatha movement and members of the majority leaning toward, or actively engaged in, the ANC (in no small part Xhosa). This was described in shorthand as "black-on-black" violence. Some commentators have been inclined to see an element of racism in the term, insofar as it might suggest either that the events in question were less important—although in quantitative terms, such black-on-black violence certainly entailed more death and suffering in this period than there was directly between whites and blacks—or imply some sort of general violent disposition.[7] True, one hardly ever saw the counterpart term "white-on-white" violence, to refer to those instances in earlier times when the terror machinery of apartheid killed or maimed oppositional South Africans of European descent. Yet the black-on-black formulation has hardly been used elsewhere in African reporting; and in the South African context of the period, it was certainly above all an indication of a concrete news judgment—what was black-on-black was understood as a sideshow to the main drama, the story line of black-white conflict (to which it was not unrelated, since internal conflicts among black South Africans suited the apartheid government in its final years quite well).

As the twenty-first century began, acute black-white conflict came back in reporting from southern Africa when in Zimbabwe, President Robert Mugabe tried to shore up his crumbling power base by allowing "war veterans" to occupy white-owned farms and turn violent against anyone resisting. In this case, however, although the white farmers had their notable part in it, the real story was clearly that of the emergence of an effective, largely black opposition to the Mugabe regime. Indeed, conflicts in postcolonial sub-Saharan Africa have mostly been, at least overtly, black-on-black. But that description is not used, because in these contexts it carries no significant information. Instead, the recurrent news motif has been "tribal" conflict; and to the extent that there has been a critique of media reporting out of Africa, it has come to dwell largely on the handling of this theme.

Part of it has simply involved terminology: Europe has ethnic groups, Africa has tribes, with all the primitivist overtones of the latter term. "Tribe" is a term in widespread use in Africa itself, so it is a little unfair to place all the blame for its occurrence in reporting on the correspondents and their editors. More subtly, however, critics note that the understanding of ethnicity at hand here tends to be of what scholars in the field now describe as the primordialist variety—ethnicity is viewed as a largely unitary phenomenon, involving fundamental, everlasting, almost quasi-biological sentiments.[8] One of the academic Africanists who have developed critiques along such lines, the British anthropologist Richard Fardon (1999), points out that the scholarly preference is now for more situationalist, constructionist understandings of ethnicity and suggests that the latter may be seen, using a term brought into anthropology by Needham (1975), as a "polythetic" category—it involves a set of characteristics so internally variable in their occurrence that particular instances may turn out to have no shared characteristics at all. The point is not, then, that ethnicity is unimportant in African conflicts or for that matter in African life. It is rather that precisely *what* it is, and *how* it is important, must be understood in different ways in different places; and news reporting seldom offers much insight into these differences. This also means that it has little to say about the routine, mostly peaceable working of ethnicity that is after all a large part of African everyday life.

A pessimistic view would be that the chances for more subtle portrayals of ethnicity in news work are not great. If you are a parachutist flying into a new battle zone with limited preparation, the tool kit of primordialist assumptions and clichés is perhaps just too conveniently available. Moreover, in reporting, with just so many minutes on the air or a limited number of column inches, teasing out the local realities of a conflict messily organized in ethnic terms is no easy task. There is a risk, consequently, that essentialism will become standard operating procedure.

Even so, the tribal theme may not have been taken quite so much for granted in recent reporting from Africa. It could be that newspeople have been learning a lesson here, not only in Africa but also noticeably from 1990s Balkan reporting, where a story line that began as heavily primordialist tended to shift with an increasing realization that critically important active parts were played by politicians, warlords, and criminals who escalated and maintained conflicts for their own gain. By the beginning of the new century, the *New York Times* correspondent in Nairobi, Ian Fisher (2000), could discuss the past and present of Hutu-Tutsi relationships under the headline "If Only the Problem Were as Easy as Old Hatreds." Fisher summarized the precolonial history of the Great Lakes area of Africa, then emphasized the impact of colonialism, German as well as Belgian, in creating a more rigid and hierarchical ethnic order (leaning here on several academic authorities), and argued that the formula of "ancient tribal hatreds" has been convenient for the outside world because it "lends a patina of logic to indifference—to saying that there is little that outsiders could do." In general outline, Fisher suggested, "the conflicts in Africa are quite like those in the Balkans: ancient divisions, even animosities, exist, but it takes a political elite to seize on them and transform them into something far more violent as politicians seek power for themselves."

Despots and Victims

If "tribalism" is now not quite so central in stories from Africa, what else is there to shape the Africa of the news consumer's imagination? One motif, for several postcolonial decades, has been that of the murderous, self-aggrandizing despot: Idi Amin, Emperor Bokassa, Mobutu, and some others of lesser reputation based on particular mixtures of violent practices, pomposity of style, and banality of greed. That motif, too, is perhaps now in decline. Even the more ruthless, mendacious power holders in later years have usually not showed off quite so much. But there are occasions for a return to it. Scott Kraft, back at the head office when I met him, but in Nairobi and Johannesburg for the *Los Angeles Times* during an extended period in the late 1980s and early 1990s, remembered that one of his early excursions out of Nairobi had been to the trial of Bokassa in Bangui, capital of the Central African Republic (no longer "Empire"). It was some eight years after Bokassa's overthrow by French paratroopers but soon after his unexpected return from exile in Paris. Bokassa was no longer a striking figure, yet as one of the headlines over Kraft's reporting (1987) put it, the trial proved to be a "stellar attraction." According to another headline, it offered "Lurid Tales of Cannibalism, Torture."

Nine years later, this ex-emperor is remembered once more. Late in 1996, the *New York Times* Abidjan-based West Africa correspondent Howard French (who moved on, not much later, to Tokyo), reports that Bokassa has died peacefully from a heart attack in his own country, having served his prison term (1996b). The stories of assassinations, hidden corpses, and alleged cannibalism are told briefly once more, and again it is noted that in his days in power, Bokassa made gifts of diamonds to his friend the president of France, with whom he used to go big-game hunting. The obituary concludes: "Mr. Bokassa, who married several times, is survived by as many as 60 children."

About a year after that, French's contemporary as a West Africa correspondent, James Rupert (1997) of the *Washington Post*, goes to visit Berengo, Bokassa's home village. The concrete runway of his airport is still there, maintained as an emergency landing strip for the French air force. Village youngsters jump from the balcony of his villa into the rain water that half fills his swimming pool. Around the villa are guest houses, barracks, watchtowers, garages, a radio station, a small plant for making phonograph records, and a movie theater. But weeds, rust, and mold are also everywhere. The bronze, four-meter-tall statue of Bokassa rocks if you push it. Bokassa's grave is marked only by a concrete slab—but it is said that his family plans a real monument. And under that rough slab, there is supposedly a two-room tomb: a tiled chamber for the coffin and a small parlor containing Bokassa's favorite armchair, reading glasses, and a Bible. Rupert tries to suggest some understanding of the "African Big Man" type of leadership, comparing it to that of American political bosses of the past. In his heyday, Bokassa was an energetic builder. He brought electricity to Bangui, and he paved roads. But also, according to a local journalist whom Rupert quotes, "he knew how to command and had the strength to do it." A senior Western diplomat, with a background of extensive service in Africa, points out to Rupert that the Big Man is forgiven many vices, including corruption, "as long as he takes care of his own, as long as he receives the people who wait in his courtyard with a problem for him to solve."

Other correspondents go to other places similar to Berengo. After

Mobutu's overthrow, one could visit Gbadolite, another Big Man home village, likewise with an air strip and a dilapidated palace (which turned out to
have been disappointingly cheaply furnished for having been described, previously, as "the Versailles of the jungle"). Then again, not all recent participants in African battles for power have been so ostentatious in their display.
A few months before he can report on Bokassa's death, Howard French
(1996a) visits Foday Sankoh in his room in one of Abidjan's best hotels and
writes "African Rebel with Room Service." Sankoh, Sierra Leonean warlord
and leader of the Revolutionary United Front, is in town to participate in
peace talks. "Every chateaubriand he eats will be a meal for peace," is the enthusiastic comment of a senior Western diplomat (presumably not the one
Rupert met in Bangui, but of the same favored category of correspondent
sources), who proceeds to speculate that after years in mosquito-ridden
camps, the comforts of ironed clothes, hot showers, and fine food will make
a resumption of the guerrilla war increasingly unlikely. Sankoh, however, has
his bitter story to tell the correspondent, about his childhood poverty, his
slow advancement in the colonial army under the British—six years to reach
the rank of corporal—the several times he has been arrested, and the years
he has spent in horrible prisons on charges of participating in varied coup
plots. Yet his movement, he says, does not build only on his personal griev-
ances. According to French's summary, it draws much more widely in Sierra
Leonean society on "the bitter experience of corruption, deepening poverty
and incompetence that came with self-rule."

Sankoh may be a despot, but he portrays himself as having been a victim of a colonial and postcolonial social order. And of victims there are endless numbers in the Africa reporting of the late twentieth and early twenty-
first centuries. Some news consumers would remember the pictures of the
starving children of Biafra, around 1970. By the mid-1980s, with television reporting greatly advanced, the images of recurrent famines in the Horn of
Africa began to appear. The boy soldiers of several internal wars, including
those fighting for Sankoh's Revolutionary United Front, could surely be seen
as perpetrators of violence, but when they are described in just slightly
greater detail as orphaned, unschooled, perhaps addicted to drugs, and often
finally as physically disabled after the loss of arms and legs, there could be
little doubt that, above all, they are also victims. While missing rains have
been the problem in some parts of Africa, flooding has resulted in disasters
elsewhere, as in Mozambique in 2000. Finally, there have been the epidemic
diseases—suddenly, dramatically, but rather briefly in the eyes of the world,
the outbreak of Ebola in Zaire in 1995; much more continuously and over-

whelmingly, in large areas of the continent but particularly in southern, Central, and East Africa, the growing AIDS disaster.

Like most correspondents stationed in Africa, *Dagens Nyheter's* Leif Norrman has been writing extensively about AIDS, both in South Africa, where he is based, and elsewhere on the continent. When I meet him in Cape Town, he has just returned from a three-week reporting trip to Uganda, Malawi, and Zimbabwe, with a Swedish photographer who joined him from Stockholm for this journey. A few weeks later their first major report from the trip takes up four pages in the paper's Sunday supplement, but the greater part of the space is occupied by the somber pictures (Norrman 1998a). There is a scene from a hospital in Lilongwe, capital of Malawi. Sick people everywhere: on corridor floors; on balconies; on the ground outside, when they are too weak to stand in the long lines waiting to get in. Ambulances are not used to bring in the sick but to take away the dead. A preacher standing outside the hospital raises his Bible, intoning against Satan and sin and warning of the final judgment. Large birds and roaming dogs compete for bloody bandages and other promising items from the garbage container. Every hour of this year, twelve Malawians die of AIDS. In Uganda, the situation is possibly slightly better. The disease struck early here, but President Museveni has a strong sense of the problem and tries to deal with it actively and publicly, whereas in much of Africa, too many try to hide it behind a wall of silence—despite all those funerals that have become a part of everyday life. In Kenya, Norrman notes, bishops protest against AIDS education campaigns and burn condoms on bonfires.

Yet in Uganda, too, people are dying. A nearly full-page color photograph with Norrman's report shows Jessica Namugaya, crouching on the earth floor of her simple mud house, next to the sewing machine that should have helped her support herself and a daughter, despite the illness. By now her mind is broken, and she may have a few more days to live. Her father, walking back and forth outside the house, thinks it is rather a matter of hours. Jessica, he tells Norrman, will be his fifth child claimed by AIDS.

Norrman has also collected materials for other stories on the same excursion. In Zimbabwe, veterans from the war of independence are dissatisfied, because they feel they have gained little from their sacrifices. In northern Uganda, the Lord's Resistance Army is fighting the government from bases in southern Sudan, where it has the support of another government (Norrman 1998b). It is a war fought in large part by child soldiers who were perhaps not even born when the rebellion started. Often they have been kidnapped from villages in the war zone and marched off to the bases, where they are made to submit to strange and violent disciplines. Because some of them are recaptured by the Ugandan army, however, and then released into the camps run by humanitarian aid organizations, where Norrman meets them, some have other experiences to recount as well. Florence Anek was twelve when she was captured. A year later, she became the fifty-ninth wife of the leader of the Lord's Resistance Army. She describes him, in retrospect, as a man who could seem kind and understanding but who was also childishly unpredictable and who ruled by fear.[9]

A couple of years later, Norrman (2000c) reports out of Cape Town on a doomsday sect in another part of Uganda, where the leaders have apparently killed about a thousand followers and dumped the bodies in mass graves, discovered after a suspicious church fire. Just before that he has been to Mozambique to report on the flooding. The disaster has been building up over some time, but when finally it receives full recognition, it is extensively covered by international media. After all, their correspondents, cameras, microphones, and laptop computers are nearby in Johannesburg, and the pictures, from boats or helicopters, of people climbing into treetops and waiting on roofs for rescue, are powerful.[10] Cultivated lands are ruined by the water masses, and cattle are washed away into the sea. Probably some 350 people are killed. "The Disaster That Became a TV Show" is the headline of Norrman's *Dagens Nyheter* article (2000f). (At about the same time, a rather larger but undetermined number of people lose their lives in communal violence in northern Nigeria, but that is quite inaccessible and draws considerably less, and less precise, coverage.)

Afro-Pessimism and, Briefly, Renaissance

"The usual images are painted in the darkest colors. At the end of the 20th century, we are repeatedly reminded, Africa is a nightmarish world where chaos reigns. Nothing works. Poverty and corruption rule. War, famine and pestilence pay repeated calls. The land, air, water are raped, fouled, polluted. Chronic instability gives way to lifelong dictatorship. Every nation's hand is out, begging aid from distrustful donors. Endlessly disappointed, 740 million people sink into hopelessness." This is from a *Time* cover story on Africa by Johanna McGeary and Marguerite Michaels (1998).

"A nightmarish world where chaos reigns": this seems to summarize much of the news out of sub-Saharan Africa during the period. If "tribalism" has declined as a story line, perhaps it only means that the African scene appears even less organized. Chaos itself may become a story line by default, a story line only where there is no story line offering a firmer grasp of events.[11]

For some time in the 1990s, "Afro-pessimism" served as a covering term for all that was wrong, and would probably continue to go wrong, between Sahara and the Limpopo River—or even all the way to the Cape of Good Hope. In a way, Afro-pessimism was epitomized in Keith Richburg's *Out of America* (1997b)—the book already referred to in chapter 1, where the *Washington Post* correspondent concludes that as a descendant, he is glad that the slave ships took his black ancestors away across the Atlantic.

In the autobiographical first chapter of his book, Richburg reminisces about the day in the hot summer of 1967 when his father took him, nine years old at the time, to see the riot ravaging Detroit, their home city. "I want you to see what black people are doing to their own neighborhood," his father had said. A twelve-year-old white girl also saw the Detroit fires, with her father and brother, from the roof of the baseball stadium where for a moment they worried about being blocked from their escape route back to the suburb. Thirty years later, the same year when Richburg's book appeared, the journalist who had been this girl, Patti Waldmeir, likewise published a book, *Anatomy of a Miracle* (1997), an account of South Africa's transition out of apartheid. It was a book many of the correspondents whom I met in Johannesburg and Cape Town referred to. Waldmeir was by then no longer around, but she had been the Johannesburg bureau chief for the *Financial Times* for several years.

Waldmeir did not seem to harbor any Afro-pessimist inclinations. One of her first jobs had been as a university lecturer in Ghana, where she was "overcome by the warmth and hospitality of black people"—it was "a seductive continent; for a girl from Detroit, raised in a world of racial hatred, its warmth proved addictive" (Waldmeir 1997, x). Before going to South Africa, Waldmeir reported on African affairs out of Lusaka, Zambia, where she made the acquaintance of ANC leaders in exile before they were able to go home.

There was, then, another view of Africa, a bit more Afro-optimist, held notably by those who were impressed by the democratic breakthrough in the south. Leif Norrman (1997a), reviewing Richburg's book in *Dagens Nyheter,* concluded that Richburg had a darker view of Africa than his own. Norrman had been present at many of the crises Richburg wrote about, but whereas Richburg had barely spent any time at all in South Africa, Norrman felt that he himself had been the witness at close hand of what he—like Waldmeir—referred to as a miracle.

At least for a while in the later years of the 1990s, Afro-pessimism did give way to a theme of "African renaissance"—pushed by Thabo Mbeki and others and coinciding strikingly, in American media, with President Clinton's swing through the continent in March 1998. Indeed, it seemed as if the theme was enunciated rather more fervidly by the journalists traveling with Clinton's entourage than by resident correspondents. Yet the renaissance was celebrated in news commentary on Africa elsewhere in the world as well. The *Time* cover story by McGeary and Michaels quoted above, entitled "Africa Rising," is from this period and coincided with the Clinton visit; the paragraph of utter gloom was there to contrast with the better times ahead. The weirdest dictators seemed to be gone, and there was "a new generation of leaders"—well, perhaps not always quite democratic, but apparently honest, rational, and progressive. Some countries were showing indications of respectable economic growth, and feature stories began to appear portraying new entrepreneurs, impatient with corruption and inefficiency. In Johannesburg, Marika Griehsel was thinking of doing a story on the growing cooperation between business and unions in South Africa—but how would she get good television pictures, not just talking heads, out of that?

Gloom was never far away, though. Some wars were referred to as "forgotten" (Angola, Sudan), but this did not mean that they had ended; if they did end, they left ruined lands behind. Others began—a strange border war between Eritrea and Ethiopia and what some commentators described as "Africa's first world war," in which perhaps a half dozen governments sent troops to fight in the Democratic Republic of Congo as the government of President Kabila failed to establish its authority. In Zimbabwe the repression increased. And AIDS only continued to spread.

Before and after the renaissance interlude, there were suggestions, from journalists and other commentators alike, about what to do with Africa. Some asked for relief from the debt burden or the creation of regional peace forces. Others came up with what might have seemed an utterly unmentionable scenario: rolling back history, placing large parts of the continent again under some form of tutelage. As the new millennium began, the correspondent for *Svenska Dagbladet,* Ola Säll (2000), made a modest proposal: couldn't all the international aid agencies get together and buy up all the Kalashnikovs and the handguns—and have them destroyed publicly, so that they would not just end up in the hands of other warlords?

Dateline Timbuktu

Not all stories from Africa are about tribes and troubles, or despots and victims, or overall hopelessness, or new hope. Wildlife stories are popular. Foreign correspondence from this continent probably has the highest animal-human ratio in the world—meet the chimpanzees, gorillas, lions, elephants, rhinos, hippos, giraffes, crocodiles . . .[12] But these were sometimes victims, too, of local poachers and the international market for trophies and aphrodisiacs.

Back in Los Angeles from his posting in Nairobi, John Balzar told me how this sometimes worked. The *Los Angeles Times* had two bureaus in Africa, in addition to the one in Cairo. The bureau in Johannesburg dealt with the southern part of the continent, and Balzar, as Nairobi correspondent, was left to deal with the rest, on his side of the Sahara—East, Central, and West. He might take a swing through West Africa and come back to Nairobi to write up the stories. Usually there was no real hurry. But in between he could arrange some lighter local travel and take his wife along so that she could see some of Kenya, wildlife reserves, for example. Balzar might really be more interested in other stories himself, but at home the audience was at least as interested in stories about animals as in anything else— so he would report on elephant management. (This was when he was not busy covering the Great Lakes conflagrations, with the more harrowing experiences described in chapter 2.)

A remarkable number of correspondents, too, sooner or later make it to Timbuktu (Timbouctou, Timbuctoo . . .). One may wonder why, but perhaps it is because there are two or three Timbuktus: the real one, in Mali, and one or two in the more or less popular Northern imagination.[13] For some, as the *New York Times* foreign affairs columnist Thomas Friedman (1998a) notes, the city is "a synonym for the most obscure spot on earth." For others, it stands as a symbol of a glorious African past of empire, trade, and learning. And for others yet, it may be both at the same time, or at slightly different times.

John Balzar (1995) and Howard French (1995) both report from Timbuktu. They note the sand. Timbuktu is brown-on-brown. Balzar sees more hoofprints of camels and donkeys than tire tracks in the loose sand outside Tarif's Bar. French observes the souvenir merchants, "wearing turbans against the fierce sun and fine grit borne in the breeze." But the tourist business is extremely slow—as French discovers, "the museum's curator stays home these days, leaving the museum, with its 500-year-old manuscripts and other relics of a great but distant past, boarded shut." The population was probably one hundred thousand five hundred years ago and is about twenty thousand now. It is difficult to get to Timbuktu by car after the first downpour of the rainy season, and yet there may be too little water in the Niger River nearby to allow river traffic to get going. Not too many visitors are likely to come in on the two weekly Air Mali flights, since there is trouble between the sedentary townspeople and the Tuaregs, who have been mounting hit-and-run attacks from their camps. There is a lot of time, instead, French realizes, for the "older routines of elaborate greetings and whispered snippets of news exchanged in spots of coveted shade over never-ending doses of sugary tea in tiny cups." And Balzar agrees that Timbuktu is "as far from the rat race as one is likely to get." "What do we do?" says Toure, a hotel proprietor. "We like to talk. We like to listen. We're good at that. Have a seat." The reggae music of Bob Marley howls on a scratchy loudspeaker.

Travels in Newsworthy Africa

As a term, "Afro-pessimism" has hardly entered African vocabularies. As a sentiment and worldview, however, something like it seems to have become rather common in recent times. Manthia Diawara (1998, 38), film maker– scholar and a member of the African intellectual diaspora in the United States, argues that "we Africans have naturalized Afro-pessimism as a way of life"; it is a condition in which "the evil part of human beings dominates their good side," resulting in internal violence and a continued reign of misery. And he goes back to Guinea, where he spent his childhood, to discuss the matter with local thinkers.[14] The anthropologist James Ferguson (1999, 234– 54), returning to classical anthropological territory on the Zambian Copper-belt, describes a sense of "abjection," of being thrown out, expelled from a world of progress and prosperity and of humiliation and debasement. And he notes that when his acquaintances comment on this state of affairs and their feelings about it, they refer to themselves not as Zambians but as Africans. On the one hand, he concludes, this identification "evoked all the images as-sociated with Africa in contemporary international media discourse—pic-tures of poverty, starvation, and war; refugees, chaos, and charity." On the other hand, it brings back to mind the old colonial usage denoting a stigma-tized race category.

One may wonder how much the street-level Afro-pessimism, by any name, is affected by foreign media coverage, in the same way as Western Ori-entalism is said to have provided an Orient with a self-image. And although there is no doubt that the representation of Africa as a peculiarly troubled region of the world reflects some very concrete realities, should the combi-nation of themes of war and disaster with the recurrence of wildlife stories and Timbuktu datelines not also now raise a question about ways in which the spatial practices of Africa correspondents may influence our view of the continent?

Remember again that concentration of news organization offices in Richmond, the Johannesburg suburb. A considerable proportion of Africa correspondents from the media of the North are there, or nearby, or in Cape Town. And again, there is at present another smaller concentration in Nairobi and yet fewer correspondents based in West Africa, in Abidjan.

In post-apartheid reporting out of South Africa, from the area closest to the correspondents' home base, we find a large variety of topics. The transition from apartheid offers a frame for many of them, but there is still a notable breadth in the exploration of its nooks and crannies. The boundary between hard news and feature stories is often blurred, but many stories are clearly in the latter category, such as Chris McGreal's report on the Miss Gay South Africa pageant or Suzanne Daley's portrait of the equestrian enthusiast in Soweto.

Clearly some media organizations allow more scope for feature stories generally than others do, out of Africa or anywhere else. Some of the Johannesburg-based correspondents indeed manage to do a fair number of such stories. But one can discern an uneven distribution of types of reporting in the wider landscape of news, a varying balance between hard news and feature stories. It may be illuminating to look again at the three foreign news beats we are mostly dealing with here. Since for reasons of cost as well as geography, one would usually not place an overall Asia correspondent in Tokyo, a posting there tends to be responsible largely for reporting on Japan (although often with Korea coverage included as well). And Japan coverage tends to be very Tokyo-centered, with exceptions for such events as the Kobe earthquake. Thus a congruency of origins can often be seen between hard news and feature stories. The tendency may be similar in reporting from Jerusalem. Although the correspondents there are frequently designated Middle East correspondents, the Arab-Israeli conflict has most of the time been so dominant as a theme in regional news that the area to be covered is really understood as quite compact. Here too, consequently, the same area is likely to serve as the source for different types of reporting, hard news and feature stories. But it is true that when reporting is from elsewhere in the Middle East, hard news stories tend to become more dominant.

Turning to Africa again, many correspondents there agree that large parts of the continent are generally underreported. One correspondent, from a small European country, remembered trying to persuade his paper that he should be allowed to report on the plight of some hundred thousand people fleeing from a battle scene in southern Sudan. But the paper was not interested—not until several weeks later, when the United Nations identified the need for a major humanitarian assistance effort in the area. (In contrast, he reflected, if there had been only a single small bomb in a street in Jerusalem or Tel Aviv, a few hours away from Sudan, immediate media attention could have been guaranteed.) Although media organizations may see the need to send a correspondent off from Johannesburg, or for that matter directly from headquarters, to report on hard news elsewhere in Africa, however, they often appear much less willing to allow costly travel for the purpose of feature stories. Unless correspondents make an effort, and have an opportunity, to do an occasional such story as an often serendipitous by-product of their crisis travel, much of the continent thus risks being reported on only when there is hard news—that is, conflict and disasters; then the area in question is visited by parachutists literally looking for trouble.

Apart from sheer distributional aspects, such a preponderance of fireman coverage may have further implications. Foreign correspondents, one of my Pulitzer Prize–winning informants said, do some of their best, most inspired work out of hotel rooms. If that is so, it may be that the sheer eyewitness aspect of dramatic breaking news helps them to reach toward such heights—no "going stale" here. But the hurried itinerary of parachutists, often combined with a lack of opportunity for advance preparation with regard to knowledge of local circumstances, would seem to make it difficult to report in depth, and interpret, and explain. Going beyond that witnessing aspect with its direct appeal to the senses, the parachutists may come to rely heavily on received wisdom: established regional interpretive frames and preconceptions brought in from elsewhere.

Whatever sources a parachutist will draw on beside personal witnessing may also have to be assembled on the spot. There is little or no long-term or medium-term cumulative networking to draw on. Some correspondents are no doubt more skilled and conscientious than others in developing varied sources. The tendency in parachutist practice, though, is that one has to rely on fewer sources, not very carefully selected. They may be one's multipurpose local fixers who, chosen perhaps in haste as a matter of immediate practicality, introduce an element of chance into the picture; or the parachutists may identify some seemingly authoritative commentator who is willing to offer them the local perspective on everything. Some of them would note that this kind of person often knows how to turn a phrase or what goes well as a sound bite and enough about the ways of the wider world to have an idea about what an audience might want. But with regard to particular concrete knowledge, such people could well be sources of limited value.

Not a few correspondents turn quickly to the diplomatic representatives of their home countries, if there are any. When James Rupert, writing about Bokassa, and Howard French, writing about Sankoh, both cite a "senior western diplomat," one suspects that this is someone at the local American Embassy who does not want to be easily identifiable. Such diplomatic sources are at times very well-informed; yet among them are also people who make the correspondents, afterward, shake their heads and roll their eyes. And then especially in Africa, where governments are weak and not too efficient in handling either information or visitors, the staff of United Nations agencies or international nongovernmental organizations (NGOs) often become very prominent sources—they may already serve as the parachutists' local fixers. Such organizations have access to accommodations and means of transport, if their infrastructure is already set up, and under the stressful circumstances of crisis reporting, they may offer a haven of friendly (often other expatriate) faces and understanding. Furthermore, they speak familiar languages.

To reiterate, not all news out of Africa, away from the centers of reporting, is crisis news. The Africa correspondents, or southern Africa correspondents, working out of Johannesburg certainly sometimes do feature stories on a variety of topics from other countries included in their assignment. Chris McGreal's portrayal of the lodge of Orangemen in Accra, in the *Guardian,* as noted in chapter 1, is one example of this. A report by Suzanne Daley (1995) on the huge Roque Santiero marketplace in Luanda, Angola, in the *New York Times,* is another. The market stretches for more than a mile along the seafront. You can buy toothpaste resqueezed from discarded tubes into new ones; you can buy leopard skins; one destitute woman was arrested for trying to sell her children. The Coca-Cola cans are from France or Thailand, and there are Japanese stereo systems and French champagne. The market, Daley notes, is named after a Brazilian soap opera hero who was once falsely accused of stealing. This is a joke, since Luandans do not doubt that most of the merchandise is either stolen or smuggled.

If crises do not entirely monopolize Africa reporting, however, a tendency in that direction still combines with a fact for which the media can hardly be blamed. Toward the end of chapter 1, I commented on differences in news embeddedness. Southern Californians, with their own interests in Japan and with experiences of the country, might respond differently to reporting from there than East Coast Americans might. And reporting from Jerusalem might resonate in audience minds with what is remembered from the holy scriptures. In contrast, it is likely that for a great many people, the media are almost entirely dominant as a source of understanding of contemporary Africa. People have learned little about it in school, they have mostly not traveled there, and they probably do not know personally anybody who has spent much time there, whether African or expatriate. So what they know, or believe they know, about this continent is almost entirely based on what they read, or hear, or see as media consumers. This places an unusually heavy burden on the media depiction of Africa.

Home-Related Stories, and Foreign Is Fun

Among foreign correspondents, to repeat, there are spiralists and there are long-timers. Compared to Jerusalem or Tokyo, Johannesburg seems to have few of the latter kind. The people reporting from there for larger Western media organizations are mostly spiralists, expecting to remain for some years but not forever. They were somewhere else a couple of years ago and will move to yet another location soon enough in the future. Moreover, as I have noted before, correspondents in Johannesburg often point out that partly because of the divisions in South African society, they associate primarily with other expatriates.

Perhaps such constraints on networking and the consequent limitations on their range of local experiences make the spiralist correspondents more dependent on the conceptions of the beat that they brought from home and on the suggestions of their editors at headquarters. When feature stories out of Africa noticeably often deal with topics like wildlife and places like Timbuktu, one may venture to guess that what was brought from home was not only that fresh perspective, the "sense of wonder," but a certain more specific baggage of ideas. Looking back on his Timbuktu trip, John Balzar told me this was the first place in Africa he ever heard of when he was a child.

Whether from Africa or elsewhere, it is not unusual that foreign news stories appeal to particular interests of the home audience. Sometimes, as in the instances just mentioned, they have to do with audience conceptions of what is generally interesting about a particular place or region. At other times, they are about particular connections between home and abroad.

Writing from Jerusalem, Joop Meijers of the *Algemeen Dagblad* expects some interest in Israeli agribusiness news among readers in the Netherlands, with its large industry of the same kind. Although Jörg Bremer's personal interests may be elsewhere, he has to be prepared to write something for the *Frankfurter Allgemeine* about Israeli soccer before the arrival of a German team. Simonetta Della-Seta and Ramy Wurgaft, writing for Italians and Spaniards, probably pay more attention to news of Christian sites, of graves and relics, than do the northern Europeans and the Americans. McGreal's Accra Orangemen story, referred to in chapter 1, certainly has its British connection. In Johannesburg, just as I met her, Marika Griehsel was busily reporting to Swedish television about the two Swedish tourists who

had just been found murdered in Durban. A couple of American correspondents told me they had in mind doing feature stories on the experiences of
African Americans who had settled in South Africa, and Dean Murphy, the
Los Angeles Times correspondent, had done one on the complexities of getting a South African driver's license that he thought his southern Californian
readers should find interesting. When Suzanne Daley (1998c) reports under
the headline "Of Leaders and Lovers: A South African Epidemic" on the
new romantic involvements of several of the country's recent presidents—
Nelson Mandela, 79; P. W. Botha, 82; and F. W. de Klerk, 61—this, too, is in a
sense a home-related story. It is the time of the Monica Lewinsky scandal in
the United States. But the story obviously also sets out to draw on the comical side of the local carryings-on. South Africans, Daley writes, have been absorbed by "their own presidential soap operas"—"Will Nelson marry Graca?
Will F. W. divorce Marike? Will P. W. stay out of jail long enough to see his
wedding day?"

Yes, humor is another genre of foreign correspondence. Foreign can be
fun. From Tokyo for the *Washington Post,* Mary Jordan and Kevin Sullivan
(1997) describe an American diplomat's visit to the bathroom in a Japanese
home. Suddenly he realizes that he does not know how to flush the toilet. The
colorful array of buttons is just baffling. But he pushes one of them: "He hit
the noisemaker button that makes a flushing sound to mask any noise you
might be making. He hit the button that starts the blow-dryer for your bottom. Then he hit the bidet button and watched helplessly as a little plastic
arm, sort of a squirt gun shaped like a toothbrush, appeared from the back of
the bowl and began shooting a stream of warm water across the room and
onto the mirror." Thus a promising young foreign service officer finds himself
frantically wiping down a Japanese bathroom with a wad of toilet paper. No
doubt this is another diplomatic source who does not wish to be identified.

Jordan and Sullivan's story goes on to discuss other aspects of Japanese
bathroom high technology, one more variation on the theme of Japanese
weirdness; certainly many other stories in this category are also intended as
entertainment. The comical element is also present in some of the reporting
on the Israeli religious split, as in Marjorie Miller's account of the controversy surrounding Gil Kopatch, the television satirist. Even Werner Vogt, in
Johannesburg for the normally very sober, business-oriented *Neue Zürcher
Zeitung,* cannot resist passing on a bizarre tidbit. One of his favorites is about
a thief who, being caught in the act, flees across a fence—and finds himself in
the Johannesburg Zoo, in the gorilla grounds. His two pursuers enter the
same area and are attacked by a male gorilla, while the thief lies down, pretending to be dead.

Here is some African farce, then, that happens also to connect after a fashion with the wildlife motif in other stories from the continent. The established regional theme of Middle East reporting becomes even more attenuated with a story that Jim Lederman, the Jerusalem author of *Battle Lines* and commentator on story line phenomena, likes to remember. During his years in the Middle East, Lederman has done some rather different kinds of reporting. One of the benefits of a period of writing for the popular British tabloid the *Sun,* he notes, was the chance to do some "off-the-wall" stories— good for cleansing the brain, like the story about the pelicans. A kibbutz in Galilee sought an insurance payment for a "natural disaster." Since Israel is on a major route of birds migrating between Europe and Africa, numerous pelicans would come by. The pelicans discovered that this kibbutz was raising fish in ponds and apparently were in no hurry to move on. Pelicans eat a great deal, relative to their own weight, so the kibbutzniks found themselves losing a lot of fish and tried to chase the pelicans away. Pelicans, however, according to Lederman's *Sun* story, are intelligent birds. They found a way of taking revenge. They would go fishing, then dive from the air toward kibbutz roofs and drop those heavy carp, causing considerable damage. So here, after all, was a kind of bombing that did not fit with the Jerusalem story line.

Voices Heard and Not Heard

Over the years, anthropologists have become increasingly concerned with polyphony in their writing. It is no longer considered entirely appropriate, as it was in a fairly unreflective way before, to claim that "the Nuer" do this and "the Balinese" think that. Ethnography should mirror the diversity of experiences and viewpoints likely to be found in any human community. Many voices should be heard. As critics note, however, in obvious or not so obvious ways, one voice is almost inevitably dominant: that of the author, who is there administering the polyphony.

The same is true of foreign correspondence. Not that it is uncontroversial—there are well-known correspondents who make themselves fully visible in their stories and let their audiences know about their feelings, but many of their peers frown on such reporting styles, and major news agencies in particular permit little such self-indulgence. Malcolm Browne (1993, 184), having moved from the Associated Press to the *New York Times,* notes in his autobiography that he has been through "the wringer of wire service indoctrination, which unequivocally suppresses the injection of personal opinion into news stories."

Nonetheless, someone is there exercising a degree of choice in deciding on stories and in putting them together. Sheryl WuDunn of the *New York Times,* when I met her in Tokyo, said that although there is an ideal of objectivity in reporting, it is impossible not to interpret; making any selection is an act of interpretation. The goal, she concluded, could only be to be "balanced and fair."

Many foreign correspondents also obviously relish the opportunities they have, especially when it comes to feature stories, to pursue their own interests and make their own discoveries. For one thing, so much of what is at hand can be expected to be unknown to the home audience; and for another, the correspondents mostly do not have to fit into the sort of minute division of labor that is required in the office at home. One can be more or less a jack-of-all-trades. Bill Orme, who was the director of the Committee to Protect Journalists when I met him in New York—later he went to Jerusalem, as part of another husband-wife team, to write for the *New York Times*—reminisced about his experiences in reporting from Central America as a stringer for a number of American and British papers.[15] Foreign correspondents, he said, could be the last great amateurs. He had written about cooking, about theater, and about differences between legal systems. In Jerusalem, Jörg Bremer, with a personal commitment to religious ecumenicism, tries to do stories on each major Jewish holiday, to acquaint his *Frankfurter Allgemeine* readers with these (and he has also told them about the teaching on the Holocaust in Israeli schools). In the same city, Simonetta Della-Seta, reporting to several Italian media but also a professional historian by background, has described Palestinians' attempts to reconstruct their national heritage and discussed the changing historiography of the Crusaders. She has written on night life in Tel Aviv but has also made a special effort to report on Israeli scientific and medical news (such as the no-pain childbirth story mentioned in the previous chapter).

The correspondent's voice is heard, then, sometimes very directly, sometimes perhaps through ventriloquism of one kind or other. But apart from that, with whom have foreign correspondents been talking? Nicholas Kristof's reporting from Kobe, in the aftermath of the earthquake, is in a way strikingly polyphonic. An array of real people are heard on aspects of the disaster: among them, Narumi Nakagawa, embarrassed by too many gifts of rice balls and apples; Toshika Hakenaka, who cannot wait to get into the bath; and Miss Takada, the apprentice geisha. But generally they are not allowed to utter much more than one-liners. Kristof orchestrates them skillfully as stylistic devices, livening up stories, suggesting immediacy and presence, and beyond that perhaps as a means of persuading the reader that common humanity can be recognized across great distances. Anxiety, coquetry, happiness, pride: all appear by way of small but unmistakable signs. Partly because the emphasis in Japan reporting is so often on difference (also in Kristof's own writing), it is a tendency one may find appealing.

If we consider the notion that foreign correspondents should be interested in societies, not only in states, however (as formulated by one foreign news editor, Bill Keller, and cited in chapter 1), and the goal that reporting should be "balanced and fair," then not only the weighting of the familiar and the alien, but especially absences and imbalances in the polyphony become problematic. Certainly this is so particularly when, in a reporting situation of conflict or ambiguity, some voices are heard but not others.

Does this affect the coverage of the story lines we have dealt with here? In foreign correspondence out of Jerusalem, with regard to the current divide between the secular and the ultra-Orthodox, we do not very often find the latter appearing as full-size, developed personae, unless they are renegades, people who have left the faith. One senses that most correspondents are more at ease among the secular Israelis.[16] With regard to the divide between Israelis and Palestinians, to which the main story line of the region is linked, the question of equal hearing must naturally be asked against the background of the characteristics of the Jerusalem foreign correspondent corps—made up in considerable part of Jewish journalists who have come from many places to settle in the national home. Is there any difference between the ways the expatriate, spiralist correspondents and these long-timers deal with the divide?

The correspondents in Jerusalem hold different, and subtle, opinions on this issue and argue about it among themselves. One expatriate suggested that it really must be difficult to be impartial if your son is, say, an Israeli paratrooper. Yet it is possible to find immigrant correspondents who seem to have as good contacts on the Palestinian side as just about any spiralist, and they may also be as sharply critical of their own government as anyone else.[17] In a comment on relationships between the Israeli government and the press in *Dagens Nyheter,* Nathan Shachar (2001) suggests that the government is really quite unhappy that so many foreign media are represented in Jerusalem by long-timer Jewish reporters, who may be less receptive to government interpretations of events simply because they have accumulated more local knowledge.

In some part the asymmetry of reporting on Israelis and Palestinians is a question of language. Not many correspondents in Jerusalem speak both Hebrew and Arabic. Some of the expatriates speak neither, but if they speak one, it is almost invariably Hebrew. The Jewish long-timer correspondents are almost all fluent in Hebrew, whereas only a few speak Arabic as well. This is not balanced by the fact that among those few who as Middle East correspondents report on Israel and Palestine but are based elsewhere (e.g., Cairo), some may speak Arabic but no Hebrew. Of course, a great many Israelis speak English, as do an increasing number of Palestinians. But apart from this, most correspondents have to work through intermediaries and depend on the translation services as they form their understandings of Palestinian life and opinion.

Aside from the language imbalance, the correspondents who reflect on the question also point out that Israel has a much wider, more varied, and generally more developed media scene of its own. Beyond what is directly available in print or on radio or television, there are also local colleagues to interact with, to check interpretations or facts with, to seek out for opinions. On the Palestinian side, there is still the clear tendency for media to become organs of the national struggle, and the freedom of the press has hardly been total either under Israeli occupation or under the Palestinian Authority. Palestinian colleagues, then, are often rather guarded in expressing personal views. Things may be changing, however—younger Palestinians, in and outside of politics, it is said, seem to be more media savvy than both their elders and their counterparts elsewhere in Arab countries.

Again, the asymmetry in coverage does not necessarily translate simply into a pro-Israeli, in the sense of pro–Israeli government, stance on the part of the correspondents. It is rather a matter of reporting more fully on Israeli internal debate and conveying a sense of the diversity of Israeli voices. When I was in Jerusalem, the correspondents' opinions of the government of Benjamin Netanyahu were often quite unfavorable. Yet the story line tends to be more densely contextualized on the Israeli than on the Palestinian side.

Changing continents and beats, what voices are heard in African reporting? In South Africa, once more, a somewhat greater variety. Yet hardly a cross-section of the society—the worries of white people in the post-apartheid era seem overrepresented. The correspondents from western Europe and North America seem inclined to turn to the people who are most like themselves. There is no overemphasis on difference here. When correspondents go to Zimbabwe, too, usually from Johannesburg, to report on farm occupations, it is the white farmers rather than the black "war veteran" occupants who are foregrounded. But then the latter, in a situation marked by a potential for violence, may not seem particularly approachable.

In the African context, however, there is a particular reason to reflect again on the prominence of representatives of international organizations as sources in parachutist reporting. As I watched the television coverage of the Mozambique flood disaster, I thought not only about the fact that so much reporting capacity had been available nearby, in Johannesburg. It also struck me that so many of the faces appearing on the screen did not belong to local people, but to expatriate relief organization personnel. And then perhaps a couple of days later, Leif Norrman (2000e) complained in his newspaper that he had lost his hotel room in Maputo, the capital: all available accommodations were required for the bureaucratic staff of the aid organizations, now moving in to place people on lists, introduce ticket systems for planes and helicopters, and make pronouncements on security matters. And he wondered why disaster aid in Africa so often ended up getting so clumsy.

John Balzar, reminiscing about his own East and Central Africa reporting, said he sometimes wondered about the numerical estimates of deaths and suffering people that he got from relief agencies—was there really any way of knowing? As we were told in chapter 2, he felt like "a cog in the world's humanitarian machine," but he had his misgivings. Like some of his colleagues and some other observers, he saw the uncomfortable possibility that the organization spokespeople also had an interest, parallel to that of the correspondents and their news organizations, in dramatizing disaster. With a somewhat cynical Darwinist twist, the saying goes that news cameras aimed so as to appeal to compassion around the world work to ensure "the survival of the cutest." Critical observers would even argue that in instances of civil conflict, an intricate, partly symbiotic structure of relationships could be set up between strong international NGOs, weak governments, rapacious warlords, news media, and benevolent metropolitan audiences. And it might end up serving mostly the material interests of the warlords.[18] That issue aside, we may at least wonder whether, in combination with the general tendency toward crisis reporting on the African beat, the prevalence of disaster relief workers as sources plays a part in the development of Afro-pessimist themes.

Moreover, while these are often expatriate voices, the Africans themselves tend to remain mostly silent, faceless, anonymous. True, there are the despots and warlords, the Bokassas and the Sankohs; and there are sometimes named victims, like Jessica Namugaya in the Ugandan village, about to die from AIDS, in Leif Norrman's story. Yet there is a problem of recognizing and acknowledging human agency here: it seems that media audiences comparatively seldom have the opportunity to experience ordinary Africans actively shaping their own lives. It is perhaps true that idioms of agency, in situations where there is simply too much overwhelming structure, can become a facile way of blaming the victims for their condition. There is ethnographic evidence at hand, however, that even crisis news could be different in this regard.[19] And when we do come across Enos Mafokate with his Soweto riding academy and the Accra grand master of the Orange Order, we may sense that we are getting a rather infrequent glimpse of the practicality and the inventiveness and the sheer diversity of life in Africa's towns and villages.

Alternative Story Lines, and Writing against Story Lines

The usual story lines are, in Jerusalem reporting, conflicts between Arabs and Israelis and between the secular and the Orthodox; from Tokyo, stories of difference, even weirdness; from Johannesburg, apartheid and its undoing and, on a larger African stage, perhaps tribalism, chaos, despots, and victims. But some other kinds of stories come up as well. What more or less informed critical stance can we develop toward story lines as thematizations of regional news flow? Do they constrain our understandings of distant places and regions too much? Are there alternative story lines or ways of writing against the story lines?

I had a long conversation about such matters with Jim Lederman in a Jerusalem café that had excellent pastries. We agreed that since he had written his book *Battle Lines,* the political and cultural split between secular and ultra-Orthodox Jews had emerged at least as a supplementary story line in reporting out of Israel. He felt, however, that this emphasis might, in turn, serve to conceal the growth of an even wider diversity in Israeli society, and in Palestinian society as well. Probably foreign correspondents had not done enough to report on, and interpret the implications of, the late-twentieth-century influx into Israel of Russian Jews—often highly qualified in educational and professional terms, mostly of secular inclination, and with their previous experience in a different political culture. There were also the Ethiopian Jews, whose arrival and continued presence on the margins of the Israeli economy and society made race a more salient category than it had been. On the West Bank, there was the growing prominence of affluent Arab-American entrepreneurs in the expansive urban center of Ramallah. These changes in the composition of the local society had not been entirely disregarded, Lederman said, but their long-run significance probably did not receive the weight it deserved in reporting.

Possibly in part because he was now doing much of his work for an exclusive newsletter of limited distribution, with a strong analytical emphasis, Lederman was even more emphatic that some basic features of the regional economy were not covered well in the mainstream media. Israel, he argued, was turning into an export-oriented high-tech society, a process that had begun with new enterprises forming as spin-offs from defense industries. This led to a widening social cleavage between the more highly educated Israelis, who could best take advantage of the new opportunities, and the less educated. The divide tended to coincide with the one between the secular and the religious and between the more recent Russian immigrants and the Sephardim of North African or Middle Eastern background. In addition, there was always the question of the scarcity of water in the Middle East. As a possible story line, it was perhaps slightly deficient, since it might not generate a continuing series of new, lively stories. Nonetheless, it was something audiences should be kept aware of.

Even if Lederman had felt when he wrote his book that the story line of Arab-Israeli conflict as conventionally developed before the intifada had neglected the growing Palestinian generation gap, and if he had presented me with a more multifaceted understanding of the current and emergent situation, he would hardly have tried to argue that the story line of Arab-Israeli conflict was mistaken or arbitrary. The series of new tangible manifestations goes on and on, offering materials for hard news stories as well as feature stories. Much the same could certainly be said, for a long time, about the story line of black-white conflict in South Africa. If Jerusalem and Johannesburg have been attractive correspondent postings, this has surely had much to do with the viability of these story lines. In sheer undeniability they perhaps compare favorably with one or another of those regional gatekeeper concepts in anthropology to which they were likened early in this chapter.[20]

Yet though these two central-twentieth-century story lines indisputably represent major structural facts and chains of events, perhaps the representations themselves can still entail misrepresentations. There can be a critique within story lines here, rather than of the story lines themselves. In cases of major, enduring conflict such as these two, with a continuous partisan, vocal scrutiny of the reporting of foreign correspondents on both sides, charges of biased reporting are only to be expected. I will come back to this in the next chapter. Yet a story line may be charged with misinterpretation or incomplete interpretation, even when no obvious partisanship is involved. The critique of reporting on the theme of African tribal conflict is of this type, arguing for a less primordialist view of ethnicity. In some African reporting, too, there is an internal hint, such as in Rupert's story on a visit to the home village of the late Emperor Bokassa, that the theme of African despotism may leave some facets mostly unexplored, such as the web of benevolent relationships that has often accompanied bigmanship.[21]

And then we have, in reporting from Japan, the overarching theme of difference, even weirdness. As a kind of story line, it is perhaps to a degree a story line by default—a bit like that of chaos in Africa. When correspondents find much of Japanese political and economic life opaque, difficult to narrate or even grasp, conspicuous otherness is there to write home about again and again. The theme is in a way overdetermined, through Japanese home-grown Orientalism as well as the Occidental discovery of an alternative modernity. But as a characterization of an entire society, it cannot be anything but incomplete.

A major problem with regional story lines is obviously that they concentrate too much attention on some single set of characteristics. Generally, if there were more feature stories, there could probably be more room for diversity, and a greater density of correspondents in the landscape of news would also help (especially in Africa). By drawing on special kinds of inspiration, some favored genres in foreign correspondence to which we have already pointed also occasionally involve a centrifugal force vis-à-vis story lines. The more or less idiosyncratic personal interests of correspondents, the fact that their reporting is somehow tailored for home audiences, wherever these are, or even their humorous items may exercise a pull in other directions. Yet at other times they interact supportively with regnant story lines.

We could note, furthermore, that some correspondents—and possibly some kinds of correspondents more than others—also to some extent struggle against the story lines, trying to keep them from becoming too dominant, too simple. It is partly on such grounds that long-timers and spiralists in Jerusalem—although they might sometimes be critical of one another—often reserve their more scathing private comments for the parachutist journalists who now and then come for a flying visit to their territory.[22] One of them suggested, a bit provocatively, that the bar of the American Colony Hotel was where one might go to hear these visiting journalists swap speculations about Israeli affairs on the basis of shared ignorance. This is where the story line would be promulgated in its most stripped-down version.

In the period of relative calm when I talked to her, Cordelia Edvardson, in Jerusalem for Stockholm's *Svenska Dagbladet,* felt that more ought to be reported about the growing collaboration between Israeli and Palestinian authorities, for example over security in Hebron. She had done a portrait of an Orthodox Jewish peace activist and another of a Palestinian father whose seven-year-old son lay brain-dead in a Jerusalem hospital after having gotten in the way of an Israeli soldier's bullet (Edvardson 1997a). The father had allowed the Israeli doctors to use his son's organs for transplants, and it did not matter to him whether the beneficiaries were young Palestinians or young Israelis. A child is a child, he said. Reminiscing about his own stint as the *New York Times* correspondent in Johannesburg, Bill Keller suggested that his strategy had been one of "looking for things that don't fit comfortably." Even the apartheid period did not just involve a white minority oppressing a homogeneous black majority. He had reported on the South African Communist Party to point to a tradition of nonracial politics, and by the time Nelson Mandela emerged from jail to become perhaps the world's favorite grandfather figure, Keller had pointed out less saintly sides of the man as well.

In other words, there is some attempt to subvert to established story lines. But story lines are not likely to go away altogether—they are simply too useful to journalism, and particularly to foreign correspondence. Perhaps it is sometimes better and more realistic just to ask for more of them, taking a step or two in the direction of a broader frame for continuity in regional news work. Jim Lederman's comments on the current scene in Israel and in the Middle East, again, seemed to suggest other, at least complementary themes for more reporting, with some potential for giving coherence, bringing out a "narrative thread." One can imagine more such guiding conceptions for news beats elsewhere.

But all story lines, all themes, need not be bound to regions. The parallel with recent commentary on anthropology's gatekeeping concepts may again be instructive. When Appadurai (1988, 46) comments on these, he returns (like Richard Fardon in his discussion of ethnicity also referred to here) to the notion of polythetic comparisons. There may be resemblances between places in some ways but not in others, and the chains of resemblances can modify contrasts that might otherwise be too rigidly drawn. One can loosen the grip of the gatekeeping concepts, he suggests, by being aware that they may entail a localization of ideas brought from elsewhere and by increasing emphasis on the diversity of themes that can be pursued in one region and at the same time in many regions. In chapter 6 I will discuss some such possibilities.

Some kinds of activity just seem to involve uniquely individual enterprise and talent, although at least behind the scenes, they really depend greatly on the participation of many people, organized into complicated patterns of interaction. Scientific awards exemplify such celebration of individual achievement. Every year, for example, several committees are at work trying to make plausible the singling out of one researcher, or at most two or three, to receive a Nobel Prize, dramatizing progress in some field of scientific activity. Often it is generally understood, however, that the achievement has involved a great many people, each one climbing on another's shoulders; sometimes they achieve eventual consensus on who should be on top, but in the meantime some of the participants may engage in more or less unbecoming struggles to reach there. In his seminal book *Art Worlds* (1982), the sociologist Howard S. Becker has pointed in a related manner to the way imageries of art often emphasize individual creativity, whereas a collective structure of activities and relationships is actually altogether indispensable for artworks to come into being and become available to publics. There is a division of labor, much of it not very visible and in part quite mundane, behind the masterpiece.

The news business, too, and foreign correspondence specifically, has an inclination to foreground individual skill and success. The real stars of recent times have been television reporters like CNN's Christiane Amanpour or BBC's John Simpson—roaming around the world, from one hard-news spot to another, their faces appearing time and time again on the screen against the background of one dramatic scenery after another. Radio voices are not quite so readily identifiable; and most readers may pay little heed to who is who in print news. Ethan Bronner, *Boston Globe* Middle East correspondent, whose stories often appeared on the paper's front page, humbly reminded himself that his own parents began to pay attention to newspaper bylines only after their son became a journalist. American print journalism has its annual round of Pulitzer Prizes, though, and probably just about any country with a well-established, reasonably sizable, and independent media industry has its own counterparts to them.[1] It is not really just a matter of honor, either. For individual award winners, the receipt of an award may tangibly affect their market value, and as one foreign editor remarked, if the management seems to waver in its commitment to foreign news gathering, cutting it down is more difficult if it earns a prestigious prize now and then.

Furthermore, when they write about their craft, the correspondents are a bit preoccupied with themselves, or they portray some fairly undifferentiated communitas of parachutist peers. The preceding chapters, however, have already offered some of the evidence for a more elaborated conception of the network of activities and relationships that are routinely part of the correspondent's existence. The purpose of this chapter is to map some further aspects of the everyday social matrix of foreign news work: forms of cooperation and support, but also sources of conflict or minor irritation. The emphasis will be on more or less local life in the places where correspondents are based—on interactions with colleagues and competitors, on native helpers, on the information environment surrounding the correspondent, on relationships with the powers that be. Nevertheless, one translocal relationship is also always present in its own way, never to be ignored—that with headquarters, with the foreign desk at home, with influential and possibly opinionated editors. So we begin there.

Distant Desks

James Cameron (1969, 83–84), the great British correspondent whose reporting life (for the *Daily Express* and the *News Chronicle*) extended over decades spent largely in Asia and Africa, reminisced in his memoirs that his newspaper had been an establishment to which he "was attached by tenuous cable-links and by little else." It had given his editor pleasure "to devise for me abrupt and intricate changes of location all over the world involving logistical problems of great complexity and expense," while it gave Cameron "pleasure to accomplish them, as often as not to no greater end than our mutual gratification at the solution of a problem." He concluded that his relationship with his paper could best be compared with that of an insignificant, very remote curate to the Holy See. He accepted its authority and paid no attention whatsoever to its doctrine.

Some poetic license can be allowed here, perhaps. Yet the question of foreign correspondents' relative autonomy seems capable of forever provoking new comment. Once you are physically out of reach, operating in an environment about which your editor may recognize that he or she does not know all that much, how much more freedom do you have, compared to a journalist, say, at the metropolitan desk at home? In Hong Kong for the *Washington Post,* Keith Richburg did not mind being twelve time zones away from Washington and "a thousand miles away from the office." If he really needed to talk to someone there, he would do it close to midnight, before lunch on the American East Coast, but mostly he kept in touch with the office by overnight E-mail messages. And in Hong Kong he more or less *was* the bureau—he did not surround himself with anything much in the way of a local office. That way he was maximally free to do what he pleased and write about what he chose.

What correspondents frequently noted (as I did in chapter 2), especially if they had been in the business for a long time, was that the technological revolution had changed their contacts with the office at home a great deal. In the past it could be difficult to get hold of a telephone line, and telex machines were not particularly effective means of communicating intricate meanings quickly and securely. Arrangements might even have to be made to fly out one's materials, perhaps carried by someone who was leaving the country. Consequently, the expectations of editors for quick and frequent contacts were at a modest level. Communication satellites, satellite phones, modems, laptops, and faxes have changed much of that. And as the *Los Angeles Times* foreign editor Simon Li said with a light smile, when bosses are more in touch, workers become less independent.

This is partly a matter of scheduling—more will be said about this in chapter 7. The question, however, is not just when to deliver but also what to deliver. Here the correspondents I talked to mostly said they still had considerable freedom. Over essential hard news stories, there could be little argument. Their professionalism gave them a sharp sense of what to go for. With other stories, they felt that they more often suggested the topics. Editors at home might have questions and ideas about angles, and with a manuscript at hand, as Scott Kraft (deputy foreign editor at the *Los Angeles Times* for a while, after returning from a series of correspondent assignments) put it, they might put in a little extra effort to "make the story say what it wants to say." But the correspondents felt that the stories were still theirs. To reiterate, one could suspect that since so many correspondents have already been socialized within the organization, there is a good chance that consensus on what is a good story comes easily and that editors have a built-up trust in their emissaries abroad. The present more continuous contact with the office at home also meant that one would not often do an entire story and then find that it was not used. Unless sudden breaking news turned out to consume much of the space, the editor would usually be able to offer an opinion on what there would be room for, and how much of it. Sometimes the foreign editor would sense that the audience at home felt a bit confused by recent news and needed some more clarification. When Barton Gellman was in Jerusalem for the *Washington Post,* he was told that many readers did not quite understand how a hawk like Prime Minister Netanyahu could have agreed to the withdrawal from Hebron—would Gellman do a story going over that once more, please?

It is inevitable, however, that relationships such as those between correspondents and their editors also have their moments of strain and their elements of ambivalence. Tom Kent, the international editor at Associated Press, who had worked in both capacities, said the difference in perspective between them was as predictable as that between car drivers and pedestrians—and could shift equally quickly, as a person moved from one position to the other.[2] For a correspondent, "having a good foreign editor is as important as having the right family," said Roy Gutman of the New York *Newsday,* when I met him early in my study. When he was the paper's European correspondent (stationed in Bonn, but spending most of his time in the Balkans), Gutman earned a Pulitzer Prize on the basis of his part in the discovery of the Serb-run concentration camps in Bosnia. He worked very closely with Jeff Sommer, his editor, before they decided they were ready to go with the story. Sommer, whom I also talked to, said that he had been cautious and sent Gutman back for more detail and that although there might have been moments of tension between them, above all they respected and trusted each other. Sommer, as a former Asia correspondent, was certainly no stranger to the particular problems of foreign reporting from situations of upheaval. Generally, correspondents are likely to find some editors more laid-back and others more hands-on. At times, they find themselves dealing with a colleague at home who has previously been in their posting; although this occasionally prompts a not-so-welcome element of backseat driving, it can be helpful in working out an understanding of the situation. Ethan Bronner had a five-day visit by the editor of the *Boston Globe* just as the peace process was in high gear and Yassir Arafat was about to return to the Palestinian territories; Bronner took him on a trip to Gaza and felt the editor showed a greater personal interest in the region after that.

There may be particular reasons to grumble about how some submitted reporting has been handled. Although my partners in conversations have included nobody whose main current connection is with *Time* or *Newsweek,* there were those who on the basis of previous or vicarious involvements referred to the alienating experience of feeding one's text into a remote, seemingly industrial apparatus that would reshape it into its own characteristic unispeak. More specifically, a Johannesburg newspaper correspondent remembered the time when he had done a story on Winnie Madikizela-Mandela, arguing that in South Africa's Cinderella story, the mother of the nation was turning into the evil stepmother. But it was a weekend, and the young staff member on duty at the foreign desk at home may not have been too clear when he summarized the story over the telephone to the editor. So the editor suggested changes, and one mythical allegory was somehow transformed into another: the evil stepmother became Joan of Arc, to the correspondent's great surprise when he found out later.

Having inexperienced, not sufficiently knowledgeable staff as contact persons or engaged in editing at home could certainly cause some irritation. Some correspondents would be displeased when they discovered that their own grammatically correct sentences had been turned into something ungrammatical. They might find it more acutely troublesome when their cautious wording had been shifted into something that, at least in the territory they were dealing with, could be provocative or unacceptable, as when their "freedom fighters" become their editors' (and readers') "terrorists." One Africa correspondent said it would be helpful to have a mixture of people on the foreign desk at home, more pure editor types as well as ex-correspondents who could bring to the job more understanding of the practicalities of reporting and would not make unrealistic demands. This might relate, for one thing, to office responses to expense claims, especially involving parachutist excursions. Another correspondent on the same beat remembered the time when he had to support a colleague for several weeks after the latter had his wallet stolen in Goma, as they were heading into Zaire to witness the dissolution of the Mobutu regime. In line with proper procedure, the office at home requested an official form showing that the theft had been reported to the local police—as if, noted the two parachutists, there had been a functioning police office in Goma ready to help with such matters, at a moment of total chaos.

And then, there was another source of dissatisfaction to which correspondents often more or less resigned themselves, something I already pointed to in the introduction: a certain deficit in the response to their work. Especially after staff cutbacks, which affected some organizations more than others, they were not getting the continuous informal feedback on their efforts, and the commentary on the state of affairs in the world and in the business, that would be part of the daily round in the office at home. Those brief exchanges by E-mail or on the phone were often devoted to forward planning rather than to review and did not always involve the people whose opinions one would be most eager to seek anyway.

Local Helpers

Meanwhile, closer at hand are other collaborators of various kinds. The arrangements are indeed diverse. The term "bureau" might suggest little more than the reasonably durable presence of a staff correspondent; but then there could be a great deal more than that, as in the example of Nicolas Tatro's Jerusalem bureau of the Associated Press. That, however, is a major news agency in an area of constant news flow; most correspondents are part of much smaller local outfits. If one reports to an affluent organization such as the *New York Times* or the *Frankfurter Allgemeine,* one may have a colleague in the bureau, or even two; in a place like Jerusalem, this might also allow the bureau to include both spiralist and long-timer staff. When I was there, Serge Schmemann as well as Joel Greenberg reported for the *New York Times,* and Walter Rodgers and Jerold Kessel for CNN, in such teams. More often, probably, although alone in the place as a full-fledged news professional for the organization, the correspondent is involved in other kinds of division of labor.

John Balzar, in Nairobi for the *Los Angeles Times,* had a South African woman working with him as office assistant. A messenger seemed to spend most of his time standing in line at different offices, a driver also did various other tasks, and as the more professional shaded into the more domestic in a way characteristic of expatriate life in an African city, there were other kinds of helpers around the house. Balzar found himself drawn into dealing continuously with the ramifying kinship connections and obligations of his staff, often puzzling to him, and found that such efforts, as well as other practical aspects of doing correspondent work, took a lot of his time. Another news veteran, heading a slightly larger bureau, also hinted at a certain dissatisfaction with distracting tasks—"I could spend a day paying bills, attending to E-mail, having a leak in the roof repaired, and then think I have done something that day, which I haven't."

There are correspondents who for such reasons are wary of having much in the way of an office establishment at all and, even when their organizations could afford another setup, insist on having their office divided between their pockets and a corner of their living quarters. They want to maximize time "out there," immersed in the beat. Yet particularly the spiralists, shifting from one assignment to another within the worldwide news landscape and vulnerable (at least to begin with) in their lack of local contacts, local knowledge, and local memory, frequently find that some organized help from people more rooted in the place is of great value in mediating connections.

The relationships thus set up are often not very narrowly defined. The *Washington Post* bureau in Tokyo, Kevin Sullivan noted, had for twenty-five years had the same Japanese office manager, of great value to the series of correspondents who had been there during that time. Now there was also a new, very bright Japanese woman on the staff; she had been told that she could do some interviews and writing for the paper but must also be prepared to wash teacups. In the small offices in the Beit Agron building in Jerusalem, for example Anton La Guardia's or Ethan Bronner's, one might find a local woman employee in the outer room, functioning as receptionist but also listening more or less continuously to the radio so as not to miss breaking news, going over Israeli newspapers, and perhaps occasionally doing some writing as well. Bronner and La Guardia, good friends as well as neighbors in the Beit Agron corridor, also shared in employing a young Palestinian woman journalist on a regular basis. Although she had never lived anywhere but Jerusalem, she impressed them by speaking nearly flawless American English, picked up mostly at the movies. She had worked for Arab publications but saw little future there, so she left her résumé in the correspondent pigeonholes at Beit Agron, and that was how Bronner had found her.

It could often be a knowledgeable veteran on the local office staff who would find out for the correspondent whom to see or what to read for a story —and who would perhaps remember whether one of the correspondent's predecessors had already done a similar story, and dig it out from the files. In Jerusalem and Tokyo, with national media operating in languages in which the expatriate correspondents were often not proficient, translation can also be a significant part of the work of local employees. In the Tokyo office of the *Los Angeles Times,* Sonni Efron—who after all knew Japanese quite well— had one staff member going through dailies and weeklies for her, marking passages she thought Efron ought to read and annotating them to make them more accessible. (She knew quite precisely what Efron might find difficult.) In Jerusalem, Marjorie Miller, Efron's counterpart, had two translators in the *Los Angeles Times* office, one for Hebrew and one for Arabic. But one of these might be leaving to become a reporter at the Associated Press bureau. Doing a little bit of everything, but especially translating and interpreting, as a local employee in a sojourner correspondent's office can thus be an apprenticeship, a stepping-stone to a journalist career. In Jerusalem, correspondents who did not have translation help of their own were not necessarily cut off from the local press. There were commercial translation services, Hebrew-

English as well as Arabic-English, to which one could subscribe and which made available (when I was in Jerusalem, primarily by fax) the most important stories from the newspapers.

As in anthropology, where over the years the field workers' multipurpose local research assistants have mostly been left invisible in the resulting ethnographies (cf. Sanjek 1993), the critical importance of local helpers in foreign news work tends not to be acknowledged.[3] But in earlier chapters here, the polymorphous category of fixers has already shown up a number of times. Anton La Guardia was himself a fixer in the Philippines, as he started out on the path that would take him to the *Daily Telegraph*. The fixer that Vincent Dahlbäck of Radio Sweden hired in Kinshasa during his wait for Mobutu's fall, we remember, was a local teacher with an old car, who may have done well enough from his parajournalist interlude to set himself up as a pig farmer. The young Palestinian woman working for La Guardia and Bronner really functioned in no small part as a fixer: knowing the language as well as the territory, making introductions, serving as a guarantee to villagers and townspeople of the goodwill of those foreign journalists.

Because fixers are often picked up by correspondents on parachutist missions, for single short-term engagements, their qualifications and their conditions of work can vary greatly—if not enormously. As they ask around, perhaps at hotel desks or among taxi drivers, sometimes correspondents have very little choice, and they may find that they have made a mistake. Vincent Dahlbäck remembered the time in Rwanda when he ended up with a Hutu fixer and a Tutsi driver. They were very suspicious of each other and made a difficult reporting trip even more difficult. But in the rural areas of Africa, having a fixer was essential, he felt, if only to alleviate the shock of people who had barely seen a white person before. In a city like Nairobi, he usually did not really need one. There, however, it might be easier to find one, since even highly qualified people could be unemployed or underemployed: you could encounter academics driving taxis.

But there are also places that correspondents return to repeatedly, for one story or another, and there longer-term relationships with fixers can be set up. Dahlbäck, based in Cape Town, had one regular contact in Soweto who would insist on coming into Johannesburg to pick him up when he was there and wished to do some township story. Dahlbäck also had arranged for his Soweto fixer to take occasional Swedish visitors on a kind of alternative sightseeing tour. Over several years that had contributed to the savings this Sowetan needed to accumulate to pay bridewealth for his wife-to-be. Ethan Bronner, as Middle East correspondent, would fly into Cairo with some regularity for one reporting job or other. So he had maintained a relatively enduring link with a fixer in that city, who would get a hundred dollars a month as a retainer and an additional fee for each actual job they did together.

Being a fixer for foreign newspeople can turn out to be a durable niche for some, in certain places, and also a risky one. Anna Husarska (1998), who observed Balkan crises through the 1990s, has noted that Serb politicians during the Milosevic years would at times make threatening remarks about Serbs who served as fixers; they were accused of being traitors because they helped hostile foreign media. They could earn as much in a day as some Serbs made in a month. One young Bosnian Serb, according to Husarska, "probably had more influence on the way the world views the Republika Srpska than any other person." He had a rickety car and a command of English, was courageous and intelligent, and understood situations and behavior that to his visitors seemed utterly illogical. He would allow them to pick his brains, and he would take them to talk to his friends in the cafés. It was another fixer who heard himself named as a traitor on state television, grabbed his passport and some underwear, and next called Husarska from a neighboring country.

Colleagues, Competitors

Do foreign correspondents make up a "community"? The term obviously has a mixed tradition of strict and loose usages, but there are ways in which correspondents may form a community even on a worldwide basis. No doubt there is a certain "consciousness of kind," a sense of sharing particular types of experiences and values. In more relational terms, this is clearly not a population in which all the individuals involved are ever in face-to-face contact, or even known to one another. But there are frames of relative cohesion that, as they intersect with each other, may create an overall network of relationships.

I am reminded of an experiment with the "small world problem" that the social psychologist Stanley Milgram conducted in the 1960s.[4] Taking his point of departure from the widely shared experience of people who meet as strangers but find that they have mutual acquaintances—"small world!"—Milgram asked how many links of acquaintanceship it would actually take to connect two randomly chosen individuals within the United States. It turned out that as letters were passed along such links toward a target person, identified by name, address, and some other limited information, it would take on the average 5.5 links for one American to connect with any other American. I would not be surprised if within the transnational network of foreign correspondents, most individuals would be indirectly in touch by way of a chain of, say, 4 or 5 linkages of personal acquaintance. Nationality, organizational affiliation, and the cumulative series of postings are no doubt among the significant factors of organizing such a network. (My own strategy for minimizing the number of linkages would be to get the letter quickly to a bureau chief of one of the major news agencies, since these are represented in many correspondent sites and have well-developed local contacts.)

Within any particular locality where foreign correspondents are based, of course, there could be a more tangible community. Yet it is not necessarily the case that everybody knows and interacts closely with everybody else. In cities such as Jerusalem, Johannesburg, and Tokyo, whatever there is of a foreign correspondent community is segmented and loosely structured along various lines. Definitely there is a division along lines of nationality, so that correspondents representing media organizations in the same country are likely to know each other or at least know of each other. They may follow each other's reporting to some degree and run into each other at gatherings at the country's embassy. How much they actually cultivate relationships with each other, in pairs or in small groups, depends partly on the relationship between their organizations. If they write for newspapers in the same city or region, the relationship may be rather ambivalent, or even one of avoidance. Colleagues become competitors. But there is certainly also a question of personal compatibility and wanting to be in touch. In Johannesburg, Dean Murphy would occasionally have lunch with Terry Leonard or with Suzanne Daley, and now and then their families might go for a swim together. As a relative newcomer, Murphy also sought his colleagues' advice about practicalities—when he went on a reporting trip to Zimbabwe the first time, for example, it was good to have someone to ask about visa requirements, and how the Harare airport worked, and where was the best place to rent a car. In Jerusalem, apart from running into them on various other occasions, Serge Schmemann of the *New York Times* might telephone his two rather younger bureau chief counterparts at the *Washington Post* and the *Los Angeles Times,* Barton Gellman and Marjorie Miller, once in a while, but that was usually for sociable exchanges—". . . and how are the kids?" And he made the point that despite the difference in age and personal background, and without discussing work very much, they would often still do similar stories. Some suspicious readers might see a conspiracy in this, he said, or ideology; but it was really just a matter of professional logic leading to parallel invention.

Physical proximity also matters. Many foreign correspondents operate out of their homes, which may be somewhat scattered over a city and its surroundings, but as we have seen, in some places a number of them have their offices concentrated at the same address: Beit Agron in Jerusalem; those two buildings in Richmond, the Johannesburg suburb; the eighth-floor corridor of the *Yomiuri Shimbun* building in Tokyo. So on the basis of sheer neigh-borliness, one might get acquainted, stop by to gossip, and have a cup of cof-fee. Anton La Guardia said he had come to know the *Le Monde* correspon-dent, who was also in Beit Agron, but not really the *Libération* man, who was elsewhere. (And again, as we saw, those who only came in to check their pi-geonholes at the Beit Agron for messages would not rub shoulders with col-leagues there so much after most such messages started to be sent by E-mail.)

Correspondents covering the same beat might also be familiar with each other by way of their reporting, but this would not always work out sym-metrically. Through their products, those who represent major organizations, publishing or broadcasting in the world languages (mostly English), are more visible, or audible, than others. One might also recognize, and develop at least a nodding acquaintance with, the people regularly showing up to cover the same events. And even if one knows little or nothing about their skills as reporters or news analysts, since their work appears only in a language one does not know or in some news market far from one's own, one may develop a respect for their ability as they ask questions in news conferences, or find them funny or a bit obnoxious.

Generally speaking, many correspondents would say that in cities where there were few of them, and especially when they were living under tough conditions and perhaps in an adversarial or at least closely guarded relation-ship with the host society and especially its government, they were likely to stick together more closely. This was the case rather more in South Africa during the apartheid period, in the Soviet Union before glasnost and pere-stroika, in China also in the past more than the present, and in Nairobi re-cently. Göran Leijonhufvud of *Dagens Nyheter,* one of the first generation of Beijing correspondents in the early 1970s, remembers that there were about thirty of them altogether at the time, all living in a foreign quarter sur-rounded by walls, where Chinese people were allowed only by special per-mission. They were not allowed to make contacts on their own, and their ac-cess to Chinese publications was also restricted (two dailies and a magazine), so they had each other to turn to, for company and to practice the local coun-terpart of Kremlinology. Just after Leijonhufvud arrived, a major annual mil-itary parade had suddenly been canceled, and they all wondered why—not accepting the official claim that it was just a matter of saving money. Some-how word came out that Lin Piao, minister of defense and Mao Tse-tung's likely successor, was in disfavor; and a Yugoslav correspondent, who had a re-fined habit of interpreting signs in a totalitarian society, wondered what would happen to the "Little Red Book" that Lin Piao had compiled. Leijonhufvud went out to look for it in the shops—and indeed, it was no longer on the shelves.

In contrast, where life is comfortable, and correspondents do not feel at all beleaguered, they tend to see less of each other except when business brings them together. Those plum assignments in major western European capitals, or Washington or New York, are more like that. Jerusalem is also held to have some of the characteristics in question, and besides, the long-timers in that city and in Tokyo who perhaps identify less intensively with their correspondent work and who are more assimilated into local circles would also be little concerned with any such entity as a foreign correspondent community.

One kind of tie with colleagues is perhaps especially important. When correspondents go on a reporting trip, especially out of town, they often prefer to go with another correspondent. This is practical, because they can split the cost of a driver and of a fixer-interpreter if one is needed. Sometimes when going to difficult reporting sites, one may feel safer traveling with a partner. Talking to different people and noticing different things, the two can pool information. And, as Anton La Guardia pointed out, "when one gets bored, the other can keep mental energy flowing."

Such partnerships are usually not exclusive. In preparing for a trip, a correspondent asks around among a few colleagues she or he enjoys going with. When I first met Marjorie Miller, she had recently been to Hebron with Barton Gellman, who a few weeks later went to Amman with Ethan Bronner, who would often travel on the West Bank with Anton La Guardia. Partners may be from the same country, provided no direct competition is involved, but they are not always. Leif Norrman remembered that in the period when more correspondents were stationed in Harare, he would call from Cape Town to a Canadian colleague there, and they would agree on teaming up somewhere in Africa, often on some parachutist mission. Personal chemistry certainly matters in these partnerships, but also a sense of equality of knowledge and resources and similarity of working style. One long-timer correspondent in Jerusalem, with decades of professional experience and extensive knowledge of Israel, said she was not enthusiastic about traveling with newcomers, because she would be exploited, turned into an instructor and a "source" rather than a colleague. A Jerusalem stringer suggested another constraint on what would be feasible partnering. Sometimes one of his good long-time friends, a woman with a stable tie to a European newspaper, would ask if he wanted to come along for a story. He had no reason to doubt that she would be able to get it into her paper. But for him the market was more uncertain, and so he would regretfully decline going for a story he could not be sure to sell.

This sort of temporary partnership mostly involves print journalists, but print and radio people might also be able to work well enough together. TV is different. Television crews are often so large that there is little room for any teaming up among them or with them; but when they charter an entire plane to take them to some out-of-the-way spot, it may be possible for a few print correspondents to catch a ride with them. Generally, however, print journalists are happiest when there are no TV people around. As in Kinshasa in 1997, TV crews have a way of drawing too much attention, getting themselves into trouble and also disturbing the work setting for everybody else. To repeat, you can be less conspicuous with just a notebook and pencil. This incompatibility between television and other media may decrease as new technology allows smaller reporting teams.

Television, however, can entail other kinds of cooperation. Marika Griehsel of Swedish TV would sometimes team up somewhat indirectly with other television journalists, because her photographer-husband Simon Stanford would also do the camera work for them. This could involve more extended reporting trips as well; normally such jobs would be initiated by Griehsel and Stanford. She sometimes found that visiting Swedish colleagues were a little surprised by the amount of cooperation among media organizations; they were inclined to think of stories as "exclusives." But she pointed out that such cooperation was usually between organizations that were not in the same home market.

For print reporters, too, traveling with a photographer is another kind of partnership (but rarely, like Yuji Yoshikata, Africa correspondent for the *Yomiuri Shimbun,* they do their own photography). Those who are in a larger bureau may have photographers of their own. Especially for hard news, though, their offices at home may be just as likely to use pictures from some major agency. For other work, notably feature stories, they may link up with some local photographer who is in business for himself. There are times when correspondents become acquainted by way of a photographer whose services they share. And sometimes, if the photographer is more locally rooted than the correspondent, the line between photography and fixing, and even interpreting, might get a little blurred. Suzanne Daley was very pleased to have a photographer of Portuguese background and long African experience and developed social skills with her on her frequent reporting trips to Angola, especially.

Members of the Club

One institution that certainly plays a part in turning the foreign correspondents in a place into something like a community is the foreign correspondents' club, existing under that or some similar name. There is one in most
places with any sizable number of resident correspondents, although the
clubs' scales of operation differ considerably. The most famous one is probably the Foreign Correspondents Club in Hong Kong—it is depicted primarily as a watering hole in the John Le Carré novel *The Honourable Schoolboy.*[5]

At the time of Le Carré's description of the Hong Kong club, it was on
the waterfront, in a building that has since then been torn down. The current
location is a climb up the Hong Kong hillside, in the old thick-walled Ice
House from the colonial days, white and brick with "FCC" in large black letters over the entrance door. Its facilities are well developed, but what is most
important is obviously still the bar, immediately to the left when one enters
the building, with the counter as an island in the middle. All the correspondents I met with during my brief visit to Hong Kong suggested we should see
each other there. The walls are adorned with photos of old Hong Kong and
with memorable newspaper front pages relating to the city.

Keith Richburg, who was president of the club at the time, said he had
taken it on because "someone had to do it"—and besides, it was the period
of the transition from British to Chinese sovereignty over the territory, and it
had seemed better not to have a Brit heading the club right then. He pointed
to the visiting speakers' program as an especially strong and useful aspect of
club activities to the correspondent members: among the visitors there had
recently been local officials, dissidents from the People's Republic of China,
a Philippines presidential candidate, a prominent banker discussing the Indonesian economy, and academic Asia specialists passing through . . . but also
a Hong Kong sexologist, on the Valentine's Day program.

Not all of the members of the Hong Kong FCC were now working foreign correspondents. With its central location, its bar and restaurant, and
generally a sophisticated, worldly ambience, it was attractive to many others
as well, expatriates as well as Hong Kong businesspeople and professionals.
And so, on special recommendation, these were also allowed to join the club
in special membership categories—paying considerably higher fees than the
actual correspondents, who also made sure they would still be in control of
the club. Without these other members, however, the organization would
hardly be viable and able to afford its facilities.

The FCC in Hong Kong came into being when Mao Tse-tung's revolutionary army was gaining control over mainland China and it became clear

that for the foreseeable future, Hong Kong would be the main site for China watching. The Foreign Correspondents Club of Japan (FCCJ) had been founded just a little earlier, in the aftermath of World War II, as correspondents began to arrive soon after Japan's surrender.[6] I visited its premises on the upper two floors of an office tower in central Tokyo. The bar and restaurant on the twentieth floor are popular meeting places for correspondents, but also for a number of associate members—like its Hong Kong counterpart, the club attracts a wider set of people, in this instance many from Japanese media and advertising industries. But again, the regular members, the foreign correspondents themselves, remain in control.

One of the facts of journalist life in Tokyo that, over the years, has made foreign correspondents feel a bit excluded is the institution of kisha clubs, groupings of reporters assigned for an extended time to cover government ministries and other major organizations.[7] The Japanese members of kisha clubs are treated favorably by the offices to which they are attached, and in turn they develop a loyalty to them, getting together among themselves to treat news originating on their beat with a certain delicacy—the kisha clubs, in other words, have been a part of what is often seen, by outside commentators and others, as a great machinery of national consensus. In the past, foreign correspondents have been excluded from the kisha clubs. Now, although this is no longer strictly the case, foreigners who are not fluent Japanese speakers and cannot in any case devote so much time to any single Japanese news setting are still handicapped in the places where kisha clubs are active. But in a way, the FCCJ is something like a kisha club of the foreign correspondents' own. And a number of club facilities are particularly useful to them.[8] There is a library that offers access to the Internet and data banks; radio reporting facilities; and a dozen workrooms, which some members use on a regular basis, as well as books and current newspapers. And like the club in Hong Kong, this one schedules visiting speakers for special luncheon events: leading Japanese politicians and bureaucrats as well as other prominent local people from business, academia, and other circles, and visitors from outside Japan. On these occasions, it is the foreign correspondents who have privileged access to news and commentary, although unlike the members of the Japanese kisha clubs, they are not very likely to huddle together afterward to agree on a shared story. It was the merciless questioning of Prime Minister Kakuei Tanaka concerning his finances at an FCCJ luncheon in 1974 that soon after led to his downfall.

The FCCJ takes itself to be the largest organization of its kind anywhere in the world. Tokyo, of course, is a world city, with a great many foreign media representatives. A veteran member also points out that the relative inaccessibility of Japanese society to foreigners makes an organization of this kind more of a haven than its counterparts in many other places, embedded in more familiar environments, would be. Some members are said to spend virtually all day at the FCCJ.

Nevertheless, the club does not count all of Tokyo's foreign correspondents as members or active users. Some of those whose postings to Japan are not long, and who represent large and powerful media corporations, simply have little use for it. The young, busy staffers of the financial wire services hardly have time for the club, and their employers do not pay their membership fees, as the more established general news organizations are likely to do. Stringers also often have to pay for the FCCJ membership out of their own pockets, and so a number of them stay away.

In Jerusalem and Johannesburg, doing without eating, drinking, and meeting facilities of their own, the foreign correspondent organizations are not equally prominent in local life but operate more strictly as professional entities; they also have some of their membership in Tel Aviv and Cape Town, respectively. When I was in Jerusalem, Nicolas Tatro, bureau chief of the Associated Press, chaired the Foreign Press Association. He acknowledged that it had had its ups and downs. What it did, he said, would depend in large part on the tastes and the degree of commitment of its elected board members. Here, too, there would be meetings with visiting speakers, as recently when the American ambassador came to discuss the current state of the peace process. But the association also functioned as a kind of ombudsman for the foreign correspondents, making sure that they were not ignored in press conferences and on tours of high Israeli officials. Occasionally, too, it had to complain when Israeli police or military personnel tangled with its members. Werner Vogt of the *Neue Zürcher Zeitung* had recently taken over the presidency of the Foreign Correspondent Association in Johannesburg from Alec Russell of the *Daily Telegraph* when I met him. He did not see it as a very close-knit group, but it offered some new contacts, and the visiting speakers, from politics, business, and local think tanks, could be useful. (Mandela and Mbeki had both been there.) Moreover, as in Jerusalem, if remonstrations had to be made with government offices, for example, they were more effective if the correspondents could speak with one voice through their association. And for events where only few newspeople would be allowed—such as when President Clinton came to South Africa, a few weeks later—it was important to argue that some of the resident foreign correspondents must be among those invited.

Secondhand News

When Bill Keller, as foreign editor of the *New York Times*, said he liked to have correspondents with "a taste for street reporting," he pointed out that in many sites they would not find available the kinds of materials they would have at home, such as opinion polls. So when Deng Hsiao-Ping had died, just before my conversation with Keller, the Beijing correspondent had to be ready to go out and interview twenty people in a day about how they felt.

Some assignments call for more of this than others. Africa correspondents at times mention that they find it exhilarating to be "barefoot journalists," really involved in the creation of new knowledge from raw reality. But no foreign beats are without their own storehouses of more or less ready-made, recorded or textualized information and their machinery for producing and assembling it, there for correspondents to draw on, or perhaps disregard at their peril. And because they are responsible for covering such large areas, correspondents had better be prepared to work much more than those at home with secondhand materials, with retrieving and recycling.

I have not asked correspondents systematically about their reading habits with regard to books and periodicals, but I gained some sense of them on the basis of what came up in conversations and what I could see lying around on desks or shelves in their workplaces. I could glimpse piles of newsmagazines like *Time, Newsweek,* and the *Economist,* as well as the *International Herald Tribune* and magazines directly relating to the region they were in, which would help one stay abreast of current events and informed comment on them: *Jerusalem Report, New African, Far Eastern Economic Review.* About book reading it would be difficult to generalize: some correspondents obviously were bookworms more than others (and for not a few, writing reviews of books about the region for their papers at home was more or less a part of the assignment). Some read fairly widely in the academic literature of the region. On Ethan Bronner's shelf in his Beit Agron office, I spotted S. N. Eisenstadt's *Transformation of Israeli Society* as well as Smadar Lavie's *Poetics of Military Occupation.* Many kept their eye on biographies. Among the correspondents in Johannesburg and Cape Town, probably few had not read Nelson Mandela's *Long Walk to Freedom.* And as I noted in the previous chapter, several mentioned Patti Waldmeir's *Anatomy of a Miracle*—Waldmeir was president of the foreign correspondents' association in Johannesburg when she was there. They had not missed Keith Richburg's *Out of America,* either. (Some of those who had been around in Africa for some time remembered meeting Richburg in the early 1990s, when they were all reporting from Somalia or Rwanda.)

Although several past Jerusalem correspondents had written books looking back at their experiences, the one that remained in most correspondents' awareness tended to be Thomas Friedman's *From Beirut to Jerusalem*. No single book stood out as having captured the Tokyo correspondents' attention, although several had at one time or another read an anthropological classic—Ruth Benedict's *Chrysanthemum and the Sword*. Generally, correspondents seem inclined to favor books by other journalists and would often know if their colleagues in the organization had something going on; Sheryl WuDunn, in Tokyo, knew that her *New York Times* colleague Thomas Friedman was just finishing a book on globalization (*The Lexus and the Olive Tree*, 1999). We will come back to that.

Some reading had to be more of a bread-and-butter nature. Africa correspondents mentioned continent-wide reference books, updated annually or so—it was, they admitted, difficult to keep track of the histories, politics, economies, and who's who of the several dozen countries included in their assignment. And certainly much attention to texts and images had to be primarily of the moment, not looking back much, and directed toward the next story.

This worked out in different ways in different places. Sonni Efron compared her two most recent postings: in Moscow she could be sure what was the story of the day, but the information she needed for it was often unavailable or incorrect, whereas in Tokyo it was the other way around. Most correspondents would agree that Jerusalem was an extremely information-saturated beat and that this had a major impact on the correspondents' work. You would not have to seek the information—it would come to you. Rather, you must filter it. (We may remember, too, from chapter 2, Barton Gellman describing Israel as an "echo chamber.") Marjorie Miller was struck by the fact that even high government officials would be so eager to be accessible that you would find their home phone numbers listed in directories. One would get materials from the Palestinian Authority, from human rights organizations, from groups representing Jewish settlers in the Occupied Territories, and from a variety of other organizations. Your own friends and tipsters let you know what they knew—and here it mattered that Israel has a high density of both public telephones and personal cell phones. Nothing important would happen in Israel or the Occupied Territories, said Serge Schmemann, that he would not hear of within ten minutes—by telephone, on the beeper connecting him with the Government Press Office, or on the radio. When the two helicopters crashed into one another close to the Lebanese battle zone, his photographer was in her car nearby and actually saw the crash in the air. Of course she was on the telephone with him almost immediately. When two rather primitively constructed bombs went off in a Tel Aviv bus station, he had seven calls about the event in five minutes. In addition to himself and a colleague and staff in the Jerusalem office, he had stringers in Tel Aviv, the West Bank, and Gaza, but there were also a number of other people who kept in touch.

Filtering must involve, for one thing, having an eye for what local news should be turned into international news. In 1997 the "Bar-On affair" was an example of a story that was big in Israel but might or might not turn out to be of international significance. An Israeli television channel accused the government of having attempted a shady deal: in exchange for supporting the Hebron agreement, which had resulted in partial Israeli withdrawal from that city, the Shas party, a minor partner in the governing coalition, would get a questionably qualified jurist-politician (after whom the affair was named) appointed attorney general. And from that position, it was alleged, he in turn could then arrange a lenient treatment of a leading Shas politician accused of corruption.

Was this something that would interest the world? Despite the large headlines in the Israeli press, many of the correspondents were not entirely sure. Yet there was the possibility that the governing coalition would fall apart as a result, and if that occurred, it would surely be international news. So apparently most of them decided to play it safe, reporting on the affair at least briefly at this early stage. (And it did indeed become major news some months later, even though the cabinet did not fall.)

Sometimes, in Jerusalem, the massive information flow also meant that you had better not try to be out there as a street reporter. The Saturday night when Yitzhak Rabin was murdered in Tel Aviv, Anton La Guardia, working alone for the *Daily Telegraph,* at first saw the question of going down to the other city or staying in as a dilemma. How much would be gained by being on the spot, and how much would be lost in travel time and by not being fully in touch with the news and commentary that through many channels would reach his Jerusalem office? He decided quickly that he would not gain much by heading for Tel Aviv. In a day or so, somebody could fly in from London to assist him in the continued coverage, but the nearest deadline, for the Monday paper (the *Daily Telegraph* does not publish on Sundays), he would have to handle alone. So on Sunday he was in his office continuously from 7:00 A.M. until midnight. Writing from the top of his head to a large extent, drawing on stored-up knowledge, while at the same time following local newscasts, he did seven stories, which would take up almost three pages in the following day's paper.

Local media could be major sources for such somewhat derivative

reporting—we noted before that correspondents and their helpers in Jerusalem offices would listen continuously to radio news bulletins and that
they, like their Tokyo counterparts, would go through newspapers and have
them selectively translated as well. When Serge Schmemann came across
something particularly interesting, he might make a lunch appointment with
the writer and occasionally even suggest that the latter do something for the
New York Times Op Ed page, to bring a new voice in. The Jerusalem correspondents were generally quite favorably impressed with the three main Israeli dailies, *Haaretz, Maariv,* and *Yediot Aharonot,* and sometimes had their
own acquaintances among those papers' journalists and columnists whom
they would call on for background commentary or quotable statements. In
Johannesburg and Tokyo, correspondents found the local papers generally
rather dull, except for the weekly *Mail and Guardian* in South Africa, which
many mentioned respectfully for its commentary as well as its investigative
journalism.[9]

In Israel and the Occupied Territories, there are not only the local television programs to consider. If CNN, BBC World, or Sky TV are also on a
news site very quickly with a live broadcast, particularly print correspondents
might feel it less necessary to be there in person as well. They can report on
what they witness, even if they see it on a screen. There is also the possibility
of using news agency materials, since the agencies, with their large staffs and
their obligation to report quickly by way of their head offices to the world,
will often have the news first.

There is a logic depending on technologies and personnel resources in
this, but the resulting division of labor is not entirely clear-cut; it generates its
own strains and problems of professional morality, as well as instances when
choices have to be made. Most of the newspapers in western Europe and
North America that have a serious commitment to foreign coverage will use
the news agencies for some of their materials, for example in those ubiquitous columns titled something like "News in Brief," a kind of buffer device to
briefly cover events that are not deemed to deserve more space. Some major
news may also be handled by using the agency reports. But what will the editors at home do when they also have their own correspondents in the places
from which news agency materials are coming in?

Marjorie Miller remembered how she and the *Los Angeles Times* foreign desk had agreed, not long before I talked to her, that the paper might as
well use the available agency report on those curious bus station bombings in
Tel Aviv (the ones that Serge Schmemann also referred to above). Then her
paper's managing editor was confronted in a public appearance before a Jewish group in Los Angeles, with angry readers who felt that the paper had thus

played down what they saw as another instance of Palestinian terrorism. Like many other observers, Miller was actually not so sure about this. The bombs had been of a very primitive type, not anything like what one expected by that time from the Palestinian groups involved in bombings; and in that neighborhood in Tel Aviv, one might alternatively guess that the bombings were part of local underworld violence. All in all, it did not seem to require an effort from one of the paper's own writers.

Some media organizations are more inclined than others to use their staff correspondents with their personal bylines for as much coverage as possible, even if they simply parallel the agency reports, and sometimes even for those "News in Brief" items. British papers seem more likely than American papers to do so. Jörg Bremer, in Jerusalem for the *Frankfurter Allgemeine,* thought that his paper also preferred to demonstrate how self-sufficient it was through its own well-developed, prestigious correspondent network. There could be staff correspondents and stringers as well who would be anxious to show their value to the foreign desks and would take it upon themselves to get their own versions into the paper rather than that of the agency. Perhaps they could add a twist of some sort, an observation or some background, a little context and color that could make it a "value added" alternative. Other organizations feel that their own correspondents should be used first of all for major stories, allowing more reporting in depth and more analysis. Jeff Sommer, international editor of the New York *Newsday,* thought he should use his handful of correspondents to work on stories that the more powerful and well-endowed competitors were not doing—with a baseball metaphor, "Hit them where they ain't." This was a successful strategy, resulting in several Pulitzer Prizes. With rather few foreign correspondents on its own staff, the *Boston Globe* must also rely largely on agency reporting, but someone like Ethan Bronner would therefore be expected to complement it with high-profile stories specific to the paper. Bronner thought he was privileged compared to some of his local British colleagues, who had to handle more of the continuously event-driven reporting from Jerusalem themselves.

Being in an information-saturated environment could also be seen as a temptation to cut corners. The first professional impulse of the journalist, after all, should be to be out there as an eyewitness, doing firsthand reporting—and so correspondent lore has more than a few anecdotes about newspeople who really inserted themselves into the news chain rather later than they had laid claim to. Martin Bell (1996, 162), the BBC television correspondent, vividly remembers a *Daily Mirror* reporter who covered the 1960s Nigerian civil war from the bar of the best hotel in Lagos, to which other correspondents would regularly return from the battlefronts: "He was generous and they were thirsty, and he had a knack of filing their stories even before they did. Such was his way with words and his economy with the truth that by the time he had finished it was as if *he* had dodged the Biafran bullets, and *he* had swum the crocodile-infested rivers. (In the coinage of Fleet Street in those days all rivers were crocodile-infested.)" And in her brief memoir of growing up with a foreign correspondent father who was mostly a parachutist (killed in action in El Salvador), Anna Blundy (1998, 49) remembers, from a Jerusalem visit when she was twelve, spending most of her days at the swimming pool of the American Colony Hotel with "the tabloid hacks" while her father was out doing his stories. When her companions, listening to the BBC World Service, heard anything newsworthy, they would rush upstairs to file copy. One minimal construction of a story sent home, quipped another Jerusalem correspondent (whose own taste certainly ran more toward street reporting), would be "I was there . . . blah, blah . . . fear and loathing . . . blah, blah (please add agency materials)."

Perhaps like stories of witchcraft and cannibalism in some societies, these are scandalous tales of the kind of immorality taking place in "the next village," recurrently talked about but not really occurring all that frequently. What sometimes irritate correspondents more than such stories, true or not, are the times when the compact information flow complicates their relationships of trust with editors at home. Although they do not necessarily spend much time looking sideways at what others in the same place are doing, they may keep an eye on the work of the immediate competition, because they know that their editors are doing likewise. Moreover, well-equipped foreign desks usually have access not only to their own correspondents' reporting but also to what two, three, or four news agencies distribute from the same place; and nowadays, when one visits the editors in charge, one is likely to find that they have both CNN and BBC World on continuously as well, on separate monitors. That could all be helpful, in their quick telephone or E-mail exchanges with their own correspondents over what needs to be done. A correspondent may be a bit upset, however, when it seems that their editor will not accept that a story is worthwhile until it has also been received from one of these standard news services. In chapter 2, we heard Yuji Yoshikata comment that Japanese editors might alter their own correspondents' stories if they differed from agency materials. Along similar lines, it can happen that when one major agency plays up a news item that the staff correspondent has disregarded, the latter has some explaining to do. One long-timer correspondent in Jerusalem remembered an occasion when an Associated Press newcomer, rather gung-ho about the importance of his own work, reported somewhat breathlessly and at length about a Palestinian Authority event in a West Bank town—and then as the story spread over the world, this veteran had to convince his editor that it had really been a quite routine affair.

Friends or Adversaries in High Places

Few relationships can be as critically important to foreign correspondents as those with the government in the place where they are stationed—although, depending on what government it is, the everyday conduct of the reporting business may be affected very little.[10] Frequently these relationships are entirely benign. In Tokyo, especially stringers, who find the membership fees of the Foreign Correspondents Club a bit steep, find a functional substitute in the government-supported Foreign Press Center, which offers a reference library, access to a national news service, and a helpful staff. But the Foreign Press Center caters primarily to the needs of more temporary visitors, by producing handouts on varied topics and by setting up appointments. Staff members at the Government Press Office in Jerusalem, on the second floor of Beit Agron, also describe themselves as first of all "facilitators." For touring journalists, for example those accompanying a visiting head of state or government, they may turn into something like a specialized travel agency, arranging itineraries and encounters; and it helps that the staff has members of varied national backgrounds, so that journalists from India can be met by someone who grew up in Bombay or Russian journalists by a Russian immigrant. The media stars flying into Jerusalem for a brief reporting fling will also show their credentials at the Government Press office—"so we see them here." In contrast, said one official a little ruefully, among the correspondents who are in Jerusalem for a longer assignment, there is sometimes the idea that "you get your accreditation and run like hell!"

Even at the best of times, there is likely to be some ambivalence built into this kind of relationship. In Israel, one does not even have to be accredited and obtain a government press card, although the people at the Government Press Office would suggest that it is sometimes useful for access and for staying out of trouble, for instance if one is taking photographs in the Old City of Jerusalem. And the news service is useful: bulletins are sent out by E-mail, and correspondents may be alerted to breaking news by way of a rented beeper and a press office access code. (Even the Foreign Press Association at times finds it practical to relay messages to members by way of the press office channels.) Some correspondents who have been long in Jerusalem recall useful bus tours organized by the Government Press Office, and veterans in the Beit Agron corridors can also remember especially fondly an earlier head of the office who loved to share political gossip with them and who, it seemed, "couldn't tell a lie."

Yet a government office must be expected to push the government point of view, especially in circumstances of conflict; so Jerusalem correspondents working continuously under such circumstances tended to feel that presentations from the Government Press Office—or those other wings of government that also had their own spokespersons—were part of that massive information flow that it was their duty to filter. In order to maintain one's autonomy, then, one must keep a certain distance, if only a friendly distance, from the people at the press office.

In other places the relationship could be more strained, or even directly hostile. Asia correspondents, again, suspected that the rather authoritarian government of Singapore would be most tolerant of having them as residents there if they did not report much on Singapore itself—if they did, they or their organizations might be harassed in big or small ways. In Johannesburg, I asked George Alagiah of the BBC about Kenya, because I remembered a rather tense interview he had done with President arap Moi. Yes, Alagiah said, at a political rally arap Moi had pointed to the BBC crew and warned them, and the crowd had started shouting at them. In South Africa itself, the foreign correspondents seemed at the time to have little difficulty with the government, even as the latter was becoming more explicitly critical of the press at home. Some high ANC officials apparently remembered that the foreign press had been a useful ally in the struggle against apartheid. On the whole, though, the correspondents in Johannesburg felt that the government now paid little attention to them and that its various offices were sometimes rather awkward and neglectful in responding to correspondent approaches.

Things were certainly very different in the apartheid era, for some of the organizations that were represented in South Africa then (instead of basing their Africa watchers elsewhere). Joseph Lelyveld, who later rose to become executive editor of the *New York Times,* describes in his book on his South African reporting experience, *Move Your Shadow* (1985), how he was declared persona non grata at one time, so that his paper for a time closed its bureau in the country, and how he later returned for another stint. At the *Los Angeles Times,* Michael Parks, another former Johannesburg correspondent who became executive editor, could remember how the government, beleaguered and scared when he was in the country in the 1980s, had arrested him on several occasions, had tried to have him deported, and had complained to his management at home that he was a Communist agent and a member of a "cell." But the paper fought back. He was under continuous surveillance—

officials later explained that they were concerned that "something could happen to him"—and the South African police had three large cardboard boxes of materials about him. Indeed, he had visited the ANC office in Zambia several times, but mostly he had to limit his travel outside South Africa, because there was a strong risk that he would be denied reentry into the country. Serge Schmemann, also in South Africa during some of this period, acknowledged when I talked with him about it in Jerusalem that "Michael Parks was the one they really wanted to get rid of." When Scott Kraft went in to succeed Parks in Johannesburg, he found that the entire *Los Angeles Times* office had been bugged.

Parks had begun his correspondent career with the *Baltimore Sun* in Saigon in 1970 and had then been based for various periods—apart from his work in Johannesburg—in Cairo, Hong Kong, Beijing, Jerusalem, and Moscow (twice, in the 1970s and again in the late 1980s). He thought Moscow in the 1970s was not as difficult as Johannesburg in the decade after. But the Soviet government of the Brezhnev era did not want the society contaminated by foreigners, and correspondents would sometimes find themselves pushed around by thugs.[11] Parks himself suspected that once, on a visit to Tbilisi in Georgia, he had been drugged. Then in the 1980s, during the perestroika, the Moscow reporting scene changed dramatically—and Parks felt that Bill Keller, *New York Times* correspondent there at the time and soon a Pulitzer Prize winner, had played a major role in the renewal of Soviet coverage under the new circumstances.

Even in less dramatic times, correspondents may find out that someone in a government office is watching what they do. Göran Leijonhufvud, in Beijing, might run into an official at some public reception who would point out that a story on Tibet had not "contributed to understanding and friendship between the peoples"—although in this case, he believed that the most provocative formulation had been in a headline or in a picture caption over which he had not had any control. The Chinese government still had a number of restrictions on correspondent movements in force on paper, although they did not seem to be applied—except perhaps when an excuse was needed for expelling someone. It would still also try to steer the choice of stories, but such attempts were not particularly successful. Leijonhufvud relied in no small part on serendipity. When he was encouraged to visit a commercial mushroom grower as an example of a successful entrepreneur and found five small children lined up in the living room, he thought it was evidence that the official one-child policy was not entirely successful.

Changes in communication technology clearly play a part in a government's capacity to control news. Another veteran of Asia reporting, Bruce

Dunning of CBS News, could remember from the hectic days in Beijing leading up to the Tiananmen Square massacre how his bureau heard through the
local grapevine of a skirmish in a town just south of the capital and how he
sent his staff out to report on it. Then within fifteen minutes after the local rumor reached him, the CBS office in New York called him about it, following
a tip-off from a Chinese student in Texas who had received a fax message
from someone at home. With Internet and cell phones now added to the information armory, Dunning concluded, China could never be closed again.

In Jerusalem, once more, the Government Press Office usually finds out
from the country's embassies abroad how Israeli, or somehow Israel-related,
events are reported. The office representatives say that they take a tolerant
view: people are entitled to their opinions. But they are concerned with
"fair" coverage, so if the coverage by some Jerusalem correspondent seems
anti-Israeli, there might be a telephone call to point out which other voices
ought to have been heard. Occasionally, it is also true, something more than
impartiality (however defined) may be at issue. At one extreme, the official
Israeli reaction to items of foreign reporting may still involve censorship—as
I noted in chapter 2, Beit Agron, the press building, also houses the office of
the military censor. Accredited foreign correspondents sign a statement that
they are aware of censorship restrictions, but on the whole, these now play a
limited role in correspondents' work—partly because military aspects of Israel's relationships to Arab countries are no longer quite as prominent as
they once were, and partly because here as well, new communication technology makes effective censorship more or less impossible.[12] In the late
1990s, when a new director of the Israeli secret service was appointed, his
name was made public; that had never happened before. When Barton Gellman reported on this in the *Washington Post,* he also mentioned the name of
the previous director—but that appointment had never been announced. For
his infraction, he was called to a hearing, at which Gellman pointed out that
the name had been mentioned on Internet Web sites as well as in graffiti on
local house walls and must surely be known to Palestinians. He was told that
a second meeting would be held to determine his punishment, but he never
heard anything more about it.

Regarding such incidents generally, one long-timer in Jerusalem commented that it might be all right for an organization with expatriate correspondents to break censorship rules, since even if such a correspondent is
expelled, it is easy to send in a replacement. A resident stringer, in contrast,
could hardly afford to risk expulsion. Someone at the Government Press
Office suggested that Israeli journalists would sometimes plant a news item
with a foreign colleague and then cite it as reported elsewhere in the world—

a way of circumventing censorship rules. The triangular relationship between government, local media, and foreign correspondents has had its uses elsewhere as well. From his reporting trips to distant Soviet provinces for the *Washington Post* during the early perestroika, David Remnick remembered that local journalists had often been wonderful sources. They knew all about the skeletons in nearby closets but could not yet mention them in their own media.

Talking Back

What about readers, listeners, and viewers? Fergal Keane (1996, 53), the BBC correspondent, had just crossed the border from Uganda into Rwanda with his crew and came upon a group of rebel soldiers, automatic rifles at the ready. Most of them looked like teenagers. Keane was not entirely at ease. One of the soldiers introduced himself as the "escort" of the crew. "I listen to the BBC all the time . . . *Newshour* on the World Service . . . dah dah dah." Those first notes of the program's signature jingle were familiar to BBC listeners across the world.

To a large extent, the media are engaged in asymmetrical, even one way communication. Audiences answer back in rather limited ways—remaining faithful to a paper or switching to another channel—and much of the time in no noticeable way at all. But we should consider some of the routine or not-so-routine ways in which they can show up and make themselves more tangible parts of the foreign correspondents' habitat.

Hans-Henrik Landsvig, Jerusalem correspondent for the Danish paper *Berlingske Tidende,* mentioned to me that in one small but concrete way he had noticed that media communication is not all a one-way flow. In the period when the correspondents were regularly watching Hebron, before the agreement about a partial Israeli withdrawal was signed, he and a couple of other foreign journalists were sitting at what they had come to think of as "Riot Square." It was afternoon, the schools were letting out their pupils, and one young Arab boy came up to them and asked who they were. And then, for their edification it seemed, he picked up a stone and threw it at the Israeli soldiers on watch. It made Landsvig think once more about what influence media coverage itself had on the everyday shaping of the conflict.

These are instances of responses from the beat itself, after a fashion, to foreign correspondent work. The intensity of such response is very uneven, and on the whole, foreign correspondents mostly seem to expect rather less feedback from audiences than they would receive at home, covering national or local news. This is another part of the sense of feeling a bit alone or free-floating. It is a somewhat predictable aspect of the intensity of the Jerusalem news environment, however, that correspondents there are made aware that others besides the Government Press Office take note of what they do. When he came in as the new bureau chief at the *New York Times,* Serge Schmemann found himself invited to lunches just about daily, by people who wanted to make contact. Barton Gellman of the *Washington Post* was also shown clearly enough that people were aware of the influence of his paper. In 1996, with the Israeli election campaign in full swing, an appointment that he had with the opposition's prime ministerial candidate, Benjamin Netanyahu, was abruptly canceled, and he was told by someone on the candidate's staff that "Netanyahu would never talk to the *Washington Post* again." Gellman had just reported in the *Post* (on the basis of an interview with a childhood friend of Netanyahu's) that at one time when Netanyahu was living in the United States, he had seriously contemplated staying there instead of returning to Israel. Since such thoughts were hardly what one would expect of a candidate for the prime ministership, the Netanyahu camp was quite upset; after the election, however, this did not prevent the new prime minister from calling up Gellman very soon again. Gellman also noted that some of his Israeli journalist acquaintances often tried to get him to make statements for publication on Israeli affairs—preferably unfavorable comments on politicians. It was difficult to flatly refuse, on collegial grounds. So on such occasions, he just tried to be as dull and unquotable as possible.

Schmemann and Gellman represented the presumably most politically influential newspapers in the United States, with which Israel had a special relationship, and it could hardly be surprising that representatives of such organizations would get some special treatment. One European old-timer saw this structure of attention, and perhaps also the greater resources of at least some of the colleagues from across the Atlantic, as leading to a stratification among the correspondents: "First the Americans, then comes nothing, then nothing . . ." This was also true in what was for a period an institutionalized local expression of the interest in foreign media: a column in the *Jerusalem Post* where its sometime executive editor David Bar-Illan systematically polemicized against what he perceived as unfair, anti-Israeli reporting.[13] One correspondent suggested that Bar-Illan became a sort of pet enemy, someone whose attacks the victims would see as badges of honor. Although Americans stood a better chance of catching his gaze and earning his animosity, Cordelia Edvardson, Swedish, of *Svenska Dagbladet,* and Jörg Bremer, German, writing for the *Frankfurter Allgemeine,* were pleased that they had also succeeded at least once.

But then a part of the audience reaction is from readers, listeners, or viewers at home. Some among them are just ordinary variously informed citizens. Others are more or less professional media critics. An Africa correspondent in Cape Town received complaints that he was neglecting a particular country that deserved more publicity; it happened to be one where many people from his own country had served as volunteers, and now they were apparently its fans forever. Foreign correspondents certainly become particularly controversial, however, when some portion of the audience thinks they have become turncoats, advocates, or apologists for what is taken to be "the other side"; in the history of foreign correspondence, there have been some notable examples.[14] War correspondence can of course be particularly vulnerable to such charges, when it departs from the habit of staying with the troops from home, in its travel or with its unequivocal sympathies. Some of the American reporting on the Vietnam War reminds us of this, as well as Peter Arnett's reporting for CNN from Baghdad during the Gulf War. And there were those in Britain who were less than happy with John Simpson of BBC, on the television screen from Belgrade while the Kosovo campaign was on.

Such controversies over reporting have often reflected general divides, for example left-right, among home audiences. Not so rarely these days, however, the people at home who pay attention to correspondent reporting most closely are members of diasporas; and some diasporas are larger, more widespread, and more vocal than others.[15] Recall that when Marjorie Miller and her editor in Los Angeles decided not to make much of the bus station bombing in Tel Aviv, there were angry Jewish readers for her managing editor to deal with. And "there are people who read the *New York Times* as if it were a second Talmud," said another Jerusalem correspondent. He and his colleagues were well aware that there is a Palestinian diaspora in the United States as well, but they felt that with remarkable exceptions, such as Edward Said, it was much less audible.[16]

When the *Washington Post* received "letters to the editor" concerning his reporting, Barton Gellman said, he would be asked if he thought the paper should publish them. Generally, he told the editor to go ahead—his voice was being heard, so why not those of his commentators? But then, he reflected, perhaps the letters would have been printed even if he had objected. As a rule, correspondents seem to expect that their editors at home will back them up in such conflicts. One of them, whose editor at home had evidently not always been so loyal, was resentful of the betrayal. Here, then, is another possible source of tension between those abroad and those at home.

Japan reporting, too, could result in strong reactions. After Sonni Efron had done a portrait in the *Los Angeles Times* of a well-known right-wing ideologue at the University of Tokyo, a conservative Tokyo newspaper responded critically under the headline "The Insolence and Arrogance of a Great American Newspaper." Again, however, some of the response could come from the diaspora, as shown in a flurry of controversy over the Japan coverage in the *New York Times*. The lively, energetic reporting by Nicholas Kristof and Sheryl WuDunn provoked Zipangu, an organization of Japanese diaspora journalists and artists in New York, to publish a highly critical bilingual volume, *Japan Made in USA* (1998). It discussed a number of the couple's feature stories and contained interviews with some academic specialists and commentaries by others, as well as a response by Kristof. Perhaps some of the Zipangu criticisms were overly defensive and not always persuasive. Yet the volume drew some supportive comment in Japanese newspapers, and there were other foreign correspondents in Tokyo as well who, though often appreciative of Kristof's and WuDunn's skills, were less enthusiastic about some of their stories. An occasional Japanese observer would label them "Orientalist."

By the time of my visit in Tokyo, Kristof and WuDunn were approaching the end of their Japan assignment. To a certain extent, Kristof's interests had already turned in other directions—he had recently done a series of articles titled "Global Contagion," which was not very much Japan-related at all (see chapter 6), and on excursions from the Tokyo beat, he had been to Central Africa at the time of the Mobutu-Kabila transition and to Jakarta for Suharto's fall. There were still articles by both of them on some of the oddities of Japanese culture and society—one by Kristof (1999b), for example, on the now extinct Japanese namba style of walking, with the right arm moving forward with the right leg and the left arm moving with the left leg—but by and large, most of the controversial stories seemed to be from their first year or so in the country.

We can remember how it had begun with Kristof's coverage of the Kobe earthquake, as dramatic an event as any. In the period that followed, however, one may suspect that Kristof and WuDunn found Tokyo in some ways a less satisfying journalistic experience than their previous posting in Beijing, where their reporting on the Tiananmen Square protests had earned them a Pulitzer Prize.[17] When I met Sheryl WuDunn at the *New York Times* office on the ninth floor of the *Asahi Shimbun* building, home of another major Japanese daily (close to the famous Tsukiji fish market), I asked her to compare the couple's Chinese and Japanese experiences. She thought the sensibilities were entirely different. In China, people had been engaged in a struggle to come up from hardly anything to seize their chance in life. In Japan there was none of that sense of drama. There was some agony, perhaps, in a period of economic recession, but Japan was an affluent country, and there were things the Japanese already had that would not be taken away from them. Apart from that, she felt, in Japan there were always shades of gray.

What this definition of the reporting situation had led her and Kristof to do, it seems, was to engage less with the "native's point of view," which seemed so curiously difficult to extract, and to focus on what, to the foreign sojourner, was indeed different. This had taken them to the stories that had irritated the Zipangu collective. One was on the high-pitched voices of Japanese women, as a sign of gender inequality. Another was on sexual molestation in the Tokyo subway—in fact, one molester had published a book of his own on the topic. Yet another story dealt with rape fantasies in a women's comic-strip magazine. And then, because Kristof felt that too much Japan reporting had become entirely Tokyo-centered, he took to visiting a small rural town for stories; from there he reported on beliefs in "fox devils" in the computer age.

Perhaps there were elements in WuDunn's and Kristof's Japan reporting of intrusions into what the anthropologist Michael Herzfeld (1997) has referred to as "cultural intimacy"—people may be embarrassed by some elements of their national culture and try to limit their visibility to the outside world. It is only fair to note that several of WuDunn's and Kristof's colleagues in Tokyo, from the United States or elsewhere, at one time or other filed stories on the same topics or at least made reference to them in some way. Yet there may have been something special in the couple's reporting style—close-up, personalizing, and, more often perhaps in Kristof's stories, somewhat ironical, gentle mocking. Again, however, probably the international eminence of the *New York Times* also had something to do with the Zipangu reaction.

Let us return, finally, to Jerusalem for an instance of a correspondent's suggestion that a critical voice was, after a fashion, welcome. In early April 1997, there was a brief exchange in *Svenska Dagbladet,* one of Stockholm's two major morning papers.[18] A volume of Edward Said's writings on Palestine had just appeared in Swedish translation, and the writer of a new introduction to the book, Mikael Löfgren, had argued there that Swedes, like much of the Western world, tend to see the Israeli-Arab conflict through Israeli eyes. One reason for this, he suggested, was that the people reporting to Western media were frequently immigrants to Israel. This could lead to a conflict between their roles as professionals and as citizens. As an example of such a "naturalized Israeli," he mentioned Cordelia Edvardson, *Svenska Dagbladet*'s correspondent in Jerusalem.

Edvardson commented in her paper that she was not an Israeli citizen and that she had indeed not sought Israeli citizenship precisely in order to avoid such a conflict. In his response to this some days later, Löfgren suggested that the real problem was the absence of autonomous Palestinian voices in Swedish reporting from the Middle East. And then in her final reply, Edvardson noted ironically that in a way she was grateful to Löfgren for claiming that her reporting was pro-Israeli. Over the years, "friends of Israel" in Sweden had kept complaining to her paper about her pro-Palestinian reporting—even to the extent of suggesting that she was in the pay of the PLO or had a Palestinian lover. If only to balance such suspicions, she concluded, it was good to have some criticism from the other side.

6 World Stories

Remember Tom Kent, the international editor of the Associated Press, from chapter 1: "In the past, if there had been a war between the Hutu and the Tutsi, our first question would have been, who is ours and who is theirs?" For several decades in foreign news, the cold war was a global story line.[1] Like other story lines, it assimilated some events to itself—thereby perhaps transforming them—while it ignored others. Unlike the regional themes that were the topic of chapter 4, it could readily cross boundaries and move between continents. The globalization of war, or of the threat of war, seems to have captured the sense of the world as a single place earlier and more effectively than any story grounded in a world at peace, or at least not dominated by the idea or the reality of armed conflict.

Yet as transnational connections grew in the late twentieth century, it became increasingly evident that there were other themes likewise entailing routes through the news terrain that would not always be confined within regions. In fact, some of the varieties of storytelling described in chapter 4 seem in one way or another to spill over the edges of their regional containers. In this chapter we will sample some of the ways that foreign correspondence has recently taken world interconnectedness into account, mostly in feature stories, and then consider further implications of that interconnectedness for news work. If the accumulated result of the thematizations sketched in chapter 4 is to suggest diversity in the world, with different regions pulling in different directions, the stories here may contribute, all in their own ways, surely not to an overall image of homogeneity, but to an image of an internally complicated, hardly entirely orderly coherence—pieced together by markets, migrants, and media; people and things from home found abroad; warriors and learners; and correspondents uniting around shared reporting projects.

Changing into Pinstripe

As president of the Foreign Correspondents Club in Hong Kong, Keith Richburg (1998) wrote a column in the club magazine, the *Correspondent,* on the
changing content of reporting—and on the garb of the reporter. He had spent
his career mostly as a political reporter, which often meant dealing with coup
attempts, insurgencies, guerrilla wars, and military crackdowns. This had
been a time for the safari jacket and the photographer's vest with lots of
pockets. Now it seemed the safari jacket was out and pinstripes were in: "Instead of romping through the bush with armies, we're conducting interviews
in brokerage houses and corporate board rooms." Yet he still thought that in
the end it would be necessary to combine economic with political reporting,
at least on the Southeast Asian assignment that he shared with many of his
Hong Kong colleagues.

    Nonetheless, there is the question what kind of writing one can do in a
pinstripe suit. "Globalization" itself has become a major story line—but in
large part as a kind of folk concept, narrowed down to that more limited and
yet fuzzy sense of the expanding reach of market logic. This story line is certainly big on the financial pages and in business news programs, but how does
one make it come alive in stories elsewhere, for more general publics?

    Although no longer appearing in the regular news pages of his paper,
Thomas Friedman, *New York Times* foreign affairs columnist and thrice a
Pulitzer Prize winner, has been grappling with the question. Friedman was a
correspondent in the Middle East in the 1980s, and his *From Beirut to Jerusalem* (1989) is probably the best-known more or less recent book on the region by a foreign correspondent.[2] Since the mid-1990s, in his present position—"actually the best job in the world," he claims (Friedman 1999, 5)—he
has been free to travel and has turned himself into a kind of global parachutist with a license to opine from anywhere.[3] In his second book, *The
Lexus and the Olive Tree* (1999)—to which we will return in this chapter as
well as the next—he portrays the coming of a new world shaped by the market. And at least with regard to vivid phrasing, Friedman does for this world
something reminiscent of what Marshall McLuhan in his day did for the electronic global village. In his book, we meet with the Electronic Herd: "mil-
lions of investors moving money around the world with the click of a mouse"
(Friedman 1989, 11)—whatever you do, do not get in its way. And there is the
Golden Straitjacket, the defining political-economic garment of the era: to
thrive, a nation has to accept a package of some sixteen measures, which
taken together mean that "your economy grows and your politics shrinks"
(87), even if there is still a role for the state in managing these changes.

Friedman's newspaper columns continue to provide a running interpretation of human affairs under globalization. As the George W. Bush administration took office, Friedman (2001) wondered if the new secretary of state, Colin Powell, would be a "wall man" or a "web man." For the couple of years just before his new appointment, Powell was on the corporate board of America Online; but before that, as a military man, he had spent thirty-five years with what Friedman calls "America Onduty," the cold war organizational complex preoccupied with walls—erecting them, defending them, bringing them down. The favorite movie of wall people, he argues, is *A Few Good Men,* where Jack Nicholson as a tough marine colonel in a pregnant moment points out that in a world that has walls, those walls must be guarded by men with guns. Web people prefer *You've Got Mail*—a Manhattan romantic comedy that tells them that in an integrated world, E-mail may bring messages from strangers with the potential of changing our lives. In America, then, wall people will focus on who is on the list of terrorists; web people will focus on who is on the buddy list or can be brought onto it.

More in the genre of reporting than of columnist commentary is an early-1999 series of articles in the *New York Times,* "Global Contagion," with Nicholas Kristof as the main author (Kristof 1999c; Kristof and Wyatt 1999; Kristof and Sanger 1999; Kristof and WuDunn 1999). It is at a time when Kristof is finishing his period as Tokyo bureau chief and moves around now and then on other assignments. (He had already spent a considerable part of 1998 reporting on the turbulence in Southeast Asia.) It is also a time to begin to look back on the economic upheavals that marked the preceding years.[4]

This is a complex story built up through fairly long articles, and it moves between many settings in several continents. It begins as we are taken back in time to a 1991 steak dinner in a private room at the 21 Club in New York, with top Democratic executives from Wall Street—indeed, "serious men, prosperous and pinstriped"—doing a job interview of sorts with young Governor Clinton of Arkansas, who impresses them with his willingness to embrace free market policies. For the first time the prospective presidential candidate makes the acquaintance here of the banker Robert Rubin, later to become his treasury secretary, in "a close partnership that has left an enormous imprint on the global economy." Clinton, Rubin, and their allies pressed hard for free trade and the free movement of capital. At least based on hindsight, commentators would say that the free capital flows could overwhelm countries where banking and legal systems were weak; but bankers, officials, scholars, and journalists all had their part in celebrating what began as phenomenal growth—and what seemed to turn into "the Asian Century."

The scene shifts to Muang Thong Thani, a new satellite city outside Bangkok, once planned for seven hundred thousand inhabitants. But when the story takes its readers there, it is almost empty, a ghost city. The Asian crisis that began with a run on Thailand's currency in 1997 left the project without funding. And then on to the third floor of the U.S. treasury, where Robert Rubin now presides in a spacious office, to give the authors a setting for sketching a dogmatic insistence on free capital movement, which allowed a flood of money to enter Asian economies in the early years of the 1990s and an almost equally massive amount to flow out some years later. The second article in the series begins at the GUM department store in Moscow, "just across from the mausoleum where Lenin lies in state like an old biological curiosity preserved in formaldehyde." A classic Soviet institution, GUM was privatized early and became an upscale shopping mall, with forty-some international retailers paying the highest rents in Europe. A great success story — until the crisis hit Russia as well, and GUM stock fell to less than 5 percent of its earlier value. "Overnight we were made paupers," says the chairman of the board, Yuri Solomatin. In Asia, countries that the American president had hailed as turning from dominoes into dynamos became dominoes again, falling over each other. Barton Biggs, investment strategist at Morgan Stanley in New York, who some years earlier had been involved in igniting the Asian investment boom, now told investors to sell their Southeast Asian holdings. Thailand, Korea, and Indonesia went into precipitous decline as investors withdrew from what had been taken to be "emergent economies." In Indonesia, the currency lost 85 percent of its value, riots cost more than a thousand lives, and hunger was widespread. Then it was Russia's turn.

Later in the series, we are in a small Illinois town with Charles Burrus, a hog farmer whose hogs would usually have ended up in small pieces between chopsticks somewhere in Asia. Local bankers are eyeing the hog farms somewhat nervously. In Modjokerto, in Indonesia, the rickshaw driver Salamet has been unable to pay for painkillers for his mother, who just died from breast cancer. Yet Salamet and his neighbors still feel that despite everything, things are better than they were ten years ago when the boom years began. There is electricity and television, and there are toilets and paved roads. In Bangkok again, Sirivat Voravetvuhikun, an ethnic Chinese Thai property developer who went to college in Texas, had borrowed heavily to build twenty-eight luxurious and highly desirable homes in a golf resort, but after the market collapsed, there was no longer anyone around to desire them. So Sirivat had to start from scratch again, peddling sandwiches. His wife made twenty of them that first day, and in six hours they were sold. Sirivat Sandwiches now sells 550 in a day, and Sirivat aims at becoming the sandwich king of Thailand.

And then finally we witness an encounter between Clinton and Rubin again, now on the third floor of the White House. The president is in cowboy boots, in his favorite chair by the fireplace, impatient and annoyed. The treasury secretary sits directly opposite, so that he can look the president in the eye. The president wants to attack the crisis more directly. Yet it is far from clear what precisely is to be done.

A commentator from the banking world notes that the preferred metaphor tends to be "a new financial architecture"; yet what is really needed, he argues, is not so grand, but rather meticulous attention to what would correspond to plumbing and electricity. It is also true that elsewhere, in Asia, Russia, and other places, people are now more critical of the American role in the global economy. Meanwhile, back in the Illinois town, Mary Jo Paoni is getting ready to retire from her secretarial job. Her pension fund lost on its Indonesian stocks and was even involved with the GUM department store in Moscow, but it has still done well in the booming American economy. Nevertheless, she is aware that she is linked to the global crisis: "There's always some tentacles out there. Asia will definitely have an effect on Iowa and Illinois."

In Kristof's polyphonic narrative, then, we see the Electronic Herd moving through the world. (In *The Lexus and the Olive Tree,* Thomas Friedman confesses that he himself was part of it when the Thai currency sank, he called his broker to get his own money out of those "emerging markets.") Moving out from the 21 Club on Manhattan through Thailand, Indonesia, and Russia, we come back to the graying denizens of the American heartlands. It is, as one could expect from Kristof, a vivid story. Yet one may sense that it is not always easy to translate globalization in this sense into a story with faces and events. It seems to have become more approachable after it has been joined by its counterconcept, "antiglobalization." With it, another battle front extending through the world is introduced, although of a rather different nature than that of the cold war. At the height of the 1998 Asian crisis, it was dramatized by the shouting match between the financier George Soros and "Dr. M," the Malaysian prime minister Mahathir Mohamed. Since just before the beginning of the new century, it has accumulated its own classic datelines in news reporting: Seattle, Genoa. Davos, with its annual World Economic Forum, had already been there for some time; but if Davos has been primarily for the pundits, Seattle and Genoa have also been for the street reporters. Antiglobalization is clearly not only that, but it has had moments of the carnivalesque, with street music, costumes ranging from the brightly outrageous to the darkly threatening, demonstrations and protests finally breaking into violent confrontation—for one thing, as it has been covered, it has shown both the strengths and the weaknesses of television.

Small Wars as Global Form

Momentarily, it seems, Keith Richburg (1999) was back in the safari jacket. The conflict over East Timor, as it finally broke away from Indonesia, was a typical parachutist situation. Journalists arrived from everywhere, crowding into a handful of hotels in Dili, the capital. It turned out to be a dangerous assignment for them. One Dutch correspondent lost his life, shot when trying to escape from a roadblock, and others were beaten up. Eventually, deciding that the risks were just too great, many of them left on a chartered plane for Australia.

For Richburg, who had the blunt side of a militiaman's machete brought down across his back, it reminded him of his African years. The memories came back when the van in which he and some of his colleagues were traveling was "stopped at a checkpoint by wild-eyed, angry militiamen with machetes, daggers and at least one pistol" and again, he writes, "when I was in my room at the Turismo Hotel in Dili, barricading the door against intruders, pulling the mattress to the floor to avoid stray bullets, positioning a tree branch near the bed to use as a last defense in case they made it through my flimsy fortification" (1999).[5]

In a way it could seem as if the events in East Timor were something out of an earlier period of the twentieth century—a liberation struggle and the final violent stand of the departing colonizers. Yet with the terror against a civilian population, its implications of identity politics (largely based on religion, along a Muslim-Christian divide), and the involvement of undisciplined militias seemingly doing the dirty work of the state, the conflagration became more like a contemporary kind of war.

Toward the end of the twentieth century, in particular after the cold war, it has been argued, warfare was reconfigured. The political scientist Mary Kaldor (1999), a central commentator on the subject, suggests that the "new wars" typically involve a blurring of the distinctions between war, organized crime, and large-scale violations of human rights. In their frequently ostentatious preoccupation with identity politics, they may appear to be intensely local phenomena and replays of very old battles. Nonetheless, in Kaldor's view, they are generated out of current circumstances, of which the intensification of global interconnectedness is one. They often involve crumbling state machineries, even "failed states," with little control over their territories, little capacity or desire to do anything for their citizens, and consequently little legitimacy. Regular soldiers, mercenaries, warlords with their bands, vigilantes, gangsters, and revolutionaries cannot always be readily distinguished from one another. The flow of weaponry across borders is essentially out of control. The combatants may be deeply involved with global consumer culture: Mercedes cars, Rolex watches, and Rayban sunglasses are displayed among the prizes of predation. Diasporas overseas may play a part in keeping the conflicts funded and propagandized. Frequently, however, the economic foundations and motives of these violent conflicts have to do with smuggling and with access to the natural resources of the land.

As another political scientist, Myron Weiner (1996), puts it, these wars mostly occur in certain "bad neighborhoods": the Balkan region, the Caucasus, Central Asia, the Horn of Africa, Central Africa, and parts of West Africa. The news media of the world pay varying attention to them. The wars of the Balkans in the 1990s received much coverage, and in the end they played a major part in the conceptualization of this family of phenomena. Others become those "forgotten wars" that are revisited now and then. Wars of this kind are inherently difficult to report on. Getting into the middle of them may be impossible, or at least dangerous and very uncomfortable. Correspondents are perhaps at hand instead to meet the floods of refugees, or to witness victorious troops as they emerge from the hinterland—marching into Kinshasa as after Mobutu's fall, for example—or to interview someone like the Sierra Leonean warlord Foday Sankoh, as he slips into the capital of a neighboring country for an attempt (not necessarily his own) to negotiate a peace.

Even so, there are ways in which the global contexts of conflicts in those bad neighborhoods can be illuminated in news reporting. Karl Vick (2001), Nairobi-based correspondent for the *Washington Post*, visits the Pokot pastoralists of northwest Kenya and finds that the ethnic battles and the cattle raids have changed as the price for Kalashnikovs has gone down. In the late 1960s, when the Pokot bought their first rifles, they were of World War I vintage and the going rate was sixty cows apiece. Now the Kalashnikovs were down to five head of cattle each and could be bought from the backs of the trucks of ambulating arms merchants. Because the rifles were acquired mostly by young hotheads, power in Pokot society was passing away from the elders, who had wielded it more cautiously in the past. In a recent raid of several hundred young Pokot on a nearby community of the Marakwet people, forty-seven people were killed, most of them women and children, who would have been spared in an earlier era.

Vick writes on the eve of a United Nations conference in New York, where delegates from some 180 nations are to negotiate a treaty to reduce the illicit trade in small arms. Discussing the same occasion, Gunilla von Hall

(2001), a roving correspondent operating out of Geneva for the Stockholm paper *Svenska Dagbladet,* is reminded that in that city she has encountered one arms trader who spends his days in the lobbies of the luxury hotels, selling arms to anyone who is ready to pay.

Reflecting on the global linkages of current modes of collective violence, one might wonder whether much current news of the troubles of Africa could be organized—at least as usefully as through the primordialist imageries of tribal hatreds—more explicitly and systematically around a story line of the battle for Africa's mineral assets. This comprises the civil war in southern Sudan, where the northern-based regime battles the Dinka and the Nuer over old cattle-grazing lands under which new oil wealth lures.[6] It includes the stream of incidents in southern Nigerian oil country, with its severe environmental blight and its local political upheavals (connecting, for one thing, with the internationally conspicuous human rights story of the execution of the writer-politician Ken Saro-Wiva).[7] The civil war in Sierra Leone, in no small part over access to its diamonds, and related conflicts in neighboring countries are also a part of the story, as is the war in Angola, even more clearly after the cold war angle is gone. If the late 1990s conflagrations in Congo (formerly Zaire) deserved being called "Africa's first world war," it was not only because of the number of African countries involved but also because of the value of its precious stones to international business.

Such a story line may now be emerging, even though it can yet become both more explicit and more comprehensive. In the German *Die Zeit,* Bartholomäus Grill (2001) reports from the border zone between Liberia, Sierra Leone, and Guinea on the "deadly synergy" of robber presidents, drug-crazed teenage soldiers, ethnic militias, and greedy diamond dealers. One can get a good glimpse of the possibilities of the theme, too, as Blaine Harden (2000), a *New York Times* (and formerly *Washington Post*) veteran of foreign correspondence, coordinates one long (5,424-word) story under the title "Africa's Gems: Warfare's Best Friend," to which four other correspondents also contribute. Here is demonstrated the complexity of one part of the theme of the social life of African minerals. Not only can the large news organization include reporting from Sierra Leone, Congo, Angola, and Botswana—it also visits the diamond bourse in Antwerp, seen by some as a diamond smuggler's dream, and reaches to where the story, for most of its readers, is no longer foreign news: an electrician from Staten Island stands with his fiancée at a diamond counter on Forty-seventh Street in Manhattan, a few blocks from the *New York Times* headquarters, eyeing a $5,500 ring. Not only warfare's best friend?

Home News Abroad

Home-related stories, we noted in chapter 4, make up a genre of foreign news that sometimes cuts across regional story lines. Coming back to the point, we see here that they also contribute to the web of transnational connections that foreign correspondents depict. Much classical war reporting has been of this kind, even to the point of seeming rather like an extension of domestic news. At times, just about all of it is reporting on the activities and experiences of "our boys"—not on the enemy and not on the civilian population.

In any case, the variety of linkages, small-scale or large-scale, that connect distant places to the familiar and to "home" continue to provide topics and angles for correspondent work. On one of her excursions to Angola for the *New York Times,* Suzanne Daley (1998e) finds an American cultural enclave run by Chevron, the oil company: hot dogs, chocolate chip cookies, golf course, and all. But American employees are not allowed to go outside the fence, where bandits roam, and when they go on home leave (four weeks, then back to Angola for another four weeks of twelve-hour days), they are helicoptered to the airport twelve miles away. It is a story that again ties in with the African story line just suggested.

When the political temperature rises in Zimbabwe in early 2000 and white-owned farms are threatened by occupants, one can recognize that this, like the flooding in Mozambique described in chapter 4, is in reporting territory easily accessible from the correspondents' bases in South Africa. There could also, however, be some home-related stories. Leif Norrman (2000b) interviews the Swedish-born wife of a tobacco farmer whose lands have been occupied. A week later the occupants kill the farmer with a shot to the head, and Norrman (2000g) files a story from Cape Town, which appears in *Dagens Nyheter* under the front-page headline "Maria's Husband Murdered." He gets back to Zimbabwe in time to report from the funeral (Norrman 2000h) and then a few weeks later does a lengthy interview with the young widow, detailing her path from a Swedish provincial town, by way of volunteer work for what turns out to be a somewhat dubious Scandinavian aid organization, to involvement, together with her South African–born husband, with the Zimbabwean opposition movement (Norrman 2000a).[8] Meanwhile, reporting for the *Daily Telegraph* on some other farmers' eyewitness accounts of the assassination, Anton La Guardia (2000) makes no mention of the victim's wife or of her national origin.

Reporting for *Dagens Nyheter* from Tokyo in January, when the Christmas season is over at home and all Santa Clauses vanish until next December,

Påhl Ruin (2001) finds that one small Swedish company, Santaworld, working closely with its Japanese agent, manages to market Santa goods throughout the year. Not belonging anywhere in particular in the Japanese calendar, Santa Claus becomes just another sweet character, like something from Walt Disney or any other comic strip, and an all-weather type. The Santa logo is on swim trunks, T-shirts, and overcoats and on tablecloths, plates, and stationery. The Santaworld company, based in the small Swedish town Mora, also realizes that its Japanese sales help attract Japanese tourists to its modest amusement park at home. Mostly they come in the summer. Now Santaworld has expanded its sales efforts into Korea and is casting a glance at the Chinese market as well.

Marjorie Miller (1996a) informs her *Los Angeles Times* readers of a local Jerusalem change of scenery: the Atara Café is closing down. Atara has been there since the days of British rule in Palestine. It was modeled on the classic central European café, where one would catch up on the news and carry on conversations for hours. In the final years of the British mandate, this was where the Jewish freedom fighters of the underground Hagana force used to meet and brainstorm. More recently, as the street outside has been closed to car traffic, the new café tables outdoors have filled early on Fridays, with regulars watching the swirl of pedestrians: "shoppers buying fresh flowers and twisted challah breads for the Sabbath; young men and women soldiers on leave for the weekend; ultra-Orthodox elders offering prayer boxes to nonbelievers; students with orange hair, snakeskin pants and pierced bellybuttons." Now Atara is to be replaced by a Burger King.

Serge Schmemann (1997) reports that the bagel, the real New York bagel, has also arrived at Zion Square, Jerusalem. The shop design at Bonkers Bagels is distinctly American, and the signs are all in English; this epitome of Jewish food in the United States has somewhat shifted identity in Israel. The immigrant entrepreneurs, one of them a New Yorker, hopes to have fifty franchises soon. But the business faces the competition, from a block away, of a new Dunkin' Donuts outlet—"reared on falafel, Israelis are not easily scared by deep-fried food." Meanwhile, another *New York Times* writer, Amy Wu (1999), finds bagels in Beijing as well. They are served in a small café with red-checkered tablecloths in an obscure industrial area, but behind the café is a factory that produces two thousand bagels a day for hotels, embassies, international schools, and other customers around town. The proprietress, Lejen Chen, is a Chinese-American who grew up in Brooklyn. Curious about her roots, she made her way to China, where she worked briefly as a guide for a group of young Americans attending a kite festival; they told her that they missed their breakfast bagel. And then as she stayed on and went into business, her Chinese engineer husband helped convert an old noodle maker into a bagel presser. The bakery and café now use Canadian wheat flour, Korean sugar, French yeast, California raisins, Australian cream cheese, and Norwegian salmon.

Americanization as a (Mixed) Success Story

With the bagels in Jerusalem and Beijing, and particularly with a Burger King replacing the Atara café, we approach another genre of globalization stories that are popular especially in American media: the spread of American popular and consumer culture. It used to be that you could not go home again, because things would no longer look the same; but now, argues Thomas Friedman (1998b) in one of his columns, you cannot leave home. Everywhere will look the same, like home.

The *Washington Post* does a series of articles with Washington, Los Angeles, Kuala Lumpur, Tehran, and Paris as datelines; the first installment is titled "American Pop Penetrates Worldwide: Nations with New Wealth, Freedom Welcome Bart Simpson, Barbie, and Rap" (Farhi and Rosenfeld 1998). Movies, music, television programs, books, and computer software, the authors point out, have become the country's biggest exports. Blockbuster Video has two thousand outlets in twenty-six foreign countries, Tower Records seventy in fifteen countries. And every day, around the world, six new McDonald's restaurants open their doors. It all has much to do with increases in leisure time and spending power (and in that connection, it could be inserted, we find many more stories of this kind relating to Asian than to African countries), but also with widespread political deregulation. As far as the particular border-crossing appeal of American popular culture is concerned, Farhi and Rosenfeld suggest, beyond "its glitz and gloss, its sex, speed and violence," it reflects themes like "individuality, wealth, progress, tolerance, optimism." A former French minister of culture argues that American entertainment "finds the soul of the child in the adult."

In Tehran, then, the *Post* Middle East correspondent John Lancaster (1998) finds a young man who is enthusiastic about *Titanic,* circulating in Iran's cities on bootleg video cassettes and originally taped inside movie theaters with handheld cameras. Although the United States is still denounced as the Great Satan, the mullahs are unable to keep American culture out. Even the Ministry of Guidance has allowed heavily expurgated translations of Danielle Steele, John Grisham, and John Gray's *Men Are from Mars, Women Are from Venus.* Since they need not worry about American copyright laws, Iranian publishers pay nothing for the materials. From Malaysia,

Megan Rosenfeld (1998) reports that lewd jokes are censored from the David Letterman show; and she, too, has run into a *Titanic* fan, a ten-year-old girl in baggy denim overalls. At a concert held to benefit a local orphanage, the orphans, in national dress, perform a dance seeming to synthesize a mind-boggling number of influences. The music is "a traditional Malaysian song vamped up with a loud disco beat."

Thus the *Washington Post* writers come to the conclusion that the spread of American pop culture is, after all, not so uncomplicated. They seek their own metaphors to formulate what they see. "And so the culture here is in many ways a hybrid, a synthesis. East and West are not just meeting, they are dancing together to a driving beat, toward a future in which defining one's own native, personal, national culture becomes increasingly difficult," comments Rosenfeld (1998) from Kuala Lumpur. "Consuming countries pick and choose what they like from the cafeteria of American cultural products, to adapt it to their tastes and uses, to plagiarize and imitate in their own tongues and styles—and of course to reject it and move on," writes Charles Trueheart (1998); "in any case, in country after country the evidence is not of cloned Americana but of native translation. What first looks like an American cultural overlay eventually seeps into the native woodwork. It is as if the United States had exported, along with much else, the idea of the melting pot into which it is bound to slowly disappear." There is the rejection of American political as well as cultural influence, which Trueheart reads into the bombing of a Planet Hollywood restaurant in a fashionable Cape Town shopping district. But there is no less the adoption and modification of originally American cultural formats, through which, soon enough, local products—music, TV sitcoms—compete very successfully with the imports.

Meanwhile, from Los Angeles, Sharon Waxman (1998) contributes the observation that when the American cultural industries become conscious of the markets for their products abroad, this influences their decisions. In Hollywood, some see a risk of a cultural thinning out, with less responsiveness toward America's own internal diversity: assembly-line violent action movies travel more easily across borders than what is "ethnic," "inner-city," "sports-driven."

As other correspondents take on topics of American cultural influence, more or less similar points are made. Howard French (2001) of the *New York Times* attends the premiere of the movie *Pearl Harbor* in Tokyo. Since it has already been a bit of a box office disappointment in the United States, the reception in Japan, the second most important market for Hollywood films, may determine its overall success or failure. And so both editing and marketing have been carefully tailored for a Japanese audience: no references to

"Japs" and at the end, a toned-down soliloquy about the American victory. In China, the Walt Disney Company has been doing very well, with an almost infinite local appetite for animated features like *The Lion King*. But then, writes Seth Faison (1996), also of the *New York Times*, Disney runs into trouble because a subsidiary is involved in the production of a film about the Dalai Lama. The film is being shot in Morocco and will certainly not be distributed in China, but the Chinese government makes it clear that it is unhappy with the glorification of an adversary. For one thing, consequently, the new Disney theme park planned for somewhere in south China may no longer be welcome. A little later, when it turns out that Hong Kong is being considered as a location for the Disney park, Evelyn Iritani (1999) of the *Los Angeles Times* reports that not everybody there is pleased. A member of the legislature writes in a newspaper column that "a Disney theme park that does not capture and reflect the local heritage and vibrancy would be a pointless parody of American kitsch."

In India, a local beauty is crowned Miss World 2000, and it happens to occur shortly after another young Indian woman has become Miss Universe. Moreover, the Miss Worlds of 1994, 1996, and 1999 were also from India, Barry Bearak (2000) of the *New York Times* writes from New Delhi. The trouble is, people are beginning to think that this is too much. Is the Miss World pageant turning into a Third World affair? In 2000 it was not televised at all in the United States and only on a down-market channel in Britain. The well-known author Khushwant Singh scoffs that "we Indians send out some bimbo and she returns with the prize, and we act like we've conquered the world." Jerry Springer, Bearak also reports, was a less-than-dignified host of the show. He asked the bewildered Miss Turkey, "Tell me, what do you eat on Thanksgiving?"

Among the global symbols of the success of American popular culture is Barbie, the high-living, curvaceous doll. Not even her acceptance, however, turns out to have been entirely without obstacles. Andrew Pollack (1996), in Tokyo with the *New York Times*, discovers that although Barbie was even originally manufactured in Japan (in 1959), she has long been in a modest second place in the doll market there, after Licca, a local product. Licca is a smaller girl, not exactly Japanese-looking either, but with the big doe eyes that the Japanese recognize from their comic strips. Yet now Mattel, the world's largest toy company and the creator of Barbie, hopes to move ahead again in the Japanese market with its famous girl model. To succeed in Japan, Barbie has had to learn to keep her mouth shut. That toothy smile does not work in a country where women politely cover their mouths with their hands when they laugh.

At the same time, Japan has been successful in promoting its own popular culture products elsewhere. Calvin Sims (1999), also of the *New York Times,* has a Taipei dateline for his account of the popularity of Japanese music, movies, television, fashion, and food among youth across East Asia. At the local Tower Records store, it turns out to be an upbeat Japanese ballad, used as background music, that makes the Taiwanese teenagers scream and begin to sing. Kang Hun, a Korean cultural critic who teaches popular culture at one of the universities in Seoul, tells Sims that "culture is like water. It flows from stronger nations to weaker ones. People tend to idolize countries that are wealthier, freer and more advanced. And in Asia that country is Japan." But if Kang Hun finds some of the reasons for the spread of Japanese culture in the cultural affinities between Japan and other East Asian countries, he suggests also that "much of Japanese popular culture is Western culture with an Asian face."

It is evident, then, that not all transnational flows of popular culture are American; and some Japanese popular culture has been reaching even further. On one of the last days of the twentieth century, Påhl Ruin (1999c) looks back in *Dagens Nyheter* at the striking success of the Tamagotchi and Pokemon figures among the world's children and forecasts the arrival of a new, cooperative little monster, Digimon, fighting against evil in the world. In Japan it is already available in computer games, animated television programs, collector's cards, and as soft, cuddly toys. Ruin sees a new business generation moving in to handle the expansion of the new cultural industries, as the predecessors who sold Japanese cars, TV sets, and tape recorders to the world prepare to retire.

The Uses of English: Backpacker Tutors and Silver Volunteers

In the TOEFL exam, the international test of proficiency in the use of English as a foreign language, Kathryn Tolbert (2000) of the *Washington Post* reports, Japan has now pulled ahead of Cambodia and Afghanistan but has fallen behind North Korea.

The spread of English as the totally dominant lingua franca in the world is also now mostly a part of the story of Americanization—but when correspondents raise this topic, it, too, entails its own complications. In rather large part, it is a theme in East Asian reporting. Although the region is intensely involved in global interconnectedness, prominently in the marketplace, it does not have a colonial past, and consequently it has not historically had the widespread use of English as an official language imposed upon it. So the sense that this is now a problem to deal with becomes especially urgent there. (If somehow, according to those TOEFL results, the Japanese seem to care less than the North Koreans, one may suspect that those who take the exam in North Korea constitute a much smaller but more select group than in Japan.)

Kathryn Tolbert notes that the prime minister, Keizo Obuchi, has released a list of Japan's goals for the twenty-first century and that one of its proposals is to make English the official second language. That is actually less radical than the suggestion of an 1870s cabinet minister that the country should abandon Japanese and switch to English altogether. The current idea, however, is still meeting some opposition. One University of Tokyo professor says that it is more important that the elites speak good English than that every Japanese do so; and though businesspeople now understand this, bureaucrats are lagging seriously behind. The author of a book on how "lack of English ability is destroying the nation" argues that the vagueness of the Japanese language allows people to hide their opinions and that by learning English, leaders will be forced to say what they think. (Foreign correspondents, so often frustrated in their attempts to interview Japanese politicians and get something quotable out of them, would probably like that.)

In South Korea, Mary Jordan (1997) of the *Washington Post* finds that the English-language boom has created something like an underground economy for language instructors. The government has been aiming at more egalitarian educational opportunities, so that the children of rich parents will not have too much advantage. This has created an enormous demand for private education. Major companies offer their employees free English lessons. Spouses of American military officers are stopped in grocery stores by strangers who beg to be taught English, and every weekend waves of South Korean school children pass through the gates of the American military bases to seek out their freelance instructors. Now the government has banned private tutoring in any subject taught during the regular school day (except art and music), and although no parents have yet been prosecuted for illicitly arranging English lessons for their progeny, an effort is made to expel "backpacker tutors" or "cowboy tutors" who arrive in South Korea on a tourist visa and then earn a small fortune teaching their native tongue. Money changers are asked to check the visa status of foreigners possessing large amounts of Korean currency.

Back in Japan again, though English in school has its problems, it does well in many other contexts—but is it English? Nicholas Kristof (1995e, 1997b) turns to the topic at least twice. He discovers that a *poke beru* is a "pocket bell"—but what is that? A beeper, it turns out. There is *wasei* English, made-in-Japan English. English words are taken to be particularly useful as euphemisms. Talking about the elderly and their particular needs and doings, gray hair is "silver" (*shirubaa*), and so the elderly can live in *shirubaa hauzingu* (retirement housing) and serve part-time as silver volunteers (*shirubaa vorantia*). A manager at a large advertising agency in Tokyo notes that what sounds good and has a special flair to a Japanese audience may sound awful to native speakers. A popular health drink that replaces the minerals lost in perspiration, available through Japan's ubiquitous street-corner vending machines, is Pocari Sweat.

Kristof points out in his second article that the young like English especially, as part of hip talk. A casual greeting, something like "Hi there," is *chekaraccho* (Check it out, Joe). Any cool teenager wears *roozu sokusu* (loose socks), and *wonchu* (I want you) is a rather direct approach by a boy to a girl. With regard to that "cultural invasion" as a whole, it is worth noting that the Japanese language easily allows turning foreign words into verbs: *deniru* means to go to a Denny's restaurant and *hageru* to visit a Häagen-Dazs ice cream outlet. Even in the use of English, as foreign correspondents listen in on it, there is perhaps some of that Japanese weirdness.

The expansiveness of the English language, however, is not entirely an East Asian story. Visiting Azerbaijan, Raymond Bonner (1995) finds that when old Communist restrictions have become a thing of the past, and when foreign oil companies offer salaries that seem astronomical by local standards, students flock to English courses. At the State Institute of Foreign Languages, however, there is a serious shortage of up-to-date teaching materials, or any contemporary reading matter at all. A Soviet-age textbook pulled from the shelf at random suggests that television in "bourgeois society reduces the human personality to the level of a puppet, a robot which is not even aware that its life is devoid of any creative content and meaning." It is a problem that the American embassy in Baku, the capital, cannot do much to help. The conflict with Armenia over the Nagorno-Karabakh enclave is on at the time, and the Armenian-American lobby in the United States has succeeded in getting the U.S. Congress to ban aid to Azerbaijan for the time being.

In contrast, in India, which has had English since the days of the British Raj, some would be happy to get rid of it. Writing from Madras for the *New York Times,* Stephen Kinzer (1998) refers to a speech by a minister who vows that he and his followers "will not rest until English is driven out of the country." The rise of smaller parties based on region, religion, or caste has entailed a fragmentation of Indian politics in which attacks on English as a national language may bring in some votes. In addition, the masses tend to see English as the exclusive property of selfish elites. The defenders of the language point to its historical role in the building of the Indian nation and the struggle for freedom and also to its role as "a vital tool in the modern world."

Screens Everywhere

Screens have been spreading, screens of the kind that belong with the communication and information revolutions of the twentieth century. In the 1990s, some foreign correspondents could still report on the introduction of television in outlying parts of their beats. Kevin Sullivan (1999) of the *Washington Post* travels from Tokyo to Bhutan, the mountain kingdom in the Himalayas. For Suzanne Daley (1996b), as southern Africa correspondent, television provides a reason to go to Malawi, a country that is part of her assignment but which she otherwise seldom gets to visit.

Malawi is actually still waiting for television. It would be an element of opening up the country, after decades under a repressive one-party regime. But the new government's plan to import used equipment for a public television station from Malaysia has fallen apart, and so the postmaster general, who is in charge of introducing the new medium, has had to put it off again. There are still those who doubt the wisdom of it all and see it as a force of Western cultural imperialism. Daley quotes a polytechnic lecturer who feels that television is "bound to accelerate the degeneration of moral decency now eating at the very heart of our society." Others retort that everything else has been brought from the West to Malawi anyway: religion, the legal system. In any case, the government expects to start out modestly, with six hours of broadcasting a day, mostly of news and educational programs provided by relief agencies. There probably will not be many viewers, either, since the cost of a set equals about three and a half months' wages of an average Malawian viewer. Perhaps if the government could open even a couple of hundred local community centers, with the help of some foreign donor, the postmaster general says, people could go there and watch educational programs on topics from health care to deforestation.

In Bhutan, Kevin Sullivan also finds that the coming of television is a part of opening up a country that is still perhaps of two minds about the wisdom of this. Two world wars went by largely unnoticed by the farmers, monks, and yak herders of Bhutan. Tourists were banned until 1974, and there are still not many of them. Nepalese immigrants have been chased away. The only newspaper in the country urges strict government regulation of the new medium and predicts that "if we were to record the language pattern, interests, sense of humor, values, fashions and behavior of our children now and repeat it six months later, we will see a dramatic difference." Indeed, notes the visiting correspondent, "living rooms across the nation are being rearranged to face the new family television set." The Bhutanese foreign minister tells him that "the whole world is getting smaller, and we need to be part of the global village, but how to do it while maintaining our traditions is a challenge." The minister, it turns out, has a master's degree from Pennsylvania State University. His Majesty the king of Bhutan (who has four wives, all sisters) has supported a variety of changes in his kingdom. He has given away much of his power: the national assembly can now remove him with a no-confidence vote, and his subjects need no longer bow nine times when they see him. The first broadcast would show the twenty-fifth anniversary of his ascent to the throne.

On the eve of a Super Bowl game, the *New York Times* also notes that the television set has turned into a "focal point of much modern ritual behavior," and so it asks a number of its foreign correspondents what viewers eat and drink in front of the screen where they are based (Kuntz 1997). In Russia, it is simply vodka; at the famous Soweto shebeen Wandie's Place, the proprietor says that what unites South Africans is beer; in Mexico, when people sit down to watch prime-time soap operas, they eat sandwiches with leftovers from the big midday meal and hot chilies, washing it all down with hot cocoa or *café con leche.* And in the Philippines, correspondent Seth Mydans finds the word play more charming than the snacks themselves. Adidas are grilled chicken feet, Walkmans are pig's ears, and IUD's are skewered chicken intestines. The national passion, however, is *balut,* unhatched duck embryos, boiled and eaten from the shell.

As Kevin Sullivan reports from Bhutan, however, not only television is being introduced. The kingdom has also launched its own Internet server. And the growth of the Internet, even more than the spread of television, has been a recent global news theme. Not so far away from Bhutan, Göran Leijonhufvud (1999) reports, in the most recent half year six Internet cafés have opened in Lhasa, Tibet. Mostly the customers are foreign tourists checking their E-mail; there are also some Chinese businessmen. But some Tibetans are surfing, as well. Back in Hong Kong, he notes that in China, there are at the time of writing some 20 million registered Internet users, in addition to those who use the Internet cafés (Leijonhufvud 2001). As a means of formulating and communicating public opinion, he suggests, wall posters were in a way the Chinese precursors of the Internet. But the latter reaches out much faster and farther and is more difficult for the authorities to control. It is impossible now to hide accidents and disasters the way it could be done earlier. As a long-time China watcher, Leijonhufvud remembers that after 230,000 people were killed when a dam burst in the mid-1970s, it took twenty years for the story to get out.

The Middle East, apart from Israel, seems to have taken to the Internet rather slowly. Writing on the Arab Middle East for the *Washington Post,* Howard Schneider (1999, 2000) does stories on the topic from Cairo and from Damascus. In Cairo he finds a young soldier in an Internet café browsing movie ads, generally seeming more interested in popular culture than in politics. The Egyptian government seems fairly lax in its attempts to control Web access, as so few people use the Internet or can afford it. What is censored in the printed pages of newspapers may still appear on the papers' Web sites. In Tunisia, the government blocks the Web site of Amnesty International. In Saudi Arabia, the government acknowledges proscribing pornography, but it turns out that sites critical of the royal family are also rendered inaccessible. As he reaches Damascus, Schneider visits another cybercafé and finds one quality Israeli newspaper, a CIA report on Syria, and "all-nude, all man-to-man sex" available on the screen. But then it is suggested that this café owner may have particularly good political connections.

From her part of the Middle East, Marjorie Miller (1996d, 1997a) likewise has Internet stories. In Ramallah, the town where returning members of the Palestinian diaspora in North America tend to reroot themselves, she finds the first Internet café on the West Bank. It is an addition to a café that sells hamburgers, draft beer, and cappuccino, and those who log on can enter both a "virtual Palestine" extending across continents and an Israeli chat room, where they may surprise other visitors. Meanwhile, Rabbi Benjamin Weiss, in the ultra-Orthodox community of Bnei Brak just next to Tel Aviv, sees no reason why his coreligionists should not use the Internet. But they should be able to do so while staying safely within the faith. So he has helped start what Miller describes as a Kosher online service, the Toranet. The logo is a Torah scroll spread across the globe. On Toranet you can access more than twenty thousand pages of Jewish texts but will not find best-seller lists, pictures of scantily clad women, or Darwinist views of creation. You can pay by credit card for goods on sale, but not during the Sabbath, when you will find only a picture of candles if you try to sign on.

Evidently there are now, in the columnist Friedman's terms, a great many "Web people" — even Web peoples? — in the world, but not everybody is there yet. On the eve of a United Nations meeting focusing on the role of information technology in the world economy, *Dagens Nyheter* in Stockholm surveys the problem of the "digital divide" between rich and poor nations. Leif Norrman (2000d), the Africa correspondent, contributes a brief piece in which he says that despite physical decline and worn-out infrastructures, in most larger African cities one will these days find an Internet café. But only a small elite, mostly in business, will be connected. Wonderful speeches are made about how the Internet will help jumpstart the "African renaissance," but even South Africa, much better off than other countries of the continent, demonstrates its own internal divides. If township schools have any computers at all, they often end up getting stolen. A professor of computer science at the University of Cape Town finds that many students are poorly prepared to take on a field like this when they come to the university—and those who do best may leave the country after they finish their training.

Human Passages

Not only messages and merchandise cross borders, then; people do, too, and newspeople get stories out of many of the present-day varieties of human mobility. Some of them are indeed stories of brain drain. In the *New York Times,* James Glanz (2001) notes that with just 5 million workers, information technology generates about one-third of the economic growth in the United States and that out of those 5 million, more than 1 million are foreign born. In the global market for knowledge and expertise, the United States has so far been the one big winner.

Possibly, however, that is beginning to change, and the *New York Times* occasionally now also runs stories on reverse brain drain, mostly involving Asia. In Taiwan, reports Ashley Dunn (1995), it is called *rencai huiliu* (return flow of human talent). When David Chiang left Taiwan in the late 1970s, there was not much opportunity for a young engineer with an advanced degree. Taipei still produced mostly cheap clothes and cut-rate electronics. Chiang therefore continued his training at the University of Cincinnati, and he found a job nearby working in aviation technology. There were lots of engineers there, however, and few chances of moving up into management. On a visit to Taiwan, Chiang found that the island country had changed greatly. He had a job interview with a new center for aviation and space technology, returned to the United States to put his Cincinnati home on the market, and then came back to Taiwan. Both he and his wife had always hoped that sometime they would live closer to their parents again. Their two youngest children were small enough to cope with the move easily. The eleven-year-old had a more difficult time, but when a McDonald's restaurant opened only ten minutes away from their new home, it seemed to tell her that the distance between Taiwan and America was not so great after all.

In India, Celia Dugger (2000) shows, the image should perhaps really be one of brains in circulation between native and adopted countries. For several decades, graduates of six elite Indian institutes of technology have been in a hurry to move on to the United States, where they have often been wonderfully successful. In Silicon Valley alone, they run more than 750 technology companies. Now that they have money to spare and the Indian economy is no longer so state-regulated, some of them seek out ways of combining their commitments to two continents. Kanwal Rekhi, in his fifties, has made $300 million in Silicon Valley. Now he is engaged in fund-raising for those Indian institutes of technology, and the one in Mumbai (Bombay) has a new school of information technology named after him. Rakeesh Mathur, some ten years younger, is a graduate of the same institute. He and his business companions sold their Internet enterprise to Amazon.com, and Mathur ended up $90 million richer. Purpleyogi.com, his new company, has offices in Bangalore and in Mountain View. He also takes time out to be a mentor for institute students in Bombay who come up with business ideas of their own.

Some people travel just for fun and experience, and tourism offers other correspondent stories. From Khao San Road, Bangkok, a hub for budget travelers in Southeast Asia, Thomas Crampton (1999) reports in the *International Herald Tribune* that the guest houses serving the street's famous banana pancakes and fruit shakes have also been getting wired and that many of the backpackers now go on line several times a day to stay in touch with home and with one another, read a paper or two, and plan their further journeys. Also in Thailand, Seth Faison (1998) finds a quickly increasing number of Chinese tourists. Planeloads of tourist groups, made up of young professionals as well as retirees, arrive to fill hotels, restaurants, and tourist shops. A local tourist official notes that tour guides used to be trained to speak Japanese and Korean, but now they needed Mandarin. The arranged itineraries include a wildlife park with elephants, a transvestite show, and a traditional medicine store where one can buy capsules of snake oil; one of the Chinese tourists asks in the information meeting whether she can use her Visa card for shopping in Thailand.

And then there is Keith Richburg. When Hong Kong is for just a couple of weeks more a crown colony and is to become part of China again, Richburg (1997a) portrays that army of young British expatriates who are in low-end Hong Kong jobs as waiters, bartenders, airport construction workers, sandwich delivery boys, even shoeshine boys in the streets. Some of them are backpacking through Asia, just staying long enough in the city to make some money so that they can move on. The young Britons feel that they are doing reasonably well, but by Hong Kong standards their incomes are hardly impressive. Some of the locals derisively refer to them as "white coolies"— or, even less pleasantly, FILTH—Failed in London, Try Hong Kong. Soon, however, it is the end of the empire for them as well. Many are on their final twelve-month residence permits, and when these expire, there will be no place for people like them in China.

Some years later, having himself moved on from Hong Kong to the Paris bureau of the *Washington Post,* Richburg (2001a) crisscrosses through much of western Europe for his stories and reaches one of its most distant outposts, the Spanish enclave Melilla, on the North African mainland. Two tall metal fences, five meters apart and topped by razor wire, he notes, separate the promise of Europe from the poverty of Africa. Nonetheless, every night some Africans manage to get past the obstacles, and if they do not succeed the first time, they are likely to try again and again. Some go all the way down to the Mediterranean coastline and swim past the fence. Those illegal migrants who come from Morocco, which surrounds the enclave, will be unceremoniously turned back to their country if they are caught. Those who come from farther away cannot just be returned to Morocco, which will not accept them. Some of them are housed and fed in an immigrants' center and are even given Spanish lessons. Others have to beg in the streets of Melilla or get some meals at a local mosque.

So here, once more, Richburg makes contact with the misery of his old African beat that he described so graphically in his book. The new arrivals in Melilla are often from sub-Saharan Africa—from Nigeria, Mali, Sierra Leone, Cameroon, Mauritania—refugees from Afro-pessimism (although some are also from lands yet farther away, such as Iraq or Kashmir). Most of the sojourners in Melilla hope to reach mainland Europe, across the straits. From then on anything seems possible. Abdul Amr Obaid, from Basra in Iraq, smuggled to Melilla on a crowded ship, says he is a physician and hopes to reunite with his wife and children in Oakland, California.

News Beats of the Global Ecumene

These are some of the kinds of stories of recent years that we may describe as global stories, themes of world interconnectedness. Is this a world we recognize? (That question, of course, assumes that we also have other sources for our views of it.) Do we miss anything in particular? What are the implications of such stories for the conduct of foreign correspondence? Do the news beats of the global ecumene imply any particular organizational arrangements, whether already in place or imaginable and desirable?

One type of story, it seems, can be told in almost infinite variety: a story of juxtaposition. Something from home shows up abroad, something new appears in an old place: Burger King in an ancient city, Kalashnikovs among cattle herders. There is a surprise element in this, and even if the specific details do not make the audience feel happy, there is an element of infotainment in the structure. We may surmise as well that the preponderance of such stories can have something to do with the selective attention patterns of the innocent "fresh eye" that spiralist and parachutist correspondents bring to their work. In the sea of things and events that are less familiar, what the correspondent recognizes, and what the audience at home will recognize as well, yields a certain kind of pleasure.

For American audiences, the stories of the spread of American popular culture (and perhaps related stories about television and about the English language) may have a similar effect; and if the surprise element in the long run is weakened, there is probably the sense of being collectively a part of a success story. The authors of the *Washington Post* series do, in fact, go on to point out that realities may be a bit more complicated. Along the lines anthropologists and other academics have been arguing in the same period, the correspondents also recognize in different terminologies that there are hybridizations and even outright resistance. Yet on the whole, these are stories of acceptance. Anti-Americanism, which has after all long been fairly widespread (in mild or virulent forms or with a streak of ambivalence) has rarely been the topic of probing articles in American foreign correspondence — at least until after "9/11," when audiences were perhaps not well prepared to be confronted with a different line of inquiry: "Why do they hate us?"[9]

It might seem as if there is generally some bias toward good news in stories of world interconnectedness, but certainly this is not entirely the case—the story on the migrants in Melilla is at least as much one of flight from misery as one of hope for the onward journey, and that on the Pokot and their new Kalashnikovs does not tell of wonderful technological progress. Not even home-related stories are all pleasurable. For Swedish readers, the story from Zimbabwe of the murder of a young woman's settler husband amounts to more bad news out of Africa. But perhaps the good news, the feature stories that bring entertainment, are frequently more immediately accessible. The stories that tease out problematic transnational linkages, such as that by Blaine Harden and his colleagues on the relationship between African wars and the European and American demand for diamonds, may often take more effort both to produce and to consume.

How do newspeople organize themselves to do the globalizing stories? In the stories referred to above, we can see that one manner of dealing with them is largely in line with the way that anthropologists have usually dealt with "the local and the global": the reporter is in one place, describing the ways that locale is affected by influences from the outside world, and perhaps its own ways of responding to these. Richburg's story of the confluence of migrants and refugees at Melilla is of this kind, as are Barry Bearak's on the Miss World contest in India, Marjorie Miller's on the Internet café in Ramallah, and Karl Vick's on the Pokot pastoralists in Kenya, in their different ways. These are local stories with a global twist, and they may seem only marginally different from other foreign correspondent work.

There are also other ways of handling connections, wherein reporting capacity is deployed differently in the global landscape. It is not entirely obvious from the coauthored articles in the *New York Times* "Global Contagion" series what has been the division of labor between the authors, but it certainly appears that Nicholas Kristof himself did much of the traveling between the reporting scenes that appear in the story. (Moreover, when I met one of the coauthors, his wife Sheryl WuDunn, she commented that in general, she was more likely to stay in Tokyo and take care of the children.) In a combination of journalist and anthropologist vocabularies, one might briefly describe the working style in its purest form, perhaps, as individual multisite reportage by way of serial parachuting.

In early 1995, at about the time I began my scrutiny of foreign correspondence, I found another multisite reporting arrangement also demonstrated by the *New York Times,* as it orchestrated its coverage of the elusive life on the run, and the eventual arrest, of Ramzi Ahmed Yousef, suspected of having masterminded the 1993 bombing of the World Trade Center in New York.

As it turned out, Yousef had just been caught in a rooming house in Islamabad, Pakistan, rushed through deportation procedures, and whisked off on an American military plane to New York. But American investigators had actually picked up his trail in Manila some time before. On February 12, the Southeast Asia correspondent Philip Shenon (1995) could thus report that Yousef—in the Philippines under the name Naji Haddad and identifying himself as Moroccan—had fled from his Manila apartment after an explosion occurred in his kitchen, probably as he was preparing a bomb. The investigators found evidence, part of it on the laptop computer he had left behind, that he had been planning to bomb American passenger airliners and also preparing to assassinate the pope, who was due for a visit in the Philippines. The apartment was ideally located for that, with its view of a major thoroughfare on which the papal cavalcade was expected to pass. The man known as Haddad had not been very obvious about his religion and had engaged actively with Manila night life.

On the same page, there was a report from the *New York Times* South Asia correspondent John Burns, datelined Islamabad, that Yousef had apparently been located there and seized after a tip from a South African Muslim student at the Islamic University of Islamabad. At the local rooming house (rather unexpectedly named *Su Casa*), he had shown a Pakistani identity card, giving his name as Ali Mohammed. In more stories the next couple of days, Burns expanded on the theme of Yousef's arrest, as described by Islamabad neighbors, and also had more to say about the rather enigmatic South African, who had apparently been taken into protective custody, to appear later as a prosecution witness (Burns 1995a, 1995b, 1995c). It seemed the South African and Yousef had shared links with an Afghan Muslim group (with ties, in turn, to Saudi Arabia) and might even have fought together in the 1980s war against the Soviet occupants of Afghanistan. And then on February 15, Bill Keller (1995), at this time *New York Times* correspondent in Johannesburg, reported that the South African informer's family and Muslim friends in Cape Town were upset to learn that he had betrayed a fellow believer to the Americans.

Three correspondents, in different parts of the world but coordinated from the head office on Forty-third Street, Manhattan, were thus able to quickly focus on a joint topic. The arrangement is similar to that for the "Africa's Gems: Warfare's Best Friend" five-correspondent story described above, with several African countries but also Europe and the United States involved, and the one for the *Washington Post* series on American popular culture abroad.

For an organization with an extensive network of correspondents, drawing on several of them is thus one way of putting together a coherent transnational story. George Marcus (1995), who has been especially active in pointing to the possibilities of multisite research in anthropology, has suggested six strategies: follow the people; follow the thing; follow the metaphor; follow the plot, story, or allegory; follow the life or biography; and follow the conflict. These are perhaps not always easily distinguished and can surely overlap, but one can see the Ramzi Ahmed Yousef story as one that follows a life and the story on African diamonds as one that follows the thing, in a quite concrete sense. Kristof's "Global Contagion" series is, in these terms, an instance of following the plot.

All these involve structures of social linkages and passages that make the stories cohere. A slightly different kind of story that organizations with a number of correspondents also like to pull together uses contrasts and comparisons between sites. We recognize this type in the *New York Times* story about what people eat and drink when watching television, in Moscow, Johannesburg, Manila, or elsewhere. The *Los Angeles Times* (March 16, 1997) uses it in its Sunday magazine section, in a kind of "at home abroad" feature, when it asks its correspondents what they do when they feel homesick and need "a dose of Americana." Dean Murphy, still in Warsaw (not yet in Johannesburg), heads for the Malibu restaurant, operated by a former Los Angeles surgeon and a former Beverly Hills clothier; Marjorie Miller escapes from the somber Sabbath in Jerusalem and piles into the car with the family, heading for the Mediterranean beachfront of Tel Aviv—"after a week of hummus we are ready for Pizza Hut or Ben & Jerry's." *Dagens Nyheter* in Stockholm has basically the same organizational concept—and no doubt shares it with a great many other news organizations on the same day, January 1, 2000—when its correspondents report together on the local arrival of the new millennium. From Jerusalem, Nathan Shachar notes that there was disappointment in Bethlehem because so few tourists showed up in a period of political tension; from Hong Kong, Göran Leijonhufvud reports that there were crowds as usual at the horse races, where luck in the first race would mean luck during the entire year—and, who knows, the entire millennium? Påhl Ruin, in Tokyo, says that most people celebrated at home and that cell phones stopped functioning because so many people tried to call each other with greetings at the same moment. Such reporting opportunities may be highly predictable and are not difficult to plan. They offer a way of demonstrating that the paper, the radio station, or the television network has far-flung reporting capacity, and they also dramatize the interconnectedness and simultaneity of the world.

The organization of newspeople for global reporting may not be just a matter of the spatial deployment of personnel, however. When I talked to Tom Kent at the Associated Press about the demise of the cold war story line, he also pointed out that one of its consequences could be a certain amount of journalistic retooling. There might be more interest now in stories on environmental, cultural, and scientific topics, and people with skills in such fields might be more sought after.

This may be true in other, more regionally oriented kinds of foreign correspondence as well—it would fit with the argument that the reporting should be about "societies, not just states." Thomas Friedman, however, has some reflections in *The Lexus and the Olive Tree* (1999, 14–24) on his own self-education precisely as a global analyst, and whether one shares his view of globalization or not, they seem instructive. "You need to do two things at once," he says, "look at the world through a multidimensional, multilens perspective and, at the same time, convey that complexity to readers through simple stories, not grand theories" (15). So he tells stories, but in the process he does what he calls "information arbitrage."

"Arbitrage" is a market term, Friedman points out; it refers to making a profit from unequal prices and unequal information. But it can be applied to many fields. "The key to being a successful arbitrageur is having a wide net of informants and information and then knowing how to synthesize it in a way that will produce a profit" (1999, 15).

It is an approach he arrived at by accident. As a Middle East correspondent, he started out dealing largely with two dimensions, politics and culture, reporting on "the mother of all tribal wars." Then he became a diplomatic correspondent and had to learn about matters of national security, superpower competition, international alliances, arms control, and geopolitics. That came together as a third dimension. The next step followed when his paper assigned him to covering "foreign affairs and finance"—and he discovered that such a beat had not really existed before. There had been two separate sets of reporters for it, but after the end of the cold war a great deal of news would be generated at the intersection. Financial markets thus became his fourth dimension. But he went on to realize that advances in technology were to a large extent at the heart of globalization; so there was the fifth dimension, and he added Silicon Valley to the list of world capitals he should visit at least once a year to keep up with things: Moscow, Beijing, London, Jerusalem. And finally, there was the environment. He began adding side trips to understand how ecosystems were affected by globalization and what were the global implications of their degradation. There was his sixth dimension of global reporting.

Among the people he now finds it most worthwhile to talk to, Friedman notes, are some hedge fund managers, because they have become highly skilled at arbitraging multidimensional information—only their job is making bets on stocks and bonds, not writing commentary. Otherwise, Friedman also suggests that some retooling is desirable. Strategists, who are responsible for shaping the world, and journalists, who are in charge of explaining it, must learn globalist thinking. He quotes a theoretical physicist and Nobel laureate with an interest in complex systems as saying that the big picture has been relegated to cocktail party conversation, while during the working day specialists in academia, bureaucracies, and elsewhere concentrate on something much narrower. Yet that cocktail party stuff is a crucial part of the real story.

Here, then, is a recipe for dealing with world stories that provides food for thought, points of departure for further speculation. One must keep an eye open for new places that need to be added to itineraries—or which could even require their own correspondents, in that changing landscape of news and configuration of assignments that a foreign editor must be ready to rethink continuously. Silicon Valley may be one. Perhaps in the structure of center-periphery relationships, which has a significant part in ordering global interconnectedness, there are organizations and institutions that deserve continuous coverage. Most New York–based foreign correspondents probably have coverage of the United Nations as an important ingredient in their assignment; the *New York Times* has recently had veteran foreign correspondents serve as United Nations correspondents.[10] Should there be correspondents in Washington concentrating similarly on the World Bank and the International Monetary Fund, with a mandate to travel to cover those institutions' decisions, policies, and operations and the consequences thereof?[11]

Moreover, clearly some of the sites that draw newspeople now are not so much localities with a newsworthiness of their own but "translocalities," significant because of the people who pass through them, either all the time or for particular events.[12] Melilla is of the former kind, Davos of the latter. This is one indication that some stories now belong not in places or even regions, but in entities better seen as networks, centering on particular issues and topics and extending through transnational space. Global interconnectedness often blurs the distinction between foreign and domestic news, as the story in an American paper on the passage of gems from African war zones to New York reminds us. How, then, might news work deal with networks, especially when the investigation and illumination of the latter demand some particular kind of knowledge?

Thomas Friedman's conception of the globalist reporter-commentator suggests the buildup of personal capacities to integrate understandings of several kinds. As an alternative or a complement to that strategy, media organizations could handle some of the information arbitrage in the office, by combining their specialized staff resources and creating new cross-cutting linkages. Many organizations now have specialists in fields like education, health, crime, environment, and consumer affairs, but mostly they are home-based. The foreign correspondents rarely see them; they do not come to visit. At home they are probably accountable to other editors.

Should there be a greater place for them in doing some of the network stories, reporting on some of the transnational comparisons and connections? Assignments of this kind do occur. In recent times, for example, AIDS may have tended to become an African story, but in its links to international organizations and to the medical industry, it is also a world story rather like some of those described in this chapter. And it is sometimes handled as such, by medical correspondents. Nevertheless, although it may be a good thing to be able to draw on the knowledge of such specialists in covering foreign or global news, perhaps they are best used not as single parachutists traveling from one site to another within their topical networks. Teaming up, when the opportunity is at hand, with correspondents who have local knowledge may allow greater depth in coverage. Do we see an instance of this as Nicholas Kristof, in one installment of his "Global Contagion" series, has a *New York Times* White House correspondent, David Sanger, joining him as coauthor?

Finally, we might ponder the fact that Thomas Friedman, in his concern with information arbitrage, sees an affinity between his efforts and those of hedge fund managers. One might think that there is an important difference: the journalist reports on what has happened; the people in hedge fund management try to understand what will happen, and they make bets on it. But that contrast would be much too simple. News is not just about the recent past or even the present. We are interested in it also because it is a gateway to the future, and that is true most of all when the news is about the world. Therefore the topic of the last chapter is the ways in which news work deals with time.

7 Writing Time

Anthropologists of Lewis Henry Morgan's generation, we have been told, experienced a "revolution in ethnological time." It was in the mid-nineteenth century that new discoveries of early human remains extended the knowable human past indefinitely backward (Trautmann 1992). And the emergent discipline formed itself as an engagement with universal history—but then it shrank, during a large part of the twentieth century, to that particular form of presentism which, for parts of the world at least, somehow took time and change out of its thinking and writing. It focused on "the ethnographic present," "cold societies," "equilibrium." A year of fieldwork represented eternity.

The notion of news could seem to involve quite another variety of presentism, one that leaves time in—but not much of it. "Our job is like a baker's work—his rolls are tasty as long as they're fresh; after two days they're stale; after a week they're covered with mould and fit only to be thrown out," writes Ryszard Kapuscinski (1990, 141). We see these two presentisms contrasted in Liisa Malkki's comment (1997, 93), noted in the introduction, that news and culture operate in such different temporal registers that they could seem to repel one another "like oil and water." Yet Malkki goes on to argue that it may be worthwhile to think about ways of addressing the distance between the two and thereby also that between journalism and her discipline of anthropology. Clearly that suggestion also reflects that anthropology has come some distance from merely assuming, at least for descriptive purposes, the timelessness of culture.

It seems useful, then, to return to the idea of news and to some issues briefly raised in chapter 1. The work of foreign correspondents and of newspeople generally has a great deal to do with managing temporality.[1] We could say that theirs are lives of "writing time" (if they are print people, at least, but often the same is true for others—radio and TV people often have manuscripts), but there is an ambiguity built into that phrasing. On the one hand, it can refer to the practical, urgent fact of the deadline: it is time to write, to get your stuff ready for delivery. On the other hand, there is the sometimes more, sometimes less obvious understanding that something about temporality is said, or implied, or assumed, in just about anything you offer to your audience. In the former interpretation it is a matter of regimentation; in the latter, one of representation. What time, what point or period in it, do newspeople report on? And with regard to the informed citizen—is it the past, or the present, or even the future that he or she is informed about by way of the daily ritual of scanning the flow of news?

Technologies and Time Zones

Not all media are print media; and as I noted in chapter 1, they differ in the way they handle time. Although these differences may not really be built into their technologies, what the latter at least make possible tends to influence the scheduling of news reporting. It is a fact of news work that television and radio can engage in instant communication, which the print media cannot do. News organizations adapt to such opportunities and conditions.

We should understand that the contrast is not entirely simple. There have been times and circumstances when the electronic media have not worked so fast, particularly over distances. Bruce Dunning, the CBS News veteran of Asia reporting, was in Vietnam during the war there, when films had to be flown back to the United States; and he was in Beijing during the Tiananmen Square events, when the Chinese authorities closed down the direct transmission facilities of foreign broadcasters, and film again had to be smuggled out through Hong Kong (while lower-rung government personnel seemed to helpfully look the other way). Moreover, Dunning notes, even now he mostly supplies materials from Tokyo, by way of the communications satellites over the Pacific or the Indian Ocean, for the regular American morning and evening news programs and for weekly magazine programs. Whereas some radio stations and television channels—most famously, CNN—have concentrated entirely on news broadcasting, older-style television networks like CBS may have become a little more ready to break into regular programming with especially important news. But on the whole, the twice-daily news slots involve a scheduling not wholly different from the once-daily routine of most newspapers. Besides, when newspapers also operate Web sites, the differences between the work habits of their news staffs and those of television and radio stations may become a little more blurred.

Even so, there are characteristic contrasting tendencies. By and large, the correspondents of daily newspapers have a deadline each day. That day may be busy or not so busy, but at least in that way there is a certain predictability, a certain time to plan ahead for. We may remember from chapter 3 Chris McGreal's comment that this was one reason why he preferred print journalism over radio, where he had started out. Certainly when there is breaking news to deal with, that daily deadline may still keep the correspondent very busy; and it may count, then, as someone said, that "I write faster than those who write better, and better than those who write faster." A weekly newsmagazine has a different rhythm. On radio and television, if hard news and live broadcasts are involved, you may need to be on the air for a brief spot every hour. When the negotiations between Palestinians and Israelis over an Israeli withdrawal from Hebron were reaching a climax, Lyse Doucet was on the air on BBC World Service radio every hour from midnight to 9:00 A.M., from the Erez Crossing between Israel and Gaza, the site of the meeting. She found it exhilarating. Martin Bell (1996, 209), of the BBC, reminiscing about covering the Bosnian war, notes that his colleague Peter Arnett of CNN had forty minutes between appearances; this did not leave much time for new fact-finding in between. Even when there is no really major story to keep watching, however, a radio correspondent may have a rather steady, dense reporting schedule. Cecilia Uddén, in Washington for Radio Sweden, finds herself doing usually two pieces a day, seven days a week, for straight news programs or for magazine programs of one kind or another. That is more than she would usually have done from Cairo, her previous stationing, and there are days when she hardly gets out of her studio office at all, but spends her time reading four newspapers and various magazines, watching television, and doing her reporting on that basis. Since the foreign news section of Radio Sweden had spent so much of its overall travel budget that year in the Balkans, she had not been funded to go to the dramatic World Trade Organization meeting in Seattle in 1999. Instead she recorded street sounds from the live coverage of one of the American TV networks and inserted them into her own reporting from the office on the other side of the continent—not fraudulent, she noted, since she did, after all, sign off "Cecilia Uddén, Washington." At least she approximated a kind of "I was there," and it became better radio that way.

The implications of technologies may not be all that different for foreign correspondents than for other newspeople. What often makes a difference with regard to deadlines, however, is one's location in space: there may be many time zones between the head office, the audience, and you. Scott Kraft, back at *Los Angeles Times* headquarters, remembered the time when he was the Johannesburg correspondent and learned that a famous South African author had died that morning. He wrote the obituary immediately, and when it appeared in the paper in the morning, it could still say "Alan Paton died today." When David Remnick was in Moscow during the busy perestroika period, there were things to report and comment on just about every day—he found himself filing three hundred stories in a year. Under any circumstances, such a writing schedule would be hectic. But it was also a component of the situation that he would start out working the normal Moscow day—and then as that day came to an end, the *Washington Post* head office in the United States, eight time zones away, would begin its new day, and he often found himself working its eight hours as well, getting feedback and negotiating over stories. He did not actually wear a second wristwatch for American East Coast time, he said, but it was constantly on his mind.

The working day of a foreign correspondent, then, may be ordered by two clocks, the one at home and the one on the beat. Keith Richburg, in Hong Kong, as we saw in chapter 5, argued that the maximum twelve-hour difference between him and Washington really gave him additional autonomy. Nicholas Valéry of the *Economist* compared his Tokyo and Los Angeles experiences: in Tokyo, he had a full working day behind him and accomplishments to show by the time the editors met in London. When he was in Los Angeles, in contrast, the editors, eight time zones ahead of him, sometimes seemed more inclined to tell him how they wanted him to spend the day. Even though he worked for a weekly, there appeared to be that kind of difference in the balance of power. Often, correspondents expecting to deliver on a regular daily basis would routinely have one early contact with the foreign news desk at home, for a quick exchange about what should be done, and then return with a story meeting the deadline. Also more or less regularly, they might be expected to give the editors an overview of what would be coming up locally, to the extent that significant events could be forecast, and of what feature stories they would plan to work on if time allowed.

But for some correspondents, there are no real deadlines. The people working for the major international news agencies know that every hour around the clock there are papers going into print or people going on the air somewhere around the world—even though the newspeople are especially conscious of the timetables for their most important concentrations of customers. The international office of the Associated Press in New York has its daily routines, but in the fourth floor newsroom, with its several rows of desks with computer screens, preparedness is a continuous, twenty-four-hour thing. Nonetheless, Nicolas Tatro, AP bureau chief in Jerusalem, thought the city was ideally located on what he described as a "time/power continuum" in relation to the American East Coast, since his bureau would normally be best prepared to deliver just as the customers there were getting their editorial machinery going. For radio people with regular news slots at home to plan for, the time calculus might take into account not only being ready for these, but also one's position in relation to other regions of the world. It was not an accident that—as I described in the introduction—the Hong Kong–based Asia correspondent for Radio Sweden reported, time and again, as I was having breakfast in Stockholm. Not only had the day ended in East Asia, but it would also normally be true that there was not yet much fresh domestic news, which would tend to take precedence, or from anywhere else in Europe, where the day was beginning, or from Africa for that matter. And only if there had been news breaking in the evening in North America would it offer fresh stories in the morning in Europe. In the competition for time among the regular news programs, the morning program was Hong Kong's best bet.

Event Crowding

There could be times when the correspondent checks in with the foreign desk at home, suggesting a story, and is told not to bother. Too much is going on in other parts of the world that day, and since the time or space devoted to foreign news usually remains more or less constant, there is not room for everything. Some things will not be reported at all, or only perhaps through the "News in Brief" column, with a few lines from an agency but without background or analysis. As Bruce Dunning of CBS News in Tokyo concluded, news can be "feast or famine"—too much or too little at any one time.

In Jerusalem, Nathan Shachar of *Dagens Nyheter* suggested that during the fall of 1996, one could almost use the opportunities for reporting on Hebron to measure the temperature in other crisis zones—when things cooled down in the others, there were more column inches for the ever-available West Bank town. Shachar's local BBC colleagues, for their part, once found an Internet Web site suggesting that their supposedly pro-Israeli reporting was due to the fact that they were all Jewish—although in fact, not one of the three was. Another critic, from the opposite camp, claimed that their supposedly anti-Israeli stance was shown by how little attention BBC had given to the tragic military helicopter collision near the Lebanese border. In that regard, one of the BBC correspondents noted, one should keep in mind that the crash had occurred on the same evening as President Clinton's State of the Union address (the first after his reelection) and the verdict in the O. J. Simpson civil trial. And the crash was, after all, an accident, with no suggestion of foul play and no immediate international repercussions. At the London headquarters, this correspondent concluded, there had probably been a question of priorities.

Sometimes little is thus made of an accident, however dramatic, or of continuous skirmishes in a town made famous by the Bible. Another time it might look as if an entire continent is placed on the back burner. On New Year's Eve 2001, Leif Norrman (2001), in Cape Town, had a reflective piece in *Dagens Nyheter,* occasioned by a telephone call he had received from a young woman from a Swedish radio station. She was doing a program on foreign correspondent life (I was also on it) and asked him how his experience compared to that of foreign correspondents in the movies. He felt a bit embarrassed because it was not much like that. The movies would have nothing about the correspondent making the rounds to the banks to try to obtain some functioning currency, or standing in line at some hopeless Ministry of the Interior to extend a work permit. Yes, there were times of fright, and uncertainty, and the stench of dead bodies. But the most destructive part of a correspondent's everyday life, he concluded, was emptiness: the emptiness that comes when one's beat is out of focus, when nobody seems to care what happens there. Norrman was writing at the end of a year when for months, just about all the attention had been on Central Asia and the Middle East (and the United States, wherever such news would be foreign news), and African news had been in little demand.

We can call this event crowding. Much of the time the amount of space or time allotted to foreign news in the media is not very flexible. There are occasional major exceptions, but often everything must go on, let us say, the same two pages. Or if not everything, whatever is deemed most worthy. Sometimes, in the news business and among its significant others, the response to such constraints, or to the limited capacity of news organizations to attend to things, is to manage the news flow by careful scheduling. In his discussion of how American journalists handle time, Michael Schudson (1987, 81) notes that as a kind of fetishism of immediacy, they prefer news that comes as close to the deadline as practically possible; and politicians who are aware of this plan public appearances and press conferences to fit with filing times. Astute press secretaries, in government or in business, also know how to schedule events to match the weekly round of the press and identify the days when few other stories will compete for media attention. Conversely, I would add, the suspicion is occasionally voiced that media-savvy people in business or politics may try to insert controversial or embarrassing items into the news flow, if these have to go in there at all, on days or at hours when they can hope that they face strong competition from more important and more attractive stories. But such intentional news management works best at a local or national level. Planning for newsworthiness on the global scene is in most cases presumably a great deal more difficult.

It is also widely held that it is difficult for foreign news stories to compete with important domestic news—or even with domestic trivia. Among American newspeople and media watchers, there seem to be a number of variations on the theme of how O. J. Simpson and the characters and events surrounding him seemed to get more attention than perhaps the rest of the world put together. Moreover, event crowding can be a matter of sheer reporting capacity. In April 1994 there certainly were a handful of reporters in Rwanda, or trying to get into it. But as we saw in chapter 2, a number of the Africa correspondents, responsible for covering forty-some countries on the continent, were in South Africa, witnessing the transition and the accession of Nelson Mandela to the presidency. They could hardly leave their most important, most long-running story line right then. Even, as it turned out, for genocide.

The First Draft of History

The notion that they do "the first draft of history" is one that many newspeople seem fond of. They are there witnessing, but they are also there reporting, formulating. As people of action and of the present, many of them may intend the phrase to convey a sense of wonder and excitement and do not necessarily think any more about it. Nonetheless, it is worth some more scrutiny. It suggests a quick move between past and future. It is prospectively retrospective, looking forward to looking backward, in claiming that what happened yesterday will be deemed important, scrutinized, perhaps reformulated, beyond tomorrow. When Mandela, former freedom fighter and long-term jail inmate, is installed as head of state, the event stands for the end of an era and the beginning of something new. It must remain a date in history. "Events" and "eras," however, are terms suggesting different slices of temporality.

We turn to an eminent historian for an overview of certain varieties in writing time. Fernand Braudel (1980, 25 ff.), master of the French *Annales* school, distinguished simply, something like a half century ago, between three kinds of history writing involving three time spans—as it were, three speeds.[2] There was event history (*histoire événementielle*), and there was the history of the *longue durée,* which was his own specialty. But between them there was something that he termed "conjunctural history," or what we may call medium-term history, covering a decade, a quarter century, or at the outside a half century. Event history, Braudel noted, has accustomed its readers "to the headlong, dramatic, breathless rush of its narrative." An event is "explosive"—"Its delusive smoke fills the minds of its contemporaries, but it does not last, and its flame can scarcely ever be discerned" (27). Yet as short-time-span history, event history should also more generally be understood as "proportionate to individuals, to daily life, to our illusions, to our hasty awareness." It is "the time of the chronicle and the journalist"; and lest we fall into the trap of taking event history to be synonymous with political history, Braudel went on to point out that the daily paper would also offer readers "all the mediocre accidents of ordinary life: a fire, a railway crash, the price of wheat, a crime, a theatrical production, a flood" (28). In contrast, for the historian, accepting the *longue durée* "means becoming used to a slower tempo, which sometimes almost borders on the motionless" (33). Perhaps for anthropologists, again, that sense of the almost motionless comes close to its traditional "ethnographic present," of time frozen. (And we might then want to add as a fourth time span that knowable human past in which Morgan's generation of anthropologists might be seen as preoccupied with ordering periods of *longue durée* vis-à-vis one another.)

Devoting his own time to other matters, Braudel did not do much with events, or event history. And though he was continuously interested in building bridges between history and social science, he concluded that "social science has almost what amounts to a horror of the event" (1980, 28). That seems no longer so true. One theorist of historical sociology, William Sewell (1996), has taken up the challenge of trying to pinpoint what is really "a historical event"; in anthropology, Sally Falk Moore (1986, 1987, 1994) has come back to the analytical role of events in several publications, and Veena Das (1995) has identified "critical events" as useful foci of attention in grappling with the coming into being of new cultural and social forms, extending widely and complicatedly through Indian life.

Sewell is clearly not concerned with all the trivialities that Braudel noted would go into the daily paper, even if they were historical in the sense of having occurred in the past. In brief, his historical events are those that have momentous consequences, which in some sense change the course of history. He elaborates his view by inspecting how the French Revolution was invented around the taking of the Bastille. Most important, Sewell insists that events change history and thus, in a manner of speaking, enter history by the way they relate to structures (not a favorite concept among writers of traditional event history). In other words, there is an interaction between the short term and something that is, by some measure, longer-term. There may have been a cumulative buildup of pressures and relatively inconspicuous changes over some time, but as the historical event occurs, some rupture

results in a ramifying sequence of occurrences that are recognized at the time
as notable, release new creativity and make possible new combinations, and
result in a durable transformation of structures.

Moore asks how anthropological fieldwork can be seen, and done, as
current history, and she argues for attention to "diagnostic events"—events
that display competing and contrary ideas and actions having contradictory consequences. They show how conflict, ambiguity, and uncertainty are
worked out. Each one of them hardly seems to be of major import, but then
"events are to processes what categories are to structures." And, Moore pro-
poses (1987, 736), "this is the time for processual ethnography."

Does this have anything to do with the way contemporary foreign correspondents engage with events and see themselves as writing that first draft
of history?

Story Lines and the Varieties of History

If news work is a business, events are the prime merchandise, but some
events are worth more than others. Perhaps in the 1990s, in a couple of the
places prominent in this book (although slightly earlier than the period with
which it mostly deals), there were indeed some historical events that would
fit with Sewell's criteria or any strict sense of the term: in South Africa, Mandela's release from imprisonment as well as his election to the presidency; in
Israel, the assassination of Yitzhak Rabin, undermining an already uncertain
peace process. And after the turn of the millennium, September 11, 2001, has
quickly come to stand as a date when a new battlefront, however it was to be
understood, was drawn through the world. Surely the newspeople reporting
on these events could rightly feel that they were producing documents for future history. Yet events come in various sizes, with various weights, and it is
not always so obvious what difference they will make in the long run. Foreign
correspondents may not so often have to be bothered with those mediocre accidents of life that, Braudel noted, will also be in the daily paper, but they
could still have to worry about that "delusive smoke" of events, the difficulties of discerning their "flame."

We can return to the notion of story lines here, as a way of handling
such difficulties. Jim Lederman, the Jerusalem correspondent I quoted on the
subject in chapter 4, described the story line as a frame that simplified the
journalist's narrative by giving coherence to what could otherwise seem like
random occurrences. Generally, to repeat, there is the problem with story
lines that they can organize attention and lack of attention in ways that may

turn out to be treacherous. But let us concentrate now on their time dimension. Given the on again, off again nature of the news flow, we should briefly reflect on what it could mean that the story line is a contextualizing device literally to be kept in mind. Note that it is a frame that relates to time not only with regard to the stable or shifting realities of the beat out there—Johannesburg, Jerusalem, Tokyo—but also to the life and career of a correspondent and to the stored conceptions of the news consumer.

To some extent, story lines may come to serve as institutional memories. One way in which foreign correspondents of the rotating variety often prepare themselves for a new assignment is to study the stories of their predecessors. This seems like a mechanism for preserving existing story lines, at least until something occurs that dramatically upsets them. The spiralist correspondents do not really arrive on their new assignment with their minds quite as fresh as they or their editors sometimes would like to think.

But then because the correspondents can only claim very limited time or space for each of their reports in their media outlets, they must try to make effective instant claims on audience memories, hoping to find the contexts for new items already available there. The reporting themes we have identified in previous chapters come out of a bundle of mainstream media based in several countries, and we may be inclined to think of those themes as becoming very securely established in audience minds. Perhaps we should then remind ourselves of the media consumption habits suggested in chapter 1: even archetypical informed citizens, unless they are pursuing some special interest, are likely to read one daily paper and attend more or less distractedly to one or two radio or television news programs in an ordinary day. If the news out of the media is embedded, as we have noted before, in other kinds of experience—it is about a city we have been to, a country where relatives live—it can perhaps do with less contextualization in the reporting itself. Otherwise, however, there may be less redundancy and recall in communication than our consideration of the story line phenomenon leads us to assume. The details of story lines, and sometimes even the survival of story lines, may be at risk. It could seem that moving beyond them or ignoring the need to recollect would beneficially emancipate audiences, allowing them a broader and less fixed view of distant places and people; but then it could also lead to disorientation, a sense of being rather less at home in the world. David Remnick told me that during his Moscow correspondent days, in those intensive times of glasnost and perestroika, he learned that he must not assume that from one day to the next, his readers would be able to identify any Soviet individual other than Mikhail Gorbachev. Somewhat playfully, he put on a particular key on his computer keyboard the phrase that for a time he could use almost every day about Nagorno-Karabach—"a disputed mountain enclave within Azerbaijan, inhabited mostly by ethnic Armenians."

Again, however, the questions are how story lines contribute to internal narrative coherence in the flow of reporting and what time has to do with it. Perhaps story lines can vary from static to dynamic. In reporting from Japan, it could seem that the story line, if one can call it that—or, at least, the theme—of difference (weirdness) is a report from the *longue durée,* or out of the ethnographic present. It presents a durable, essential Japanese-ness. It is a theme that is usually not made fully explicit, even if there may be little room for mistake over what it consists of. To a considerable extent it is composed from feature stories and does not really revolve so much around events and hard news. Yet as we have seen, when Nicholas Kristof had a very real dramatic event, the Kobe earthquake, to report in the *New York Times,* it too became an opportunity to investigate Japanese-ness: "the way people or nations react to disasters can open a window on their souls."

I talked to David Remnick about how reporting on the Soviet Union, for as long as it lasted, had related to time and events. At its beginning, of course, stands a monument to historical event reporting—John Reed's *Ten Days That Shook the World* (a book that, with the movie *Reds* later linked to it, must have done as much as any to foster the heroic popular image of the foreign correspondent)—and then there was that period marked by what became known as Kremlinology, news work and interpretation carried out under very restrictive circumstances.[3] In the 1970s, Soviet society evidently became a more accessible beat, as shown in books by several Moscow correspondents for western newspapers—*Russia* by the *Washington Post's* Robert Kaiser (1976) and *The Russians* by Hedrick Smith (1977) of the *New York Times* were the most prominent examples.

I remember that as I read these books almost thirty years ago, they seemed a lot like ethnography, at a time when they had hardly any competition from a professional anthropology of everyday Soviet life. The back-cover blurb of Kaiser's book said that it would tell readers "how the Russians feel about their government, the West, the housing situation, the new Russian Fiat car, schools, marriage, abortion, children, premarital sex, sports, crime, drink, the quality of consumer goods, books, food, prices, war and peace—in short, about life." On Smith's book, the blurb said about the author that "he has talked all night beside a steaming samovar in cramped flats and dirt-floored peasant *izbas* . . . he has gone to the people, made friends with them, studied their customs and government at close range."[4]

When we talked about these books, David Remnick's own book *Lenin's*

Tomb (1993) had recently been published. It had been very well received and had won him a Pulitzer Prize. But he was aware of the difference between his book and those of his predecessors. At their time, ordinary Soviet life and experience, in what may at least have felt like a Soviet *longue durée* (on hindsight, one may question whether there was such a thing), was unfamiliar to readers in the West and therefore had news value. And as this was part of that extended Brezhnev period which we have later come to label one of stagnation, there were perhaps fewer newsworthy events—a little like Tokyo in the 1990s. By the late 1980s and early 1990s, Kaiser's and Smith's kind of Moscow reporting had already been done—quite a lot of it—so it had little news value any more. Besides, the speed of history had accelerated, and the perestroika kept generating significant events. So Remnick's own book, as well as his newspaper reporting, dwelt rather more on these.

The *longue durée* could also be understood to play a significant part in setting story lines, however, even though hard news stories are more visible. Such a privileging of the long-term, almost timeless, in the construction of a story line can be recognized in the kind of Africa reporting (by now perhaps too compromised) that links "tribal wars" to "ancient hatreds"—and where parachutist reporting often has not drawn on much knowledge of previous local events. One might even argue that in its most general terms, the story line of Arab-Israeli conflict appears to involve events infinitely generated anew out of a lasting structure. In a particular way, event history relates to structure here, yet one might not reach so eagerly for the "first draft of history" trope if that history, without particular direction or sense of dramatic transformation, seems to be just a chronicle of one damn thing after the other.

That, however, may be an interpretation that develops most readily if one has no precise grasp of the sequentiality of those events. "An event can if necessary take on a whole range of meanings and associations . . . Infinitely extensible, it becomes wedded, either freely or not, to a whole chain of events, of underlying realities which are then, it seems, impossible to separate," wrote Fernand Braudel (1980, 27–28). One part of the building and maintenance of a more recognizably cumulative story line would seem to entail placing events in that chain and thus indicating at least some minimal associations between them. Events—if not "historical," then perhaps at least "diagnostic"—become building blocks for processes. In the Middle Eastern instance, in the late 1990s, there was some speculation that the peace process might succeed, that one was indeed reporting on an accumulation of events moving in one direction. Correspondents could do that mixture of hard news and feature stories in which the latter often were dependent on the former and at the same time supportive of them, by filling in details and offering background. But again, as the BBC correspondent Lyse Doucet said, it all resembled working with a Rubik's cube: somewhere something would go wrong. The chain of events could go on and on. At times the correspondents in Jerusalem even felt overburdened by events that could not be ignored, even if they did not do much to change the overall story, and which hindered the correspondents from spending time on feature stories. In South Africa during the apartheid period, the situation may have been similar, with another deep divide generating events, even though the event density much of the time was lower than in the Middle East. In addition, perhaps there was in the South African case continuously a sharper sense that the sequence of events would eventually reach some kind of climax—although it was darkly uncertain what would be the nature of the major historical events involved in it. (The fact that most of the world media had a stronger sense of where their sympathies should be in this conflict may have played a part in such assumptions.)

Then it should be understood that there can also be directionality in less conspicuous ways—and the question may arise how as a newsperson you handle this. Characteristically, I had some interesting conversations on this topic in Tokyo. On the Japanese news scene, to reiterate, there is little local event crowding to speak of, involving news of a dignity that would draw international attention. The correspondents on this beat, consequently, may have given some particular thought to the condition of living with event scarcity.

Selling the theme of Japanese otherness was one way out, but another was a skilled use of pegs. Through pegs one can turn a process momentarily into an event; something like a feature story can become an entity resembling hard news. In the end, of course, pegs are organizing devices for drawing audience attention, but before that correspondents can find them useful in negotiating with editors at home. In a field of competing news, again, something that does not seem urgent may just never make it beyond a hurried, skeptical, tough-minded editor's desk. If it is an interesting story that attaches itself to an event, though, even if the latter is not in itself earthshaking, it may seem worth having right at that moment.

When I met Nicholas Valéry in Tokyo, it was a couple of weeks after the *Economist* had published his cover story on the continued debate over Japanese defense (mentioned in chapter 4—"Japan's Constitution"). He had persuaded the editor in London of the value of the story about a month in advance, since he knew the subject was about to come up in the Diet, so that he would have some "spot news" to hang the story on. Until then, he thus had a few weeks of thinking and preparation. He took the story from the end of

World War II, through various wranglings over the Japanese constitution, into the present preoccupation with the North Korean threat and current attempts by political parties to position themselves before the upcoming elections. In a similar way, Sonni Efron of the *Los Angeles Times* felt that many potential stories out of Japan were really matters of process—you kept watching them but would not necessarily be quite sure when to do them. One of her predecessors in the bureau had said they were like a toothpaste tube: you have to decide yourself when to stop squeezing. She took a particular interest in technology stories, but she found it very difficult to predict precisely what innovations would have the greatest long-term impact, and the experts often disagreed among themselves.

Valéry had thought about how to describe Japan in the present period. He reflected on famous past attempts to grasp the nature of Japanese culture and society. Ruth Benedict's *Chrysanthemum and the Sword,* published at the end of World War II, had been interesting but wrong; the Dutch correspondent Karel Van Wolferen's more recent *Enigma of Japanese Power* (1989) had been quite good, although it perhaps exaggerated the weakness of the center in the Japanese political system. But Valéry had also pointed out to Van Wolferen that significant changes were now occurring at the peripheries. For decades, he said, the society had been built on the premise of expansion, but this no longer worked. Japan had actually been in a phase of maturity since 1973. The senior Japanese generation, people in their sixties, were slow to recognize this, but there were people a generation younger who understood it. Now he saw the present as "the beginning of the end of denial" and thought this was the big story to be told.

Between the *longue durée* and event history, we remember Braudel pointing out, there can be a medium-term history. It seems to be something like this that Valéry and Efron are grappling with, and looking again at foreign correspondence out of Japan, we can perhaps recognize it in a range of stories. When Efron (1999) reports on the passage of Japan's first freedom-of-information law, she sets it against the background of twenty years of struggle by citizens' groups—and one gets some sense of cumulative change away from the old opacity of Japanese power. When Påhl Ruin (1999f) describes the revolt of Japanese youth, their rejection of the ideals of lifelong employment and loyalty to the corporation and their shift to expressive cultural styles, we sense that a generation is rearranging its relationship to the economy. When Mary Jordan and Kevin Sullivan (1999b) begin a story on "classroom chaos" with a visit to Miss Sato's collapsing second-grade class, where "one child has broken windows four times; hits other children, walks on the desks, urinates off the veranda and spits on the floor," and "[a]nother scribbles all over the room and lies down on the desktops," it is clear that something other than individual misdemeanors is involved. Is an old authority structure failing? And when the same writers find that "Japanese Retirees Fill 'Second Life' with Second Jobs," it becomes obvious that what they identify as the world's fastest-aging and longest-living population is fitting itself into the economy, and into family life, in changing ways (Sullivan and Jordan 1999). We realize perhaps as well that some of the stories on family and gender in Japan noted in chapter 4 are not just about difference but also about the medium-term making of history.

Into the Future

The varieties of writing time that we have borrowed from Braudel may not differ only in the time spans they cover. They could also turn out in practice to involve different views and combinations of past, present, and future. In the *longue durée,* reporting tends to merge the three. Much event reporting of a rather mundane kind describes an immediate past and hardly suggests any particular implications for the future. But reporting on what are perceived to be "historical events" does suggest that these are, in a manner of speaking, events with a future. Medium-term histories, for their part, may quite often not just take in a bit more of the past but implicitly or explicitly place themselves across the divide between past and future. Observing what appear to be processes, what has been happening for some time, becomes a resource for, if not predicting, then at least speculating and debating about what will come next.

Braudel was not rigid about what he would count as medium-term: a decade, a quarter century, a half century. Objectives and contexts may determine pragmatically what goes into writing time here, for newspeople, historians, or anthropologists. Some would focus on economic cycles and waves. Another time span also fairly readily suggests itself as a general possibility: generations and lifetimes, what you remember and what you are likely still to be a part of, the more personal and subjective looking backward and looking forward of the media consumer. Since at any one time the audience may include those who are rather young as well as those who are rather old, with different time horizons, marking off the medium term here may need to involve some compromise, but one could argue that to draw on people's own memories and experiences and cater to their curiosity about what may still be in their own future, two or three decades in each direction could be a reasonably user-friendly medium-term history.

Informed citizens, whom we identified in chapter 1 with a little help from Alfred Schutz, would seem to be likely consumers of medium-term history. Sensing that zones of relevance have blurred boundaries, that they are within reach of remote others and their actions, they do not mind receiving some early warning. They may try to discern the signs themselves in the passage of event history, but they will be interested in coherent interpretations from others, especially those whom they would acknowledge as experts. They certainly pay attention to emergencies, but they also want to know about emergences.

Newspeople certainly sometimes acknowledge that such stories may not get told. "By swarming to events, we correspondents miss the developments which are the basic factors of change," writes Mort Rosenblum (1993, 22), the Associated Press veteran. "Because of the press of daily events, journalists are forced to ignore what otherwise might be significant stories, and correspondents tend to lose continuity in their reports because they have to run from one dramatic event to another," notes very similarly Jim Lederman (1993, 115), whose comments we have already heard on what longer-term developments Middle East and Israel reporting may be missing out on: shifting ethnic composition, changing class structure in a growing high-tech information society, water scarcity.

Lederman's point of departure in writing about the first intifada, we have seen, was also precisely that because the news media had defined the story line too narrowly, they had not attended to the tensions accumulating within Palestinian society. The historical event of September 11, 2001, is similarly worth thinking about in this connection. In Sewell's analysis of such events, he noted that they set in motion new and ramifying chains of events. Indeed, in the enormous coverage of that particular event and its aftermath, the point was made often enough that it created a new situation, extending throughout the world. But Sewell also pointed out that historical events could already have behind them less dramatic changes, pressures building up slowly. After that meaning-saturated date, news audiences received stories portraying such a buildup—distributed intriguingly over a network of people in Koranic schools in Pakistan, technical schools in Germany, mosques in Great Britain, flight academies in the United States, and various other locations. But that occurred only afterward: what might have been a major global story line for some time, and most certainly has become one now, was mostly constructed retrospectively. Some multisite reporting on the sentiments, expressions, and milieus of anti-Americanism and sectarian Islamism could perhaps have provided some earlier warning of the accumulating danger.

Yet news media also try to respond to an interest in the emergent in various ways. When I met the New York *Newsday*'s Roy Gutman after he had

returned from that harrowing, almost too eventful assignment as Europe correspondent that had also earned him his Pulitzer Prize, he had become his
paper's "international security correspondent"—his task was to try to figure
out where new dangers were arising. And it was clear to him, just as it is to
various other observers, that the notion of international security does not
now refer only to military phenomena, but to everything from drug cartels to
damaged environments, to whatever one may now associate with "risk."
Whether they employ the label "international security correspondent" or
not—and it is not a job label invented only for Gutman—many newspapers
and other media organizations certainly tend to use experienced foreign correspondents, after they have returned to headquarters, as analysts and commentators with a mandate to concentrate at least partially on longer-term
tendencies and often with comparatively easy access to travel money. Thomas
Friedman's *New York Times* position, as discussed in the previous chapter, is
an obvious further example.

There is also a pattern of fitting such longer-term summarizing, reflective work into the rhythm of audience habits. Newspapers obviously often
steer overviews and interpretations of things to come, along with assorted
other feature stories, into weekend editions. If, according to Hegel, the newspaper is the modern man's substitute for morning prayers, at the end of the
week there may be time for a sermon. Then, however, there is also that wider
division of labor between the news media that becomes evident here. As Roy
Gutman pointed out when we talked about his new assignment, radio and
television are faster with event reporting but biased toward concrete, dramatic imagery and sometimes have trouble knowing what to do with processes; investigation and interpretation can therefore become a niche for
print journalists. Among them, one could add, those who write for weeklies
and monthlies may still selectively chronicle recent events, but often they relate better to the logic of doing medium-term, partly future-oriented history.

I sat in on a meeting of the foreign news staff of *Dagens Nyheter* in
Stockholm on a Friday afternoon, the day before a new project was to be
launched. It had been the foreign news editor's idea. There was no widely
read newsweekly in Sweden, she pointed out, and thus *Dagens Nyheter* ought
to make an effort to give some regular space to the kind of comprehensive
reports and analyses on durable topics that one would tend to find in such
publications elsewhere. Preparations were made, and the following Saturday
would be the premiere for the new effort, "Outlook," which was to be a steady
item every Saturday morning, on the back page of section 1.

Much of the meeting that afternoon, at the end of May 1997, was devoted to reporting and commentary within the group on incoming event news

and what to do with it. NATO foreign ministers were meeting in Portugal to discuss just how much they should open up the organization to new eastern European members. There was a French election campaign going on; a free-lance photographer who had been retained by the paper had sent in some excellent pictures, but the technical costs for this coverage had turned out to be greater than anticipated, and there was some joking about this. Since president Yeltsin was due in Ukraine, the Moscow correspondent would do something about the conflict over the Crimean peninsula. In Israel a minister had said something about how much of the West Bank his government intended to keep; this was from a news agency, but since the *Dagens Nyheter* Jerusalem correspondent Nathan Shachar was traveling elsewhere, there would be no further comment from him. The Taliban, again, had suffered a setback, as some warlord had changed sides once more. In Indonesia, President Suharto had won the election (it would turn out to be his last) with 75 percent of the vote, which even the government evidently thought was a bit much. But Göran Leijonhufvud in Hong Kong wanted to wait and hear a little more before writing an analytical piece.

There was some exchange over items in the "News in Brief" column. Half of the text of one possible item was about Reuter reporting that a national news agency had reported that a local newspaper had claimed that . . . Too much on the chain of news links, too little substance, someone said. It was sometimes necessary to add more background explanation. The foreign news editor gave an example — one item the other day had referred to "one of the prime ministers of Cambodia." So how many are there, and why?

Nevertheless, the focus of attention was on the new "Outlook" series. The first article was about the international arms trade. The author, Bengt Albons (1997), a long-term foreign correspondent who had served as foreign news editor before and who was now the "security correspondent"—at the moment he was in Portugal reporting on the NATO meeting—discerned that the trade was actually declining. Someone fetched a page proof. There was little discussion of the text itself but some favorable comment on the graphics, although someone said that they were perhaps a little complicated. And there was some argument about the headline: a bit dull, no real action. But attempts to remake it came up against the obstacle that "arms trade" in Swedish is one long word, which would have to be hyphenated and run over two lines. For this series there really should be headlines running across the entire page, one staffer proposed. Concluding the meeting, the foreign news editor said that whoever would represent them as the front page was laid out that evening must battle to make sure that the "Outlook" premiere was prominently featured.

Indeed it was—a blurb for the new series (with a small picture of a Kalashnikov) was in the top left-hand corner of the front page, the best possible location. On later Saturday mornings, for a long period, there were other extensive "Outlook" reports, on topics such as the emerging strategy of the United States, as remaining superpower, for combining security and trade politics; new working styles in diplomacy; the international drug trade, with the Cali Cartel as a case study (allowing more nice graphics); and, as a 1997 end-of-the-year overview, the prospects for democracy in the world. After some years, however, the series began to appear less regularly and basically stopped being a series. There was a new foreign news editor who was perhaps less committed to the idea; perhaps also there was a beginning dearth of promising topics; and in any case, a newspaper should keep renewing itself.

Conclusion: Hedge Fund Managers, Scenarios, Anthropologists

So who can take citizens with a desire to feel informed from the present into the future? "Security correspondents" may be a claim from inside the news media apparatus. "Hedge fund managers," suggested Thomas Friedman, the *New York Times* columnist, in *The Lexus and the Olive Tree* (see chapter 6); at least he found that their power of combining heterogeneous information made them unusually interesting to talk to about how things were coming together in the world and about probable outcomes and futures. What, then, about academics? Anthropologists?

Early in his book, Friedman notes that it belongs in the same genre as some other well-known examples that appeared not long before his own: Paul Kennedy's *Rise and Fall of the Great Powers* (1987); Francis Fukuyama's *End of History and the Last Man* (1992), Samuel Huntington's *Clash of Civilizations and the Remaking of World Order* (1996). He points out that "various essays and books" by Robert Kaplan also belong on the same short list—we may want to identify *The Ends of the Earth* (1996) and *The Coming Anarchy* (2000) in particular.

Perhaps we can cast a glance at these books and this genre—also involved in writing time, in later drafts of history. In the introduction, I suggested that studying foreign correspondents for an anthropologist was—well, possibly studying up, but more important, studying sideways, trying to understand the workings of a neighboring group engaged in a somehow parallel pursuit. Reflecting over these books may again seem like a matter of studying up, but once more I prefer to see it as studying sideways. How does what they say about the world relate to what anthropologists say? Or at least could say?

We are leaving the everyday work of mainstream media foreign correspondents here, the people of datelines and deadlines, and entering the borderland between journalism and academia: a political science professor at one leading university (Huntington, at Harvard) and a history professor at another (Kennedy, at Yale); a think-tank intellectual (Fukuyama, then at Rand Corporation); a journalist publishing most regularly in a monthly magazine (Kaplan, in the *Atlantic Monthly*); and Friedman himself, at probably the world's leading newspaper. Moreover, several of the books are of the kind that grew out of an original journal or magazine article. No real divide here, it seems, but various approaches within one genre. And what is the genre? Friedman (1999, xviii)—while trying tentatively but not quite persuasively to edge out of it himself—identifies it as "The One Big Thing."

The timing of these books is obviously central. The Kennedy book identified by Friedman could seem just slightly too early to fit in, but even when it appeared, one could see the writing on the wall. And then the wall— The Wall—fell, and Friedman makes the point that this was when we got a born-again world. So what we deal with are macroscenarios for the post-cold-war period.[5] They are attempts to launch, with their respective "one big things," new story lines, whether chaos, the triumph of liberalism, civilizational clashes, or something else, to substitute for the one just lost. If Kennedy's book could at least have seemed, on the face of it, to be looking backward, he was more unequivocally in the future-writing mode with his following book, *Preparing for the Twenty-First Century* (1993). One may assume, in addition, that the books are intended not only for experts but also for the many informed citizens who want to get a handle on what has been going on and what will happen next (if anything—the end of history?). The authors, it would seem, are the next step up from international security correspondents. Their books also happen to have been published during, or just before, the period when I was having my conversations with foreign correspondents and editors and keeping track of their writing time. (Huntington's book was indeed mentioned once, in passing, as Bill Keller explained why it would be good to have a *New York Times* correspondent in Istanbul.)

There is no need to go into detail here with regard to these particular books or to provide a critique of them. Each has been extensively reviewed and debated already, and the immediate post-cold-war period that they came out of is fading away. I cannot claim to be fair as I use a line or two to sum up what their respective "big things" are, but this would be by way of reminder. Fukuyama argues that now liberal democracy and the market have conclusively shown their superiority and that nothing will be quite so important after that. Friedman's emphasis, we have seen, is a bit related: beware, do not get in the way of the Electronic Herd stampeding through the global market! Huntington discerns that after the end of ideologies, the world can return to older cleavages. Cultural differences will be fundamental, world politics will be a politics of identity—"we know who we are only when we know who we are not and often only when we know whom we are against" (Huntington 1996, 21)—played out between half a dozen or so civilizations (the number is a little uncertain), and one cannot be sure that this will be a peaceful politics. Kaplan seems to be on a journey to a coming dystopia. "The years that follow an epochal military and political victory such as the fall of the Berlin Wall are lonely times for realists" (Kaplan 2000, xi). Hardly the end of history, since democracy may turn out to have been only a moment. The world population grows much too quickly, the environment deteriorates, and hordes of young thugs roam through the streets, so do not trust human nature to be any good. Less drastic in his choice of vocabulary, but still worried about what is coming up, Kennedy in his later book also focuses on issues of demography, ecology, energy, and technology. In the end, though, he suggests that leadership will matter—we face "a troubled and fractured planet, whose problems deserve the serious attention of politicians and publics alike . . . [T]he pace and complexity of the forces for change are enormous and daunting; yet it may still be possible for intelligent men and women to lead their societies through the complex task of preparing for the century ahead" (Kennedy 1993, 349).

The time perspectives built into these scenarios seem to vary, although they are not always entirely obvious. Kennedy notes that for demographic reasons he feels most secure in discussing the next thirty years; this, we see, is a medium-term history of the future. So, perhaps, are Kaplan's and Friedman's. Huntington, with his civilizational interpretation, is rediscovering an old but ongoing *longue durée*. Fukuyama is evidently forecasting a new one.

Even if these books, as Friedman suggests, are all in one genre, they differ in the way they assemble their materials and present them to their readers, and this tends after all to betray the positions of their authors on the academia-to-journalism continuum. Fukuyama and Kennedy seem mostly to stay in their studies, close to their bookshelves and file cabinets. Friedman describes himself in a chapter heading as a "tourist with an attitude"—we can suspect that as a globetrotting *New York Times* columnist, he finds most doors open to him. Kaplan's writings frequently show him approaching the coming anarchy, in West Africa or Central Asia or wherever, in a bush taxi, with a rucksack. Huntington, thinking on a large scale about civilizations, may again appear most at home in his office, with Toynbee and Spengler (and Braudel) on the shelves and a geopolitical map on the wall, although after his

most famous book appeared, he has surely been doing a global round of conference centers—a case of traveling theory again. Yet (the plot thickens) as
Robert Kaplan (2001, 75) interviews him in the *Atlantic Monthly* apropos the
September 11 events and suggests that Huntington has been right most of the
time, he also claims that "more than other academics, Huntington pays attention to ground-level realities."[6] In his footnotes, writes Kaplan, Huntington has "displayed an academically atypical fondness for quoting on-
the-scene observers." "There are no academic sources for recent events,"
Huntington tells Kaplan; "there is only academic opinion."

Again, what about us anthropologists—what could we say about recent
events, medium-term history, the future? True, we may not be likely sources
for hard news. That "little bunch of madmen" struggling to get in where sane
people are trying to escape are newspeople, most likely without any academic ethnographers among them. And by the time the parachutists pull out
of the news site, and its lights perhaps go out as far as the news media are concerned, anthropologists, in the logic of academic production, may at best be
polishing the first draft of a research proposal to a funding agency.

When it comes to placing events within processes, however, doing anthropology rather more as a medium-term history of the present, there are
greater possibilities. If major events involve a rupture with new ramifying
consequences, someone should look into what happens after the parachutists
leave. Occasionally they return to find out for themselves. Schudson (1987,
103), in his interpretation of time in news work, notes that the *New York
Times* came back to Bhopal, India, to do a story a year after the Union Carbide industrial disaster; he places it in his class of "anniversary stories." Yet
such inquiries can be taken further—that slow-motion research proposal may
be worth doing, after all. Veena Das (1995, 137–74), considering Bhopal as
one of her "critical events," concentrated largely on pursuing it in discourses
as the related cases entered American and Indian courts, but she could thus
show how it developed as more than a local story.

Even when there are no major events, however—or where they are yet
to occur, although one may just possibly discern a buildup—there is the opportunity to portray, again, the emergent rather than the emergency.[7] How do
the sheer temporal practices of foreign correspondents as well as anthropologists affect possibilities here, we could wonder. Leaving parachutist work
aside, among newspeople, the long-timers rather than the spiralists ought in
principle to be the more privileged observers of things that take a bit more
time to become noticeable. At least, that is, as long as they really do pay attention to them, rather than merely absorbing them into everyday experience. But it would not be surprising if a spiralist who returns to a previous

beat after a period of absence, as sometimes happens, was more acutely aware of what has changed and what is cumulatively going on. (It seems not accidental that Nicholas Valéry of the *Economist,* who was such a returnee in Tokyo, did reflect on slow change.) Among the anthropologists, the classic one-year period in the field should again allow a better sense of medium-term process than the brief visit of a parachutist. All the same, we should remember "the ethnographic present," the classic inclination to translate that year into eternity—it is not self-evident that such process will be recognized. More longitudinally oriented research formats, with continuous involvement and repeated visits to the same field, would seem advantageous for such purposes. Yet to a degree, it probably matters less whether one is in a place for a brief or an extended period, only once or many times. What makes the difference may be simply a cultivated sensitivity toward the passage of time: the medium-term history of the present as a state of mind.

"Portraying" the emergent was the phrasing we just allowed ourselves. What role does it suggest for ethnography in grasping the meaning of the passage of history? It is noticeable that the prominent commentators on "one big thing" (or two) frequently focus on demography and environment. Undoubtedly these dimensions are important as one attempts to gaze into troubles of the future, but there is also some tendency among commentators to give them a larger-scale, rather abstract sort of treatment. As he reflects on his own presentation of twenty-first-century tendencies, Paul Kennedy (1993, 16) recognizes this. It could seem as if he were paying insufficient attention to "intangible" and "nonmaterial" dimensions of human existence, he writes, but when he gets to his regional case studies, it should become clear that "the most important influence on a nation's responsiveness to change probably is its social attitudes, religious beliefs, and culture." One could still feel that he does rather little with the insight, at least until he gets to his chapter on the United States, where as an academic immigrant (from Britain), he allows himself certain more critical and probably more personal impressions.

Samuel Huntington, with his argument that cultural fault lines are what ultimately matter and his conviction that civilizations and identities can now and more or less forever be tied to one world religion or another, is probably the "one big thing" author who comes closest to issues in which anthropologists feel that their scholarly capital should count (and the one who has therefore, I believe, drawn the most criticism from them).[8] But despite his presumed fondness for local sources, his book also largely leaves real people out—unless they are the historical personages of a cultural fundamentalist branch of *Realpolitik.*

What would Huntington do with these scenes in chapter 1—the street

argument in Jerusalem, the Ghanaian Orangeman, the young Chinese jump-
ing up and down in the Beijing discotheque? Bringing people back in will often show that culture tends not to be a long-durable consensus but a shifting although sometimes distracted debate. That there are many different
ways of being more or less Christian, more or less Confucian, more or less
Hindu, or more or less Muslim, and that people can at the same time be a
number of other things, outside religion, with which they might likewise identify more or less strongly. Again, newspeople, in their feature stories especially, sometimes come close to doing ethnography, even when they have to
fit it into a few column inches. It can be argued that Kaplan and Friedman,
the two journalists among the authors identified above, are also those who
are most consistently inclined to bring people back in, even when it is only
through the hurried, worried glimpse from the bush taxi.

Ethnography can thus play a part if anthropologists choose to enter the
public culture, approaching in one way or another the genre of macroscenarios. But it can do so in different ways. It can give a human face—better yet, a
number of different faces, and voices—to large-scale, too easily anonymous
processes and offer an understanding of what human agency has to do with
them. If a desirable thick cosmopolitanism is a matter of feeling at home in
the world, ethnography can cultivate that sense by allowing a breadth of vicarious experience. At the same time, ethnography can be a tool of critique.
Probably there is a widespread skepticism among anthropologists against
many of the varieties of "one big thing" scenarios. These latter seem to generalize too boldly and broadly across the global scene or simply to ignore
parts of it. Rather than supporting the "one big thing" formulations and filling in their details, ethnography can sometimes be trusted to express and
underpin, eloquently and on its own, our doubts about both scenarios and
sound bites—not so unlike those correspondents who, impatient with the
story line for their beats, set out at least occasionally to write against it.

Yet we should perhaps avoid getting into too celebratory a mode with
regard to our ethnographic predilection. To do a better job of turning the citizens of the world into readers of ethnography, do anthropologists have to
give some renewed thought to what this ethnography should look like and
what it needs to go with?

"You have to write more seductively," we may remember a correspondent saying, confronting the problems of making readers engage with foreign news after the end of the cold war had removed their major worries.
Perhaps the relative consensus among anthropologists on the value of ethnography—"rich," "fine-grained"—is to a degree a result of the inward-turning
of the academic discipline. It is an appreciation that comes naturally to the

connoisseurship of skilled craftspeople and their apprentices in training. If anthropologists want to contribute more effectively to a public culture, in which audiences may just be somewhat impatient with their in-house enthusiasms, however, they may find that their ethnography needs to be fitted into more mixed genres. Small facts can speak to big issues, we have learned (from Clifford Geertz, 1973, 23), and we need not deny this. There is still a risk, though, that the small facts sometimes speak only to small issues or even appear to suggest that those big issues just are not there. We may accomplish little by just responding to "one big thing" stories, eloquently formulated and not immediately implausible, with myriads of little facts. Even as we try to persuade our audiences that things are a bit more complicated than just "one big thing," the alternative must also be clear and accessible. Leaving an intellectual vacuum behind is not much of a public service.

And then there is the question of what to do with the future.[9] For one thing, you cannot really do the ethnography of what has not yet happened. Moreover, anthropologists tend to have their doubts about predictions and may be inclined to think that this is what scenarios are about.

Even if some scenarios, on one scale or another, imply a predictive power, however, this is too restrictive a view of what writing toward the future can be about. In his essay on the varieties of time in writing, Michael Schudson (1987, 106–8) suggests another opening, as he describes two *Los Angeles Times* feature stories—for their readers these are domestic rather than foreign news, but this does not matter for our purposes. One of them seems at first to be about Rick Higgins, but really it is about telecommuting. Three days a week Higgins is the ordinary kind of suburban commuter, spending forty minutes each way on his car ride to the downtown office. The other days—his telecommuting days—he may even take a bike ride after breakfast before sitting down to work. The other story comes out of Dayton, Ohio, and reports that three years after toxic waste was found in local water supplies, nobody, at any level of government, has acted on the problem. An odd news story, one might think, in that it reports on inaction, on what has not happened. But the point of it, Schudson argues, is that it is not really about Dayton. It is about the threat posed by tens of thousands of toxic waste sites across the country, some of them probably nearby.

Schudson calls this "subjunctive reporting"—the subjunctive form, according to his dictionary, is used to express supposition, desire, hypothesis, possibility. The telecommuting and toxic waste stories show glimpses of possible futures, of what may happen "if certain trends continue" or if nothing is done about them. Some of the feature stories referred to above about generational and technological changes in Japan, for example, similarly seem to be not just about the medium-term, processual making of history, but about also stretching it forward. So, to an extent, is Nathan Shachar's feature story from Jerusalem, described in chapter 4—concluded with an interview with a demographer about the future dominance of the Orthodox, who have many more children than secular Israelis. (But then the demographer says he cannot be sure, since something unexpected will always happen.)

If we want to engage with those informed citizens in their search for conceptions of what may come next, or later on, it may be worthwhile to experiment with forms of subjunctive anthropology as well, at the level of complexity we find necessary. Thomas Friedman's favored interlocutors, the hedge fund managers, know as well as anybody else that making bets on the future involves risk taking, and the necessity of approaching times ahead with a certain intellectual humility, emphasizing the tentativeness of one's assumptions and expectations, is understood among scholars as well. "Conjectures about the future . . . become an implicit part of the understanding of the present," writes Sally Falk Moore (1987, 727, 731), going on to argue that analyses in the mode of current history "must be more candid about what cannot be predicted."

Under such circumstances, rather than focusing on a single scenario, we are perhaps better off with multiple scenarios, complementary or alternative, on various scales, each with its own critique, with one possibly destabilizing the others. The argument has been set forth, especially with regard to Huntington's about the clash of civilizations, that scenarios can become self-fulfilling prophecies. A matching insight is that if they are scrutinized and if people act against them, they can self-destruct as well. Perhaps Alfred Schutz, drawing his contrast between the informed citizen and the man in the street, thoroughly at home in a very small world, would have accepted the notion that one role of scenarios could be to replace the certainty based on ignorance with an uncertainty based on understanding. In any case, if a public culture brings newspeople and scholars—let us for the moment forget the hedge fund managers—together to explore what is going on now and what may happen later, that, for informed citizens, should help make the news just a little less foreign.

NOTES

Introduction

1. A number of the writings resulting from this phase are included in Hannerz 1996.

2. Several of my Stockholm colleagues were thus likewise pursuing the possibility of transnational occupational ethnography—see Garsten 1994; Dahlén 1997; Wulff 1998.

3. I will note here, however, that I mostly follow ethnographic practice in not detailing each interaction I had with individual members of the collectivity ("tribe") and not even identifying each member I have met with—sometimes also for reasons of integrity and discretion. Yet I try not to overgeneralize, as older ethnographies tended to do, about the beliefs and practices of the group involved, but to give attention also to its internal diversity.

4. The notion of contact zones is drawn from Pratt (1992, 6–7), perhaps in a wide sense of "spatial and temporal copresence of subjects previously separated by geographical and historical disjunctures, and whose trajectories now intersect," and not limited to colonial situations as Pratt mostly has in mind.

5. I have commented on these various kinds of neighbors a little more elaborately in Hannerz 1998b.

6. In an American domestic context, Ortner (1999) touches on similar questions in a discussion of the imagery surrounding Generation X in public culture.

7. Among those, Swedish, British, and American correspondents form a large proportion of my interlocutors, reflecting my own general habits of media consumption, but I have tried to include a number of others as well. The main gap is certainly France; due not least to its imperial past, French media international coverage has its particular characteristics.

8. Thus we now have a critical literature in anthropology scrutinizing our ways of "writing culture" (e.g., Clifford and Marcus 1986; Geertz 1988; Archetti 1994; MacClancy and McDonaugh 1996; James, Hockney, and Dawson 1997).

9. Although the study is thus in large part interview-based as far as fieldwork goes, there have been some other ingredients. I sat in on a daily staff meeting of the foreign desk at *Dagens Nyheter* in Stockholm (see chapter 7), and I have described a reporting trip on the Palestinian West Bank with Ethan Bronner, then of the *Boston Globe,* elsewhere (Hannerz 1998a, 93–95). More field materials of such types would undoubtedly have been

valuable, but for practical reasons I did not pursue some such possibilities, using the time at my disposal rather to ensure diversity through the interviews.

10. One might observe that some of the most dramatic action in foreign correspondence during this period was in Europe or on its outskirts: the Balkans, Chechnya. With a greater interest in reporting to the Occident from elsewhere in the world, however, I have largely disregarded these events and the literature of war correspondence they generated.

11. In the words of Morrison and Tumber (1985, 445), in the context of a study of London correspondents but making a more general point, "[t]here is no absence of material on foreign correspondents, but studies are rare. Most of the literature which exists consists of the trade, in the beloved tradition of journalism, writing about itself, usually in the most colourful detail and most often by individuals who consider their journalistic careers and associated personal lives to be marked by special interest . . . The result is a somewhat grand presentation of both role and occupant at the expense of more mundane and characteristic features of the occupation."

But there certainly are some studies. Especially in its coverage of organizational themes, the book by Hess (1996) to a certain extent parallels my interests here, although it deals specifically with American correspondents. Hohenberg's well-known book (1995, first edition published in 1965), again focusing on American journalists, chronicles the history of foreign correspondence from its eighteenth-century beginnings, with an emphasis on hard news and famous names. The Associated Press veteran Mort Rosenblum's *Who Stole the News?* (1993) is a breezy overview of many aspects of foreign news reporting, drawing on a wealth of knowledge of prominent recent practitioners.

12. For prominent early studies of news work at home by sociologists, along more or less ethnographic lines, see Schlesinger 1978; Tuchman 1978; and Gans 1979. A much more recent anthropological study of a Hindi-language newspaper in Lucknow, India, is Ståhlberg 2002.

13. The idea of multisite fieldwork has drawn sustained attention in anthropology particularly through the efforts of George Marcus (e.g., 1989, 1995). With a number of my Stockholm colleagues, I have discussed experiences of multisite field research in Hannerz 2001; see also Hannerz 1998c.

14. When I was still testing the possibilities of studying foreign correspondence and not yet quite committed to it, I wrote a paper drawing largely on such autobiographical materials; it was later published as a chapter in my book *Transnational Connections* (Hannerz 1996). See, however, note 11.

15. For a classic discussion of people treating relationships with others through the media as personal relationships, in "parasocial interaction," see Horton and Wohl 1956.

Chapter 1

1. As Resek (1960, 121) has it: "Setting down everything from the method of serving breakfast in England to the procedure involved in buying a pair of binoculars in Vienna, he had filled, by the time he returned, six husky volumes with closely written, and for the most part useless, observations."

2. On the reception of Morgan in Communist thought, and more specifically Soviet anthropology, see Znamenski 1995. Siu-lun Wong (1979, 88), in an overview of research on ethnic minorities in China in the early years of the People's Republic, notes that "Morgan's *Ancient Society* was virtually the only western anthropological treatise available in translation."

3. On the global ecumene, see Hannerz 1992, 217–67; 1996, 6–7. I use the term with a bow of acknowledgement to another of the ancestral figures of anthropology, Alfred Kroeber (1945).

4. Schutz, whose essay was first published in 1946, actually used the form "well-informed citizen," but the briefer form I prefer seems to convey the same meaning. His analysis elaborates on the issues of knowledge distribution in a way that I cannot do justice to here. Schudson (1995, 169) suggests that in terms of sheer quantity and intensity of news flow, there may now, more than ever before, exist an "informational citizen," although he takes care to contrast this notion with that of the informed citizen, with a more integrated point of view and civic commitments based on it. Schudson does not comment specifically on the supply of foreign news.

5. In one particularly corrupt usage, "cosmopolitans" has been a term of disapproval, to place a dark cloud over minorities who are suspected of divided loyalties. The political variety of cosmopolitanism has also sometimes been depicted as elitist, in either of two ways, or both at the same time. On the one hand, the cosmopolitan is seen as escaping from local or particularly national contexts and constraints, avoiding rather than accepting responsibility, not sharing in a common burden. On the other hand, cosmopolitanism may be understood precisely as creating another burden for ordinary people, a mode of domination yet further removed from control from below than anything previously encountered. My own first discussion of cosmopolitanism, emphasizing the experiential and lifestyle aspects, is in Hannerz 1990; I returned briefly to the topic in Hannerz 2002. For other more recent perspectives see, e.g., Vertovec and Cohen 2002.

6. The political scientist Benjamin Barber (1996, 33) argued that she had understated "the thinness of cosmopolitanism . . . [T]he idea of cosmopolitanism offers little or nothing for the human psyche to fasten on." Opined Michael McConnell (1996, 81), law professor, "Teach children . . . to be 'citizens of the world,' and in all likelihood they will become neither patriots nor cosmopolitans, but lovers of abstraction and ideology, intolerant of the flaw-ridden individuals and cultures that actually exist throughout the world." And Robert Pinsky (1996, 34), poet, concluded that "global citizenship demands of its patriots levels of abstraction and disembodiment most women and men will be unable or unwilling to muster, at least in the first instance."

7. On ethnic/primordial and civic nationalism, see, for example, Kohn 1945; Ignatieff 1994. Primordialism is sometimes taken to indicate something "given," almost biological, as contrasting with "socially constructed." Geertz (1963, 109), sometimes referred to as a source for such an understanding, actually distances himself from it; see on this also Appadurai 1996, 139–44; Goldmann, Hannerz, and Westin 2000, 12–13. I will return to the notion in the context of African ethnic conflicts in chapter 4.

8. Less than a year after those events, what amounts to the gossip column in the *International Herald Tribune* (August 28, 2002), reports that Dan Rather, CBS anchorman, told *TV Guide* in an interview that there was again a lack of emphasis on such reporting. "The public has lost interest," Rather says. "They'd much rather hear about the Robert Blake murder case or what is happening on Wall Street. A feeling is creeping back in that if you lead foreign, you die." For more extended discussions of post-cold-war and post–September 11 journalism, see, e.g., Seib 2002; Zelizer and Allan 2002.

9. In fact, a question about big-power influence on the Hutu-Tutsi conflict probably still could have been formulated along such lines—focusing on the clashing Francophone/Anglophone interests in Africa, with a history going back at least to the confrontation at Fashoda in 1898, long before the Soviet Union had come into existence. Malkki (2001, 339–41) notes such an interpretation among Hutu exiles in Montreal; see on this

also, e.g., Huband (2001, 307–26). Yet Malkki's Hutu informants also alternatively resorted to a view more in line with what I will identify in chapter 4 as Afro-pessimism—the world is indifferent as Africans kill each other.

10. For an interpretation along such lines, in terms of a shift from "broadcast" to "narrowcast" foreign news, see Utley 1997.

11. One could elaborate here on the notion of news consumption as ritual. James Carey, the media scholar, has argued prominently (1989, 20) for a "ritual view of communication" (as contrasted with a "transmission view"), whereby, for example, reading a newspaper is understood as a dramatic act in which one engages with a particular portrayal of the world. Benedict Anderson's emphasis (1983) on the role of print capitalism in the formation of "imagined communities" is not far from this view.

12. Rosenblum (1993, 151), also reporting on a conversation with Li, notes that for years there was a sign at the *Los Angeles Times* foreign desk admonishing the staff to "Consider Gus" (a character probably much like that bus driver), to make stories clear even if they were complex: "A low common denominator loses the informed readers and does little to educate those who would like to be informed."

13. One should be reminded here that the news media are not always, strictly speaking, in the marketplace. In Europe the state tended to play a strong part in the development of radio and television, and its presence is still often noticeable, even though there may be strong traditions of autonomy and "public service" in government-related media. There can be other arrangements as well: the *Frankfurter Allgemeine* is run as a business-supported foundation.

14. For a critical analysis of the Gulf War coverage, see, e.g., Taylor 1992; and for a *Washington Post* woman correspondent's experience of the American military management of the coverage, see Moore 1993. Peterson (2000, 111–15) offers comparable experiences from Somalia in 1993.

15. Another BBC correspondent, Fergal Keane (2001, 8–9), reminisces about responses from audiences to his reporting from Africa: "When I made a film on the plight of a mother and her five children struggling in a squatter camp, the British public dug deep into their pockets to build her a house. Likewise in Rwanda, where the viewers of BBC1 purchased a small herd of cows for a village decimated by genocide. There was a palpable concern for the oppressed that crossed political boundaries; the Radio 4 audience was, politically speaking, a very broad church, united, I would suggest, by a view of the world that believes we must act according to principles of fundamental decency."

16. The correspondent was Elaine Sciolino; see Moeller 1999, 9. For further discussions in other disciplines on relationships between distance and morality, see the sociologist Boltanski (1999) and the geographer Smith (2000).

17. For ethnographic studies of media reception, see, e.g., Lull 1990; Abu-Lughod 1993; Mankekar 1999.

18. Perhaps such views were not entirely new at her paper. In the 1970s, when an age set of more or less radical young journalists went out to describe the Third World for *Dagens Nyheter,* their rather uniform reporting commitments led commentators at the office to identify a main type in their stories, a bit derisively, as "the DN peasant."

19. Some anthropologists and anthropology watchers have recently also turned their interest to, or at least commented on, the place of the senses in ethnography and an anthropology of the senses—see, e.g., Stoller 1989; Howes 1991. One should not forget here that much of the writing in contemporary print media also appears in immediate connection to news photography, which can add importantly to the impact of words.

20. Such a critique of a long-established tendency toward "allochrony" or "denial of coevalness" in anthropology has been most fully elaborated by Fabian (1983).

21. I will come back to Richburg's book when discussing 1990s Afro-pessimism in chapter 4.

22. Gwertzman's memorandum is reprinted in a book by Japanese writers who are critical of recent *New York Times* reporting from their country; we will return to this in chapter 5 (Zipangu 1998, 38).

Chapter 2

1. Leonard said he had this quote from the *New Yorker.* Mort Rosenblum (1993, 1), another Associated Press veteran, begins his book on foreign correspondents with it and attributes it to H. R. Knickerbocker.

2. Morrison and Tumber (1985, 447), who have attempted to enumerate the foreign correspondents in London, have some illustrative figures. Out of a little more than four hundred correspondents, those from western Europe and North America made up about 57 percent. There were about 11 percent from the Far East, mostly Japanese, and some 8 percent from Australia and New Zealand. Also around 8 percent were from the Third World, but of these a mere handful came from other countries than India, Pakistan, and Brazil.

3. For recent work, see, e.g., Golding and Harris 1997; Boyd-Barrett and Rantanen 1998.

4. But Hohenberg (1995, 317), who reports this figure, notes that many of the visitors who had sought such accreditation may not actually have been working journalists.

5. A veteran British "diplomatic correspondent," John Dickie of the London *Daily Mail,* has described his thirty years of touring the world in the company of his country's foreign secretaries in a book entitled *The Boys on the Bongo Bus* (1997).

6. Several Africa correspondents, such as Fergal Keane (1996) of the BBC; Mark Huband (2001), representing several British newspapers over time; Scott Peterson (2000) of the *Daily Telegraph;* Keith Richburg (1997b) of the *Washington Post;* and James Schofield (1996) of the Australian Broadcasting Corporation, have reported in books about their experiences during this period.

7. Back in the United States, he wrote a noted account of the Yukon Quest International Dog Sled Race (Balzar 2000).

8. These are the postcolonial names of these cities; during the period of Belgian colonialism and its immediate aftermath, Kisangani was Stanleyville, Lubumbashi was Elisabethville, Kinshasa was Leopoldville. In the tumultuous period of the early 1960s, another generation of correspondents had reported from the same cities with these old names in the datelines. See, for example, a large part of Kapuscinski, *The Soccer War* (1990).

9. Munnion's slightly mysterious book title refers to a dateline (place and weekday) that neither he nor any other correspondent apparently ever managed to use. Banana, a coastal Congolese town, is not a news site very often, and it seems nobody got a story out of there on a Sunday before dateline conventions changed.

10. This is from my own conversation with Norrman, although he also reported on his experience in *Dagens Nyheter* (1997b).

11. Laurent Kabila, it turned out, had once been visited by Che Guevara when the latter was looking around for revolutionary potential in Africa; but Guevara had gone away disappointed, finding Kabila too attracted by quite unrevolutionary diversions.

12. A *gaijin* is a foreigner, especially someone from the West.

13. On Lester House, see, e.g., Richburg 1997b, 29.

14. Russell's book *Big Men, Little People* (1999), focusing on encounters with African political leaders, draws mostly on such reporting experiences.

15. McGreal's inquiries in Ogoniland resulted in a long report in the *Guardian,* suggesting that Saro-Wiwa's political activities had not been entirely innocent (McGreal 1996).

Chapter 3

1. He also felt he knew more about the area than he could ever use in his newspaper writing and was giving some thought to writing a book—which eventually he did (La Guardia 2001).

2. The general, overarching conception of careers I employ here draws on the writings of the sociologists Howard S. Becker (e.g., 1963, 24–39) and Everett C. Hughes (e.g., 1971, 124–31).

3. For a "do-it-yourself" perspective on stringing and freelancing, see Goodman and Pollack 1997. For a revealing account of two journalists' experience as stringers in (and outside of) Korea, a country with few resident regular staff correspondents, see Leyden and Bank 1991.

4. This is not to say that agency correspondents are necessarily anonymous within the news business. When the Reuter correspondent Kurt Schork lost his life in an ambush in Sierra Leone in early 2000, obituaries written by correspondents who had known him appeared in the newspapers in many countries. For a brief sketch of Schork's place in the press corps in Sarajevo during the Bosnian war, see Bell 1996, 51–52.

5. Hanna later moved from Johannesburg to report for CNN from Jerusalem and Moscow.

6. An interview with the publisher of the *Phnom Penh Post* suggests that the route that Arnett followed has not changed so much: "Phnom Penh has always been a 'rucksack' journalists' town. These days, international newspapers do not base correspondents there, and [the publisher] employs people from a constant flow of young westerners wanting to work in journalism" (Dalby 1998).

7. Hess (1996, 74–78) notes that foreign-born, non-Commonwealth correspondents are more involved in reporting to American media from less central news sites abroad, but on the whole their presence is fairly marginal, and a number of them are no doubt stringers who also work for local media organizations.

8. The Bonner affair has been discussed by Massing (1983, 1993), Danner (1994), Binford (1996), Diamond (1995, 244–45), and Pedelty (1995, 93–97).

9. In a later period, Bonner has been back writing for the *New York Times.* He was among those reporting from Zaire at the time of Mobutu's fall, and in chapter 6 we will find him describing the problems of learning English in Azerbaijan. In October 2001, in the period between the September 11 events in the United States and the campaign against the Taliban in Afghanistan, he reported from the strategic news locations in Pakistan.

10. The sociologist Gaye Tuchman's study (1973), in a local television station and a morning newspaper in the United States, of how newspeople "routinized the unexpected" by categorizing types of news, is relevant here.

11. In this connection one may also note a reflective story by Marjorie Miller (1999), looking back at her just-completed Jerusalem assignment. When she arrived there,

although she was Jewish, she felt that she had no more stake in the Middle East conflict than she had had in the Central American civil wars that she covered in the 1980s. She had not practiced a religious rite since she left her parents' home twenty years earlier. But then while in Israel, various experiences, more often involving ethnic culture and history than religion, made her feel in some ways part of "the Jewish family." As a professional, nonetheless, she remained a spiralist. When her new assignment came through, she called her parents and said, "Well, Dad—next year in London."

12. One expatriate correspondent commented ironically that Jerusalem was a curious posting in that so many of its foreign correspondents pretended to report from abroad when they were actually at home.

13. Joop Meijers, of the Dutch paper *Algemeen Dagblad,* is another long-timer in Jerusalem. He weighed the pros and cons of his situation when I met him. When in the Netherlands, he had been active in a Zionist organization and eventually decided to move to Israel. As a psychologist, he found a part-time position at Hebrew University, but he also maintained a contact with Dutch media and gradually increased his media work (some radio and television as well) and decreased his academic involvement. But his psychologist background continued to be useful. Since he had worked as an army psychologist, he could readily do a story on Israeli youths' attitudes toward military service, and he also valued a professional relationship with a Palestinian psychologist who was, for one thing, engaged in advising Palestinian negotiators in the peace process. Generally, he felt that the breadth of his Israeli involvements were very helpful in his journalist activities. Indeed he was aware of the risk of "going stale," but he tried to avoid it by traveling frequently, to arrive back in Israel with a refreshed view. He suspected, however, that if it had been economically feasible, a paper like his might have preferred to have a staff correspondent of its own in Jerusalem, of the spiralist type.

14. Hess (1996, 79–86) devotes a chapter to the language skills of American foreign correspondents.

15. A veteran Swedish newspaper correspondent, Ulf Nilson (1976, 212), has commented on the particular position of the United States in contemporary imagined worlds as something he had had to take into account in his reporting out of New York: "[I]t is as if every country on earth had built an electronic bridge to the USA and found the messages it carries so fascinating that one has decided to shut out those from more nearby."

16. Hess (1996, 15–27) has an extended discussion of the changing involvement of women in American foreign correspondence. In an earlier series of articles on foreign correspondents in the *Los Angeles Times,* the paper's media correspondent David Shaw (1986) devoted one article to problems of marital stress, but the picture offered there now seems somewhat out of date.

17. See, for example, May 1985 on Higgins; Rollyson 1990 on Gellhorn; and Sebba 1994 on British women correspondents more generally.

18. Adie established her reputation as a foreign correspondent through her coverage of the American bombing of Libya in 1986 and went on to report, for example, from Tiananmen Square in 1989 (see especially Adie 2002; also, e.g., Wallis and Baran 1990, 210–15; Sebba 1994, 264–75). Amanpour, a little later, first became visible in CNN reporting from the Gulf War and reached stardom with her presence on the Bosnian war scene (including a remarkable long-distance confrontation with President Clinton); for a selection of celebrity portraits in the press, see Kinzer 1994; Bennetts 1996; and Nordland 1996.

19. One should perhaps keep in mind here that the Bosnian war has become a prototype for a "new war," in which much violence is directed against civilians (see chapter 6), and this could be taken to indicate that the changing nature of war itself, rather

than the gender of reporters, made the occurrence of sexual violence more noticeable in reporting—but then again, could the characterization of such wars as an emergent type depend to a certain extent on the emphases of available news coverage?

20. As it turned out, after Johannesburg he returned to the United States and joined the *New York Times.* His reporting on the September 11 attack on the World Trade Center also resulted in a book (Murphy 2002).

21. Horwitz (1992, 5), in his account of freelancer experiences in the Arab world while married to the staff correspondent Geraldine Brooks, notes that "some men follow their dreams, some their instincts, some the beat of a private drummer. I had a habit of following my wife."

22. For some discussion of such matters, see Shaw 1986; Hess 1996, 20–23.

23. This, one might note, can be financially advantageous for the employer, compared to having two unrelated individuals in the bureau—it is necessary to meet the considerable costs of accommodation, travel, and other fringe benefits for only one household, rather than two.

24. A book by a veteran Swedish radio correspondent, looking back at his Balkan experience, offers insights into this (Abrahamson 1995).

Chapter 4

1. For comments on Nihonjinron, see, for example, Iwabuchi 1994; Morris-Suzuki 1998.

2. Enz was not alone among the correspondents I talked to in suggesting that Japanese public figures would feel little compunction about such different pronouncements. Note here again the difference reported by Moeran and cited in chapter 3, between *tatemae,* the public language of principle, and *honne,* language coming from the heart.

3. There have been other exceptions, and they are apparently always found noteworthy. One has been the controversial, nationalistically inclined politician Shintaro Ishihara, who coauthored the book *The Japan That Can Say No* and later was elected governor of Tokyo; but then Ishihara first earned fame as a novelist. For another apparent exception, see Kevin Sullivan's portrait (1998) of another 1990s prime minister: "He had a sassy mouth and memorable hair. He was a macho master of kendo sword fighting who smoked with a cigarette holder and wore stylish suits. Women voted for him because they thought he was sexy . . . a leader with pulse, a streak of color in the bland parade of interchangeable party hacks who normally occupied the chair." And then in 2001, Junichiro Koizumi became prime minister, drawing attention both for his apparent commitment to reform and for wearing his hair longer than most politicians.

4. In her study of coverage of the earthquake by Japanese news organizations, MacLachlan (2001, 114) suggests that such criticism was more prominent in foreign media and that Japanese media actually drew somewhat on foreign reporting in discussing issues of this kind.

5. But a little after the musical chairs game, at the same party, Kristof notes, little Chitose-chan and another girl got into an argument over a toy, and Chitose-chan slugged Naoko-chan in the mouth. Younger Japanese, perhaps, are becoming more competitive than their parents. Kristof concludes, "Perhaps that's globalization." One could note that some of these parents seem competitive enough: Howard French (1999), coming in as Kristof's successor as *New York Times* Japan correspondent, reported on a gruesome Tokyo murder story in which a two-year old girl who had passed a highly desirable entrance exam for a kindergarten was strangled by the jealous mother of another little girl who had failed.

6. Some also point out, however, that especially for smaller black businesses, such departures create new opportunities, new spaces. On the decline of central Johannesburg and hopes for its revival, see Suzanne Daley 1996a; Alex Duval Smith 1999.

7. For comments on the "black-on-black" phrase, in the context of a general critical discussion of Africa coverage in American media and the image of Africa among the American public, see Fair 1993, 14–15.

8. On primordialism, see chapter 1, note 7.

9. The Lord's Resistance Army had its roots in the movement led by Alice Lakwena among the Acholi people in the late 1980s. While thousands of her followers were killed, Lakwena fled to Kenya. The leader in the late 1990s, when the Lord's Resistance Army received considerable international publicity, was said to be a relative of hers. Ola Säll (1998), Norrman's closest competitor as correspondent for *Svenska Dagbladet,* the other Stockholm morning paper, was in northern Uganda a few months later and wrote a story largely paralleling Norrman's.

10. The Mozambique flood coverage became controversial when a BBC correspondent argued that the "media circus" endangered lives—the air turbulence caused by the helicopters, for one thing, may have blown people out of the treetops where they had sought refuge (Wells and Morris 2001).

11. Not really a part of the corpus of regular foreign correspondence, but still a contribution to mainstream reporting from Africa, the writer Robert Kaplan's well-known article "The Coming Anarchy" in the *Atlantic Monthly* in 1994 is probably the best-known example of the chaos theme. Kaplan offers an epidemiological view of social breakdown, spreading through the world but with Sierra Leone as an early example. Kaplan, whose work we will briefly return to in chapter 7, is also widely understood to have had an important role in promoting an "ancient hatreds" conception of ethnicity and nationalism through his book *Balkan Ghosts* (1993).

12. In early 2001, it is true, the animal-human ratio increased in European news reporting, at the time of the mad cow and foot-and-mouth disease panics.

13. The novelist–travel writer Bruce Chatwin (1997, 27) distinguished between two Timbuctoos, the "administrative centre of the Sixth Region of the Republic of Mali" and the place of the mind—where "he has gone to Timbuctoo" really means "he is out of his mind." His account of his visit to the physical Timbuktu, originally published in *Vogue* in 1970, rather like Balzar's and French's brings together the glorious past and the dreary present. He finds the Librairie Populaire a bridgehead of international socialism but also recognizes that torn pages from the complete works of Mao, Lenin, Marx, and Lenin are used in the marketplace for "wrapping little packages of dye, chili pepper, snuff, chewing tobacco, the crushed leaves of the baobab tree used as an abortive, or charms to counteract *djinns.*" Ryszard Kapuscinski (2001, 287–88) also made it to Timbuktu, looking for the Tuaregs, and found a house with a plaque announcing that Heinrich Barth, the German explorer, lived there from September 1853 to May 1854. And Henry Louis Gates Jr., W. E. B. Du Bois Professor of the Humanities at Harvard University, writing of his own visit to Timbuktu in the *New Republic* (1998), notes that in the early sixteenth century the Arab geographer Leo Africanus suggested that in this city more profit was made in the book trade than in any other line of business (tell that to the Librairie Populaire). Gates reminisces about first reading about Timbuktu in the Sunday paper during his West Virginia childhood—probably in Ripley's "Believe It or Not." The men gathering habitually at Mr. Combie Carroll's barber shop saw the item, too, and speculated that the white man just would not want them to know about such a center of learning in black Africa. Now, after an arduous three-day river trip on the Niger—the only alternative route, he says, would have been a ninety-day camel caravan across the Sahara—in the private home of a

new acquaintance, Gates finds a huge collection of ancient manuscripts, squirreled away centuries ago by prominent Timbuktu families. And he wishes that Mr. Combie Carroll and his customers and friends were also there to see it.

14. Among others, the novelist Williams Sassine, whose books Diawara feels portray Afro-pessimism eloquently; especially the novel *Le Zéhéros n'est pas n'importe qui*.

15. The Committee to Protect Journalists is an organization supported by foundations and news organizations to give aid mostly to local journalists working under difficult conditions in countries where press freedom is not well established or where they are under other sorts of threat; when I met Bill Orme, there was a concentration of cases in ex-Soviet Central Asian republics.

16. A more rounded, relatively more inside view of ultra-Orthodox life in Jerusalem can be found in Samuel Heilman's ethnography (1992).

17. A striking historical example of a Jerusalem foreign correspondent who indeed did engage closely with Arab life is Leopold Weiss, a correspondent for the *Frankfurter Zeitung* (a precursor of today's *Frankfurter Allgemeine*) in the 1920s. Weiss, coming from a family line of rabbis in Poland, traveled widely in the Middle East, converted to Islam, and took the name Muhammad Asad, under which he became a well-known writer (see Windhager 2002).

18. For critical perspectives on the role of international organizations in African and other crises and their interaction with news media, see, e.g., Benthall 1993; de Waal 1997; Birnbaum 2000, 329–30.

19. The anthropologist Carolyn Nordstrom's aptly titled *A Different Kind of War Story* (1997, xviii), which depicts a Mozambique torn by years of foreign-induced violent conflict, begins by drawing attention to creativity: "[I]n the midst of terror-warfare, ordinary citizens were undertaking a remarkable process of revitalization: mourning and healing wounds both physical and emotional, combating the insidious hegemony of violence in their daily lives, and repairing ruptures in cultural viability maimed by the atrocities of lethal conflict."

20. If "honor and shame" had not seized the anthropological imagination of one or two pioneers in Mediterranean studies, for example, would that complex of ideas and practices have come to have the centrality in research in the region that it did for a long time? There may be a measure of arbitrariness in such choices, a commitment with elements of both conformism and competitiveness, that may go along with a certain blindness toward other topics. Can we discern here some of what in critiques of the news trade would be referred to as "pack journalism"—sticking with one's colleagues in the intense pursuit of a collectively prioritized story, instead of striking out on one's own?

21. But perhaps it is not entirely fair to demand from the sojourner news workers in Africa a well-rounded, and at the same time easily communicated, overview of the current situation, when it does not really seem as if academic specialists have arrived at any consensus here either—even on whether any comprehensive story line is really worth looking for. For recent academic points of view relating to current styles of politics in sub-Saharan Africa, see, e.g., Chabal and Daloz 1999; Mbembe 2001.

22. There is an intriguing parallel here with Fardon's comment (1990, 28) that specialists in regional anthropologies tend to be less than enthusiastic about quick visits in their territories by distinguished senior colleagues. The latter seem often to use regional materials with panache to make some general theoretical point, which becomes influential even if it perpetuates stereotypes and involves an uncertain grasp of context.

Chapter 5

1. The more scholarly literature on foreign correspondents also has a rather individualist slant. Hohenberg's *Foreign Correspondence* (1995) is subtitled "The Great Reporters and Their Times," and Hess's in many ways admirable *International News and Foreign Correspondents* (1996) has little to say about the contextual matters considered in this chapter.

2. Going further, John Simpson (1998, 71–72) claims humorously that the differences between reporters and editors are a matter of character: the former are "slap-happy and take risks; they wear rumpled suits and stained ties; they always mean to check the terms of their insurance policies but never get around to it; they drive fast and are subject to multiple divorces," whereas the latter are "careful, unadventurous people who wear cardigans, work at desks, make adequate financial provision for themselves and their families, drive safely, and mate for life like swans." Simpson feels he was born to be a reporter.

3. The movie *Killing Fields* is a striking exception, with its celebration of the close yet problematic relationship between an expatriate correspondent, Sidney Schanberg of the *New York Times,* and his local Cambodian assistant, Dith Pran. When Schanberg receives a prize in New York while Pran is still lost in Cambodia, and perhaps no longer alive, there is the conventional celebration of individual journalistic heroism—and then one of Schanberg's old peers from Cambodia accuses him, in the washroom, of betraying and sacrificing Pran.

4. See Milgram 1969; Travers and Milgram 1969; and comments in Hannerz 1980, 194–96.

5. Le Carré's foreword to his novel shows that he did a sort of field research in preparation for it, following in the shadow of the *Washington Post* correspondent David Greenway through Southeast Asia. One of the legendary Asia correspondents of the twentieth century, Richard Hughes, appearing in the book rather lightly disguised as "Craw," was fictionalized at least twice—he also inspired the "Dikko Henderson" character in Ian Fleming's James Bond story *You Only Live Twice.* Hughes's biography has been written by Macswan (1983).

6. The volume published by the Foreign Correspondents Club of Japan (1998) to celebrate its fiftieth anniversary offers detailed information on the history of the organization. See also comments by Neilan (1995, 310–13).

7. On the kisha clubs, see Van Wolferen 1989, 93–95; Neilan 1995, 313–15; Hall 1998, 45–79; De Lange 1998.

8. I am indebted to Robert Neff, a contributing editor of *Business Week* and president of the FCCJ at the time of my visit to Tokyo, for discussing the work of the organization with me and for showing me its facilities.

9. The *Mail and Guardian* has its ancestry in liberal white oppositional journalism in the apartheid era.

10. For war correspondents in the field, the most relevant government has of course often been their own, actively engaged in the war; I touched briefly on controversies arising in such circumstances, from the Vietnam War onward, in chapter 1.

11. In a memoir of his rather brief stay in Moscow in the early 1980s as correspondent for *Newsweek* (ending with his expulsion), Andrew Nagorski (1985, 56) notes that this was another reason for correspondents to team up for travel: it was important to have a witness of any "incident" that might be staged.

12. On the decline of censorship in Israel, see Lederman 1993, 51–60.

13. A collection of such media comment by Bar-Illan (1993) has been published in book form.

14. Walter Duranty, an Englishman working for the *New York Times* in Moscow for a long period beginning in the 1920s, came under a cloud of suspicion with his remarkably well-informed reporting from Stalin's Kremlin; and Herbert Matthews of the same paper, who reported on the early years of the Cuban revolution, from the hills of Sierra Maestra to Havana, had to defend himself against accusations of having misled the American public with reporting favorable to Fidel Castro. We have already taken note, in chapter 3, of Raymond Bonner's reporting for the *New York Times* from El Salvador. Matthews (1971, 337–65) has discussed the controversy over his Cuba reporting; on Duranty, see Bassow 1988; Taylor 1990. Arnett (1994, 408–10) discusses American reactions to his Baghdad reporting.

15. See, for example, a volume published at the time of the first intifada that states in the introduction that "in 1988, a new level of moral, intellectual, and physical flaccidity was reached by Western journalists" (Karetzky and Frankel 1989, xi).

16. Said's early commentary on Western media reporting on the Middle East is in *Covering Islam* (1981).

17. For their experiences in reporting on China, see Kristof and WuDunn 1994.

18. The articles in *Svenska Dagbladet* are by Edvardson (1997c and 1997d) and Löfgren (1997). Edvardson, German-born and a survivor of Nazi concentration camps, decided to live in Israel after, somewhat accidentally, she had been sent by a Swedish paper to report on the 1973 Yom Kippur war, which started very badly for the Israelis. Her autobiographical account (1984) of her childhood and youth has been translated into several languages, although not into English.

Chapter 6

1. For a multifaceted view of the role of the cold war in American journalism, see Hallin 1994.

2. The closest competition, from a different perspective, may be the British correspondent Robert Fisk's book *Pity the Nation* (1990), on the war in Lebanon.

3. After the events of September 11, 2001, when attention to Friedman's columns grew abruptly, a *Washington Post* portrait quoted a White House official's view: "We ignore him at our peril . . . He's a very thoughtful guy with more than a dash of Tabasco. Sometimes what he writes is important and sometimes it's drivel. But his audience is really important" (Kurtz 2001). Much of Friedman's writing after September 11 (and some relevant previous writing) has been collected in another book, *Longitudes and Attitudes* (2002).

4. Kristof and WuDunn cover some of the same ground in their book *Thunder from the East* (2000).

5. Then in November 2001, Richburg was also among the parachutists covering the Afghanistan crisis and could report on a horse ride across the mountains, through ice and snow (no safari suits here), with three cousins in the jewelry business, one relief agency worker, and two other foreign journalists. One horse slipped and fell into a river, taking sleeping bags, satellite phones, and laptops with him. "Of all the dumb things reporters have done to get a story, this definitely was one of the dumbest" (Richburg 2001b).

6. For an anthropological view, see Henderson 2000.

7. See the brief reference to this event in chapter 2, in connection with one of Chris McGreal's reporting trips to Nigeria.

8. The coverage of the affair in *Svenska Dagbladet,* the other Stockholm paper, initially makes a little less of the Swedish connection, although its correspondent, Ola Säll (2000), has a full-page interview with the widow a little later.

9. A couple of articles on Chinese youth by Patrick Tyler (1996a, 1996b) of the *New York Times* are examples of reporting on sentiments more critical of the United States.

10. In one of her United Nations stories, Barbara Crossette (2000) adds to the "war and diamonds" theme as she reports on a study commissioned by the Security Council. One of the entrepreneurs in the shadowy world of arms and diamond trade, the study notes, is Victor Anatolyevich Bout, born in Tajikistan, who has at least five aliases and as many passports (two are Russian, and one is from Ukraine), is involved in Angola as well as Sierra Leone, and currently resides in the United Arab Emirates. Returning to New York from Jerusalem, Serge Schmemann became for some time Crossette's successor at the United Nations.

11. One should perhaps remember here, however, how Simon Li, *Los Angeles Times* foreign editor, had to give up on getting Californians to take an interest in the intricacies of the European Union. If you want to write seductively, an international bureaucracy may not seem like a promising beat.

12. On translocalities, see Appadurai 1996, 192.

Chapter 7

1. Schlesinger (1977) offers a pioneering treatment of the topic, based on his study of radio and television newspeople at BBC.

2. Although the reference is to a volume of translations of Braudel's essays, the article drawn on here was originally published in *Annales* in 1958.

3. Bassow (1988) chronicles American foreign correspondence from the Soviet Union from its early years to the beginning of the perestroika.

4. Both the blurbs quoted are from the paperback editions.

5. The authors are all based in the United States, and one could wonder why the genre has been so dominantly American, even though it has also had a wider impact. Perhaps aside from taking it to be another example of the general strength of American influence in the world, one should again be aware that the American public has possibly been even more in need of post-cold-war scenarios than people elsewhere. It might also have been worthwhile to compare these works to those of a handful of contemporary social theorists—Manuel Castells, Anthony Giddens, Ulrich Beck, and perhaps some others—who have somewhat similarly attempted to provide "big pictures" of the present and the future. On the whole, however, these writers have not received an equal amount of public attention outside the academic context.

6. And as if to let the plot thicken even more, Kaplan also notes that Francis Fukuyama is a former student of Huntington's.

7. Roger Sanjek (1991, 616–17), discussing the ethnographic present and the ethnography of the present, states his preference for such a processual view over more past-oriented historical anthropologies—for those who "struggle in the present," engaged in advocacy and political action, it can be of operational relevance. Sanjek's own study of borough politics in Queens, New York, *The Future of Us All* (1998), is an obvious example.

8. See, among others, my own comments (Hannerz 1999).

9. On the whole, anthropologists have commented extensively on time and on conceptions of the past but have said rather little about the future; see, however, Wallman 1992.

REFERENCES

Abrahamson, Kjell Albin. 1995. *Balkan betyder berg.* Stockholm: Fischer.

Abu-Lughod, Janet. 1991. Going beyond Global Babble. In *Culture, Globalization, and the World-System,* ed. Anthony D. King. London: Macmillan.

Abu-Lughod, Lila. 1991. Writing against Culture. In *Recapturing Anthropology,* ed. Richard G. Fox. Santa Fe, NM: School of American Research Press.

———. ed. 1993. Screening Politics in a World of Nations. *Public Culture* 5:463–604.

Adie, Kate. 2002. *The Kindness of Strangers.* London: Headline.

Albons, Bengt. 1997. Handeln med vapen halverad. *Dagens Nyheter,* May 31.

Anderson, Benedict. 1983. *Imagined Communities.* London: Verso.

Appadurai, Arjun. 1986. Theory in Anthropology: Center and Periphery. *Comparative Studies in Society and History* 29:356–61.

———. 1988. Putting Hierarchy in Its Place. *Cultural Anthropology* 3:36–49.

———. 1991. Global Ethnoscapes: Notes and Queries for a Transnational Anthropology. In *Recapturing Anthropology,* ed. Richard G. Fox. Santa Fe, NM: School of American Research Press.

———. 1996. *Modernity at Large.* Minneapolis: University of Minnesota Press.

Archetti, Eduardo P., ed. 1994. *Exploring the Written.* Oslo: Scandinavian University Press.

Arnett, Peter. 1994. *Live from the Battlefield.* New York: Simon and Schuster.

Balzar, John. 1995. In Timbuktu, Even the Camels Idle. *Los Angeles Times,* September 2.

———. 2000. *Yukon Alone.* New York: Holt.

Barber, Benjamin R. 1996. Constitutional Faith. In *For Love of Country,* ed. Joshua Cohen. Boston: Beacon Press.

Bar-Illan, David. 1993. *Eye on the Media.* Jerusalem: Jerusalem Post.

Bassow, Whitman. 1988. *The Moscow Correspondents.* New York: Morrow.

Bearak, Barry. 2000. India, Beauty Superpower, Is Becoming Jaded. *New York Times,* December 13.

Becker, Howard S. 1963. *Outsiders.* New York: Free Press.

———. 1982. *Art Worlds.* Berkeley: University of California Press.

Behr, Edward. 1982. *"Anyone Here Been Raped and Speaks English?"* London: New English Library.

Bell, Martin. 1996. *In Harm's Way: Reflections of a War-Zone Thug.* London: Penguin.

Bennetts, Leslie. 1996. Woman o'War. *Vanity Fair,* September.

Benthall, Jonathan. 1993. *Disasters, Relief, and the Media.* London: I. B. Tauris.

Billig, Michael. 1995. *Banal Nationalism.* London: Sage.

Binford, Leigh. 1996. *The El Mozote Massacre.* Tucson: University of Arizona Press.

Birnbaum, Michael. 2000. *Die schwarze Sonne Afrikas.* Munich: Piper.

Blundy, Anna. 1998. *Every Time We Say Goodbye.* London: Century.

Boltanski, Luc. 1999. *Distant Suffering.* Cambridge: Cambridge University Press.

Bonner, Raymond. 1995. Azerbaijanis Try to Learn English, under U.S. Handicap. *New York Times,* February 19.

Bourdieu, Pierre. 1998. *On Television and Journalism.* London: Pluto Press.

Boyd-Barrett, Oliver, and Terhi Rantanen, eds. 1998. *The Globalization of News.* London: Sage.

Braudel, Fernand. 1980. *On History.* Chicago: University of Chicago Press.

Bremner, Brian, Emily Thornton, and Irene M. Kunii. 1999. Fall of a Keiretsu. *Business Week,* March 15, Asian ed.

Browne, Malcolm W. 1993. *Muddy Boots and Red Socks.* New York: Random House.

Burns, John F. 1995a. Bomb Tipster Is Reported to Hate U.S. *New York Times,* 14 February.

———. 1995b. Informers in Bomb Arrest Were S. African Neighbors. *New York Times,* 12 February.

———. 1995c. Terror Informer Reported to Get U.S. Protection. *New York Times,* 13 February.

Cameron, James. 1969. *Point of Departure.* London: Panther.

Carey, James W. 1989. *Communication as Culture.* Boston: Unwin Hyman.

Chabal, Patrick, and Jean-Pascal Daloz. 1999. *Africa Works.* Oxford: James Currey.

Chatwin, Bruce. 1997. *Anatomy of Restlessness.* London: Picador.

Clifford, James. 1997. *Routes.* Cambridge, MA: Harvard University Press.

Clifford, James, and George E. Marcus, eds. 1986. *Writing Culture.* Berkeley: University of California Press.

Crampton, Thomas. 1999. Have Internet, Will Travel on a Shoestring. *International Herald Tribune,* July 1.

Crossette, Barbara. 2000. U.N. Study of Diamonds-for-Arms Deals Focuses on Shadowy Trader. *New York Times,* December 22.

Dahlén, Tommy. 1997. *Among the Interculturalists.* Stockholm Studies in Social Anthropology, 38. Stockholm: Almqvist and Wiksell International.

Dalby, Stewart. 1998. Going into the Rouge in Cambodia. *Financial Times,* June 20–21.

Daley, Suzanne. 1995. A Market Where Anything Goes, but for a Price. *New York Times,* September 23.

———. 1996a. Downtown Denizens: Fear, and Fearless Vendors. *New York Times,* August 21.

———. 1996b. Malawi Deprived? Well, TV's on Way. *New York Times,* May 30.

———. 1998a. Africa's "White Tribe" Fears Dark Past Is Prologue. *New York Times,* February 22.

———. 1998b. Horseplay It's Not: Blacks Dream of Finishing First. *New York Times,* 16 February.

———. 1998c. Of Leaders and Lovers: A South African Epidemic. *New York Times,* 19 February.

———. 1998d. South Africa's Al Gore Tries for a Common Touch. *New York Times,* 28 December.

———. 1998e. Why This Pampered Paradise? It's Oil, Stupid! *New York Times,* June 25.

———. 1999a. Afrikaners Have a Dream, Very Like the Old One. *New York Times,* 4 May.

———. 1999b. South Africa Confronts Brutalities of One Man. *New York Times,* 19 July.

Danner, Mark. 1994. *The Massacre at El Mozote.* New York: Vintage.

Darnton, Robert. 1975. Writing News and Telling Stories. *Daedalus* 104 (2): 175–94.

Das, Veena. 1995. *Critical Events.* Delhi: Oxford University Press.

De Lange, William. 1998. *A History of Japanese Journalism.* Richmond, Surrey: Japan Library/Curzon Press.

De Waal, Alex. 1997. *Famine Crises.* Oxford: James Currey.

Diamond, Edwin. 1995. *Behind the Times.* Chicago: University of Chicago Press.

Diawara, Manthia. 1998. *In Search of Africa.* Cambridge, MA: Harvard University Press.

Dickie, John. 1997. *The Boys on the Bongo Bus.* Luton, England: University of Luton Press.

Dugger, Celia W. 2000. Return Passage to India. Emigrés Pay Back. *New York Times,* February 29.

Duke, Lynne. 1998a. Following Killing, Calls for Healing in S. Africa. *Washington Post,* April 22.

———. 1998b. Whites React Warily to Emphasis on Opportunities for Blacks. *Washington Post,* February 17.

Dunn, Ashley. 1995. Skilled Asians Leaving U.S. for High-Tech Jobs at Home. *New York Times,* February 21.

Duval Smith, Alex. 1999. Jo'burg Tries to Clean Up Its Mean Streets. *Independent on Sunday* (London), October 3.

Edvardson, Cordelia. 1984. *Bränt barn söker sig till elden.* Stockholm: Brombergs.

———. 1997a. Alla barns liv lika viktiga att rädda. *Svenska Dagbladet,* November 19.

———. 1997b. Avspärrning hot mot svårt sjuka. *Svenska Dagbladet,* August 10.

———. 1997c. Kan vi lita på Mikael Löfgren nu? *Svenska Dagbladet,* April 4.

———. 1997d. Påhopp blev bästa försvar för hedern. *Svenska Dagbladet,* April 10.

Efron, Sonni. 1999. Right-to-Know Laws Changing Shape of Japan. *Los Angeles Times,* May 11.

Fabian, Johannes. 1983. *Time and the Other.* New York: Columbia University Press.

Fair, Jo Ellen. 1993. War, Famine, and Poverty: Race in the Construction of Africa's Media Imagery. *Journal of Communication Inquiry* 17 (2): 5–22.

Faison, Seth. 1996. Dalai Lama Movie Imperils Disney's Future in China. *New York Times,* November 27.

———. 1998. The Chinese Burst onto the Tourist Scene. *New York Times,* April 8.

Fardon, Richard. 1990. Localizing Strategies: The Regionalization of Ethnographic Accounts. In *Localizing Strategies,* ed. Richard Fardon. Edinburgh: Scottish Academic Press.

———. 1999. Ethnic Pervasion. In *The Media of Conflict,* ed. Tim Allen and Jean Seaton. London: Zed.

Farhi, Paul, and Megan Rosenfeld. 1998. American Pop Penetrates Worldwide: Nations with New Wealth, Freedom Welcome Bart Simpson, Barbie, and Rap. *Washington Post,* October 25.

Ferguson, James. 1999. *Expectations of Modernity.* Berkeley: University of California Press.

Fisher, Ian. 2000. If Only the Problem Were as Easy as Old Hatreds. *New York Times,* January 2.

Fisk, Robert. 1990. *Pity the Nation.* London: André Deutsch.

Foreign Correspondents Club of Japan. 1998. *Foreign Correspondents in Japan.* Rutland, VT: Tuttle.

Freedland, Jonathan. 1999. *Bring Home the Revolution.* London: Fourth Estate.

French, Howard W. 1995. Timbuktu Journal: In a Fabled Faraway Place, No Escape from Fear. *New York Times,* January 30.

———. 1996a. African Rebel with Room Service. *New York Times,* June 23.

———. 1996b. Jean-Bedel Bokassa, 75, Ruled the Central African Republic. *New York Times,* November 4.

———. 1999. Exam Wars, Prepping, and Other Nursery Crimes. *New York Times,* December 7.

———. 2001. "Pearl Harbor" in Japan: Love or War? *New York Times,* June 22.

Friedman, Thomas. 1989. *From Beirut to Jerusalem.* New York: Farrar, Straus, and Giroux.

———. 1998a. Booting Up Africa. *New York Times,* May 5.

———. 1998b. The Mouse That Roars. *New York Times,* July 18.

———. 1999. *The Lexus and the Olive Tree.* New York: Farrar, Straus, and Giroux.

———. 2001. Powell's Perspective. *New York Times,* January 16.

———. 2002. *Longitudes and Attitudes.* New York: Farrar, Straus, and Giroux.

Fukuyama, Francis. 1992. *The End of History and the Last Man.* New York: Free Press.

Gans, Herbert J. 1979. *Deciding What's News.* New York: Pantheon.

Garsten, Christina. 1994. *Apple World.* Stockholm Studies in Social Anthropology, 33. Stockholm: Almqvist and Wiksell International.

Gates, Henry Louis, Jr. 1998. All the Way to Timbuktu. *New Republic,* April 20.

Geertz, Clifford. 1963. The Integrative Revolution: Primordial Sentiments and Civil Politics in the New States. In *Old Societies and New States,* ed. Clifford Geertz. New York: Free Press.

———. 1973. *The Interpretation of Cultures.* New York: Basic Books.

———. 1988. *Works and Lives.* Stanford, CA: Stanford University Press.

Gellman, Barton. 1996. Rock Idol Stirs Angry Chorus after Urging Israelis to Flee Country. *Washington Post,* September 12.

Geyer, Georgie Anne. 1996. *Buying the Night Flight.* Washington, DC: Brassey's.

Glanz, James. 2001. Trolling for Brains in International Waters. *New York Times,* April 1.

Golding, Peter, and Phil Harris, eds. 1997. *Beyond Cultural Imperialism.* London: Sage.

Goldmann, Kjell, Ulf Hannerz, and Charles Westin. 2000. Introduction: Nationalism and Internationalism in the Post–Cold War Era. In *Nationalism and Internationalism in the Post–Cold War Era,* ed. Kjell Goldmann, Ulf Hannerz, and Charles Westin. London: Routledge.

Goodman, Al, and John Pollack. 1997. *The World on a String.* New York: Henry Holt.

Grill, Bartholomäus. 2001. Die Chaosmächte von Westafrika. *Die Zeit,* July 26.

Gusterson, Hugh. 1997. Studying Up Revisited. *Political and Legal Anthropology Review* 20 (1): 114–19.

Hall, Gunilla von. 2001. FN-konferens ett första steg mot vapenkontroll. *Svenska Dagbladet,* July 10.

Hall, Ivan P. 1998. *Cartels of the Mind.* New York: Norton.

Hallin, Daniel C. 1994. *We Keep America on Top of the World.* London: Routledge.

Hammond, Phil, and Paul Stirner. 1997. Fear and Loathing in the British Press. In *Cultural Difference, Media Memories,* ed. Phil Hammond. London: Cassell.

Hannerz, Ulf. 1980. *Exploring the City.* New York: Columbia University Press.

———. 1990. Cosmopolitans and Locals in World Culture. In *Global Culture,* ed. Mike Featherstone. London: Sage.

———. 1992. *Cultural Complexity.* New York: Columbia University Press.

———. 1993. The Withering Away of the Nation? An Afterword. *Ethnos* 58:377–91.

———. 1996. *Transnational Connections.* London: Routledge.

———. 1998a. Of Correspondents and Collages. *Anthropological Journal on European Cultures* 7:91–109.

———. 1998b. Other Transnationals: Perspectives Gained from Studying Sideways. *Paideuma* 44:109–23.

———. 1998c. Transnational Research. In *Handbook of Methods in Anthropology,* ed. H. Russell Bernard. Walnut Creek, CA: Altamira Press.

———. 1999. Reflections on Varieties of Culturespeak. *European Journal of Cultural Studies* 2:393–407.

———. 2002. Where We Are, and Who We Want to Be. In *The Postnational Self: Belonging and Identity,* ed. Ulf Hedetoft and Mette Hjort. Minneapolis: University of Minnesota Press.

———, ed. 2001. *Flera fält i ett.* Stockholm: Carlssons.

Harden, Blaine. 2000. Africa's Gems: Warfare's Best Friend. *New York Times,* April 6.

Heilman, Samuel. 1992. *Defenders of the Faith.* New York: Schocken.

Henderson, Sharon Elaine. 2000. Nuer Ethnicity Militarized. *Anthropology Today* 16 (3): 6–13.

Here Is the News. 1998. *Economist,* July 4.

Herzfeld, Michael. 1997. *Cultural Intimacy.* New York: Routledge.

Hess, Stephen. 1996. *International News and Foreign Correspondents.* Washington, DC: Brookings Institution.

Hohenberg, John. 1995. *Foreign Correspondence.* 2d ed. Syracuse, NY: Syracuse University Press. First edition published in 1965.

Horton, Donald, and R. Richard Wohl. 1956. Mass Communication and Social Interaction. *Psychiatry* 19:215–29.

Horwitz, Tony. 1992. *Baghdad without a Map.* New York: Plume/Penguin.

Howes, David, ed. 1991. *The Varieties of Sensory Experience.* Toronto: University of Toronto Press.

Huband, Mark. 2001. *The Skull beneath the Skin.* Boulder, CO: Westview.

Hughes, Everett C. 1971. *The Sociological Eye.* Chicago: Aldine.

Huntington, Samuel P. 1996. *The Clash of Civilizations and the Remaking of World Order.* New York: Simon and Schuster.

Husarska, Anna. 1998. Danger for Serbian "Fixers," Outsiders' Eyes in Balkans. *International Herald Tribune,* October 28.

Ignatieff, Michael. 1994. *Blood and Belonging.* London: Vintage.

Iritani, Evelyn. 1999. Entertaining China; Disneyland Talks Stir Debate in Hong Kong. *Los Angeles Times,* June 13.

Iwabuchi, Koichi. 1994. Complicit Exoticism: Japan and Its Other. *Continuum* 8 (2): 49–82.

James, Allison, Jenny Hockney, and Andrew Dawson, eds. 1997. *After Writing Culture.* London: Routledge.

Japan's Constitution: The Call to Arms. 1999. *Economist,* February 27.

Jordan, Mary. 1997. S. Korean Thirst for English Irks "Language Police." *Washington Post,* April 15.

———. 1999. Captives to Tradition: Japanese Society's Deep Aversion to Adoption Exiles Children to Lives of Longing in State Homes. *Washington Post,* June 28.

Jordan, Mary, and Kevin Sullivan. 1997. But Do They Flush? Japan's High-Tech Toilets Do Nearly Everything, Even Redden Faces. *Washington Post,* May 15.

———. 1999a. A Dad in Name Only: Japan Aims to Raise Involvement at Home. *Washington Post,* May 8.

———. 1999b. In Japan Schools, Discipline in Recess: Old Order Making Way for Disorder in Formerly Rigid Classrooms. *Washington Post,* January 24.

Kaiser, Robert G. 1976. *Russia.* New York: Pocket Books.

Kaldor, Mary. 1999. *New and Old Wars.* Cambridge: Polity.

Kaplan, Robert D. 1993. *Balkan Ghosts.* New York: St. Martin's Press.

———. 1994. The Coming Anarchy. *Atlantic Monthly,* February, 44–76.

———. 1996. *The Ends of the Earth.* New York: Random House.

———. 2000. *The Coming Anarchy.* New York: Random House.

———. 2001. Looking the World in the Eye. *Atlantic Monthly,* December, 68–82.

Kapuscinski, Ryszard. 1986. *Shah of Shahs.* London: Pan.

———. 1990. *The Soccer War.* London: Granta.

———. 2001. *The Shadow of the Sun.* New York: Knopf.

Karetzky, Stephen, and Norman Frankel, eds. 1989. *The Media's Coverage of the Arab-Israeli Conflict.* New York: Shapolsky.

Keane, Fergal. 1996. *Season of Blood.* London: Penguin.

———. 2001. *A Stranger's Eye.* London: Penguin.

Keller, Bill. 1993. De Klerk's Gorbachev Problem. *New York Times Magazine,* January 31.

———. 1994. Apartheid's Gone, and Anything Goes. *New York Times,* December 28.

———. 1995. Terror Case Informer Is No Hero in His Homeland. *New York Times,* February 15.

Kennedy, Paul. 1987. *The Rise and Fall of the Great Powers.* New York: Random House.

———. 1993. *Preparing for the Twenty-First Century.* New York: Random House.

Kinzer, Stephen. 1994. Where There's War There's Amanpour. *New York Times Magazine,* October 9.

———. 1998. Nehru Spoke It, but It's Still "Foreign." *New York Times,* January 28.

Kleinman, Arthur, and Joan Kleinman. 1996. The Appeal of Experience: The Dismay of Images: Cultural Appropriations of Suffering in Our Times. *Daedalus* 125 (1): 1–23.

Knight, Alan, and Yoshiko Nakano, eds. 1999. *Reporting Hong Kong.* London: Curzon.

Kohn, Hans. 1945. *The Idea of Nationalism.* London: Macmillan.

Kraft, Scott. 1987. Bokassa Trial: Lurid Tales of Cannibalism, Torture. *Los Angeles Times,* March 15.

Kristof, Nicholas D. 1995a. An Ancient City Hopes to Reassure Tourists That It Is Safe to Visit. *New York Times,* January 24, 1995.

———. 1995b. As Kobe Comes Back to Life, Happiness Is a Bath. *New York Times,* January 26.

———. 1995c. Fault Lines and Class Lines in Japan. *New York Times,* January 25.

———. 1995d. Japan Reluctant to Accept Help from Abroad for Quake Victims. *New York Times,* February 5.

———. 1995e. Japan's Favorite Import from America: English. *New York Times,* February 21.

———. 1995f. Japan's Invisible Minority: Better Off Than in Past, but Still Outcasts. *New York Times,* November 30.

———. 1995g. Japan's Nature: A People Tremble in Harmony with the Land. *New York Times,* January 22.

———. 1995h. Kobe Chinatown Booms as Post-Quake Market. *New York Times,* February 11.

———. 1995i. Kobe's Best Problem: Too Many Gifts. *New York Times,* January 28.

———. 1995j. Kobe's Survivors Try to Adjust: Hand-Wringing, Relief, Laughter. *New York Times,* January 22.

———. 1997a. Alas, Poor Alfonse! Was He His Keepers' Supper? *New York Times,* April 24.

———. 1997b. Stateside Lingo Gives Japan Its Own Valley Girls. *New York Times,* October 19.

———. 1997c. Where Children Rule. *New York Times Magazine,* August 7.

———. 1998. Uncompetitive in Tokyo: In Japan, Nice Guys (and Girls) Finish Together. *New York Times,* April 12.

———. 1999a. Mr. "Cold Pizza" Earns Respect in Japan with Deft Tinkering. *New York Times,* April 1.

———. 1999b. Walk This Way, or How the Japanese Kept in Step. *New York Times,* April 18.

———. 1999c. World Ills Are Obvious, the Cures Much Less So. *New York Times,* February 18.

Kristof, Nicholas D., and David E. Sanger. 1999. How Clinton Wooed Asia to Let Cash Flow In. *New York Times,* February 16.

Kristof, Nicholas D., and Sheryl WuDunn. 1994. *China Wakes.* New York: Times Books/Random House.

————. 1999. Of World Markets, None Is an Island. *New York Times,* February 17.

————. 2000. *Thunder from the East.* New York: Knopf.

Kristof, Nicholas D., and Edward Wyatt. 1999. Who Went Under in the World's Sea of Cash. *New York Times,* February 15.

Kroeber, Alfred L. 1945. The Ancient *Oikoumenê* as an Historic Culture Aggregate. *Journal of the Royal Anthropological Institute* 75:9–20.

Kuntz, Tom. 1997. A Global Guide to TV Munchies. *New York Times,* January 26.

Kurtz, Howard. 2001. Thomas Friedman Comes Out Swinging in His Columns on the Middle East. *Washington Post,* December 6.

La Guardia, Anton. 1997. Suicide Bombers Who Saw Death as a Gateway to Paradise. *Daily Telegraph* (London), August 1.

————. 2000. White Farm Survivors Tell of Beatings. *Daily Telegraph* (London), April 17.

————. 2001. *Holy Land, Unholy War.* London: John Murray.

Lancaster, John. 1998. Barbie, "Titanic" Show Good Side of "Great Satan." *Washington Post,* October 27.

Le Carré, John. 1977. *The Honourable School Boy.* London: Hodder and Stoughton.

Lederman, Jim. 1993. *Battle Lines.* Boulder, CO: Westview.

Leijonhufvud, Göran. 1998. Kloten rullar en lördagskväll i Peking. *Dagens Nyheter,* August 2.

————. 1999. "Världens tak" är uppkopplat. *Dagens Nyheter,* July 27.

————. 2001. Internet öppnar stängt Kina. *Dagens Nyheter,* April 10.

Lelyveld, Joseph. 1985. *Move Your Shadow.* New York: Times Books.

Leyden, Peter, and David Bank. 1991. Be a Stringer, See the World. *Washington Journalism Review* 13 (8): 25–28.

Löfgren, Mikael. 1997. Röster som inte hörs är problemet. *Svenska Dagbladet,* April 9.

Lull, James. 1990. *Inside Family Viewing.* London: Routledge.

Lutz, Catherine, and Donald Nonini. 1999. The Economies of Violence and the Violence of Economies. In *Anthropological Theory Today,* ed. Henrietta L. Moore. Cambridge: Polity.

MacBride, Sean. 1980. *Many Voices, One World.* Paris: UNESCO.

MacClancy, Jeremy, and Chris McDonaugh, eds. 1996. *Popularizing Anthropology.* London: Routledge.

MacLachlan, Liz. 2001. Turning Seeing into Believing: Producing Credibility in the Television News Coverage of the Kobe Earthquake. In *Asian Media Productions,* ed. Brian Moeran. London: Curzon.

MacLeod, Scott. 1994. The South African Connection. *Time,* September 26.

Macswan, Norman. 1983. *The Man Who Read the East Wind.* Kenthurst, Australia: Kangaroo Press.

Malkki, Liisa H. 1997. News and Culture: Transitory Phenomena and the Fieldwork Tradition. In *Anthropological Locations,* ed. Akhil Gupta and James Ferguson. Berkeley: University of California Press.

————. 2001. Figures of the Future: Dystopia and Subjectivity in the Social Imagination of the Future. In *History in Person,* ed. Dorothy Holland and Jean Lave. Santa Fe, NM: School of American Research Press.

Mankekar, Purnima. 1999. *Screening Culture, Viewing Politics.* Durham, NC: Duke University Press.

Marcus, George E. 1989. Imagining the Whole: Ethnography's Contemporary Efforts to Situate Itself. *Critique of Anthropology* 9 (3): 7–30.

———. 1995. Ethnography in/of the World System: The Emergence of Multi-Sited Ethnography. *Annual Review of Anthropology* 24:95–117.

———. 1997. Critical Cultural Studies as One Power/Knowledge like, among, and in Engagement with Others. In *From Sociology to Cultural Studies,* ed. Elizabeth Long. Malden, MA: Blackwell.

Massing, Michael. 1983. About-Face on El Salvador. *Columbia Journalism Review* 22 (4): 42–49.

———. 1993. Bringing the Truth Commission Back Home. *Harper's,* July, 64–67.

Matthews, Herbert L. 1971. *A World in Revolution.* New York: Scribner's.

May, Antoinette. 1985. *Witness to War.* New York: Viking Penguin.

Mbembe, Achille. 2001. *On the Postcolony.* Berkeley: University of California Press.

McConnell, Michael W. 1996. Don't Neglect the Little Platoons. In *For Love of Country,* ed. Joshua Cohen. Boston: Beacon Press.

McGeary, Johanna, and Marguerite Michaels. 1998. Africa Rising. *Time,* March 30.

McGreal, Chris. 1996. A Tainted Hero. *Guardian* (London), March 23.

———. 1999a. Debt? War? Gays Are the Real Evil, Say African Leaders. *Guardian* (London), October 2.

———. 1999b. The Deeds of Dr. Death. *Guardian* (London), October 5.

———. 1999c. Pageant Puts Gay Prejudice in Africa on Parade. *Guardian* (London), November 22.

———. 1999d. Truth and Retaliation. *Guardian* (London), October 14.

———. 1999e. Ulster-by-the-Equator: They Wear Orange Sashes, They Go on Orange Marches, and They're Based in Ghana. *Guardian* (London), November 6.

McLuhan, Marshall. 1964. *Understanding Media.* New York: McGraw-Hill.

McNeil, Donald G., Jr. 1997a. Art That Condemned Apartheid Will End Its Exile. *New York Times,* August 13.

———. 1997b. Living, and Learning, in a White Racial Cocoon. *New York Times,* December 21.

———. 1998. Heavily Laden Black Chips: Empowerment Deals Thrive in South Africa, but Sniping and Skepticism Mount. *New York Times,* April 17.

Merton, Robert K. 1957. *Social Theory and Social Structure.* Glencoe, IL: Free Press.

Milgram, Stanley. 1969. Interdisciplinary Thinking and the Small World Problem. In *Interdisciplinary Relationships in the Social Sciences,* ed. Muzafer Sherif and Carolyn W. Sherif. Chicago: Aldine.

Miller, Marjorie. 1996a. The Final Days of a Landmark Café. *Los Angeles Times,* September 27.

———. 1996b. Hear the One about the Bible Interpreter? *Los Angeles Times,* November 8.

———. 1996c. Holy City's Boundaries on the Line. *Los Angeles Times,* December 7.

———. 1996d. "Kosher" Online Service Offers Judaica to the Devout—You Were Expecting Maybe Victoria's Secret? *Los Angeles Times,* November 4.

———. 1996e. "Sabbath War" Flares in Holy City. *Los Angeles Times,* July 26.

———. 1996f. When Jews Leave Faith Behind. *Los Angeles Times,* December 29.

————. 1997a. Coffee and a Byte to Eat: Café Is Gateway for People Who Hunger to "Visit" Closed Areas. *Los Angeles Times,* May 26.

————. 1997b. Israeli Women Make a Clean Sweep of the Holiday. *Los Angeles Times,* April 18.

————. 1999. To Be a Jew: An American Reporter Based in Israel Makes Peace with Her Faith and Her Heritage Even as She Covers the Conflicts of the Region. *Los Angeles Times,* January 23.

Moeller, Susan D. 1999. *Compassion Fatigue.* New York: Routledge.

Moeran, Brian. 1989. *Language and Popular Culture in Japan.* Manchester: Manchester University Press.

Moore, Molly. 1993. *A Woman at War.* New York: Scribner's.

Moore, Sally F. 1986. *Social Facts and Fabrications.* Cambridge: Cambridge University Press.

————. 1987. Explaining the Present: Theoretical Dilemmas in Processual Ethnography. *American Ethnologist* 14:727–36.

————. 1994. The Ethnography of the Present and the Analysis of Process. In *Assessing Cultural Anthropology,* ed. Robert Borofsky. New York: McGraw-Hill.

Morgan, Lewis Henry. [1877] 1963. *Ancient Society.* Cleveland: Meridian Books.

Morrison, David E., and Howard Tumber. 1985. The Foreign Correspondent: Date-Line London. *Media, Culture, and Society* 7:445–70.

Morris-Suzuki, Tessa. 1998. *Re-Inventing Japan.* Armonk, NY: M. E. Sharpe.

Munnion, Christopher. 1995. *Banana Sunday.* Rivonia, South Africa: William Waterman.

Murder and Siege Architecture. 1995. *Economist,* July 15.

Murphy, Dean E. 2002. *September 11: An Oral History.* New York: Doubleday.

Nader, Laura. 1972. Up the Anthropologist—Perspectives Gained from Studying Up. In *Reinventing Anthropology,* ed. Dell Hymes. New York: Pantheon.

Nagorski, Andrew. 1985. *Reluctant Farewell.* New York: Holt, Rinehart, and Winston.

Needham, Rodney. 1975. Polythetic Classification: Convergence and Consequences. *Man* 10:347–69.

Neilan, Edward. 1995. The New Foreign Correspondent in Japan. *Japan Quarterly* 42:307–16.

Nilson, Ulf. 1976. *Ulf Nilson, utrikeskorrespondent.* Höganäs, Sweden: Bra Böcker.

Nordland, Rod. 1996. Christiane's World. *Newsweek,* August 26.

Nordstrom, Carolyn. 1997. *A Different Kind of War Story.* Philadelphia: University of Pennsylvania Press.

Norrman, Leif. 1997a. Grym bild av Afrika. *Dagens Nyheter,* December 18.

————. 1997b. Nu har vi varnat er . . . *Dagens Nyheter,* April 15.

————. 1998a. Bakom en mur av tystnad. *Dagens Nyheter,* April 5.

————. 1998b. Barn offer och bödlar i absurt krig. *Dagens Nyheter,* March 24.

————. 1998c. Mördarna ligger i bakhåll. *Dagens Nyheter,* October 20.

————. 1999a. Rädslan försvann inte med apartheid. *Dagens Nyheter,* May 29.

————. 1999b. Valstrid och gangsterkrig. *Dagens Nyheter,* May 28.

————. 2000a. Äventyr på liv och död. *Dagens Nyheter,* May 6.

————. 2000b. Det är som under kriget. *Dagens Nyheter,* April 8.

————. 2000c. Fler massgravar upptäcks. *Dagens Nyheter,* April 3.

———. 2000d. Internet bara för eliten. *Dagens Nyheter,* September 8.

———. 2000e. Journalisterna in, byråkraterna ut. *Dagens Nyheter,* March 7.

———. 2000f. Katastrofen som blev tv-show. *Dagens Nyheter,* March 19.

———. 2000g. Marias man mördades. *Dagens Nyheter,* April 17.

———. 2000h. Mugabe måste stå till svars. *Dagens Nyheter,* April 26.

———. 2001. Filmens journalister långt från Afrikas vardag. *Dagens Nyheter,* December 31.

Nussbaum, Martha C. 1996. Patriotism and Cosmopolitanism. In *For Love of Country,* ed. Joshua Cohen. Boston: Beacon Press.

Onishi, Norimitsu. 1999. New Leaders Face a Violent and Splintered Nigeria. *New York Times,* June 10.

Ortner, Sherry B. 1999. Generation X: Anthropology in a Media-Saturated World. In *Critical Anthropology Now,* ed. George E. Marcus. Santa Fe, NM: School of American Research Press.

Pedelty, Mark. 1995. *War Stories.* New York: Routledge.

Peterson, Scott. 2000. *Me against My Brother.* New York: Routledge.

Pinsky, Robert. 1996. Eros against Esperanto. In *For Love of Country,* ed. Joshua Cohen. Boston: Beacon Press.

Poggioli, Sylvia. 1997. A Strategy of Rape in Bosnia. *Media Studies Journal* 11 (2): 131–37.

Pollack, Andrew. 1996. Barbie's Journey in Japan. *New York Times,* December 22.

Pratt, Mary Louise. 1992. *Imperial Eyes.* London: Routledge.

Remnick, David. 1993. *Lenin's Tomb.* New York: Random House.

Resek, Carl. 1960. *Lewis Henry Morgan, American Scholar.* Chicago: University of Chicago Press.

Richburg, Keith B. 1997a. Empire Ends for the Brits behind the Bar. *Washington Post,* June 16.

———. 1997b. *Out of America.* New York: Basic Books.

———. 1998. I Sing the Body Politic — and Economic. *Correspondent,* March, 4–5.

———. 1999. Horror I Thought I'd Left Behind. *Washington Post,* September 26.

———. 2001a. At Spain's Gate, Africans Dream of Europe. *Washington Post,* March 28.

———. 2001b. A Trek through the Mountains to the Taliban Front Is a Chilling Experience. *Washington Post,* November 8.

Robertson, Roland. 1992. *Globalization.* London: Sage.

Rollyson, Carl. 1990. *Nothing Ever Happens to the Brave.* New York: St. Martin's Press.

Rosenblum, Mort. 1993. *Who Stole the News?* New York: Wiley.

Rosenfeld, Megan. 1998. Malaysians Create Hybrid Culture with American Imports: Despite Government Censorship, Young People Enthusiastically Embrace Western Music, Fashions. *Washington Post,* October 26.

Ruin, Påhl. 1999a. Ensam om att vara pappaledig i Tokyo. *Dagens Nyheter,* June 29.

———. 1999b. Fuchino, 84, bor hos sonen. *Dagens Nyheter,* June 23.

———. 1999c. Japanska monster skapar hysteri. *Dagens Nyheter,* December 29.

———. 1999d. Japansk väntan på p-piller över. *Dagens Nyheter,* September 4.

———. 1999e. Nationalsången och flaggan symboler för kriget. *Dagens Nyheter,* March 28.

———. 1999f. Unga japaner revolterar. *Dagens Nyheter,* March 31.

————. 2000. Bäst vara japan i Japan. *Dagens Nyheter,* January 2.

————. 2001. Svenska tomten charmar japaner. *Dagens Nyheter,* January 14.

Rupert, James. 1997. An Emperor's Subjects Recall Good and Bad: Bokassa's Brutal Rule of Central African Republic Remembered with Less Ire at Home than Abroad. *Washington Post,* September 3.

Russell, Alec. 1998. Black Pupils Whipped as Multi-Racial Dream Dies. *Daily Telegraph* (London), February 28.

————. 1999. *Big Men, Little People.* London: Macmillan.

Said, Edward. 1981. *Covering Islam.* New York: Pantheon.

————. 1983. *The World, the Text, and the Critic.* Cambridge, MA: Harvard University Press.

Säll, Ola. 1998. De tvingades sparka ihjäl sina kamrater. *Svenska Dagbladet,* July 21.

————. 1999a. Ny president bjuder upp till valmöte. *Svenska Dagbladet,* May 29.

————. 1999b. Winnie Mandela åter i rampljuset. *Svenska Dagbladet,* April 28.

————. 2000. "Jag har aldrig varit ett offer . . ." *Svenska Dagbladet,* May 14.

Sanjek, Roger. 1991. The Ethnographic Present. *Man* 26:609–28.

————. 1993. Anthropology's Hidden Colonialism: Assistants and Their Ethnographers. *Anthropology Today* 9 (2): 13–18.

————. 1998. *The Future of Us All.* Ithaca, NY: Cornell University Press.

Schlesinger, Philip. 1977. Newsmen and Their Time-Machine. *British Journal of Sociology* 28:336–50.

————. 1978. *Putting "Reality" Together.* London: Constable.

Schmemann, Serge. 1997. American Fast Food in Israel: The Bagel. *New York Times,* March 9.

Schneider, Howard. 1999. In a Spin over the Web: Cautious Arab States Confront Challenges of Unleashing Internet. *Washington Post,* July 26.

————. 2000. Letter from Syria: The World's Commotion Arrives on Internet. *Washington Post,* June 20.

Schofield, James. 1996. *Silent over Africa.* Sydney: HarperCollins.

Schudson, Michael. 1987. Deadlines, Datelines, and History. In *Reading the News,* ed. Robert Karl Manoff and Michael Schudson. New York: Pantheon.

————. 1995. *The Power of News.* Cambridge, MA: Harvard University Press.

Schutz, Alfred. 1964. *Collected Papers,* vol. 2, *Studies in Social Theory.* The Hague: Martinus Nijhoff.

Sebba, Anne. 1994. *Battling for News.* London: Hodder and Stoughton.

Seib, Philip. 2002. *The Global Journalist.* Lanham, MD: Rowman and Littlefield.

Sewell, William H., Jr. 1996. Historical Events as Transformations of Structures: Inventing Revolution at the Bastille. *Theory and Society* 25:841–81.

Shachar, Nathan. 1996. Romeo och Julia i Jerusalem. *Dagens Nyheter,* December 29.

————. 1997. Hårt tryck på Hebrons invånare. *Dagens Nyheter,* January 7.

————. 2001. Tidning nagel i ögat på Israel. *Dagens Nyheter,* May 11.

Shaw, David. 1986. Foreign Correspondents: Job Abroad Often Fatal to Marriage. *Los Angeles Times,* June 29.

Shenon, Philip. 1995. Broad Terror Campaign Is Foiled by Fire in Kitchen, Officials Say. *New York Times,* February 12.

Silver, Eric. 1997. How Many Homelands? *Time,* January 20.

Simpson, John. 1998. *Strange Places, Questionable People.* London: Macmillan.

Sims, Calvin. 1999. Japan Beckons, and East Asia's Youth Fall in Love. *New York Times,* December 5.

Smith, David M. 2000. *Moral Geographies.* Edinburgh: Edinburgh University Press.

Smith, Hedrick. 1977. *The Russians.* New York: Ballantine Books.

Ståhlberg, Per. 2002. *Lucknow Daily.* Stockholm Studies in Social Anthropology, 51. Stockholm: Almqvist and Wiksell International.

Stern, Bernhard J. 1931. *Lewis Henry Morgan, Social Evolutionist.* Chicago: University of Chicago Press.

Sterngold, James. 1995a. Gang in Kobe Organizes Aid for People in Quake. *New York Times,* January 22.

———. 1995b. Minorities in Gritty Part of Quake City Bear Big Loss. *New York Times,* January 24.

Stoller, Paul. 1989. *The Taste of Ethnographic Things.* Philadelphia: University of Pennsylvania Press.

Stop Press. 1998. *Economist,* July 4.

Sullivan, Kevin. 1998. Hashimoto Promised a Great Deal but Delivered Too Little, Too Late. *Washington Post,* July 13.

———. 1999. Letter from Bhutan: Uplink to the Twentieth Century: Tiny Kingdom Welcomes, Worries about Television. *Washington Post,* May 19.

Sullivan, Kevin, and Mary Jordan. 1999. Japanese Retirees Fill "Second Life" with Second Jobs. *Washington Post,* July 13.

Taylor, Philip M. 1992. *War and the Media.* Manchester: Manchester University Press.

Taylor, S. J. 1990. *Stalin's Apologist.* New York: Oxford University Press.

Tolbert, Kathryn. 2000. English Is the Talk of Japan: Fears of Stagnation Spark Crusade to Teach the Language of the Internet. *Washington Post,* January 29.

Trautmann, Thomas R. 1992. The Revolution in Ethnological Time. *Man* 27:379–97.

Travers, Jeffrey, and Stanley Milgram. 1969. An Experimental Study of the Small World Problem. *Sociometry* 32:425–43.

Trueheart, Charles. 1998. With Popularity Come Pitfalls: American Pop Culture Can Be Stolen, Altered, and Even Turned against U.S. *Washington Post,* October 27.

Tuchman, Gaye. 1973. Making News by Doing Work: Routinizing the Unexpected. *American Journal of Sociology* 79:110–31.

———. 1978. *Making News.* New York: Free Press.

Tyler, Patrick E. 1996a. China's Campus Model for the 90's: Earnest Patriot. *New York Times,* April 23.

———. 1996b. Rebels' New Cause: A Book for Yankee Bashing. *New York Times,* September 4.

Utley, Garrick. 1997. The Shrinking of Foreign News: From Broadcast to Narrowcast. *Foreign Affairs* 76 (2): 2–10.

Van Wolferen, Karel. 1989. *The Enigma of Japanese Power.* New York: Knopf.

Vertovec, Steven, and Robin Cohen, eds. 2002. *Conceiving Cosmopolitanism.* Oxford: Oxford University Press.

Vick, Karl. 2001. Small Arms' Global Reach Uproots Tribal Traditions. *Washington Post,* July 8.

Waldmeir, Patti. 1997. *Anatomy of a Miracle.* New York: Norton; 2d ed., London: Penguin, 1998. Page references are to the 1998 edition.

Wallis, Roger, and Stanley Baran. 1990. *The Known World of Broadcast News.* London: Routledge.

Wallman, Sandra, ed. 1992. *Contemporary Futures.* London: Routledge.

Watson, William. 1964. Social Mobility and Social Class in Industrial Communities. In *Closed Systems and Open Minds,* ed. Max Gluckman. Edinburgh: Oliver and Boyd.

Waugh, Evelyn. 1938. *Scoop.* London: Chapman and Hall.

Waxman, Sharon. 1998. Hollywood Tailors Its Movies to Sell in Foreign Markets: Studios Say "Ethnic" Films Are Not Popular Overseas. *Washington Post,* October 26.

Weiner, Myron. 1996. Bad Neighbors, Bad Neighborhoods: An Inquiry into the Causes of Refugee Flows. *International Security* 21:5–42.

Wells, Matt, and Steven Morris. 2001. Does the Media Circus Make Disasters Worse? *Guardian Weekly* (London), April 26.

Whymant, Robert. 1999. Japanese Jeweller to Pay for Racist Insult. *Times* (London), November 18.

Windhager, Günther. 2002. *Leopold Weiss alias Muhammad Asad.* Vienna: Böhlau.

Wong, Siu-lun. 1979. *Sociology and Socialism in Contemporary China.* London: Routledge and Kegan Paul.

Wu, Amy. 1999. In the Industrial Back Alleys of Beijing, a Little Bit of Gotham. *New York Times,* April 18.

WuDunn, Sheryl. 1995a. Japan Leaders Criticized on Response to Quake. *New York Times,* January 24.

———. 1995b. Many Japanese Women Are Resisting Servility. *New York Times,* July 9.

———. 1996. Japan May Approve Pill, but Women May Not. *New York Times,* November 27.

———. 1998. Women's Work in Japan: Serving Tea, Swallowing Insults. *New York Times,* November 1.

———. 1999a. A Japanese Version of "Geisha"? Well, It May Sound Easy. *New York Times,* January 7.

———. 1999b. Japan's Tale of Two Pills: Viagra and Birth Control. *New York Times,* April 27.

———. 1999c. Manager Commits Hara-Kiri to Fight Corporate Restructuring. *New York Times,* March 24.

Wulff, Helena. 1998. *Ballet across Borders.* Oxford: Berg.

Yang, Mayfair. 1996. Tradition, Travelling Anthropology, and the Discourse of Modernity in China. In *The Future of Anthropological Knowledge,* ed. Henrietta L. Moore. London: Routledge.

Zananiri, Elias M. 1997. Betrayed Settlers and Cautiously Jubilant Hebronites. *Jerusalem Times,* January 17.

Zelizer, Barbie, and Stuart Allan, eds. 2002. *Journalism after September 11.* London: Routledge.

Zipangu, ed. 1998. *Japan Made in USA.* New York: Zipangu.

Znamenski, Andrei A. 1995. "A Household God in a Socialist World": Lewis Henry Morgan and Russian/Soviet Anthropology. *Ethnologia Europaea* 25:177–88.

INDEX